Productivity and Motivation

Productivity
and
Motivation

A Review of State and Local Government Initiatives

John M. Greiner

Harry P. Hatry

Margo P. Koss

Annie P. Millar

Jane P. Woodward

An Urban Institute Book

THE URBAN INSTITUTE PRESS · WASHINGTON, D.C.

Copyright © 1981
The Urban Institute
2100 M Street, N.W.
Washington, D.C. 20037

Printed in the United States of America

LC 80-53981
ISBN 87766-283-5
UI 0328-2

Please refer to URI 29600 when ordering

This book was printed by Braun-Brumfield, Inc.,
from type set by Typesetters Incorporated.

THE URBAN INSTITUTE is a nonprofit research organization established in 1968 to study problems of the nation's urban communities. Independent and nonpartisan, the Institute responds to current needs for disinterested analyses and basic information and attempts to facilitate the application of this knowledge. As part of this effort, it cooperates with federal agencies, states, cities, associations of public officials, and other organizations committed to the public interest.

The Institute's research findings and a broad range of interpretive viewpoints are published as an educational service. The interpretations or conclusions are those of the authors and should not be attributed to The Urban Institute, its trustees, or to other organizations that support its research.

CONTENTS

PART TWO: Performance Targeting

PART FOUR: Job Enrichment

LIST OF EXHIBITS

FOREWORD

Lyndon Johnson once said that government can never be any better than the people who work for it, the tools they have, and the people they serve. As governments at all levels find themselves increasingly beset by conflicting demands to provide more and better services, higher wages and benefits, and greater relief for taxpayers, government officials have begun to seek ways to enhance the contributions of their employees and the tools available to them.

One target of concern has been the motivation of the public employee. The potential benefits of improved employee motivation are clear: employee salaries and benefits constitute by far the largest single category of expenditures for state and local governments. Moreover, the public perception is that government is staffed by workers who are neither efficient nor effective. Five months after Proposition 13 loosed the so-called tax revolt upon the nation, a *Washington Post* poll suggested that Americans weren't nearly as angry with their tax bills as they were with how little they got from government in return. "Tax money," said the *Post* story announcing the poll results, "is seen as largely wasted by local, state and federal governments that have padded payrolls and employees who are overpaid, lazy, discourteous and inefficient."

This public dissatisfaction is often matched by that of the civil servant. Public employment has often meant "dead-end" jobs, remote and uninspired management, and little opportunity for individual recognition, autonomy, and growth. Such conditions can lead to worker alienation, frustration, and low morale, while contributing to reduced productivity.

For many years, government administrators paid little serious attention to this problem. However, the last decade has witnessed increased interest in the productivity of the government workforce. Many public administrators have begun to look toward motivational techniques as a way of maintaining service quality while getting the most from each tax dollar.

The result has been the emergence of a variety of public sector motivational efforts, ranging from the use of monetary incentives to the application of recent developments in job redesign and participatory management. However, for the most part these efforts have been isolated often *ad hoc*, initiatives. Little information has been available to interested governments on what is being tried elsewhere, which programs work, and what the obstacles to success might be.

For almost eight years, The Urban Institute has been closely observing state and local government efforts to improve employee motivation and productivity. The Institute's involvement in this area has ranged from identifying and reporting on the types of motivational innovations being used to actually participating in the design and testing of a few such programs. A continuing objective of this work has been to begin to fill in the gaps in the evaluative information available on such approaches.

This book represents an effort to update, elaborate, and synthesize the results of six years of Urban Institute research on the use of motivational techniques to improve state and local government productivity. The authors have focused on four motivational approaches that have appeared particularly promising —and in some cases, essential—for improving the productivity of public employees: monetary incentives, the setting of performance targets, performance appraisal, and job enrichment. The authors have attempted to extract and synthesize what is known from past and present trials of these approaches in the public sector, while at the same time drawing on their own observations, experiences, and data analyses.

Unfortunately, there has been little systematic research or field experimentation in the public sector to provide evidence as to the effects of those innovations that have been tried. Thus, even now there is only limited information on the impacts of motivational approaches in real-life state and local government settings. Consequently it is difficult to draw conclusions as to the effectiveness of individual motivational techniques.

Nevertheless, the authors believe that it is important to present and assess the information that is available to aid public officials faced with the necessity of making decisions on motivational programs. This information can also provide guidance for future research on public sector motivational programs. This report should help public (and private) sector management, union officials, and the research community to better understand the practices, problems, and potentials associated with using motivational techniques for improving state and local government productivity.

William Gorham
President
The Urban Institute

PREFACE

Many people believe that better motivation of government employees can be an important step toward improving the efficiency and effectiveness of public services. And many have accepted the idea that, like any good employer, a government should strive to provide an attractive work environment while trying, within reason, to enhance employee job satisfaction.

The findings described in this report emerged from a two-year examination of state and local government responses to the foregoing concerns. The study's goals were to estimate the incidence of various state and local government employee motivational approaches, assemble the information currently available regarding the impact of those approaches on productivity and job satisfaction, identify obstacles to the use of such techniques, and provide recommendations concerning future needs.

We found that many state and local governments have tried new motivational approaches of various types. The great majority of these programs have been isolated innovations by individual jurisdictions. In all but a very few cases, little effort was made to provide for a thorough, objective evaluation of the effects of these innovations on productivity and job satisfaction or to identify implementation obstacles and problems. Systematic, well-documented assessments were rare. In some instances, the programs were so new that insufficient time had elapsed for the accumulation of adequate evaluative information.

Consequently, we were often forced to rely on partial evidence and self-reports from the governments currently utilizing the motivational programs. As a result, the reader may find the discussion of impacts unsatisfying.

Nevertheless, we believe that this synthesis of the limited information available will prove helpful to government officials, who currently have little guidance in choosing between motivational programs. Although these findings are far from definitive, they provide some important insights. We hope they will lay the groundwork for future efforts by governments, universities, and other organizations to systematically explore the most promising approaches for improving both the performance and the satisfaction of state and local government employees.

The Authors

ACKNOWLEDGMENTS

This report is the product of efforts by several persons. The following individuals were responsible for the various sections of this book:

   Part One (Monetary Incentives): John Greiner, with assistance from Jane Woodward and Annie Millar;

   Part Two (Performance Targeting): Jane Woodward, with assistance from Margo Koss and Harry Hatry;

   Part Three (Performance Appraisal): Margo Koss, with assistance from Jane Woodward and Harry Hatry;

   Part Four (Job Enrichment): John Greiner and Annie Millar;

   Part Five (Factors Affecting Implementation): John Greiner, with assistance from Jane Woodward;

   Part Six (Overall Findings, Conclusions, and Recommendations): John Greiner and Harry Hatry, with the assistance of the other members of the project team.

John Greiner was the project manager for this study, and the overall effort was supervised by Harry Hatry, Director of The Urban Institute's State and Local Government Research Group. This work was sponsored by the Office of Policy Development and Research of the U.S. Department of Housing and Urban Development.

   This report has benefited from the ideas, suggestions, and assistance of numerous other persons. First, the authors wish to thank the many state and local government officials and leaders of public employee organizations who shared with us their experiences and observations regarding employee motivational programs. We are also grateful for the support and suggestions provided by staff from the U.S. Department of Housing and Urban Development's Office of Policy Development and Research, especially Alan Segal, Robert Baumgartner, Hartley Fitts, and E. Jay Howenstine of the Government Capacity Building Division.

   A number of other persons assisted with this study in various ways. Cynthia Lancer of The Urban Institute and Marc

Kahn, an intern from George Washington University, helped with data collection. Rack Fukuhara of the International City Management Association provided access to data from ICMA's 1976 survey of local government productivity improvement efforts. Robert Pajer of the U.S. Civil Service Commission (now the Office of Personnel Management) greatly facilitated our inquiries to the Commission's ten regional offices regarding potential obstacles to the use of incentives; in addition, Mr. Pajer provided information on current motivational efforts and reviewed an early draft of this report. Others who contributed reference materials, suggestions concerning the direction of the study, or information about innovative state and local government motivational efforts included Katherine Janka and Charles Morrison of the National Training and Development Service, Robert Joyce of the U.S. Civil Service Commission, and Tom White and Katrina Regan, both of The Urban Institute.

The authors also thank the reviewers of this report. They included Joseph Adler of the American Federation of State, County, and Municipal Employees; Enid Beaumont of the International Personnel Management Association; Susan Clark of the National Center for Productivity and Quality of Working Life; Thomas DeCotiis and Robert Doherty of Cornell University; R. Scott Fosler of the Committee for Economic Development; Nesta Gallas of the City College of New York; Allan Heuerman and his staff at the U.S. Civil Service Commission's Bureau of Intergovernmental Personnel Programs; Eleanor Laverson of the U.S. Civil Service Commission; Dorris McLaughlin of the University of Michigan; Chester Newland of the University of Southern California; Deborah Shulman of the National Association of Counties; Graham Watt of the National Training and Development Service; and Sam Zagoria of the Labor-Management Relations Service of the U.S. Conference of Mayors. Phillip Sawicki reviewed and edited the entire draft report.

To all who have helped, we express our deep appreciation. Of course, the findings and conclusions reported here and any errors therein are solely the responsibility of the authors.

Chapter 1

INTRODUCTION

State and local governments today find themselves in an increasingly difficult financial situation. At the same time that they are being asked to provide more and better services to citizens and to pay higher wages and fringe benefits to government employees, they are faced with demands from the public that taxes be reduced. As one way of dealing with these conflicting pressures, many administrators have looked for new methods to improve productivity—that is, for ways to provide more or better service for each tax dollar and staff year invested.

State and local governments have used several strategies in attempting to improve productivity. These have included (1) the introduction of new or improved technology, (2) improvement of operational procedures, (3) revision of organizational structures, (4) improving the work skills of employees and the managerial abilities of supervisors, and (5) intensified efforts to motivate employees.

This report deals with the last of these strategies. The potential benefits of improved employee motivation are clear. Among state and local governments, the salaries and benefits of employees constitute the largest single category of expenditures.[1] Government employees, of course, play a major role in determining the quality and effectiveness of public services. Thus, enhancing the effectiveness and efficiency of its personnel will be an important consideration in any government's efforts to achieve higher productivity.

---

1. U.S. Bureau of the Census, *Governmental Finances in 1976-77*, Series GF77 No. 5 (Washington, D.C.: Government Printing Office, 1978), p. 5.

1

There is growing concern that government service is often not conducive to maximum employee efficiency or effectiveness. Government personnel policies and civil service systems are frequently accused of stifling incentive and ignoring excellence.[2] This can lead to alienation, frustration, and poor morale among state and local government workers, as well as lower productivity.

As a result of the growing concern over worker efficiency and effectiveness, state and local governments have become increasingly interested in new methods of motivating employees. In recent years, a substantial number of these governments have adopted new motivational programs to help improve productivity. This report examines four of the principal approaches that have been used for improving motivation: monetary incentives, performance targets, performance appraisals, and job enrichment. These are addressed in terms of the following questions:

1. To what extent has each type of approach been used by state and local governments?
2. What is currently known about the impact of each kind of motivational program on government productivity (i.e., service efficiency and effectiveness) and on employee job satisfaction?
3. What are the major factors that lead to the successful introduction of such motivational programs in state and local governments?
4. What important gaps still exist in our knowledge about these motivational approaches, and how can the gaps be remedied?

Theories of Motivation

"Motivation" has been defined as "the incentives, both intrinsic and extrinsic, which initiate and sustain any given activity; a complex and ambiguous concept to denote (usually) sustained, goal-directed behavior." [3] Motivation is thus closely related to (and sometimes synonymous with) the idea of an incentive, which has been defined as "that which initiates and sustains a

---

2. See, for instance, E. S. Savas and Sigmund G. Ginsburg, "The Civil Service: A Meritless System?" *The Public Interest,* vol. 32 (June 1973), pp. 70-85.

3. Philip L. Harriman, *Handbook of Psychological Terms* (Totowa, N.J.: Littlefield, Adams and Company, 1969), p. 111.

behavior sequence leading to some reward or to avoidance of punishment." [4] Among the many theories about motivation and incentives that have been tested experimentally, the following appear to be especially relevant to the programs discussed in this book.[5]

• *Expectancy theory* [6] holds that the efficacy of additional rewards in motivating increased effort depends on the employee's perception of the value of the rewards and the employee's degree of confidence that increased effort will produce outcomes that will be rewarded. Under this conception, motivation is viewed within the context of modern statistical decision theory: decisions (e.g. to act in certain ways) are influenced by the decision maker's assessment of the expected utility (value) of each available option.

• *Goal-setting theory* [7] postulates that human actions are instigated by conscious intentions, which are expressed as specific goals. Thus, a goal is what an individual (or a group) is consciously trying to achieve and constitutes the most immediate determinant of performance. Under this theory, increased effort and better performance can be achieved by providing

4. Ibid., p. 87.
5. This outline of motivational theories draws heavily upon two reviews of the psychological literature on employee motivation, satisfaction, and pay: Public Services Laboratory, Georgetown University, *What Determines City Employees Compensation?* Staffing Services to People in the Cities No. 8 (Washington, D.C., 1975), pp. 14-23; and John B. Miner and H. Peter Dachler, "Personnel Attitudes and Motivation," in *Annual Review of Psychology,* eds. Paul H. Mussen and Mark R. Rosenzweig, vol. 24 (1973), pp. 379-402.
6. See, for instance, V. Vroom, *Work and Motivation* (New York: John Wiley and Sons, 1964); Lyman W. Porter and E. E. Lawler III, *Managerial Attitudes and Performance* (Homewood, Ill.: Irwin, 1968); and E. E. Lawler, *Pay and Organizational Effectiveness: A Psychological View* (New York: McGraw-Hill Book Company, 1971).
7. See, for example, D. P. Schwab and L. L. Cummings, "Theories of Performance and Satisfaction: A Review," *Industrial Relations,* vol. 9 (October 1970), pp. 408-430; Gary P. Latham and Gary A. Yukl, "A Review of Research on the Application of Goal Setting in Organizations," *Academy of Management Journal,* vol. 18 (December 1975), pp. 824-845; E. A. Locke, N. Cartledge, and C. S. Knerr, "Studies of the Relationship Between Satisfaction, Goal-Setting, and Performance," *Organizational Behavior and Human Performance,* vol. 5 (1970), pp. 135-158; T. A. Ryan, *Intentional Behavior: An Approach to Human Motivation* (New York: Ronald, 1970); Richard M. Steers and Lyman W. Porter, "The Role of Task-Goal Attributes in Employee Performance," *Psychological Bulletin,* vol. 81 (1974), pp. 434-452; and A. Zander, *Motives and Goals in Groups* (New York: Academic Press, 1971).

employees with clearer targets or by making targets harder to achieve (i.e., more challenging). External incentives, such as monetary rewards, are believed to affect performance by inducing alterations or adjustments in an employee's goals.

• *Operant conditioning theory* [8] views rewards and punishments as "reinforcers." [9] The effectiveness of a reinforcer depends, among other things, on its nature and its timing. This theory holds, for instance, that to be effective a reinforcer should be closely linked in time with the behavior to be modified.

• *Equity theory* [10] holds that if compensation is either above or below what an employee perceives as equitable, tension will be produced. This tension will lead the employee either to change the amount of effort expended (for instance, less effort if pay is perceived as being low, more effort—or better quality work—if pay is viewed as being high) or to seek a change in

8. See, for instance, B. F. Skinner, *Science and Human Behavior* (New York: Macmillan Publishing Co., 1953); C. B. Ferster and B. F. Skinner, *Schedules of Reinforcement* (New York: Appleton-Century-Crofts, 1957); W. K. Honig, ed., *Operant Behavior: Areas of Research and Application* (New York: Appleton-Century-Crofts, 1966); D. J. Cherrington, H. J. Reitz, and W. E. Scott, "Effects of Contingent and Non-Contingent Reward on the Relationship Between Satisfaction and Task Performance," *Journal of Applied Psychology,* vol. 55 (1971), pp. 531-536; W. R. Nord, "Beyond the Teaching Machine: The Neglected Area of Operant Conditioning in the Theory and Practice of Management," *Organizational Behavior and Human Performance,* vol. 4 (1969), pp. 375-401; and G. A. Yukl, K. N. Wesley, and J. D. Seymore, "Effectiveness of Pay Incentives Under Variable Ratio and Continuous Reinforcement Schedules," *Journal of Applied Psychology,* vol. 56 (1972), pp. 19-23.

9. Although managers are often uncomfortable with negative reinforcers, clinical evidence supports their effectiveness in modifying behavior. There is a danger, however, that a manager who administers "punishment" may generate resentment that could interfere with efforts to help employees, particularly if the manager does not balance punishments with appropriate rewards.

10. J. Stacy Adams, "Toward an Understanding of Inequity," *Journal of Abnormal and Social Psychology,* vol. 67 (1963), pp. 422-436; P. S. Goodman and A. Friedman, "An Examination of Adams' Theory of Inequity," *Administrative Science Quarterly,* vol. 16 (1971), pp. 271-286; Elliot Jacques, *Equitable Payment* (New York: John Wiley and Sons, 1961); A. K. Korman, "Toward an Hypothesis of Work Motivation," *Journal of Applied Psychology,* vol. 54 (1970), pp. 31-41; Lawler, *Pay and Organizational Effectiveness;* Martin Patchen, *The Choice of Wage Comparisons* (Englewood Cliffs, N.J.: Prentice-Hall, 1961); and R. D. Pritchard, "Equity Theory: A Review and Critique," *Organizational Behavior and Human Performance,* vol. 4 (1969), pp. 176-211.

the pay level itself. The worker judges pay in terms of both its absolute level and its relation to the pay of other employees.

● *Two-factor theory* [11] separates job factors into "hygiene factors" and "motivators." Hygiene factors pertain to the work environment. Examples include physical working conditions, supervision, pay, and company policies on personnel matters. It is differences in these "hygiene factors" that make work tolerable or intolerable. Although an employee's productivity may decline if these factors are not maintained adequately, hygiene factors are not believed to contribute to worker satisfaction and positive work attitudes. What contribute to the latter are "motivators"—factors associated with the content of the work rather than the work environment. Changes in these factors, which include achievement, recognition, responsibility, and opportunity for advancement, are considered the primary means of eliciting improved job performance from employees.

● *Need hierarchy theory* [12] postulates a five-level pyramid of needs whose satisfaction governs human behavior. In order of importance, these needs are (1) physical survival, (2) safety and security, (3) love and social belonging, (4) self-esteem, and (5) self-actualization (the full utilization of an individual's talents, capacities, and potentialities). When a lower-level need is satisfied, the next higher need becomes an individual's dominant motivating force. Thus, this theory holds that wages decline in importance once a certain level of income is reached. In an

---

11. F. Herzberg, B. Mausner, and B. B. Snyderman, *The Motivation to Work* (New York: John Wiley and Sons, 1969); V. M. Bockman, "The Herzberg Controversy," *Personnel Psychology,* vol. 24 (1971), pp. 155-189; N. King, "Clarification and Evaluation of the Two-Factor Theory of Job Satisfaction," *Psychological Bulletin,* vol. 74 (1970), pp. 18-31; and R. C. Hackman, *The Motivated Working Adult* (New York: American Management Association, 1969).

12. Abraham Maslow, *Motivation and Personality* (New York: Harper and Row, 1954); J. C. Wofford, "The Motivational Bases of Job Satisfaction and Job Performance," *Personnel Psychology,* vol. 24 (1971), pp. 501-518; C. P. Alderfer, "An Empirical Test of a New Theory of Human Needs," *Organizational Behavior and Human Performance,* vol. 4 (1969), pp. 142-175; M. G. Wolf, "Need Gratification Theory: A Theoretical Reformulation of Job Satisfaction/Dissatisfaction and Job Motivation," *Journal of Applied Psychology,* vol. 54 (1970), pp. 87-94; and Clare W. Graves, "Levels of Existence: An Open System Theory of Values," *Journal of Humanistic Psychology,* vol. 10 (Fall 1970), pp. 131-155.

increasingly affluent society, the number of persons motivated by higher needs will grow, resulting in an increased demand for jobs that provide a sense of identity, self-esteem, and self-actualization.

● *Job enrichment theory* [13] holds that by improving the content of a job—that is, by changing or expanding job tasks to make the work more interesting—the job itself will stimulate greater motivation and thus lead to improved employee performance as well as greater job satisfaction. According to this theory, job content can be improved by providing more diversity (e.g., by increasing the number of assigned tasks or the extent to which the job involves additional interpersonal relationships) or by providing greater responsibility and self-fulfillment (e.g., by giving the worker increased discretion, responsibility for handling a complete task rather than only part of it, and direct feedback on job performance). Job enrichment theory also addresses the relationship between worker and management, holding that a job can be enriched (and therefore made intrinsically more motivating) by providing the worker with an opportunity for meaningful participation in managerial decisions.[14] Recent research indicates, however, that the effectiveness of job enrichment is contingent upon numerous external considerations, including the production technology used (for instance, the degree to which the job is tied to the use of

---

13. L. E. Davis, "Job Satisfaction Research: The Post-Industrial View," *Industrial Relations*, vol. 10 (1971), pp. 179-193; R. N. Ford, *Motivation Through the Work Itself* (New York: American Management Association, 1969); J. R. Hackman and E. E. Lawler III, "Employee Reactions to Job Characteristics," *Journal of Applied Psychology*, vol. 55 (1971), pp. 259-286; Raymond A. Katzell, Penny Bienstock, and Paul H. Faerstein, *A Guide to Worker Productivity Experiments in the United States: 1971-75* (New York: New York University Press, 1977); Raymond A. Katzell and Daniel Yankelovich, *Work, Productivity, and Job Satisfaction: An Evaluation of Policy-Related Research* (New York: The Psychological Corporation, 1975); J. R. Maher, ed., *New Perspectives in Job Enrichment* (New York: Van Nostrand Reinhold, 1971); and Suresh Srivastva et al., *Job Satisfaction and Productivity: An Evaluation of Policy Related Research on Productivity, Industrial Organization and Job Satisfaction* (Cleveland, Ohio: Case Western Reserve University, 1975).

14. R. Likert, *New Patterns of Management* (New York: McGraw-Hill Book Company, 1961); A. J. Marrow, D. G. Bowers, and S. E. Seashore, *Management by Participation* (New York: Harper and Row, 1967); and M. S. Myers, *Every Employee a Manager* (New York: McGraw-Hill Book Company, 1970).

complex, interdependent machines), the employee's inner need for personal growth, and the degree to which the employee is satisfied with such things as pay, job security, coworkers, and supervisors.[15]

The seven theories summarized above sometimes overlap, sometimes conflict with, and sometimes complement each other. In general, existing research has not assigned primary importance to any single one. Indeed, a general relationship between rewards (or punishments) and performance has not yet been established empirically. At present, the relationship appears to be influenced by many factors which are not yet well understood.

Four Important Motivational Techniques

This book concentrates on state and local government use of four types of motivational techniques:

1. **Monetary Incentives.** Monetary incentives are cash awards used to induce desired behavior or results. The awards may be contingent on the performance of an individual or a group. Historically and psychologically, monetary rewards have been central to any consideration of motivation, work performance, and job satisfaction. This study concentrates on five types of monetary incentives—performance bonuses, piecework plans, shared savings plans, suggestion awards, and performance-based wage increases (including those that function through a "merit" system and those that function through other means, such as productivity bargaining).

2. **Performance Targeting.** Performance targeting is a process for developing precise statements of the desired performance of an individual or group, in quantitative terms where possible. These statements make explicit the performance that is expected. In state and local governments, performance targets have most often been used in connection with management-by-

15. See, for instance, Hackman and Lawler, "Employee Reactions"; Katzell and Yankelovich, *Work, Productivity, and Job Satisfaction*, pp. 182-184; G. R. Oldham, J. R. Hackman, and J. L. Pearce, "Conditions Under Which Employees Respond Positively to Enriched Work," *Journal of Applied Psychology*, vol. 61 (1976), pp. 395-403; and C. L. Hulin, "Individual Differences and Job Enrichment—The Case Against General Treatments," in J. R. Maher, ed., *New Perspectives*, pp. 159-191.

objectives (MBO) programs, performance appraisals (e.g., appraisal-by-objectives programs), work measurement (i.e., work standards specifying the work to be accomplished and the time allotted for it), and program budgeting efforts. Achievement of targets may or may not be tied to the provision of rewards or sanctions.

3. Performance Appraisal. Performance appraisal refers to procedures used by governments to assess employee performance. Among the appraisal techniques that have been used are management by objectives, appraisal by objectives, work narratives, various types of subjective rating scales, checklists of personal attributes, reports of "critical incidents," and various types of comparative rankings. Appraisals generally focus on the performance of an individual, but they may also be applied to a group.

The appraisal process itself, it should be noted, may contribute to—or detract from—motivation. For example, it may contribute to an employee's sense of achievement or self-esteem; it may help the employee learn how to perform better; or, conversely, it may create resentment or dissatisfaction. Appraisals may also serve as the basis for incentive plans and personnel actions (promotions, dismissals, etc.) that can contribute to employee motivation.

4. Job Enrichment. Job enrichment involves efforts to improve both employee productivity and job satisfaction by altering the job itself. This can be done in a variety of ways, including increasing the employee's autonomy (self-direction), increasing the variety of skills used or activities performed, giving the employee the opportunity to perform all aspects of a particular task rather than just part of it, allowing the employee to participate in management decisions, or increasing the direct feedback that employees receive on their job performance. Among the major approaches to job enrichment that have been used by state and local governments are job redesign, job rotation, the creation of teams, and participative decision making. Note that these job enrichment techniques have not usually been linked to extrinsic rewards, such as monetary bonuses.

There were several reasons for choosing these four motivational techniques as the focal points for this study. First, a number of state and local governments have tried different versions of each technique. An examination of the effectiveness of the techniques, and the problems experienced in implementing them, seemed likely to be of special interest to state and local government officials. Second, previous Urban Institute studies have given preliminary indications that these techniques are especially promising tools for improving productivity.[16]

A third consideration in selecting these four techniques was their pivotal role in employee motivation. No examination of motivational programs would be complete without consideration of monetary incentives, the classic motivational technique. But opinions differ regarding the applicability and effectiveness of monetary incentives in stimulating increased productivity among public employees. Consequently, it was also deemed necessary to examine the potential usefulness of the most important non-monetary approaches: performance appraisal, performance targeting, and job enrichment. Of these, performance appraisal now plays perhaps the most central role in motivating public employees. The appraisal process itself can contribute to (or detract from) employee motivation. In addition, performance appraisal is important because of its close relationship to other techniques of interest, namely, performance targeting and certain types of monetary incentives. Furthermore, problems with regard to the equity, objectivity, and validity of appraisal techniques can serve as obstacles to the introduction of other motivational procedures.

Thus, taken together, these four motivational approaches exhibit several noteworthy characteristics. They reflect a number of different motivational theories; they involve the use of monetary as well as nonmonetary rewards; and (with the possible exception of job enrichment) they exhibit some potentially important interdependencies.

Research Goals

Each of the four motivational techniques was studied with respect to the following characteristics:

---

16. See John M. Greiner, Lynn Bell, and Harry P. Hatry, *Employee Incentives to Improve State and Local Government Productivity*, National Commission on Productivity and Work Quality (Washington, D.C., March 1975); and John M. Greiner et al., *Monetary Incentives and Work Standards in Five Cities: Impacts and Implications for Management and Labor* (Washington, D.C.: The Urban Institute, 1977).

A. *Incidence*. How often has each technique been used by state and local governments, and what different forms of each technique have been used?

B. *Impact*. First, what has been the impact of each technique on employee efficiency? Have there been changes in unit costs or in work accomplished per dollar or per staff hour? Second, what has been the impact of each technique on employee effectiveness? Have there been changes in the degree to which service objectives are achieved or in the quality of service provided? Have there been unexpected benefits or liabilities as a result of using the technique? Third, what has been the impact of each technique on employee job satisfaction? What changes in overall employee morale and job satisfaction have occurred? What changes have there been in counterproductive employee behavior, such as absenteeism, tardiness, or accidents? Fourth, where employee organizations are present, have the techniques significantly affected relations between management and those organizations?

C. *Obstacles*. What obstacles have local and state governments confronted in attempting to implement these motivational techniques? How have they overcome them? What obstacles to successful implementation remain?

On the basis of the answers to these questions, recommendations are provided about the research needed to improve our understanding of these techniques and to make firmer judgments about those that currently seem most promising from the standpoint of improving employee productivity.

Study Methods

Several methods were used to obtain information for this report. The investigation began with a search for, and examination of, written materials on public sector experiences with the various motivational techniques, plus an examination of relevant material from the private sector. In addition, information was obtained from telephone interviews with personnel in jurisdictions reported to have tried or considered motivational techniques and from written reports by these and other governments on their programs and experiences.

Information about the extent to which each of the techniques has been used was obtained from a joint survey undertaken by The Urban Institute (UI), the International City Management Association (ICMA), and the National Governors' Conference (NGC) in 1973.[17] Additional information on incidence was obtained from two surveys conducted in 1976, one by the ICMA [18] and the other by the International Personnel Management Association (IPMA).[19] This information was supplemented by information obtained through two mail surveys (discussed later) and by information and references in recent issues of ICMA's *Guide to Management Improvement Projects* and other publications.[20]

The specialized information sources described above were supplemented by a number of more general sources:

- Interviews with federal officials, with representatives of public interest groups (such as the National Training and Development Service, the National League of Cities, the National Association of Counties, and the Labor-Management Relations Service of the U.S. Conference of Mayors), and with staff members of professional groups (such as the International City Management Association and the International Personnel Management Association).

- Materials and information collected in the course of several recent (or ongoing) Urban Institute studies of incentive plans, team policing, municipal management techniques, and other relevant topics.[21]

Information on several specific motivational plans was obtained from interviews with personnel from a number of state

17. See Greiner, Bell, and Hatry, *Employee Incentives*, pp. 4-7. This survey will be referred to as the 1973 UI/ICMA/NGC survey throughout the remainder of this report.

18. See International City Management Association, "The Status of Local Government Productivity" (Washington, D.C., March 1977). The survey will henceforth be referred to as the 1976 ICMA survey.

19. This information was obtained from IPMA's annual survey of member governments (there were 402 respondents in 1976). This will be referred to as the 1976 IPMA survey.

20. See International City Management Association, *The Guide to Management Improvement Projects in Local Government* (Washington, D.C., November-December 1977) and other reports in this series.

21. For descriptions of additional public sector motivational efforts, see Greiner, Bell, and Hatry, *Employee Incentives*; and Greiner et al., *Monetary Incentives*.

and local governments. The methods used for selecting these jurisdictions varied considerably, depending on the type of motivational approach under investigation, the presence of variants of special interest, and the extent of prior information. In some cases, governments were sampled randomly; in others, attention was focused on jurisdictions known to have used one of the motivational approaches. The following interview strategies were employed:

Monetary Incentives: Telephone interviews were conducted with twenty-five cities and five states chosen from an extensive list of jurisdictions believed to have planned or implemented monetary incentives in recent years. This list was developed from the sources noted above. The selection strategy emphasized programs reported to have encountered implementation problems and programs that appeared likely to be especially innovative.

Performance Targeting: Telephone interviews were conducted with a random sample of twenty-five local governments that reported in the 1976 ICMA survey that they had tried MBO. Twenty-three were selected from the 118 that reported having used MBO for longer than one year, and two were chosen from the twenty-five governments that reported terminating MBO programs.

Performance Appraisal: The personnel departments of the fifty states were requested by letter to send copies of forms, instructions, laws, rules and regulations, and evaluative studies relating to their performance appraisal systems. Twenty-five city and twenty-five county governments, selected randomly from among cities with populations over 50,000 and counties with populations over 100,000, were asked to do the same. The seven states, fifteen cities, and sixteen counties that did not reply to the first or second request were interviewed by telephone. These interviews were supplemented with relevant information from the twenty-five local governments interviewed in connection with performance targeting.

Job Enrichment: Telephone interviews were conducted with personnel in sixteen jurisdictions that had tried job enrichment. (Another eight jurisdictions reported to have had job enrichment programs were called but were found not to have undertaken such efforts.) The sixteen cases were selected from an extensive list of jurisdictions reported to have planned or implemented job enrichment efforts in recent years. In selecting jurisdictions, project staff members tried to include at least one program illustrating each of the four major types of job enrichment while giving special emphasis to those types that appeared most likely to result in significant productivity improvements (namely, operating teams and job redesign). These interviews were supplemented with additional materials and information on specific public sector job enrichment efforts, including the results of a number of telephone interviews conducted in connection with the 1973 UI/ICMA/NGC survey.

Implementation Obstacles: Information on the problems involved in implementing motivational programs was obtained in the interviews noted above. In addition, the following were utilized:

- Telephone interviews with officials of six cities in Michigan and six cities in Virginia. These states were selected as having contrasting legal and labor environments regarding public employees. The twelve jurisdictions were all reported to have tried motivational approaches of one type or another.
- In-person interviews with high-ranking state civil service or personnel officials in five states—Michigan, Mississippi, New Jersey, Virginia, and Washington.
- Information provided by regional offices of the U.S. Civil Service Commission on the legal, labor, and civil service environment in forty-four states with respect to the introduction of monetary incentives for state employment service personnel.[22]
- Interviews with officials of twenty-seven state municipal leagues.
- Telephone (and a few in-person) interviews with officials of state public employee unions and associations in three

22. This information was obtained in connection with a recent study for the U.S. Department of Labor. See U.S. Department of Labor, Employment and Training Administration, "Employee Incentives for Local Offices of the Employment Service: Prospects and Problems," a report by John M. Greiner and Virginia B. Wright, December 1977.

states—Michigan, New Jersey, and Washington. (Officials of the California State Employees' Association commented in writing on the use of monetary incentives for employees of the state's employment service.)

- Published statements and position papers by leaders of several public employee organizations on monetary incentives and other motivational programs.
- A review of state public employee laws and policies, plus an examination of selected public employee contracts and statistical studies of contract provisions recently conducted by the Bureau of Labor Statistics.

The interviews (some of which lasted over an hour) utilized semistructured questionnaires and were supplemented in some cases by additional documentation provided by respondents. Interviews which did not involve random samples have not been used to make generalizations as to incidence or representativeness. In these instances we focused on the range of situations or experiences encountered.

Because of limited resources, no new, independent program evaluations—such as examination of a jurisdiction's records to determine changes in productivity after introduction of a new motivational plan—were undertaken for this study. This constraint greatly limited the amount and quality of the information obtained. As is emphasized later, such evaluations should be conducted in the future to obtain a better understanding of the usefulness of these motivational approaches. Nonetheless, it is believed that the results of the present study can be helpful to government officials, public employee organizations, and others interested in providing effective and efficient government services as well as satisfying and rewarding jobs for public employees.

Part One:
MONETARY INCENTIVES

Chapter 2
THE NATURE OF
MONETARY INCENTIVES

A monetary incentive is a cash reward used to induce a desired type of performance or behavior by an employee. Monetary incentives hold a central position, historically and psychologically, in any study of ways to motivate employees. As Katzell and Yankelovich have noted, "the topic of 'money' is . . . fundamental to a consideration of work motivation, and its consequences of job satisfaction and performance." [1]

While monetary incentives have long played an important role in the private sector, their use in the public sector has been both limited and controversial. Of course, many state and local governments provide "merit increases," which in theory depend on good performance. And some governments have tried other ways of linking pay with performance, such as formulas for determining future salaries or bonuses on the basis of current performance and techniques for sharing with employees the savings resulting from improved employee productivity.

Such programs, however, raise a number of questions. Do they really motivate public employees? Do they reduce expenditures? Do they increase output? Do the resulting gains significantly outweigh the costs of the incentive plans?

This part of the study examines and summarizes the available information on these issues. Attention is focused on a variety of monetary incentives whose objectives include direct improvement of the productivity of government employees:

---

1. Katzell and Yankelovich, *Work, Productivity, and Job Satisfaction*, p. 288.

performance bonuses, piecework plans, shared savings plans, suggestion awards, and performance-based wage increases. Monetary incentives that only indirectly address improved performance, such as educational and career development incentives, and incentives whose primary purpose is to reduce certain types of "counterproductive behavior" (e.g., absenteeism), are excluded.

The Relevance of Monetary Rewards to Public Employees

Studies of the preferences of public employees indicate rather consistently that even though high wages are frequently not one of their major objectives, their opinions about the adequacy of their compensation are often so unfavorable that additional monetary rewards are often preferred over most other types of motivators.[2] Moreover, studies in the states of New Jersey and Washington indicate that monetary rewards can play an especially important role in efforts to improve government productivity.[3] Both studies concluded that increases in productivity depended greatly on the implementation of fundamental changes in the state system of rewards and recognition. Both supervisory and nonsupervisory personnel felt that it was especially important to establish a clear relationship among performance, compensation, and opportunities for advancement. Employees in both states suggested that the state should provide monetary

---

2. This conclusion is based on an analysis of the findings reported in Peter Gregg, "Work in the Public Service—How Employees View Their Jobs," *Network News*, National Training and Development Service, vol. 3, no. 1 (Washington, D.C., Winter 1975); F. Gerald Brown and Richard Heimovics, "What Municipal Employees Want from Work," paper presented at the National Conference of the American Society for Public Administration (Los Angeles, April 1973); Vincent J. Macri and Dina D. Paul, "Multi-Municipal Productivity Project Attitudinal Program," County of Nassau (Mineola, New York, June 1974); and State of New Jersey, Department of Labor and Industry, "Establishment of an Improved Employee Incentive Plan," Report of Committee No. 7, Employee Task Force on Morale, Productivity, and Involvement (Trenton, 1975).

3. See State of New Jersey, Department of Labor and Industry "Broadening Employee Involvement in the Department's Management Structure," Report of Committee No. 1, Employee Task Force on Morale, Productivity, and Involvement (Trenton, 1975), and State of Washington, Office of Program Planning and Fiscal Management, "Report on Inhibitors Questionnaire" (Olympia, 1974).

rewards for demonstrably outstanding performance (i.e., as measured by the achievement of valid goals).

The Potential Benefits of Monetary Incentives: Private Sector Experiences

Most of the basic research on monetary rewards in the private sector was conducted between ten and twenty years ago. A number of publications summarizing the results of that research are available. Many of the more recent research findings (through 1973) have been reviewed by Katzell and Yankelovich and by Srivastva and his associates.[4] In view of the evidence indicating that public sector and private sector employees are generally similar in terms of needs and motivation, these results are relevant to the use of monetary incentives for public employees.[5] Among the more important private sector findings on the effects of compensation are the following: [6]

- Relatively well-paid workers generally are better satisfied with their pay and jobs than are relatively low-paid workers; as a result, the former are less likely to be absent or to quit than are low-paid workers.
- Workers who are paid more than other workers for a given job are likely to have higher motivation and productivity, but only if pay is linked to performance.
- Workers who think their compensation is inequitable are less satisfied with their jobs than those who feel their pay is equitable; a related point is that satisfaction with pay is greater when pay is clearly tied to performance than when it is not.

---

4. Katzell and Yankelovich, *Work, Productivity, and Job Satisfaction*; and Srivastva et al., *Job Satisfaction and Productivity*. The remainder of this section draws extensively from the synthesis of the research literature provided by Katzell and Yankelovich.
5. A number of studies have directly or indirectly addressed the congruence between the needs of public and private sector workers. See, for instance, Lance W. Seberhagen, "What Motivates Civil Service Employees?" *Public Personnel Review*, vol. 31, no. 1 (January 1970), pp. 48-50; and John W. Newstrom, William E. Reif, and Robert M. Monczka, "Motivating the Public Employee: Fact vs. Fiction," *Public Personnel Management* (January-February 1976), pp. 67-72.
6. Katzell and Yankelovich, *Work, Productivity, and Job Satisfaction*, p. 36.

- The potentially favorable results of improved compensation are nullified if they have an adverse impact on other working conditions, such as job security or social relations.

There have also been a number of studies of the overall effectiveness of individual, group, and organization-wide incentives. Individual incentives focus on evaluating and rewarding the performance of individual employees, while group incentives use measures of overall group performance to determine the size of a reward pool that is then divided among the members of the group. Organization-wide incentives link rewards to measures of overall organizational effectiveness (e.g., cost savings by a company or by an agency) and share any rewards earned among all employees in the organization.

Numerous research findings suggest that one of the most important factors in the effectiveness of each of these incentive approaches is the degree to which pay is *explicitly* dependent on performance. The closer one comes to tying individual pay to individual performance, the greater the increase in productivity.

In an extensive review of the literature, Lawler concludes that the overall effectiveness of individual monetary incentives in raising productivity is well-documented. Even the most conservative studies indicate that individual incentives can increase productivity 10 percent to 20 percent.[7] (The reverse may also be true. One study found that elimination of an individual incentive program was associated with a 25 percent decrease in productivity.)[8]

Katzell and Yankelovich identified several factors that can limit the impact of individual monetary incentive plans:[9]

- Task interdependency and the need for cooperation among workers (individual incentives foster competition and therefore may reduce worker effectiveness when cooperation is required);
- The difficulty of specifying objective criteria which address all important aspects of the desired job behavior;
- Task complexity; and
- An organizational climate of insecurity and mistrust

7. E. E. Lawler, *Pay and Organizational Effectiveness*, p. 124.
8. Katzell and Yankelovich, *Work, Productivity, and Job Satisfaction*, p. 317.
9. Ibid., pp. 318-319.

(which can lead workers to restrict productivity despite the existence of individual incentives).

There have been relatively few investigations of the effectiveness of group incentives.[10] However, the existing studies indicate that group incentives lead to levels of productivity superior to those achieved with no incentive rewards but lower than those achieved with individual incentives. Furthermore, the size of the productivity improvement likely to be achieved under a group incentive plan tends to decrease as the size of the group increases. (This is due in part to increased blurring of the linkage between pay and performance.) Groups that share incentive rewards equally generally exhibit higher job satisfaction but lower productivity than groups which give larger shares of the rewards to high-performing members. The research findings indicate that group incentive plans are especially well-suited to situations in which worker cooperation is desired. Moreover, group plans tend to avoid certain undesirable side effects of individual incentive plans, such as restriction of output among workers covered by incentives.

Even less is known about the effects of organization-wide incentives, such as shared savings plans. So-called Scanlon plans (which incorporate profit sharing) have not consistently increased or decreased productivity.[11] Nonetheless, Katzell and

10. See James L. Farr, "Incentive Schedules, Productivity, and Satisfaction in Work Groups: A Laboratory Study," *Organizational Behavior and Human Performance*, vol. 17, no. 1 (October 1976), pp. 159-170; Gary A. Yukl and Gary P. Latham, "Consequences of Reinforcement Schedules and Incentive Magnitudes for Employee Performance: Problems Encountered in an Industrial Setting," *Journal of Applied Psychology*, vol. 60, no. 3 (1975), pp. 294-298; Alan G. Weinstein and Robert L. Holzbach, Jr., "Impact of Individual Differences, Reward Distribution, and Task Structure on Productivity in a Simulated Work Environment," *Journal of Applied Psychology*, vol. 58, no. 3 (1973), pp. 296-301; and Katzell and Yankelovich, *Work, Productivity, and Job Satisfaction*, pp. 319-320. The latter reviews much of the research on group incentives prior to 1973. For a study of group incentives in a nonprofit organization, see J. J. Jehring, "The Use of Subsystem Incentives in Hospitals: A Case Study of the Incentive Program at Baptist Hospital, Pensacola, Florida," Center for the Study of Productivity Motivation, University of Wisconsin (Madison, 1968).

11. Katzell and Yankelovich, *Work, Productivity, and Job Satisfaction*, pp. 320-321. For an evaluation of an organization-wide system of monetary incentives in a nonprofit organization, see J. J. Jehring, "Increasing Productivity in Hospitals: A Case Study of the Incentive Program at Memorial Hospital of Long Beach," Center for the Study of Productivity Motivation, University of Wisconsin (Madison, 1966).

Yankelovich suggest that such plans can serve as a useful part of broader efforts to improve productivity.

Katzell and Yankelovich found little systematic research on the relationship between monetary incentives and employee job satisfaction, and the little research that does exist shows no consistent relationship between them.[12] Instead, the impact appears to depend on factors specific to each case.

The available research on monetary incentives in the private sector also suggests that improving both job satisfaction and worker productivity at the same time is likely to be considerably more difficult than improving only one of those characteristics. Indeed, improving both simultaneously is likely to require more than just the introduction of monetary incentives.[13]

Rothe has assessed the theoretical effectiveness of a number of specific types of monetary incentives found in both the public and private sectors, using criteria developed from expectancy theory (see Chapter 1). His conclusion is that individual and group incentives are most likely to improve productivity.[14]

Lawler has compared the characteristics of several monetary incentive approaches used in the private sector and has developed ratings for plans which use different types of rewards (bonuses or wage increases), different types of performance criteria, and different employee groupings.[15] (See Exhibit 1.) No one type of program is strong in all areas, but group and organization-wide bonus plans, with rewards based on objective performance criteria, are generally rated highly. Lawler also concludes that the effectiveness of monetary incentive plans varies greatly: "What is a wonderful plan for one organization is for a whole series of reasons a bad plan for another." [16]

A related question is whether the introduction of monetary incentives is compatible with the use of other motivational approaches. As will be discussed later in this book, the linking of employee performance appraisals with monetary rewards can be counterproductive unless care is taken to ensure, among

12. Katzell and Yankelovich, *Work, Productivity, and Job Satisfaction*, pp. 328-330.

13. Ibid., pp. 23-24, 36-37.

14. H. F. Rothe, "Does Higher Pay Bring Higher Productivity?" *Personnel*, vol. 37, no. 4 (July-August 1960), pp. 20-27.

15. Edward E. Lawler III, "Improving the Quality of Work Life: Reward Systems," U.S. Department of Labor (Washington, D.C., 1975), pp. 59-65.

16. Ibid., p. 60.

Exhibit 1

RATINGS OF VARIOUS MONETARY INCENTIVE APPROACHES

Type of Reward	Grouping Used for Measuring Performance	Performance Measure Used [1]	Degree to Which Plan Exhibits Selected Characteristics Likely to Affect Productivity			
			Ties Pay to Performance	Produces Negative Side Effects	Encourages Cooperation	Meets with Employee Acceptance
Wage Increase	Individual	Productivity	4	1	1	4
		Cost effective-ness	3	1	1	4
		Subjective ratings by supervisors	3	1	1	3
	Limited Group	Productivity	3	1	2	4
		Cost effective-ness	3	1	2	4
		Subjective ratings by supervisors	2	1	2	3
	Organization-wide	Productivity	2	1	3	4
		Cost effective-ness	2	1	2	4

(Continued)

Exhibit 1 (Continued)

Type of Reward	Grouping Used for Measuring Performance	Performance Measure Used [1]	Degree to Which Plan Exhibits Selected Characteristics Likely to Affect Productivity			
			Ties Pay to Performance	Produces Negative Side Effects	Encourages Cooperation	Meets with Employee Acceptance
Bonus	Individual	Productivity	5	3	1	2
		Cost effectiveness	4	2	1	2
		Subjective ratings by supervisors	4	2	1	2
	Limited Group	Productivity	4	1	3	3
		Cost effectiveness	3	1	3	3
		Subjective ratings by supervisors	3	1	3	3
	Organization-wide	Productivity	3	1	3	4
		Cost effectiveness	3	1	3	4
		Profit	2	1	3	3

Exhibit 1 (Continued)

1. The terms "productivity" and "cost effectiveness" are not defined. Productivity measures appear to refer to such criteria as sales or production volume. Cost-effectiveness measures apparently refer to costs, profits, sales, and similar criteria.

Source: Edward E. Lawler III, "Improving the Quality of Work Life: Reward Systems," U.S. Department of Labor (Washington, D.C., 1975), p. 60. A rating of 5 indicates that a plan exhibits the characteristic to a high degree; a rating of 1 indicates that a plan exhibits the characteristic to a low degree. The ratings represent personal judgments by Lawler based on a review of the literature and his own experiences, primarily with private sector plans.

other things, that the appraisal criteria are objective, the appraisors well-trained, and the appraisal process well thought out. Performance-targeting systems (such as MBO) that meet these criteria, however, appear to be quite compatible with the use of monetary incentives.

On the other hand, the evidence concerning the compatibility of monetary incentives with job enrichment techniques is inconclusive. As noted previously, private sector applications of Scanlon plans—which combine monetary incentives in the form of profit sharing with job enrichment in the form of increased participation by employees in cost-saving decisions—have had no consistent impact on productivity. Laboratory studies by Deci have given indications that the provision of monetary rewards contingent upon performance actually decreases intrinsic motivation—that is, the worker's natural interest in, and commitment to, a task.[17] Deci concluded that when monetary incentives are introduced, workers concentrate on earning more pay rather than on performance of the task itself. (On the other hand, Deci found that monetary rewards not contingent upon performance did not appear to affect intrinsic motivation, while verbal praise increased intrinsic motivation.) However, some recent research results have not supported Deci's conclusions. For instance, Farr found in a carefully designed laboratory study that tying pay to performance did not reduce intrinsic motivation.[18] Farr concludes that a combination of proper job design and an objective system for linking pay to performance would provide the motivational advantages of *both* monetary incentives and job enrichment.[19]

---

17. Edward L. Deci, "The Effects of Contingent and Noncontingent Rewards and Controls on Intrinsic Motivation," *Organizational Behavior and Human Performance*, vol. 8 (1972), pp. 217-229.
   18. James L. Farr, "Task Characteristics, Reward Contingency, and Intrinsic Motivation," *Organizational Behavior and Human Performance*, vol. 16 (August 1976), pp. 294-307.
   19. Ibid., p. 306.

Chapter 3
TYPES OF MONETARY INCENTIVES USED IN THE PUBLIC SECTOR

In recent years a variety of monetary incentive plans have been used to stimulate the productivity of state and local government employees. These plans have varied with respect to their coverage, selection procedure, reward mechanism, and the nature of the rewards.

Coverage refers to which employees are eligible for rewards. One plan may cover managerial employees only, while another covers nonmanagerial employees only. An incentive plan may apply only to selected types of employees (clerical, for example), or it may cover only the employees of a few selected agencies within a government.

Selection procedure refers to the technique used to choose the individuals or groups that will receive awards. Employees may be chosen on the basis of a formula or rule, by subjective management decision, through competition with other individuals or groups, or in some other fashion.

Reward mechanism refers to the procedure that relates the amount of the monetary incentive to the performance required to obtain it. The size of the reward may depend on a specific schedule of awards, on some kind of formula, or on management discretion (possibly within certain limits). Plans that reward individuals on the basis of their own performance are termed "individual incentives"; plans which reward group performance and provide more or less the same reward to each member of the group are known as "group incentives."

The nature of the reward refers to how and what is provided in the way of a monetary incentive. The award may be a one-time award (a lump-sum bonus) or a permanent wage increase, and it can be given in a variety of ways—through an established merit procedure, as an across-the-board increase contingent on performance, or through productivity bargaining between the government and a union or employee association. The award may take the form of cash, savings bonds, or increased retirement benefits, among other things.[1]

Most monetary incentive plans in the public sector fall into nine major classes:

1. *Performance Bonuses* are one-time financial awards paid specifically for superior job performance.[2]

2. *Piecework Bonuses* are special kinds of performance bonuses that tie a worker's pay directly to the worker's production. Variations of this practice include payment of a specified amount of money for each unit of output produced, payment for each unit produced above a specified amount, or payment on the basis of "standard hours" (engineered time standards) earned for each unit produced.[3]

3. *Shared Savings Plans* provide a monetary reward for a group of workers based on cost savings achieved within a given period. Usually, a specified portion of the savings is distributed among the employees who contributed to the cost reduction. The distribution is usually made as a bonus (and thus can be considered as a special type of performance bonus). Shared savings plans are the

---

1. Other types of rewards, such as extra vacation or sick leave, trips, and prizes, also have monetary value and represent a cost to the jurisdiction. Since they are rarely encountered in the public sector in connection with performance incentives, they are not discussed here.

2. Throughout this book, the term "performance bonus" does not include piecework plans or rewards funded out of savings. While such programs usually do involve bonuses, they are discussed separately under "piecework" and "shared savings plans."

3. Note that the Bureau of Labor Statistics generally considers only the first of these—plans that tie a worker's earnings directly to the number of units produced—to be piecework plans. Incentive schemes that provide extra payments for production in excess of a quota or for the completion of tasks in less than the standard time are considered "production bonuses" by the BLS. See George L. Stelluto, "Report on Incentive Pay in Manufacturing Industries," *Monthly Labor Review*, vol. 92, no. 7 (July 1969), pp. 49-53.

public sector equivalent of profit-sharing plans in the private sector.

4. *Suggestion Award Programs* are intended to encourage employees to contribute ideas for ways to decrease costs, increase quality, or otherwise improve the operation of their organization. These programs usually constitute a type of shared savings plan, in that the size of the award is based on the magnitude of the cost savings produced by the suggestion in the first year of its implementation.

5. *Performance-Based Wage Increases* are permanent increases in wages or salary to reward high-quality performance as measured by output, efficiency, or work quality. Two subtypes of performance-based wage increases are especially significant in the public sector:

   a. *Merit System Increases.* This type utilizes existing civil service or merit system procedures for awarding increases. Of special interest are those procedures that focus specifically on rewarding job performance—quantity and quality—measured in concrete terms.

   b. *Performance Increases Obtained Through Productivity Bargaining.* Some governments have turned to mechanisms outside their regular merit or civil service system procedures for awarding performance-based wage increases. Of particular significance are productivity bargaining agreements that link higher pay to improved productivity. Two forms of productivity bargaining are particularly worth noting.[4] One is the "buy-out," a process through which management or a joint labor-management committee identifies changes that would improve productivity but that require the approval of the union. In return for union approval, management agrees to modify the current contract, for instance, by adding a wage increase. These rewards to workers are contingent only on union approval

---

4. See Robert B. McKersie and L. C. Hunter, *Pay, Productivity and Collective Bargaining* (London: Macmillan-St. Martin's Press, 1973); also, Committee for Economic Development, *Improving Management of the Public Work Force: The Challenge to State and Local Government* (New York, 1978), p. 80.

of the changes; the success of the changes in improving productivity has no effect on the reward.
A second form of productivity bargaining is called
"gain sharing." The bargain here is designed to
provide workers with monetary rewards only if
productivity increases. The reward often must be
funded out of savings generated by the workers. It
may take the form of a one-time bonus or a permanent wage increase.

6. *Safety Awards* involve the provision of monetary (or
nonmonetary) rewards to encourage employees to improve their safety records.

7. *Attendance Incentives* involve the use of monetary rewards to induce employees to improve their attendance
records, e.g., by reducing lateness or abuse of sick leave.

8. *Educational Incentives* are monetary rewards given to
encourage employees to take certain types of training
or to continue their formal education.

9. *Career Development* incentives are systems of well-
defined promotional opportunities linked to training
programs designed to qualify employees for the positions available.

The present study of monetary incentives focuses on the
first five techniques listed above. These five are the ones most
specifically intended to improve employee motivation and productivity (although the other four can also lead to greater productivity). Each of these five approaches is discussed in more
detail in the following chapters.

Overall Use of Monetary Incentives by State and Local Governments

The last large-scale study of the use of monetary (and other)
incentives by state and local governments appears to have been
the 1973 UI/ICMA/NGC survey. That survey showed that the
use of monetary incentives by state and local governments was
relatively rare, except for performance-based wage increases provided through merit system procedures and suggestion awards.
Among the respondents to that survey, 42 percent of the local

governments and 61 percent of the state governments reported using performance-based wage increases, while 25 percent of the local and 63 percent of the state governments reported using suggestion awards.[5] Experience with performance bonuses was reported by only 6 percent of the local governments and 10 percent of the states, with even smaller percentages for shared savings plans, piecework plans, and productivity bargaining.

Overall use of these monetary incentives does not seem to have changed much since 1973, even though more recent figures are available only for performance-based wage increases and productivity bargaining. The 1976 ICMA survey found that productivity bargaining was being used by 10 percent of the responding local governments, up five percentage points from the 1973 UI/ICMA/NGC survey results.[6] Information provided by officials of the fifty state governments and a random sample of fifty local governments in the course of this study revealed that 54 percent of the states and 48 percent of the local governments had utilized programs linking monetary rewards (bonuses, wage increases, etc.) with superior performance ratings. These results indicate relatively little change in the incidence of such programs between 1973 and 1977—a six percentage-point increase for local governments and a seven percentage-point decrease for state governments. During the same period, few new piecework plans, shared savings plans, or suggestion award programs appear to have been introduced. The 1976 ICMA survey indicated that 16 percent (sixty-one) of the local government respondents were using "management incentives,"[7] but it was not known whether these involved monetary awards.[8]

---

5. Greiner, Bell, and Hatry, *Employee Incentives*, pp. 5, 7.

6. International City Management Association, "Local Government Productivity."

7. Ibid.

8. It is also instructive to compare recent private sector trends in the use of incentives. Private sector use of monetary incentives (bonuses and piecework plans) for plant workers has not increased in recent years and may actually have declined in some areas. For instance, the overall percentage of factory workers covered by such plans decreased from 16 percent in 1963 to 12 percent in 1970, although the changes were generally concentrated in a few industries. The indications are, however, that the private sector is currently making a major effort to revise past pay plans for white collar and managerial employees, with an emphasis on tying pay more clearly to performance. Indeed, it appears that private sector pay plans based on "merit increases" are suffering from the same problems as those in the public sector when it comes to encouraging excel-

Availability of Information on the Effectiveness of Monetary Incentives for State and Local Government Employees

There is more evaluative information on monetary incentive plans than on most of the other types of motivational techniques being tried by state and local governments. Nevertheless, the evaluative information available is quite limited. The 1973 UI/ICMA/NGC survey indicated that thirty-seven local government and eight state government monetary incentive plans had been evaluated. Over half of these plans (twenty-three) reportedly involved performance-based wage increases (merit increases), and another 31 percent (fourteen) involved suggestion awards. However, on the basis of the evaluations reviewed in the course of this study, it would appear that few of them adequately address the range of criteria necessary to make a comprehensive judgment about the impact of such plans. The available evaluative information is reviewed in the next two chapters.

lence. See John Howell Cox, "Time and Incentive Pay Practices in Urban Areas," *Monthly Labor Review*, vol. 94, no. 12 (December 1971), pp. 53-56; Stelluto, "Report on Incentive Pay"; and David A. Weeks, *Compensating Employees: Lessons of the 1970's* (New York: The Conference Board, 1976).

Chapter 4

INCENTIVES INVOLVING BONUSES AND OTHER ONE-TIME MONETARY REWARDS

Four important types of monetary incentives—performance bonuses, piecework bonuses, shared savings awards, and suggestion awards—are provided on a "one-time" basis. In other words, the employee or group of employees must have exhibited superior performance each time a reward is received. Unlike performance-based wage increases, these types of incentives do not commit a state or local government to continue paying an award long after it was originally earned.

Performance Bonuses

Exhibit 2 summarizes the available information on the status of performance bonus plans used or considered by state and local governments. Among local governments, performance bonuses were reported planned or in use in thirty-two jurisdictions (6 percent) that responded to the 1973 UI/ICMA/NGC survey.[1] The existence of fourteen of those programs was verified in 1974. Another—in Fullerton, California—had been terminated, and two more (in Philadelphia, Pennsylvania, and Fargo, North

---

1. Greiner, Bell, and Hatry, *Employee Incentives*, p. 7.

Exhibit 2

PERFORMANCE BONUS PLANS
(As of March 1978)

Jurisdiction	Eligible Employees[1]	Planned (P) or Existing (E)[2]	Rejected (R) or Terminated (T)
Arlington, Tex.	All nonmanagement employees at top step of pay range	E	
Burbank, Calif.	All department heads	E	
Charleston County, S.C.	All employees except department heads	E	
Compton, Calif.	Police	E	T
Downer's Grove, Ill.	All department heads	E	
Fargo, N. Dak.	All department managers *	E	R
Fort Worth, Tex.	Automotive mechanics	E	T
Fullerton, Calif.	Nonsupervisory employees	E	
Hartford, Conn.	Police and firefighters	E	
Helena, Mont.	Drivers and collectors in Sanitation Division	E	R
Hennepin County, Minn.	*		T
Jersey City, N.J.	Streetsweeper operators	E	
King County, Wash.	All nonunion employees	E	
Long Beach, Calif.	All management personnel	E	
Mesa, Ariz.	All nonmanagement employees		
Midland, Tex.	*		
New York, N.Y.	All career civil servants	E	R

Exhibit 2 (Continued)

Location	Employees covered		
Norfolk, Va.	Waste collection supervisors and line employees	E	
Palo Alto, Calif.	All management personnel	E	
Philadelphia, Pa.	Supervisors in meter division of Water Department	E	
	Catchbasin cleaning crews		R
Pontiac, Mich.	All employees	E	
Santa Rosa, Calif.	All management personnel	E	
Torrance, Calif.	All management personnel	E	
West Hartford, Conn.	All city employees	E	T
Westminster, Colo.	All city employees	E	R
State of California	Career executives		
	Job agents		
State of California	All employees of Employment Development Department	P	
State of Colorado	All state employees	E	
State of Connecticut	All state employees	E	
State of Minnesota	All governor-appointed department heads and deputies	E	
	Senior nonmanagement employment service and unemployment insurance field personnel	P	
State of Montana	Local office employees of the division of employment security	P	T
State of Nevada	All state employees in the classified service	P	
State of New Jersey	All state employees	P	T
	Local office employees of the Department of Labor and Industry who have contact with the public		

(Continued)

Exhibit 2 (Continued)

Jurisdiction	Eligible Employees[1]	Existing (E)[2] or Planned (P)	Rejected (R) or Terminated (T)
State of Ohio	Employment service and unemployment insurance staff in local offices	P	
State of Pennsylvania	Employment security personnel in one service district		R
State of Washington	Employment security personnel in one local office	P	

NOTE: Two more bonus plans have come to our attention as this book goes to press. Since 1976, Darien, Conn., has provided bonuses for "markedly improved performance"; the plan covers all city employees. And since 1977, Montebello, Calif., has awarded bonuses to management personnel for outstanding performance as measured against quarterly targets.

1. An asterisk indicates that planning did not proceed far enough for the eligible employees to be specified.
2. "Existing" indicates that the program appears to be still in use, according to the most recent information. In some cases, however, that information is up to four years old.

Dakota) had been considered and then rejected before being implemented.[2]

Since 1974, two of the fourteen programs have been suspended (in Jersey City, New Jersey, where a key person was transferred and not replaced, and in Compton, California, where the city council refused to fund a management bonus plan after 1975). Eight local governments are known to have started bonus programs since 1973. Of the twenty-seven local government bonus programs listed in Exhibit 2, seven were for nonsupervisory personnel, eight were for managerial or supervisory employees, and nine covered employees of both groups.

The following four programs illustrate the variety among bonus programs being tried and some of the implementation problems they have encountered.[3]

Helena, Montana. Helena's program began in January 1975 and originally covered the nine waste collection employees assigned to residential collection routes. Management offered the incentive plan to the collectors (who were not unionized at that time) to help win their cooperation for a change to plastic bags and curbside pickup. Under the plan each collector is awarded an extra $5 every day that he completes his regular collection route and receives no more than two legitimate complaints from citizens. (If a collector receives more than four legitimate complaints in a given week, he receives no bonus for that week.) Since the collectors work together in three-man crews and the criteria apply to crew performance, this incentive program should be considered a group plan. The plan was designed with the active participation and cooperation of the employees.

In the first year of the plan's operation, employees qualified for bonuses on 82 percent of the available working days; by FY 1977 the figure was 91 percent (equivalent to a total annual bonus of more than $1,000 per person). City management believes that the use of incentives plus the switch to plastic bags made it possible for the division (1) to reduce the number of residential collection crews

---

2. Of the remaining fifteen programs reported in the 1973 UI/ICMA/ NGC survey, seven were then in the planning stage, two were found to have been erroneously reported, and the other six programs were not followed up at that time.

3. For descriptions of other local (and state) government bonus programs, see Greiner, Bell, and Hatry, *Employee Incentives*, pp. 52-62.

from four to two, (2) to save about $65,000 annually, and (3) to delay for three years any increase in customer service charges. Since 1975 the total number of sanitation division employees has dropped 42 percent.

The program originally created some concern among the division's commercial collection crews, who were not covered by the plan. These employees were subsequently included, and management reports that the covered employees are quite happy with the plan. No formal assessment of job satisfaction has been conducted.

There have been no major labor relations problems between the city government and the sanitation employees, but there has apparently been some dissension within the bargaining unit between the sanitation employees and other workers not covered by the plan. As a result, management has offered to introduce similar incentives for other employee groups if the employees themselves design a satisfactory plan. Productivity incentives for the city's vehicle maintenance and fire department employees are under consideration.

Compton, California. A bonus plan for Compton's fifteen department heads was used between 1970 and 1975. Up to $365 a year could be awarded on the basis of "performance," although no specific criteria for rating department heads were established. However, the city council questioned the legality of bonuses for city employees; there were equity problems (three elected department heads were legally ineligible for bonuses); and over time the awards became rather routine. In 1975 the council refused to authorize additional funds for the program.

Hennepin County, Minnesota. A proposed incentive bonus for county employees was rejected by the county board in 1973. The board felt that the concept of incentive pay tied to performance targets was not politically acceptable, and that such a program would lead to salary competition between Hennepin County and neighboring local governments.

Midland, Texas. City officials in Midland considered a bonus plan in 1973 but abandoned the idea, largely because of their inability to agree on how to measure performance.

Among state governments, four states reported experience with performance bonuses in the 1973 UI/ICMA/NGC survey.[4] Not reported in the 1973 survey was a bonus plan tried in 1971 by the state of New Jersey. Three states —California, Minnesota, and Montana—have introduced bonus plans since the 1973 survey.

As of March 1978, efforts to create bonus plans for employment security personnel were under way in five states.[5] In the state of Washington the Employment Security Department has been developing a bonus system to be tested in one local office. It would focus on staff performance in making job placements and reducing periods of unemployment. In New Jersey the Department of Labor and Industry formed an employee task force in 1975 to look into a number of personnel matters, among them the possible advantages of monetary incentives. The task force's committee on incentives suggested several incentive programs, including four types of bonus plans.[6] Since the bonus plans would have required modifications of state merit system procedures and civil service laws, the department was unable to implement them itself; however, it formally recommended them to the governor. There has been no further action on the plans. Bonus plans for employment security personnel are also being developed in California, Minnesota, and Ohio.

In Pennsylvania a bonus plan for employment security personnel was rejected during the planning stage in 1974, largely because state officials anticipated union resistance. California had a similar experience with a bonus plan for job agents in 1973.[7]

Four attempts by state governments to introduce performance bonuses are described below.

Montana. A system of performance bonuses for the approximately 370 local office employees of Montana's Division of Employment Security was introduced in 1976. The program was developed with the knowledge of the Montana Public Employees Association and continued for twelve months. The plan involved two separate types of

4. Greiner, Bell, and Hatry, *Employee Incentives*, p. 5.
5. For a description of these and other motivational approaches which have been developed for state employment service personnel, see Greiner and Wright, "Employee Incentives for Local Offices," Chapter 3.
6. See State of New Jersey, "Improved Employee Incentive Plan."
7. See Greiner and Wright, "Employee Incentives for Local Offices," pp. 16-18; and David Greenberg, Al Lipson, and Bernard Rostker, "Technical Success, Political Failure: The Incentive Pay Plan for California Job Agents," *Policy Analysis*, vol. 2, no. 4 (Fall 1976), pp. 545-575.

awards: quarterly cash performance bonuses and annual cash incentive rewards.

Both were group incentives, with the local office being the primary unit for incentive purposes. The offices were classified as large, medium, or small, and offices in each size grouping competed against each other. Under the quarterly incentive plan, a local office could earn a maximum bonus each quarter of $100 per paid position, depending on its performance relative to other offices in its group. For the annual incentive plan the maximum bonus per paid position was $50. The reward money earned by an office was shared equally among all personnel in the office.

The quarterly incentive rewards were based on each office's accomplishments with respect to targets it had specified in its annual plan of service. Three types of rankings were used to determine the rewards:

(1) Each office was ranked against other offices in its size grouping according to its achievements during the previous quarter with regard to six criteria: individuals placed, total placements, individuals counseled, counseled individuals placed, veterans placed, and veterans counseled. For each performance criterion, five "incentive points" were awarded to the office that ranked first in its size grouping.

(2) An overall level of achievement was then computed for each office by averaging the office's performance with regard to all six of the performance criteria. The offices within each size grouping were then ranked on their overall level of achievement, and twenty "incentive points" were awarded to the offices ranking first in each size grouping.

(3) Each office was given points for achieving or exceeding each of seventeen quarterly goals (individuals placed, migrants placed, individuals counseled, etc.). The results were then weighted and combined to produce an overall score. Each local office was then ranked within its size grouping according to its overall score for the seventeen goals, and fifty "incentive points" were awarded to the offices with the highest overall score in each grouping.

The total number of "incentive points" earned by an office under the various rankings, expressed as a percentage, determined what proportion of the maximum quarterly per person incentive reward the office received.

A similar procedure was used for the annual awards.

Offices in each size grouping were ranked according to their performance over the course of the year with respect to each of four quality criteria: (1) percentage of nonagricultural placements longer than 150 days, (2) average hourly wage of persons placed, (3) percentage of nonagricultural placements in professional or managerial jobs, and (4) the *change* (with respect to the previous year) in the ratio "number of individuals placed per staff year divided by the corresponding target specified in the office's plan of service." For each criterion on which an office ranked first in its size grouping it earned a bonus that was divided equally among all its personnel. Thus, if an office ranked first on all four criteria, local office staff could receive a bonus of up to $50 per person.

During the year the plan was used, incentive earnings of local office employees ranged from $159.72 to $2.96 per person. In five local offices, no awards were earned. The total expenditure for incentive rewards came to about $9,700. In an evaluation of the plan for the state's Office of Budget and Program Planning, Montana's Division of Employment Security found that all winning offices had made substantial increases in production over FY 1976. Moreover, there was an increase in *overall* agency performance during the year in which the plan was used, relative to the preceding year (e.g., a 14 percent increase in individuals placed, a 23 percent increase in individuals counseled, a 10 percent increase in job openings received). However, it is not possible to distinguish what portion of that increase reflected improved economic conditions and what portion could be attributed to the use of incentives.

According to agency officials there were a number of reasons why the incentive system was discontinued after one year, but the major problem was the standards used to measure an office's achievements. By using standards based on an office's performance during the previous year, the plan tended to reward offices which had performed poorly in the past and hence found it easiest to make substantial improvements. Another difficulty was that the incentive plan did not adjust performance levels for differences in the size of local offices *within* a grouping. Nevertheless, agency management indicated that no major complaints had been received regarding the plan and that the flaws could have been corrected had there been top level management interest in continuing the effort and had the staff time needed to develop the necessary modifications been available.

Minnesota. In 1973 Minnesota established a bonus plan for appointed department heads and their deputies.[8] The plan provided cash bonuses of up to 25 percent of annual salary for the achievement of objectives established through a management-by-objectives procedure. Assessment of achievements was made by the governor, and most of the bonuses ranged from 3 percent to 13 percent. Originally, the objectives included both work-related and personal goals, including control of such things as smoking, drinking, and obesity. Although achievement of personal goals was not a factor in determining bonuses, media reports gave the impression that the bonuses were rewards for controlling personal habits. The resulting furor led to elimination of personal goals from the plan. Subsequent salary increases for officials covered by the plan led to a further modification—the limiting of bonuses to a maximum of 10 percent of annual salary.

California. In the process of refining its "career executive" program (a plan to move top state managers out of the civil service and into a more flexible personnel system that emphasized managerial initiative and responsiveness), California in 1973 initiated quarterly bonuses for outstanding managerial performance.[9] The bonuses were ended after about a year because management felt they demanded too much paperwork while not creating much of an incentive for improved performance. But the state has not given up on monetary incentives. California's Employment Development Department is currently developing a plan to award $150 bonuses to between sixty and seventy of its employees each year for "sustained superior accomplishments," as judged by supervisors.

New Jersey. In 1971 the New Jersey legislature appropriated $1 million for a statewide program of employee bonuses. The money was allocated to all state agencies in proportion to number of employees. Except for some general constraints to ensure that clerical personnel shared in the rewards, the legislature allowed each agency to determine how to distribute the bonuses. The program

---

8. For a recent summary of this program, see James E. Jarrett and Dick Howard, *Incentives and Performance: Minnesota's Management Plan*, The Council of State Governments (Lexington, Kentucky, 1978), p. 7.

9. John Birkenstock, Ronald Kurtz, and Steven Phillips, "Career Executive Assignments—Report on a California Innovation," *Public Personnel Management* (May-June 1975), pp. 151-155, especially p. 154.

was dropped after a year, following numerous charges of favoritism and bias.

In summary, twenty-three state and local governments are now believed to be operating bonus plans. Twelve other plans either were terminated or were rejected before being implemented. Although still quite rare nationally, performance bonus plans have exhibited a net increase (from sixteen to twenty-three) since 1974. Most of that increase has been due to use by local governments. Only three of eight state bonus plans have survived, compared to twenty of twenty-seven local plans.

Of the six terminated state and local programs, three were dropped largely or partly because of the absence of clearly defined, objective, performance-related criteria for selecting recipients. Of the six programs rejected prior to implementation, three were halted primarily because of union opposition; the other three were rejected by legislators for a variety of reasons, including the absence of objective performance criteria, concern over inequities, and fear of undesirable political or financial effects.

All but one of the existing bonus plans have involved individual incentives, the exception being Helena. The only other group incentive plan to be implemented was that tried by Montana's Division of Employment Security, although the program planned for Pennsylvania's Bureau of Employment Security involved group bonuses. Group bonuses also were among the programs suggested in New Jersey.

The Carter Administration's proposed reform of the federal civil service includes bonuses for top managers. The introduction of bonuses at the federal level may encourage increased use by state and local governments.

THE IMPACT OF PERFORMANCE BONUSES

There have been few thorough evaluations of the impact of state and local government performance bonus plans. Of the plans listed in Exhibit 2, quantitative information on productivity impact was available for only four. Formal assessments of the effect of bonuses on job satisfaction were conducted in only two instances, but subjective assessments by program officials were obtained for an additional eight cases as part of this study.

Some indication of the impact of a bonus plan on productivity can be obtained from places where objective performance criteria have been used to award bonuses. Thus, seven months after the introduction of performance bonuses for auto mechanics in Fort Worth, Texas, output had increased by 23 percent. No information was available, however, about the effect of the bonuses on the quality of repairs. In Helena the introduction of bonuses designed to encourage completion of sanitation routes and reduce citizen complaints helped the city reduce the number of residential trash collection crews from four to two while delaying any increase in customer service charges for three years. Furthermore, service quality improved. In the two years after the introduction of bonuses there was a 9 percent increase in the number of days in which all routes were completed with no more than two valid complaints from residents about the work of any given collection crew. Because Helena's bonus plan was coupled with the introduction of plastic bags and once-a-week collection, however, it is difficult to isolate the motivational role of the bonuses.

A similar problem makes it difficult to analyze the impact of Montana's one-year trial of group incentives for local offices of its Division of Employment Security. Although division performance improved in comparison to the previous year (the number of individuals placed rose 14 percent, the number of individuals counseled rose 23 percent, and the number of job openings received increased 10 percent), some or all of these increases may have been the result of improving economic conditions.

A 1975 Urban Institute study of Philadelphia's incentive plan for water meter repair and installation personnel found that bonuses awarded to supervisors for controlling unit costs had no clear-cut impact on productivity. The primary role of the supervisory bonus appeared to be the maintenance of equitable pay differentials between the three supervisors covered by the plan and subordinates earning piecework bonuses.[10] One surprising effect of the supervisory bonus was to limit managerial pressure on employees; supervisors did not want to be accused of making employees work harder to increase the size of their own bonuses. The supervisory bonuses in Philadelphia (the only city in which comprehensive cost information has been devel-

---

10. Philadelphia's piecework bonus plan for nonsupervisory employees is discussed in the next section.

oped) have had an annual average cost of $5,100 since 1967. The cost of installing the program was about $15,000.

Subjective assessments by city and state officials provide most of the information about the impact of other performance bonus plans on productivity. In Jersey City, where photographic street litter standards were used to determine whether or not streetsweeper operators received bonuses, city officials reported that the streets were cleaner and citizen complaints were fewer while the bonus plan was in effect.

In King County, Washington, where bonuses were awarded to employees by supervisors on the basis of performance ratings,[11] half of the employees surveyed for their reaction felt that the plan had no effect on the way county employees worked. (These results were about the same for employees who had received awards, employees who were eligible but did not receive awards, and employees who were ineligible for awards.)[12] Another 23 percent felt that the bonus plan was likely to *reduce* job performance. Here, the results differed considerably among persons who had received awards (15 percent felt the plan would decrease performance), persons who were eligible but did not receive awards (26 percent felt performance would be reduced), and persons who were ineligible to receive awards (37 percent of whom felt that the program would decrease performance). No objective assessment was made of the plan's impact on service efficiency and effectiveness.

Officials of two cities using bonuses (Arlington, Texas, and Downer's Grove, Illinois) felt that their plans had no effect on service quality or production. In four other jurisdictions (the cities of Fullerton and Compton, California, and the states of New Jersey and California), the apparent ineffectiveness of bonus plans in stimulating productivity was reported to have been a major reason for termination of the plans. In all four, the absence of objective performance criteria was reported to be a major factor in the program's demise.

A systematic assessment of the impact of bonuses on em-

---

11. For a more extensive description of this program, see Greiner, Bell, and Hatry, *Employee Incentives*, pp. 57-58.

12. Judith Fiedler and M. Peter Scontrino, "A Study of the King County Merit Award Program," University of Washington (Seattle, 1974), p. 20. The respondents included 376 persons who had received awards, 230 who were eligible for awards but did not receive any, and 148 who were ineligible for awards. Fourteen percent of the respondents were supervisory personnel.

ployee job satisfaction was made only in Philadelphia and in King County. In Philadelphia the bonuses apparently contributed to improved job satisfaction for supervisors.[13] In King County reactions were mixed. Of those who received awards, 42 percent felt that the program would actually lower morale. This was also the view of 63 percent of the eligible employees who received no award. Among respondents ineligible to participate (for instance, employees covered by union contracts), 78 percent felt the plan would lower morale.[14]

Officials in ten other jurisdictions offered subjective views about the impact of bonuses on employee job satisfaction. In Arlington, Texas, in Jersey City, and in Mesa, Arizona, bonuses were believed to have improved job satisfaction. In Helena, workers originally excluded from the bonus plan were reportedly dissatisfied but became quite satisfied after being covered by the plan. However, officials of three cities (Compton, Fullerton, and Palo Alto, California) and three states (California, Minnesota, and New Jersey) reported significant dissatisfaction and dissension among employees regarding bonus award programs.

In summary, of the five governments where bonus awards were based on objective criteria (Fort Worth, Helena, Jersey City, Philadelphia, and the state of Montana), productivity apparently improved in all except Philadelphia. Helena, Jersey City, and Philadelphia also reported improved job satisfaction. (No information about changes in job satisfaction was obtained in Fort Worth or in Montana's Division of Employment Security.)

In jurisdictions where performance criteria were not objectively defined, the impact of bonus plans on productivity was, at best, mixed. The plans were deemed ineffective and were subsequently terminated in four of these jurisdictions. There were also indications that bonus plans caused substantial job dissatisfaction in five jurisdictions where awards were based on subjective ratings.

Piecework Plans

Exhibit 3 summarizes the status of piecework bonus plans used

---

13. Greiner et al., *Monetary Incentives*, p. 43.
14. Fiedler and Scontrino, "King County Merit Award Program," p. 19.

Exhibit 3
PIECEWORK PLANS
(As of March 1978)

Jurisdiction	Eligible Employees	Planned (P) or Existing (E)[1]
Albany, N.Y.[2]	Maintenance personnel in	E
Bridgeport, Conn.[2]	selected local public	E
Denver, Colo.[2]	housing authorities,	E
Newark, N.J.[2]	including painters, car-	E
Newport News, Va.[2]	penters, electricians,	E
Savannah, Ga.[2]	custodians, extermina-	P
St. Louis, Mo.[2]	tors, gardeners, etc.	P
Jersey City, N.J.	Meter readers	E
Philadelphia, Pa.	Water meter repair and installation personnel	E
Rochester, N.Y.	Animal census takers	E
San Bernardino County, Calif.	Keypunch operators[3]	E
State of Minnesota	University of Minnesota keypunch and clerical employees	E
State of New Jersey	Keypunch personnel in the Department of Labor and Industry	P
State of Pennsylvania	EDP personnel in the Bureau of Employment Security	E

1. "Existing" indicates that the program still appears to be in use, according to the most recent information. In some cases, however, that information is up to four years old.
2. All seven of these jurisdictions are participating in the National Work Incentive Demonstration Program sponsored by the U.S. Department of Housing and Urban Development.
3. This program involves a type of piecework bonus known as "measured daywork." (See text.)

or considered by state and local governments. Use of piecework plans continues to be low. As of 1974, piecework bonuses were being used by four local and two state governments. These bonus plans included one example of "measured daywork" (in San Bernardino County, California), a variation of piecework in which an employee's performance during one period determines bonus pay during the next period.

Since 1974, five other piecework bonus plans have been introduced at the local level, and two others are being planned. All seven of the programs, funded by the federal Department of Housing and Urban Development (HUD), are designed to test the effectiveness of monetary incentives for maintenance workers at public housing projects. As of March 1978 the programs involved about two hundred nonsupervisory employees—painters, carpenters, electricians, and others. One of the programs now in the planning stage is expected to include supervisors as well. These incentive plans are modeled after plans that have been widely used by local housing authorities in Great Britain.[15]

In these HUD-sponsored piecework plans, weekly bonuses are paid to maintenance and custodial personnel who exceed specified performance levels as defined by engineered time standards. "Performance" is measured by the ratio of "earned hours" (work output times the standard time allotted for each type of output) to actual hours spent on the job, including overtime (but excluding waiting time and time spent on assigned activities not covered by the time standards). This ratio determines the size of the bonus. A painter in Savannah's public housing projects, for example, earns no bonus if his performance ratio is 0.80 or less. For each 0.01 increment above 0.80 the painter receives a bonus equal to 1 percent of his regular earnings, up to a maximum of 40 percent.[16]

Most of the seven housing authority demonstration projects have needed cooperation from unions (usually construction trade unions). No major union problems have been encountered at the seven project sites, but Minneapolis was dropped from consideration as a possible test site because of union opposition.

THE IMPACT OF PIECEWORK PLANS

Of the eleven existing plans listed in Exhibit 4, only two—those

15. E. Jay Howenstine, Morton Isler, and John Dietrich, "Public Housing Maintenance Productivity Improvement in the United Kingdom," Paper No. 222-51-1 (Washington, D.C.: The Urban Institute, 1974).

16. More detailed descriptions of the incentive computation are provided in William E. Poulter and Robert Sadacca, "Work Incentives in Public Housing: A Proposed Demonstration Program," Working Paper 223-62-1 (Washington, D.C.: The Urban Institute, 1976); and Kent Watkins, "Quarterly Report: July-September 1977," National Work Incentive Demonstration Program, Institute for Housing Management Innovations (Washington, D.C., 1978).

in the city of Philadelphia and in the state of Pennsylvania—
have been evaluated in depth.

Under the Philadelphia piecework plan, water meter install-
ers and repairmen were paid bonuses for repairs and service calls
above the number defined as a "fair day's work" according to
engineered time standards. An Urban Institute examination concluded that the plan had contributed to significant improvements in productivity since its start in 1952.[17]

As of 1975, the number of meters serviced per repairman per
year had increased 113 percent relative to preprogram (1951)
conditions. Over the same period, staff levels decreased 40 percent while workload rose 23 percent. The division saved approximately $142,000 per year between 1968 and 1975 compared to
preprogram expenditures. Administrative costs averaged $16,800
per year over the same period. The impact on service quality
was less clear, however. While customer calls were handled faster
(the repair backlog all but disappeared), complaints about mal-
functioning meters more than doubled in the years following the
introduction of incentives.

The state of Pennsylvania's piecework plan for data-process-
ing personnel in the Bureau of Employment Security was evaluated by the bureau itself at the end of the first and second
years after the plan's implementation in 1969.[18] Under the plan,
employees were paid a bonus for each wage record correctly en-
tered into the bureau's computer system above a specified minimum. The evaluation indicated that the program had contributed to a significant and continuing improvement in productivity. The number of wage records processed per operator went up
22 percent in the first year. In addition, the EDP operation was
able to take on work previously handled by other agencies. After
allowing for bonus payments, overall net savings in operating
costs of more than $10,500 a month were realized.

By the end of the plan's second year the bureau estimated
that the equivalent of ten fewer operators (at the then average
annual salary of $5,200 each) were needed to handle the unit's
primary task of entering wage records. Average output per
worker had increased from 280 to 450 wage records per hour,
and unit costs had decreased from 86 cents per 100 records to

---

17. Greiner et al., *Monetary Incentives*, Chapter 4.
18. Commonwealth of Pennsylvania, Department of Labor and Industry, "Pennsylvania Bureau of Employment Security Personnel Incentive Plan," Bureau of Employment Security (Harrisburg, n.d.).

54 cents per 100. No information was provided regarding the program's effect on the accuracy of the records.

Other jurisdictions with piecework plans also have offered positive assessments of their programs. Jersey City's incentive plan for part-time meter readers (who were paid 30 cents for each meter read) reportedly reduced the backlog of readings needed. Minnesota reported that piecework bonuses for university keypunch personnel helped attract and retain skilled people, a result also reported by Pennsylvania's Bureau of Employment Security. Initial results from three of the cities (Bridgeport, Denver, and Newport News) using piecework incentives for public housing maintenance personnel have been positive. Program officials in Bridgeport noted that painters started work earlier and continued later as soon as they began earning bonuses. Program officials in Denver and Newport News felt that their plans were supporting themselves out of savings. Newport News reported a 45 percent increase in overall productivity, a 32 percent drop in maintenance staff size (through attrition), and net savings of $50,000 as of early 1978.[19] But the validity of such savings—that is, whether they represent "paper" savings or actual reductions in out-of-pocket costs—is still to be established.

Finally, San Bernardino County, California, reported that keypunch operators performed so well under a "measured daywork" system that a management consultant could suggest no other way to improve their output. The county began using this system for about sixty keypunch operators in 1973. An operator's output and work quality during each three-month period determine the size of a bonus added to the operator's regular wage rate for the next three months. The bonus rate increases in steps of 2.5 percent, depending on performance, to a maximum of 15 percent. Although no formal evaluation has been made, management has called the plan "very successful."[20]

There is less information on the impact of piecework plans on employee satisfaction. Only in Philadelphia was a survey of employees conducted. The survey indicated that the plan generally had no detrimental effect on job satisfaction and had, in some

---

19. International City Management Association, *The Guide to Management Improvement Projects in Local Government*, vol. 2, no. 4 (Washington, D.C., July-August 1978), Item No. 139.

20. For a recent reappraisal of the potential benefits of measured daywork plans, see Mitchell Fein, "Let's Return to MDW Incentives," *Industrial Engineering*, vol. 11, no. 1 (January 1979), pp. 34-37.

cases, improved it.[21] Although competition increased among some employees, there was less need for supervisors to urge personnel to work harder. Internal evaluations of the piecework incentive plan in Pennsylvania's Bureau of Employment Security found that turnover and absenteeism fell while employee morale and enthusiasm increased. Employees sometimes arrived an hour before the normal starting time and worked during much of their lunch hour, indicating an overall improvement in job satisfaction. In Jersey City, however, the incentive plan was reported to have led to some animosity among more senior workers (who were not included in the plan) toward younger workers earning bonuses.

Shared Savings Plans

Exhibit 4 summarizes the status of shared savings plans used or considered by state and local governments.[22] There are still only a handful of these plans in the public sector, although the number has grown somewhat in the last four years. A 1974 Urban Institute report on incentives found three shared savings plans at the local level and none at the state level.[23] Since then, the number of local efforts has risen to five, and one state government (Washington) has tried (but subsequently dropped) a shared savings plan for one agency. Another state (Wisconsin) has introduced such a plan but has yet to distribute any bonuses. A third state (North Carolina) has begun planning a shared savings program recently authorized by the state legislature.

Of the shared savings plans contemplated by local governments since 1974, one was not implemented despite extensive planning, the second has been judged a modest one-time success, and the third only recently began to provide rewards to employees. All three are described below.

Nassau County, Hempstead, North Hempstead, and Oyster Bay, New York. This plan was an outgrowth of a multimunicipality productivity program that involved Nassau County, three of its towns, and local units of the New York Civil Service Employees Association. The plan called

21. Greiner et al., *Monetary Incentives*, p. 43.
22. Although suggestion award plans can be considered a form of shared savings plan, such awards are treated separately.
23. Greiner, Bell, and Hatry, *Employee Incentives*, pp. 91-94.

Exhibit 4

SHARED SAVINGS PLANS
(As of March 1978)

Jurisdiction	Eligible Employees	Status[1]	Presence of Labor-Management Committee
Detroit, Mich.	Nearly all sanitation personnel	Implemented	
Flint, Mich.	All waste collection personnel	Implemented	
Lake Charles, La.	Nonsupervisory sanitation employees	Implemented	
New York, N.Y.	All employees covered by union contracts	Implemented	X
Rockville, Md.	Unionized park and public works employees	Implemented	X
Hempstead, N.Y. / Nassau County, N.Y. / North Hempstead, N.Y. / Oyster Bay, N.Y. }	All city and county employees	Planned but never implemented	X
State of Washington	Supervisory and some clerical employees in the state printing plant	Implemented	X
State of New York	Employees covered by contract with Civil Service Employees Association	Implemented but no rewards were ever distributed	
State of North Carolina	All employees in three pilot organizational units	Planned	
State of Wisconsin	Employees covered by contract with Wisconsin State Employees Union	Implemented but no rewards were ever distributed	X

1. Based on the most recent information available to project staff. In some cases, however, that information is up to four years old.

for 50/50 sharing of productivity improvement gains and provided that the employees' share of the savings would be put into a deferred compensation trust, with shares to be awarded to employees upon retirement. Although introduced into negotiations between the parties in 1975, the plan was not included in any final labor agreements, apparently because of union resistance to delayed benefits and because of the dissolution of the political unity previously achieved by the four jurisdictions.[24]

Rockville, Maryland. In 1975 a shared savings program was begun in Rockville as part of a contract settlement with the union representing parks and public works employees.[25] In lieu of part of the wage increase sought by the union, management and labor adopted a union suggestion that a joint committee be established to identify ways to save money, with the savings to be shared between the city and the employees. The committee met from August through October 1975. Of twenty-seven cost-saving suggestions, only two were thought likely to provide real savings. One involved doing work in-house that had previously been done by outside contractors; the other involved having truck drivers inspect and clean the interiors of their vehicles. These two suggestions were implemented. The city and the employees evenly divided the total savings of $6,200. The employees divided their half into equal parts, resulting in a bonus of $23.30 each. The procedure has not been continued, apparently because both parties felt the possibilities for significant savings had been exhausted for the time being.

New York City. In 1976, as part of the agreement under which emergency federal assistance was provided to New York City, city employee unions were required to accept a so-called "no cost" wage contract. Under this contract, any cost-of-living adjustment in city employees' salaries had to come from savings in municipal costs. Furthermore, these savings had to be achieved with no reduction in services. (This arrangement was not really a "shared" savings plan, since all first-year savings were to be given to employees. It is included here, however, as an example

24. Sam Zagoria, "An Evaluation of the Nassau County Project," Final Report, U.S. Department of Labor Contract L-74-82, Labor-Management Relations Service (Washington, D.C., July 30, 1975), p. 9. See also Frederick O'R. Hayes, *Productivity in Local Government* (Lexington, Mass.: D.C. Heath and Co., 1977), Chapter 5.

25. See Larry N. Blick, "Cost Savings Plan Breaks Impasse," *Public Management*, vol. 58, no. 9 (September 1976), pp. 20-21.

of an incentive plan in which monetary awards are paid for with savings generated by employees.)

The plan included the creation of forty labor-management committees. These helped to identify and achieve municipal savings of about $7.8 million for the six months ending March 31, 1977.[26] Although these savings were certified by the city's Emergency Financial Control Board, only about $1 million came from productivity improvements. Most of the rest came from the development of new sources of revenue.

The savings of $7.8 million financed a cost-of-living increase of $94.50 (plus $10.50 in fringe benefits) for each of the city's approximately 74,000 nonuniformed employees. Neither the union's leaders nor the rank and file were overjoyed by the exercise. As the executive director of the local AFSCME bargaining unit put it:

. . . (our members) don't like it, they don't understand it. It hasn't been explained to them and it's being done with one-shot deals. The way they are participating is almost on a punitive basis: you produce this now, you get a nickel in your contract. . . . How can they be happy about this? They'll work harder to get a cost-of-living increase after deferring salary increases one year and signing a new contract with a wage freeze. Their participation in this process so far has been to trade harder work for a chance to slow down the rate by which they continue to fall behind the cost of living. That's some bargain, some *quid pro quo.*[27]

In addition to the three shared savings plans just described, three earlier plans listed in Exhibit 4 have provided considerable information on the impact of shared savings efforts. These three earlier plans are described below.

Detroit, Michigan. In July 1973, as a result of productivity bargaining, Detroit introduced a shared savings plan for sanitation workers. During negotiations, the city offered to share the savings expected to accrue from productivity

26. See "N.Y.C. Cites Gains from Productivity," *LMRS Newsletter*, vol. 8, no. 5 (May 1977), p. 4, and City of New York, "The Joint Labor Management Productivity Committee Program to Fund the Cost of Living Adjustments for the Period October 1, 1976, to March 31, 1977" (December 1976).

27. Victor Gotbaum and Edward Handman, "A Conversation with Victor Gotbaum," *Public Administration Review*, vol. 38, no. 1 (January/February 1978), pp. 19-20.

increases resulting from longer routes and the use of larger trucks. The city also pledged that no layoffs would result from the increased productivity. A pilot test of the plan, conducted between December 1972 and March 1973, produced savings of $52,000, $48,000 of which was awarded to workers in the form of a productivity bonus (amounting to about 17 cents an hour or $350 per year per worker). The unions finally agreed to try the productivity bonus plan for a year, starting in July 1973. The plan has been included in all subsequent contracts.

Under the program, savings are split 50/50 between labor and management. The amount of the bonus depends on the degree to which the waste collectors improve their performance in terms of unit costs (paid employee-hours per ton), need for unscheduled overtime, percentage of routes completed, and collection quality (cleanliness of routes).[28] The bonuses are paid quarterly. The plan covers more than 1,100 employees—nearly everyone in the sanitation department directly responsible for refuse collection, including supervisory personnel and some union officials. The bonus is apportioned according to the time employees spend on waste collection duties.

The program has been credited with saving the city a total of $595,000 during its first year of operation, primarily from the redesign of collection routes, the use of larger trucks, staff reductions, and reductions in overtime. The net savings to the city (after deletion of bonus payments) was $298,000, excluding administrative costs. However, because of the complexities of the bonus calculation procedure and the process for determining the pool of savings distributed in any given quarter, it is not clear how much of the reported savings were true cost reductions and how much were imputed "paper" savings.

On the other hand, several changes in service efficiency and effectiveness were attributed to the program. These changes included a decrease in average paid employee-hours per ton of refuse collected, an increase in the per

---

28. For a description of this formula as well as other aspects of the Detroit program, see National Commission on Productivity and Work Quality, *Improving Municipal Productivity: The Detroit Refuse Collection Incentive Plan* (Washington, D.C., 1974); James Neubacher, "Detroit Sanitation Productivity—Everyone Wins," Strengthening Local Government Through Better Labor Relations No. 18, Labor-Management Relations Service (Washington, D.C., November 1973); Andrew Giovannetti and Theodore Opperwall, "Detroit's Sanitation Productivity Plan," Department of Public Works, City of Detroit (1974); and Greiner, Bell, and Hatry, *Employee Incentives*, pp. 82-86.

centage of collection routes completed (from 67 percent to 91 percent), and a saving of over 90,000 hours of overtime during the first year relative to the average for the previous three years. In addition, program officials reported a significant reduction in citizen complaints.

The impact on job satisfaction was mixed. Bonuses averaged between 5 percent and 6 percent of salaries during the first year of the program, and city officials reported that employees seemed satisfied when bonuses were high. At other times, however, sanitation workers have reportedly been dissatisfied with the size of their bonuses, especially when size was influenced by factors beyond employee control (e.g., makeup collections after holidays). City officials have also reported problems in getting full cooperation from field supervisors, although the plan depends on their help.

Flint, Michigan. A performance-based wage incentive program similar to Detroit's was inaugurated for sixty-six management and nonmanagement employees of Flint's Waste Collection Division in 1973. The program was negotiated between the city and union representatives in an attempt to resolve worker demands for increased pay. Under the plan the city agreed to share with waste collection workers half of the savings produced by reducing overtime and improving productivity (e.g., cost per ton). The size of the bonus was made conditional on several factors, including reduction of overtime, percentage of routes completed, and quality of work (as indicated by the number of valid citizen complaints).[29] The agreement also permitted crews to go home after six hours with a full day's pay if their collection routes were satisfactorily completed. The initial agreement was modified during subsequent productivity bargaining sessions. Among the changes were an increase in the minimum bonus (to 10 cents an hour), deductions from bonuses for unexcused absences without pay, and the addition of $2,000 to the bonus pool for each worker eliminated from the work force below a baseline level of sixty-three.

Flint's program seems to have been generally successful in reducing overtime, labor costs, and personnel requirements. Controllable overtime fell from 6,700 hours in FY 1973, the year before the program, to forty-five hours in FY 1975. During the same period, the number of em-

---

29. See Greiner et al., *Monetary Incentives*, Chapter 5, for a description of this formula and of the overall impact of the program.

ployees fell 7 percent and personnel costs (including fringe benefits) declined 3.3 percent. The city realized net savings (after subtracting bonus payments and administrative costs) of about $15,700 the first year and $22,200 in FY 1975. (Program costs came to $21,600 in FY 1974 and $33,-300 in FY 1975, including bonuses and administrative expenses.) Changes in division efficiency were mixed. Some indicators improved (such as tons of solid waste collected per employee and per employee-hour) while a few worsened (e.g., dwelling units serviced per employee). In the second year of the program overall division efficiency appeared to decline, but there was still a net improvement in comparison with preprogram conditions.

What little information there was on service quality in the first two years of the program was ambiguous. Although the proportion of route completions increased and there was an initial trend toward fewer citizen complaints, complaints increased significantly in 1975. When the FY 1975 contract related incentive rewards to number of hours of unexcused absences, the rate of absenteeism fell 17 percent.

A survey of employee job satisfaction after the program had been in operation for two years found that a majority of the waste collectors interviewed perceived no change in job satisfaction or job security as a result of the program.[30] Indicators of counterproductive behavior (separations, absenteeism, sick leave use, etc.) declined in the first year of the progam but increased somewhat in the second year, a period of increased labor unrest. (However, in most cases they did not exceed preprogram levels.) Younger and older workers had different views about the desirability of the program; generally, younger workers (who were in the majority) tended to support the plan.

Lake Charles, Louisiana. Lake Charles adopted a shared savings plan for its sanitation workers in 1973 as part of a new union contract.[31] The program was designed as a safety incentive with the goal of reducing accident costs. The city agreed to share with the employees any refunds of workmen's compensation insurance payments due to reduced accident rates. A refund of $107,000 was realized from accident reductions in the first year. This money was shared with the refuse collectors in the form of a perma-

30. Greiner et al., *Monetary Incentives*, p. 55.
31. Greiner, Bell, and Hatry, *Employee Incentives*, p. 94.

nent 5.5 percent increase over and above their regular 2 percent annual longevity increase.

In addition to these local government efforts, four state governments have initiated or are currently planning shared savings plans. These are described below.

Washington. This state's printing plant used increases in the ratio of "sold" hours (hours charged to jobs) to "bought" hours (hours worked by employees) as the basis of bonuses for supervisory and some clerical personnel.[32] (The printing operation in Washington does not come under civil service, and its employees belong to a printing trade union rather than the public employee union which represents the majority of state employees.) Rewards were computed from the change in the ratio relative to its average level for FY 1973 and FY 1974 (the two years prior to the program). Other efficiency and quality measures were also monitored (e.g., impressions per hour, spoilage, average time for washups), and a penalty for spoilage was deducted from the bonuses. Bonuses were paid quarterly. The agency reports that during the two years the program was in operation (FY 1975 and FY 1976) the ratio of sold hours to bought hours rose 7 percent. Estimated net savings over the two-year period were approximately $280,000. During that time spoilage was reduced 44 percent, and supervisors earned more than $66,000 in premiums. The benefit-cost ratio was reported to be $4.20 saved per dollar of rewards paid. The program was discontinued in March 1976. The agency indicated that this was because the targeted improvements had been achieved and would continue without incentives as a result of the introduction of improved work methods. However, the program also was criticized in an audit by the state's Legislative Budget Committee for using an invalid measure of productivity.[33] The Committee recommended that the incentive plan be discontinued.

Wisconsin. A recent contract between the state and the AFSCME-affiliated Wisconsin State Employees Union set up a joint labor-management committee to identify and implement ideas for saving money. The contract specified

32. State of Washington, Department of Printing, "Comments of Public Printer Relative to Performance Audit of the Public Printer" (Olympia, 1976).

33. State of Washington, Legislative Budget Committee, "Performance Audit: The Public Printer," Report No. 76-7 (Olympia, 1977).

that 25 percent to 50 percent of the savings (depending on changes in the cost-of-living index) would be shared with the employees as a wage increase. It appears that no cost-saving suggestions have been accepted by the committee up to this time.[34]

New York. In 1972 the state of New York and the Civil Service Employees Association representing 135,000 state employees signed an agreement which included a shared savings plan. Under the contract a joint labor-management committee was established and charged with identifying and authorizing productivity improvement programs. Twenty-five percent of the savings were to be distributed among all employees, another 25 percent were to go to those units and employees which had directly contributed to the improvements, and the remaining 50 percent were to go to the state. To encourage the state and the employee association to reach an agreement regarding performance criteria and productivity measurement procedures, bonuses of 1.5 percent of annual salary were to be paid to all state personnel if such agreements were achieved in a timely fashion.

The latter agreements were finally negotiated and the 1.5 percent bonuses were authorized, but the parties were unable to agree on any efforts to improve productivity. In fact, the union began to use the productivity clause as a reason for opposing any changes in assignment or work procedure, contending that such unilateral changes were prohibited under the terms of the contract and had to be jointly considered. The productivity clause was eliminated from the next contract, apparently to the relief of both parties.[35]

North Carolina. In 1977 legislation was passed that established a pilot program to test the effectiveness of shared savings incentives in three state agencies.[36] (Up to that time, North Carolina had been one of six states that explicitly prohibited monetary incentive awards to state em-

---

34. The Wisconsin shared savings plan illustrates the difficulty of applying this technique to a large group of employees (the Wisconsin plan covers a total of 23,000 employees in six bargaining units). For each employee to receive the equivalent of an extra cent an hour through the program, savings of nearly $1 million would be needed.

35. For a detailed description of this effort, see Melvin H. Osterman, Jr., "Productivity Bargaining in New York State—What Went Wrong?" paper prepared for the Tenth Annual Conference on Management Analysis in State and Local Government, Windsor Locks, Connecticut, October 19, 1973.

36. A similar bill has been introduced in the Montana state legislature.

ployees.) If a pilot unit reduces its expenditures for the trial year below the average for the two prior fiscal years, 25 percent of the resulting savings will be shared equally among all employees. There must, however, be a reduction in "bottom line" savings; no credit is given for improvements in service quality or for reductions only in "constant dollar" costs (which compensate for inflationary pressures). The three pilot units chosen were a highway maintenance office serving Rowan County, a highway department equipment depot in Raleigh which houses seven vehicle repair shops, and five cottages of the Western Carolina Center, a facility for mentally retarded children.

The program was scheduled to begin in July 1978 and last for one year. The legislation specifically addressed the question of effectiveness by requiring that the pilot program be designed to help determine (a) whether the incentive plans are responsible for any productivity improvements that may occur, and (b) whether the improvements are worth the cost. The performance of the three participating units was to be measured before the incentive plan began and after it ended.

In addition to the public sector examples described above, the shared savings approach has been used by several private, nonprofit organizations with counterparts in state and local governments. Two of these (Memorial Hospital Medical Center of Long Beach, California, and Baptist Hospital in Pensacola, Florida) have been extensively evaluated, and although the results are over ten years old, they appear relevant for public sector organizations.

Memorial Hospital Medical Center, Long Beach, California. At Memorial Hospital, a plan for sharing the savings arising from reduced costs was introduced in 1960.[37] The amount shared was determined by computing the ratio of total controllable expenses to total operating revenue for a given period and comparing it to the ratio for a base period (the three years prior to the introduction of the plan). The difference between these two ratios—defined as the improvement in operating efficiency—was multiplied by the total hospital payroll to determine the savings pool for employee bonuses. Several limits were placed on the size of this pool. For instance, it was not permitted to exceed 5 percent of the hospital's total an-

---

37. Jehring, "Incentive Program at Memorial Hospital."

nual payroll or 15 percent of the combined annual compensation of all employees participating in the incentive plan. The savings pool was divided among the participating employees annually in proportion to their earnings during the previous year. The bonus due each worker was invested in a trust fund and was payable on severance, retirement, or death.

In the 3½ years immediately following the introduction of the plan, total hospital contributions to the savings pool were over $900,000, indicating improved operating efficiency relative to the base period. Operating costs at Memorial Hospital during that time were generally below the average for other area hospitals. Several successful productivity improvement projects relying heavily on employee cooperation were introduced by the hospital during the period subsequont to the introduction of the incentive plan.

Evaluators found that the plan had contributed to a positive attitude among employees regarding efficiency and elimination of waste and had fostered a spirit of cooperation.[38] Interviews with a sample of fifty-five hospital workers found widespread enthusiasm for the plan, and a survey of patients found satisfaction with hospital services at Memorial Hospital to be the same or better than at other nearby hospitals.

Baptist Hospital, Pensacola, Florida. Baptist Hospital introduced a shared savings plan in 1966.[39] Each department or employee group—laundry, surgery, nursing, radiology, laboratory, etc.—functioned as an independent group for purposes of determining savings. Group norms for costs controllable by employees (labor hours, supply costs, etc.) were determined from historical records. These norms were compared monthly with the actual cost performance of the group, and savings arising from operating below the historical norm were shared with all employees in the group. The percentage of the savings shared by the employees varied, depending on the group and its performance. Bonuses were paid each month from savings accruing in the previous month.

A group's share of the savings was computed from a rather complicated reward formula designed specifically for that group. Usually these formulas involved several performance measures, providing separate payments for individual and group productivity gains.

---

38. Ibid., p. 73.
39. Jehring, "Incentive Program at Baptist Hospital."

An evaluation of Baptist Hospital's shared savings plan indicated that there had been a substantial improvement in the productivity of the various incentive groups (e.g., radiology procedures per staff-hour) since the introduction of the plan.[40] Both costs and outputs had improved, and patient surveys indicated that the hospital's level of quality had been maintained. In 1967, bonuses totaling over $78,000 were paid to employees out of savings.

There were some problems with the Baptist Hospital plan, however. The reward formulas for some groups were quite complicated, making employee understanding difficult. And there were some problems with regard to the perceived equitability of the formulas. For instance, nurses resented the fact that laundry workers were getting regular bonuses while the bonuses paid to the nurses were neither as regular nor as large.

THE IMPACT OF SHARED SAVINGS PLANS

Taken together, the ten plans listed in Exhibit 4 have a number of similarities. All but the one in North Carolina were introduced in unionized agencies, and all but two (those in the states of North Carolina and Washington) grew out of contract negotiations or productivity bargaining. Most focused on line personnel, although many also included management (only the Washington state program was primarily for management). In five of the ten cases (Detroit, Flint, New York City, Rockville, and New York State), there was no prior planning; instead, the program emerged from the bargaining process as a way to resolve an impasse. In contrast, the program in Nassau County was the product of several years' preparation and planning which collapsed at the last minute.

Most of the shared savings plans envisioned a 50/50 division of first year savings between labor and management; the exceptions were Wisconsin (where there were two possible ratios— 50/50 and 25/75), New York City (where employees could use all the savings they could generate to fund their cost-of-living adjustment), and North Carolina (which envisioned 25 percent of the savings going to employees). However, two of the eight programs that got past the planning stage never produced any savings at all. The other six efforts generated at least some savings, and some produced fairly significant improvements. All in

---

40. Ibid.

all, despite the limited number of cases on which any evidence is available, shared savings plans appear to have a relatively high likelihood of producing cost savings. Clearly, however, they are also quite difficult to introduce and sustain. And in a period of high inflation, such plans are likely to be especially frustrating if savings are assessed without adjustments for inflationary effects. Under such circumstances, even large efficiencies may not be enough to provide meaningful savings—and rewards—in the face of rapidly escalating costs.

Among the ten shared savings programs there were a few reports of employee dissatisfaction. However, in the only known systematic assessment of the impact of a shared savings plan on job satisfaction (i.e., in Flint), most of the employees interviewed perceived no change in job satisfaction or job security as a result of the program.[41]

The role that shared savings plans can play in resolving disputes over higher wages should not be overlooked. In all but two jurisdictions (the states of Washington and North Carolina), the plans emerged from collective bargaining, often as a means to resolve a wage dispute. Rockville's city manager noted that even though the program produced few savings it did help achieve a contract and avert a strike. Moreover, the subsequent search for ways to save money helped demonstrate the city's financial plight to the union and led to a better labor-management atmosphere.

Suggestion Award Programs

Suggestion award programs are related to shared savings plans. They constitute one of the most common types of monetary incentives found in state and local governments. The 1973 UI/ICMA/NGC survey found that 25 percent of the local government respondents reported the use of a suggestion award program.[42] Fifty-nine percent (twenty-four) of the forty-one states responding reported using suggestion awards, while two other states said they had discontinued award programs. Two additional states known to be using suggestion programs are North Carolina (which began its program in 1975) and New Jersey (which did not reply to the 1973 survey).

---

41. Greiner et al., *Monetary Incentives*, p. 55.
42. Greiner, Bell, and Hatry, *Employee Incentives*, pp. 5, 7.

Suggestion award plans are, in effect, shared savings programs that focus on individuals rather than groups. The primary function of suggestion award programs is to elicit money-saving suggestions. They are not designed to motivate employees to work harder. Employees are usually awarded a share (e.g., 10 percent) of the first-year savings generated by their ideas, up to some maximum amount (often $500 to $1,000).

Most suggestion award plans are similar in structure, and typical ones have been described in previous studies.[43] One recent variation has been tried in Nashville-Davidson County, Tennessee, which has explicitly oriented its awards toward productivity improvements.[44] A monthly competition is held for the best suggestions on how to improve productivity, and a $50 prize is awarded to the winner. (After the first several months of the program the prize-winning suggestions reportedly resulted in average savings of $2,500.) Among other recent variations are the use of rating scales to assess the value of suggestions with an intangible impact (suggestions to improve morale, working conditions, etc.). A number of states (e.g., New Jersey and Washington) are attempting to revamp their suggestion award programs to help improve government productivity. Among the potential improvements are simplification of the procedure for reporting suggestions, audits to measure actual savings, and revision of award schedules.

Recently, an interesting modification of suggestion award programs has been proposed.[45] The plans would be converted from individual to group rewards. Only suggestions leading to cash savings would be considered. These savings would be credited to a bonus pool on a monthly basis. As long as a suggestion continued to generate savings, the savings would be credited to the pool (in contrast to current common practice, in which only the first year's savings contribute to the suggestion award). At the end of each month the operating costs for the program would be deducted from the bonus pool, and the remainder of the savings would be shared equally between the government and its employees. The employees' share would be divided equally among

43. For example, see Greiner, Bell, and Hatry, *Employee Incentives*, pp. 95-98.
44. International City Management Association, *Guide to Productivity Improvement Projects*, Third Edition (Washington, D.C., 1976), pp. 22-23.
45. See Kristin Olsen, "Suggestion Schemes Seventies Style," *Personnel Management*, vol. 8 (April 1976), pp. 36-39.

all nonmanagement personnel (whether or not they had contributed suggestions) and awarded as a monthly bonus.

This type of program has not yet been tried in either the private or public sector, and a number of potential problems would have to be resolved before it could be judged as practical—for example, whether having to share the rewards with other employees would inhibit persons from making suggestions, the future costs and complexities of the program as suggestions accumulate, and so on. However, the plan may bear further investigation by state and local government officials, since it appears to provide a means for converting a suggestion system into a shared savings plan that could involve employees at all levels.

THE IMPACT OF SUGGESTION AWARD PROGRAMS

While many suggestion programs have become rather routine and excite little interest among employees, a number of programs have been credited with producing large savings. Private sector data compiled for 1974 by the National Association of Suggestion Systems indicated an average of $5.70 in net savings for each dollar spent on the program.[46] In the public sector, a recent survey of eight state suggestion award plans found that total cash savings in 1974 (net of the rewards paid) ranged from $4,800 (Ohio) to more than $2,500,000 (California).[47] In FY 1975 New Jersey reported savings of $102,000 through its suggestion program; in FY 1976 the figure came to $503,000.[48] The state of Washington reported that during the 1973-75 biennium its suggestion award program was responsible for $222,000 in savings.[49] Cost data are available only for New Jersey. There, program costs (including administrative expenses and employee awards) amounted to $38,000 in FY 1975 and $71,000 in FY 1976, resulting in benefit-cost ratios of 2.7 and 7.1 for the two years, respectively.

46. Milton A. Tatter, "Turning Ideas Into Gold," *Management Review*, vol. 64 (March 1975), pp. 4-10.

47. Edward H. Downey and Walter L. Balk, *Employee Innovation and Government Productivity: A Study of Suggestion Systems in the Public Sector*, Personnel Report No. 763, International Personnel Management Association (Chicago, 1976), p. 5.

48. State of New Jersey, Civil Service Commission, "69th Annual Report: 1975-1976" (Trenton, 1976), pp. 27-28.

49. State of Washington, Advisory Council on State Government Productivity, "Final Report" (Olympia, 1976), p. 12.

The validity of the savings that stem from suggestion award plans is often unclear. Many appear to involve "paper" savings based on early estimates that are unlikely to result in savings as large as projected. Thus, a careful evaluation of such reported savings by an outside authority appears to be needed to establish the overall effectiveness of suggestion award plans.

As noted earlier, most suggestion plans place an upper limit on awards and base them on estimated first-year savings. It may well be that such limits significantly reduce the incentive for employees to submit suggestions. This issue also needs careful evaluation.

Chapter 5

MONETARY INCENTIVE PLANS INVOLVING PERMANENT WAGE INCREASES

One advantage to management from using incentive plans involving bonuses or other one-time awards is that the award must be earned each time it is received. Performance-based wage increases, on the other hand, commit management to paying indefinitely for a single instance of good performance or a high rating, even if performance subsequently declines. Nevertheless, such approaches are much more common than bonuses in the public sector. This chapter discusses the two main types of performance-based wage increases—those given through a merit system and those negotiated through productivity bargaining.

Performance-Based Merit Increases

The question of whether "merit pay" is or can serve as an incentive for public sector employees is currently of considerable concern.[1] It should be noted at the outset, however, that the termi-

---

1. For example, the federal government has recently proposed a number of changes in its merit system in an effort to encourage improved performance. See U.S. General Accounting Office, "Federal Employee Performance Rating Systems Need Fundamental Changes," Report to Congress by the Comptroller General of the United States, No. FPCD-77-80 (Washington, D.C., March 1978); and "Final Staff Report: Personnel Management Project," vol. 1, President's Reorganization Project (Washington, D.C., December 1977).

nology used in connection with merit pay plans can cause confusion. Although the word "merit" is often invoked, it does not always refer to excellence. One must be careful to distinguish between the "merit system," the "merit principle," and "merit increases" (also known as "merit pay").[2]

The *merit principle* refers to the hiring, rewarding, and promoting of public employees on the basis of competence and without consideration of political factors. The *merit system* refers to the specific procedures a government has established to be sure that its managers conform to the merit principle in personnel decisions. A merit system usually includes a set of civil service or personnel rules which authorize and define the system, a fixed number of salary "steps" which define the wage increases possible within a given job classification, tests or other formalized rating procedures which serve as the basis for hiring, promotions, and some or all wage (step) increases, and formal rules (e.g., the "rule of three") for choosing among candidates for a job or promotion. In some cases an independent civil service commission administers the entire merit system.

Merit increases are salary increases obtained through a merit system. These are the step increases available for a given job classification and should not be confused with across-the-board "cost-of-living" increases or raises resulting from a change in the salary range to keep a given position in line with private sector rates.

Merit systems are widespread among local governments. In a 1970 survey of 517 counties and cities with more than 500 municipal employees (excluding educational and institutional staff), the National Civil Service League found that 84 percent of the cities and 83 percent of the counties reported having merit systems.[3] The NCSL survey also found that "performance" was reported to be the most common factor used in promoting employees. Seventy-seven percent of the respondents (including forty-five states) reported using performance as one of the factors in promoting unskilled employees, 80 percent used it in the promotion of skilled employees, 77 percent considered it in promoting office workers, and 79 percent incorporated it in the promotion of administrative and professional personnel.[4]

2. See, for instance, Marty Morgenstern, "Merit Principle, Civil Service and Collective Bargaining," *State Government Administration*, vol. XII, no. 1 (January 1977), p. 7.

3. Jacob J. Rutstein, "Survey of Current Personnel Systems in State and Local Government," *Good Government*, vol. 87, no. 1 (Spring 1971).

4. Ibid.

In the 1973 UI/ICMA/NGC survey, state and local governments were asked to report their use of output-oriented merit increases, that is, merit increases given primarily on the basis of job performance. Forty-two percent of the local governments and 61 percent of the state governments indicated that they used or had used such increases.[5] Information recently provided by officials in the fifty states and a random sample of fifty local governments—twenty-five counties and twenty-five cities—in connection with our examination of performance appraisal systems indicated that twenty-seven states (54 percent) and twenty-four cities (48 percent) provided special wage increases or bonuses for "superior" performance.[6]

These results exaggerate the actual use of *performance-based wage increases*. Job performance plays, at most, only a small role in many merit systems said to be "output-oriented." Of the fifty-one state and local governments we contacted in connection with performance appraisal systems and which provided monetary rewards for "superior" performance, eight state and eighteen local governments (51 percent) used performance ratings that gave little, if any, emphasis to output-oriented performance measures. Typically, such ratings included only a subjective assessment of the quantity and possibly the quality of an employee's work, together with assessments of numerous other employee characteristics. Usually, the ratings for all characteristics were combined (often with equal weight for each characteristic) to arrive at an overall employee rating for the purpose of awarding a raise or a promotion.

One jurisdiction, for example, evaluated employees in terms of accuracy, alertness, creativity, friendliness, personality, personal appearance, physical fitness, attendance, housekeeping, dependability, drive, job knowledge, stability and psychological fitness, judgment and common sense, and courtesy, as well as quantity of work produced. The ratings were subjective, with a five-level rating scale being used.

PROBLEMS WITH CURRENT MERIT SYSTEM PROCEDURES FOR REWARDING PERFORMANCE

There have been few systematic studies of the effectiveness of merit system rewards. Indeed, an extensive study of city person-

---

5. Greiner, Bell, and Hatry, *Employee Incentives*, pp. 5, 7.
6. See Chapter 14 for detailed results of this survey.

nel procedures in 1975 concluded that "what we learned was that evaluation studies that had been made on subcomponents of personnel systems were few in number and did not provide a basis for answering the question: Do merit systems improve public services?"[7]

Our examination of the current literature and of merit system practices in a variety of state and local governments, as well as conversations with a number of state and local government officials, revealed several types of problems with merit systems and merit increases that interfere with their usefulness as performance incentives.

1. Problems with Criteria. As noted above, the criteria commonly used in merit systems for awarding salary increases and promotions are frequently not clearly related to job performance. Instead, heavy emphasis is placed on longevity, examinations, and personal characteristics that have only a tenuous relation to performance. When job performance is explicitly considered it is usually judged subjectively, with little or no use of standards or other objective performance information. This approach puts considerable pressure on supervisors to grant regular increases, because without objective information it is hard to justify the denial or deferral of an increase. Supervisors understandably are reluctant to risk trouble with their employees over such poorly defined ratings.

2. Problems with the Rewards Available. In most cases the only rewards possible are step increases. There is usually little or no flexibility in the size or frequency of such increases (hence the amount and timing of an award cannot be tailored to the specific performance being recognized), and there is little likelihood that an increase will be withdrawn if performance deteriorates. Thus, the incentive value of such increases is compromised, and a government is faced with the likelihood of paying additional wages indefinitely for previous high performance (assuming performance is a factor at all). When performance *is* considered (in addition to longevity and other criteria), it is often difficult to distinguish a longevity increase from a performance increase. When a distinction is made between performance increases and longevity increases, the additional rewards for out-

---

7. Selma Mushkin, "Personnel Management in the Cities as a Component of Administrative Services," Public Services Laboratory, Georgetown University (Washington, D.C., November 1976), p. 5.

standing performance are often too small to be much of an incentive. Moreover, additional step increases are not usually allowed for employees who have reached the top of their pay range. Hence it is often impossible to grant performance-based step increases to long-term employees.

3. Problems with Design and Implementation. Even though some merit systems do, in principle, provide for relating pay to performance, in practice the linkage is often weak. Although merit increases are usually contingent on employees' receiving a rating of "satisfactory" or better, such ratings tend to be given almost routinely. Personnel officials in eight states reported that less than 5 percent of their employees were denied step increases for unsatisfactory performance; in five of these states, less than 1 percent of the employees were denied such increments.[8] In such situations, merit increases come to be perceived as automatic. Moreover, the weak linkage that does exist between pay and performance usually constitutes only a negative incentive— the possibility that unsatisfactory performance will mean the denial of an increase. The linkage does not usually include a mechanism for motivating employees to strive for excellence.

On the other hand, in jurisdictions where positive performance rewards are available (e.g., a step increase for outstanding performance), officials often report that managers are reluctant to recommend employees for such rewards. In part, this reluctance may reflect the absence of adequate, objective criteria for judging performance. If the criteria are inadequate, the burden of distinguishing between employees is placed on the manager. In other cases, the refusal to recommend employees for awards may represent a more general reluctance by managers to distinguish between employees or to undertake the considerable amount of paperwork necessary to justify exceptionally good (or poor) ratings. In situations where making a choice between employees is unavoidable (e.g., where managers are required to recommend the top 5 percent of their employees for performance increases), managers have sometimes tended to rotate the awards among all employees.

The problems in using existing merit systems to motivate

---

8. The U.S. Comptroller General found that about 99 percent of all federal employees rated under the existing merit system have received a rating of "satisfactory"; the majority of the remaining ratings have been "outstanding," and only a few have been "unsatisfactory." See General Accounting Office, "Federal Employee Performance Rating Systems," p. 6.

personnel were well-articulated by employees of the state of Washington who responded to a survey concerning productivity inhibitors.[9] Nearly two-fifths of the inhibitors reported concerned personnel rules and procedures and the pay system. Employees of the state's Department of Agriculture, for example, reported that lack of adequate incentives and rewards for superior achievement discouraged extra effort and reduced morale. Employees of the Department of General Administration were disinclined to work harder when such effort would only lead to more work and more problems but no additional remuneration. Highway Department personnel pointed out that exceptional performance went unrewarded while mediocre performance was protected. Officials of the Board of Industrial Insurance Appeals noted that there was no incentive to achieve greater competence under the existing pay system. And employees of the Department of Social and Health Services felt that productivity was being inhibited by the lack of adequate measures and rewards for managerial performance.

4. Problems with Budgetary Constraints. Rapid increases in the cost of living have sometimes served to limit the use of performance increases by state and local governments. In particular, the priority given to funding cost-of-living adjustments and other across-the-board pay increases may exhaust available funds and thus preclude the granting of performance increases. The impact of inflation was well-illustrated in Joliet, Illinois, where merit increases had to be eliminated because large cost-of-living adjustments to salaries were necessary. In Dayton, Ohio, and Peoria County, Illinois, however, efforts have been made to allocate funds for the support of both cost-of-living and merit increases. Without such an effort, the concept of tying pay to performance will probably not survive in periods of rapid inflation. The establishment of separate funds does not make the survival of merit increases absolutely certain, but it does make their survival somewhat more likely.

RECENT EFFORTS TO FOCUS MERIT INCREASES ON JOB PERFORMANCE

A number of state and local governments have been experimenting with modifications of their merit systems to address the

---

9. State of Washington, "Inhibitors Questionnaire."

problems identified above. Much of this innovation has concentrated on providing performance incentives for management personnel, although once established the programs are often extended to nonmanagement employees.

Four different approaches have been used to focus merit systems on job performance: (1) improvement of performance appraisal criteria, (2) other improvements within the format of existing merit systems, (3) improvements that involve moving away from the traditional merit system format, and (4) special procedures that require supervisors to focus on employee performance. Each of these approaches is discussed below. Information about them comes from a variety of sources, primarily interviews with state and local government officials. Of course, as the following examples illustrate, governments experimenting with ways to focus merit increases on performance often utilize a mixture of approaches.

1. Improved Criteria for Measuring Performance. A number of jurisdictions have tried to relate employee ratings more directly to performance by tying all or part of those ratings to precise—and sometimes quantitative—standards of performance or measures of effectiveness. A common source of performance standards (actually, performance targets) has been the personal performance goals developed in connection with such processes as management by objectives (MBO) or appraisal by objectives (ABO). The degree to which these goals are achieved becomes part of the performance rating. (These techniques are discussed in more detail in Part Two of this report.) Among the jurisdictions that have introduced such a system and linked it to the provision of monetary rewards arc Burbank, California; Dayton, Ohio; Palo Alto, California; Phoenix, Arizona; the Municipality of Metropolitan Seattle, Washington (a regional government); Ventura, California; Los Angeles, California; and the state of Minnesota. Gainesville, Florida, plans to implement such a system in 1979.

Dayton, Ohio.[10] In 1974 the city of Dayton began to develop a program that ultimately tied the compensation of department managers to the achievement of objectives that emphasize quantitative measures of efficiency and ef-

---

10. Arthur L. Lorenzini, Jr. and Rackham S. Fukuhara, *Management Evaluation and Compensation,* Municipal Management Innovation Series No. 13, International City Management Association (Washington, D.C., December 1976).

fectiveness. Each year, department managers meet with the city manager to negotiate performance goals for the next year. These include both qualitative goals (e.g., develop better relations with a particular organizational unit) and quantitative targets (e.g., limit the rate of increase of specific crimes to no more than X percent). The department head signs a performance "contract" with the city manager agreeing to the negotiated goals. The year-end performance appraisal and subsequent salary adjustments are based on a comparison of actual results with the goals specified in the contract. Five levels of performance are defined (distinguished, commendable, competent, fair, and marginal). The manager's salary is adjusted up or down within his or her salary range according to performance. Thus, a "distinguished" rating produces a higher salary, a "fair" rating a lower one. A city ordinance limits the city manager (who makes the final evaluation) to giving one "distinguished" and three "commendable" ratings in a given year (among a total of twenty-five managers). This system has, in fact, led to dismissals, decreased responsibilities, and pay cuts for some department managers.

Palo Alto, California. In order to link management salaries more closely to demonstrated performance, the Palo Alto City Council in December 1975 directed the city manager to develop a new management compensation plan covering the city's eighty-three nonappointed management positions. The result was a plan which provides considerable flexibility for adjusting management compensation on the basis of performance.[11] Within each management pay grade a control point has been established, representing the nominal salary level for the position. A manager's salary can be set anywhere from 25 percent below to 15 percent above the control point. (Most are within 5 percent of that point.) The actual salary within that range is determined by performance. The following criteria are used:

  (a) Achievement of targets specified under the city's management-by-objectives procedure;
  (b) Performance of the manager's unit as measured against quantitative service objectives; and
  (c) An annual performance appraisal by the city manager and appropriate department heads.

For newly appointed managers, longevity (growth in the job) is also a factor in awarding salary increases.

Palo Alto has supplemented its performance-based wage

---

11. City of Palo Alto, Calif., "Management Compensation Plan" (April 1977).

increases with a system of performance bonuses. Bonuses of from 1 percent to 15 percent of base pay can be awarded to managers for "extraordinary" performance, as reflected in the the achievement of MBO targets. No more than 5 percent of the managers can receive such bonuses in a given year. A manager's annual pay adjustment can therefore consist of both a performance bonus and a performance-based wage increase. However, the manager's total compensation in a given year may not exceed the relevant control point by more than 15 percent.

Ventura, California. In 1972 this city established an executive pay plan for its seven top management personnel. A salary range was established for each position, and the city manager was authorized to grant annual wage increases of 1 percent to 10 percent of a manager's salary, so long as an increase did not exceed the range specified for the position. The size of the increase was to be determined by the city manager on the basis of how well a given executive met departmental objectives.

Los Angeles, California. In April 1973 the city of Los Angeles integrated merit increases for most program managers (all but three departments) with a system of MBO performance targets.[12] Program managers were made responsible for developing short-range program targets for the coming year, based on overall program objectives. The targets had to specify what was to be accomplished and provide appropriate (preferably quantitative) criteria for measuring the degree to which the targets were achieved. The criteria had to include quality and productivity or efficiency measures and were to be coordinated with budgetary goals. A target might consist of an increase in the level of service, a reduction in the time required to process an application, and so on. For example, one Police Department target was to reduce all major reported crimes by at least 10 percent.

Managers were also required to set "management targets" that would demonstrate their ability to plan, organize, staff, direct, and control operations. Examples of such targets have included achieving certain economies and improving staff morale. Both program targets and management targets were subject to yearly adjustment.

Performance evaluations were made by the managers themselves, with assistance from citizen commissions, the

---

12. C. Erwin Piper, "Memo to the Heads of All Departments of City Government," City of Los Angeles (June 18, 1973); and Greiner, Bell, and Hatry, *Employee Incentives*, pp. 63-64.

city administrative officer, and the personnel director. The city administrative officer transmitted these evaluations, along with an assessment of the manager's achievement record, to the city council. The performance rating subsequently arrived at by the city council could lead to as much as a 5.5 percent salary increase or decrease. If a rating was unsatisfactory for two consecutive years, removal procedures could be initiated.

In November 1977, however, the council rescinded the procedure and ordered the city administrative officer to develop a new one. City officials report that a major reason for the council's action was dissatisfaction with high management salaries and the many "large" (5.5 percent) increases. In addition, problems had been encountered in using performance targets. The objectives set by managers were found to be poorly defined and too numerous to be useful for assessing performance.

To address these problems, the following system was proposed.[13] Each management position would have five salary steps. The first three steps would each be 5.5 percent apart, and managers would move from step to step if their performance was rated "satisfactory." The last two steps could be reached only with a performance rating of "outstanding." Each of the latter steps would represent only a 2.75 percent wage increase. Failure to maintain an "outstanding" rating while at either of these two steps would result in the manager's being dropped one step.

Appraisals would be conducted by the mayor, and "goal achievement" would be only one of the criteria. Others would include the achievement of economies and productivity improvements. Furthermore, "goal achievement" would be based on only one or two goals selected with the mayor's approval. These goals would have to be limited in scope, well-defined, and capable of completion within one year (i.e., before the next appraisal).

Huntsville-Madison County Mental Health Center, Huntsville, Alabama.[14] Although this mental health center is a private, nonprofit organization, its system of performance-based merit increases appears to be applicable to government service. Employees meet with their supervisors

13. C. Erwin Piper, "Executive Compensation Plan," City of Los Angeles (June 1978).

14. David C. Bolin and Laurence Kivens, "Evaluation in a Community Mental Health Center: Huntsville, Alabama," *Evaluation*, vol. 2, no. 1 (1974), pp. 26-35. See also A. Jack Turner and W. H. Goodson, "Catch a Fellow Worker Doing Something Good Today," Huntsville-Madison County Mental Health Center (Huntsville, Alabama, n.d.).

to jointly establish a set of job goals for the year. These are defined in quantitative terms, and measures of effectiveness are assigned to them. For example, therapists set goals for the progress of their clients through various stages of therapy. Performance is monitored by cotherapist reports, videotapes of therapy sessions, and examination of a sample of client files drawn from the therapist's caseload.

Five levels of performance—far exceed, exceed, meet, partially meet, and not meet—are provided for. In addition, each employee can specify some personal performance objectives (unrelated to specific work responsibilities) to encourage either the elimination of undesirable personal behavior or the improvement of specific job skills. When the tasks, criteria, and targets are agreed to, they become a "contract" between employee and supervisor. Performance data are gathered and reviewed at least quarterly. Employees are evaluated annually according to a point system. Each objective identified by the employee and the employee's supervisor as a goal for the year is ranked and assigned a certain number of points (150 for the top-ranking goal, 140 for the next, etc.). The employee is credited with earning a certain proportion of those points depending on how well he or she meets the goal—100 percent if the employee "far exceeds" the goal, 75 percent if the employee "exceeds" it, 50 percent if the employee just "meets" the target, and so on. The total points earned are divided by the total number of points possible; the result Is a quantitative performance rating based on weighted goal achievement. Salary increases are awarded on the basis of the performance rating achieved—for example, a 10 percent raise for a rating of 95–100 percent, and an 8 percent raise for a 70–94 percent rating.

There have also been some instances in which state and local governments have specified objective performance criteria without the use of target-setting procedures. The following examples illustrate some of these efforts.

Fort Worth, Texas. Streetsweeper superintendents observe and rate the routes of streetsweeper operators for cleanliness. Poorly swept streets must be redone the same day, and cleanliness ratings are used in evaluating overall employee performance and recommending wage increases.

Michigan and Mississippi. These two states have tied the pay of certain keypunch and EDP personnel to quantitative performance standards. In Michigan, a data coding machine operator must exceed the statewide average speed for processing data on a given type of machine in order to move from an Operator 04 to an Operator 05 level. In Mississippi, an entry-level Optical Character Recognition Processor Grade 02 is advanced two pay steps upon reaching a production level of 60,000 strokes per month (less errors) and two more steps upon reaching 100,000 strokes per month. (No provision is included for downgrading staff if production falls below these rates.) A similar program applies to Video Data Terminal Operators working for Mississippi's State Tax Commission.

California. State attorneys in California are assessed according to output-oriented criteria to determine their eligibility for special pay increases of 5 percent to 10 percent. In tort cases, for example, attorneys are assessed in terms of how well the state has been protected and how much money the state has lost in connection with cases the attorney has handled. In administrative cases, attorneys are rated on the "excellence" of their legal advice, among other things.

Maine. In September 1973 the Maine Management and Cost Survey (a commission of businessmen chaired by future governor James B. Longley) recommended the establishment of performance incentives for state liquor store managers and assistant managers. Legislation was then drafted that would have linked the pay of managers and assistant managers to their store's gross sales for the previous year.[15] The lowest pay level would have been for gross sales of $500,000 per year or less, the next level for sales of $500,000 to $750,000 per year, and the highest level for gross sales in excess of $750,000. The legislature's Committee on State Government recommended against the introduction of such an incentive arrangement on the grounds that it would conflict with merit principles and would represent special treatment for a small group of employees.[16] State officials report that there was also some sentiment in the legislature against offering incentives to encourage sales of liquor.

15. State of Maine, House of Representatives, "AN ACT to Establish Pay Scales for Managers and Assistant Managers in State Liquor Stores," Legislative Document 2354 (January 15, 1974).

16. State of Maine, Committee on State Government, "Report of the Committee on State Government on the Necessary Evolution of the State Personnel System" (December 18, 1974), p. 14.

The increasing use of management by objectives, performance budgets, and measures of service effectiveness seems likely to increase the utilization of objective, output-oriented performance measures. Even where subjective performance ratings are still used, recent developments in rating scales have helped make such ratings more systematic. These are discussed in Part Three of this report.

2. Improvements Made within the Format of an Existing Merit System. The following three approaches provide monetary rewards for high performance while retaining step increases.

a. Dual Systems of Rewards. In this approach, separate wage increases are provided (1) for performance and (2) for other factors, such as longevity or the cost of living. Frequently, performance-based rewards take the form of a special step increase for "outstanding performance." Fullerton, Inglewood, Riverside, and Santa Barbara, California, and the state of Wisconsin, are among the many jurisdictions that provide such rewards. Dearborn, Michigan, provides special increases of up to 10 percent for extraordinary performance, and Wyoming, Michigan, gives special merit increases of 5 percent (fewer than six of these are awarded each year). St. Paul, Minnesota, grants 5 percent increases for outstanding performance and 3 percent raises for longevity. Some potential difficulties with this approach are illustrated in the following three instances, where dual reward systems were disbanded.

Bloomington, Minnesota. In 1973 the union representing police sergeants, captains, and lieutenants in Bloomington negotiated a contract that included both annual (minimum) increases for all supervisors and quarterly increases for those with high performance. Each supervisor was evaluated (subjectively) by his superior on a variety of traits (supervision, discipline, etc.) and given a numerical rating. This rating became the basis for awarding quarterly wage increases. A majority of those covered reportedly received raises.

City management reports that the program had little apparent impact on performance but caused considerable dissatisfaction. There was concern over the inequities of the rewards and complaints about their small size. In addition, the quarterly reviews were cumbersome and time-consuming. After a year's trial, the program was dropped at the union's request.

Mississippi. Between 1974 and 1976 Mississippi awarded a one-step increase to state employees for outstanding performance. The awards were limited to 5 percent of the employees in a given department, with selection criteria left up to department officials. The State Classification Commission disbanded the program when it found that the awards had been abused (they usually seemed to go to those closest to the boss) and were creating dissatisfaction among employees.

West Virginia. As of 1974, West Virginia's Department of Welfare employed two types of wage increases. A single 5 percent step increment was available to all employees at the discretion of their supervisor. Most personnel usually received this increase. An additional 5 percent step was available for only about 20 percent of the agency's employees and was intended to be a reward for outstanding performance. In 1974, the Welfare Commissioner decided that a more objective basis was needed for distributing the limited number of outstanding performance increases. A committee of about ten field personnel, representing employees from all levels, was charged with developing a plan for distributing these increases.

The result was a procedure for evaluating the performance of each of the agency's twenty-seven area offices. These offices had about seventy-five employees each and were responsible for conducting a number of programs ranging from determining applicant eligibility for welfare benefits to various social services, such as foster care. Criteria and procedures were developed for evaluating the performance of each office with regard to seventeen program activities.[17] While many of the criteria were objective (e.g., eligibility error rates, number of persons placed in jobs, percentage of overdue case reviews), others were based on subjective judgments, sometimes by central office personnel (e.g., ratings of public relations activities, accounting practices, etc.). Performance scores on each of the seventeen program areas were computed for each office, and the offices were then ranked with regard to each program area. The rankings for a given office were then weighted by program area and added, providing an overall performance score for each office.

The twenty-seven area offices were ranked every six months according to their overall performance scores. The

17. See State of West Virginia, Department of Welfare, "Area Rankings Manual" (Charleston, June 1974 and later editions).

top nine offices each received money to fund performance-based increases for 15 percent of their employes. The middle nine offices received funds for providing increases to 10 percent of their employees, and the lowest nine offices received money to fund increases for 5 percent of their employees. (Note that funds were provided even to the lowest-ranking offices, under the assumption that even in these units there were likely to be a few people deserving of performance increases.) Within a given office, the area supervisor distributed the increments to deserving staff on the basis of performance (the criteria for appraising individual performance were left to the supervisor's discretion).

The program began in 1974 and lasted three years. It covered all 2,700 department field personnel. There was no formal evaluation of this effort, but in a telephone interview agency officials reported improvements in area office performance. There were, however, some complaints. Some employees disliked the use of subjective performance ratings, especially when they were made by state office personnel. Others reported instances of "cut-throat" competition. Agency officials reported that the program was not adequately explained initially to field personnel and therefore was widely misunderstood. The program was terminated when a new commissioner took over.

b. Phased Systems Combining Both Longevity and Performance Rewards. A number of jurisdictions provide both longevity and performance rewards in such a way that only one kind is available at any given time for a given employee. The earliest step increases are given primarily on the basis of longevity, on the assumption that the employee is learning on the job and that the employee's value to the government is increasing enough to warrant a raise based on tenure alone. For later increases, however, emphasis is placed on documented high performance, and the top steps are reserved for outstanding performers. Jurisdictions that have used this approach include Atlanta, Georgia; Newton and Wichita, Kansas; Hennepin County, Minnesota; Santa Clara County, California; and the city of Los Angeles (whose program was described previously). Alternatively, outstanding performance can be recognized by the early awarding of a regularly scheduled annual longevity increase or by reviewing more frequently than usual those persons who have received outstanding performance ratings (thus making them eligible for more frequent merit increases).

c. Provision of Performance Awards for Persons at the Top of Their Pay Range. Several methods have been adopted to reward outstanding job performance by persons who have reached the last step of their pay range. One technique is to create an extra "performance" step that is awarded only for exceptional performance. In Arlington, Texas, employees at the top step can earn a bonus (equal to a single step increase) for outstanding performance. At one time Greensboro, North Carolina, awarded an extra pay step for outstanding performance to certain police personnel. This practice was subsequently eliminated as being detrimental to overall department morale and efficiency, since only certain units were eligible.

The most extreme modification which would still retain the standard merit system format would be to base step increases only on job performance, as measured by the achievement of performance targets, levels of service quality and efficiency, and the like. No jurisdictions have been found which rely solely on such information when awarding step increases.

3. Improvements that Involve Moving Away from the Traditional Merit System Format. Some efforts have been made to link wage increases with performance by moving away from the use of traditional step increases. In general, these efforts involve giving management more discretion to award pay increases of varying amounts on the basis of a variety of criteria (a procedure that is commonplace in the private sector, at least for management and professional employees).

a. Provision of Several Possible Step Sizes. Instead of a single step size, some governments vary the size of the step, depending on the level of performance. In South Carolina, for example, employees may receive salary increases of 4 percent, 6 percent, or 8 percent, depending on whether performance is rated satisfactory, superior, or outstanding. The following two programs illustrate this type of system.

Bladensburg, Maryland. Annually, each employee of the town is rated subjectively on six factors (twelve for police) and receives a numerical rating for each. These ratings are added together to provide a single overall rating. All employees in a given department, regardless of job, are then ranked according to their overall ratings. The highest-ranking employees receive a full step increase, while those with lower ratings are given increases of only a half step. The cutoff point between full and half-step increases is determined by the town council before the rankings are obtained and is based on budgetary considerations. The town's administrator reports that persons slightly below or slightly above the cutoff score have generally increased their level of effort during the following year.

Seattle, Washington. Seattle's Metro (Municipality of Metropolitan Seattle)—a 2,000-employee regional organization managing the area's public transportation and waste water treatment systems—has developed a rather complicated system for linking pay to performance.[18] The plan, implemented in 1977, applies to forty management personnel. Performance is rated quarterly in terms of the degree to which each manager achieves the objectives he or she has established under the organization's MBO procedure. Each objective is weighted, and at the end of the year a composite rating synthesizing performance with respect to all of the year's objectives is prepared. These composite scores are grouped to create five rating categories: "extra meritorious," "meritorious," "completely satisfactory," "satisfactory," and "less than satisfactory." This rating then becomes the basis for awarding annual increases.

The annual increase consists of one or more step increases and a cost-of-living adjustment. There are twelve steps, with a 4 percent separation between the first and second steps and a 2 percent separation between the other steps. The reward system is designed to provide larger increments to persons at the lower steps and to persons with higher performance ratings. For instance, an employee at step 1, 2, or 3 who receives a composite rating of "satisfactory" gets a one-step increase in addition to the annual cost-of-living adjustment. Employees at higher steps who get only a "satisfactory" rating receive no step increase and their cost-of-living adjustment is decreased by two percentage points (e.g., if the general cost-of-living adjustment is 6 percent, they receive only 4 percent). Similarly, employees who are rated "completely satisfactory" receive the following increases, depending on their current pay step:

---

18. Terrance O. Monohan, "Management Merit-Compensation Plan," Municipality of Metropolitan Seattle (Seattle, July 1976).

Steps 1 to 3:   two-step increase + cost-of-living ad-
                justment
Steps 4 to 7:   one-step increase + cost-of-living ad-
                justment
Step 8:   cost-of-living adjustment only
Steps 9 to 12: cost-of-living adjustment reduced by two
                percentage points

Analogous increases (although generally larger for a given pay step) are provided for performance ratings of "meritorious" and "extra meritorious."

b. Elimination of Steps in Favor of Discretionary Increases. A number of jurisdictions (e.g., Peoria County, Illinois; Troy, Michigan; Simi Valley, California; Herndon, Virginia; and the state of Minnesota) have abandoned step increases based on standardized rating procedures. Dayton, Ohio, and Ventura, California—whose programs were described earlier—have also eliminated fixed step increases in favor of granting managers discretion to link the size of the increase with performance. In all of these jurisdictions, managers may recommend an increase of any size consistent with budget constraints, subject to certain guidelines (e.g., that the ratings emphasize documentable performance rather than longevity). However, in instances where no effort is made to make performance criteria explicit and objective, the process can represent a reversion to the broad management discretion that existed before the advent of civil service and merit systems. Indeed, performance-based merit increases have come under criticism in several jurisdictions where the incentive plan gives supervisors considerable discretion both in selecting the performance criteria and in choosing the size of rewards. In some of these cases there have been charges of political bias and favoritism.

It seems clear that efforts to focus pay and promotional decisions on individual job performance by increasing managerial discretion in handing out awards must, to be effective, include some central control over the criteria used. Unless clear, meaningful criteria are employed, the link between pay and performance (and the corresponding motivational power of the appraisal process) can be weakened considerably. In each of the jurisdictions we examined where management discretion over performance increases had been expanded without the creation of specific, uniform guidelines regarding performance criteria, the increases were being given primarily, or only, to nonunion personnel. This practice may simply indicate, of course, that in their initial efforts to break away from rigid systems of step increases those jurisdictions preferred to focus on managerial and professional employees. Conversely, this phenomenon may mean that state and local governments implicitly recognize the potential inequities inherent in such an approach and feel that only where employees are not protected by unions can they use a less rigorous, more subjective procedure for awarding increases. Under such circumstances, employee resistance may be understandable, and performance increases are likely to encounter major problems while failing to stimulate productivity.

The following two cases illustrate some of the techniques used and the problems encountered.

Herndon, Virginia. In 1974 department heads in Herndon were given the authority to recommend a pay increase of anywhere from 0 to 5 percent for individual employees, on the basis of a subjective performance appraisal. City officials report that the program has been difficult to sustain because of employee unhappiness with the perceived inequities of the system.

Minnesota.[19] In 1976 Minnesota introduced a new pay plan for 400 senior managers. (This was one of several management compensation systems being used by the state.) The plan linked both merit increases and cost-of-living adjustments to performance ratings. In principle, the ratings were to be based on the manager's achievement of objectives agreed to under an MBO program and an assessment made by the manager's superior of how the manager handled day-to-day responsibilities. The superior then used these factors to arrive at an overall performance rating and to recommend an appropriate increase. A committee reviewed all increases in a given department for consistency, but the final decision was the responsibility of the department head.

Both the frequency and the amount of the increases depended on the employee's position in the salary range as well as on the performance rating. Managers in the lower half of the range were eligible for larger and more frequent wage increases than were those in the upper half. Managers in the upper half, however, were eligible for one-time performance bonuses if rated "above average" or "out-

19. Jarrett and Howard, *Minnesota's Management Plan.*

standing." Cost-of-living adjustments were given only to managers rated "satisfactory" or better.

The foregoing procedures were in effect for only six months before being substantially revised. The revised plan drastically limited eligibility for performance rewards. Quotas were established for the proportions of "outstanding," "above average," "satisfactory," and "marginal" ratings. For the 1976–1977 period, the following schedule of rewards was used: [20]

Performance Rating Levels	Percentage of Eligible Employees Per Rating Level	Increase to Be Authorized
Marginal	10	0
Satisfactory	40	Up to 3 percent
Above Average	40	Up to 6 percent
Outstanding	10	Up to 12 percent

These changes were reportedly implemented in part because the governor's office believed that large salary increases for most state officials would be politically unpopular.

The foregoing system, with its performance rating quotas, lasted for about one year. In 1977 additional changes were made that increased the number of employees eligible to receive performance increases and eliminated the quota system (although departments had to justify an "excessive" number of high increases). The schedule for performance increases for 1977–1978 is shown below: [21]

| Position in Salary Range | Performance Rating | | | |
	Below Expectations*	Satisfactory	Above Average	Outstanding
Above Midpoint	No increase	No increase	0-6 percent	0-8 percent
Below Midpoint	No increase	0-4 percent	0-8 percent	0-12 percent

* "Below Expectations" includes both the "unsatisfactory" and "marginal" ratings.

---

20. Ibid., p. 5.
21. Ibid., p. 6.

In 1977 the Council of State Governments conducted a survey of the opinions of Minnesota's managers about this pay system. Responses were received from ninety-three of 200 randomly selected managers. Only 40 percent of the respondents with an opinion believed that manager performance had improved, and only 41 percent wanted the plan continued "as is." Moreover, 86 percent felt the plan was not proceeding satisfactorily.[22] In addition, an investigation by Minnesota's Legislative Audit Commission found that the plan was often used in ways that did not focus on job performance—e.g., to equalize salaries or provide increases to counter job offers from private sector organizations.[23] At present, additional revisions in the program are being prepared by state officials.

c. In-Grade Promotions Based on Performance. Another mechanism for rewarding outstanding job performance—especially by senior employees near the top of their salary range—is to create promotional opportunities that recognize consistently high performance but do not involve significantly greater responsibilities (e.g., Patrolman II to Patrolman I to Master Patrolman). Such promotions do not involve qualifying examinations. Cities that have tried this approach include Atlanta, Georgia; Bellevue, Washington; Orange, California; Portsmouth, Virginia; and Washington, D.C.

4. Special Procedures Requiring Supervisors to Emphasize Performance in Evaluating and Rewarding Employees. To overcome the frequent reluctance of managers to distinguish between employees on the basis of performance, some jurisdictions require supervisors to identify a fixed number, or proportion, of high and low performers. Performance awards are then given to, say, the "top 5 percent" of the staff (rather than to all who might qualify). Presumably, such a procedure compels supervisors to think seriously about performance, at least to the extent needed to justify their choices to their employees. At the federal level, for example, the Goddard Space Flight Center in Greenbelt, Maryland, is developing a plan that would require all supervisors to rank employees and to divide them into three

---

22. Ibid., p. 8.
23. See State of Minnesota, Legislative Audit Commission, "Department of Personnel," report to the Minnesota State Legislature (St. Paul, May 1978), p. 22.

groups: the top-rated 10 percent, the bottom-rated 10 percent, and the rest (who are deemed "average").[24] A similar quota system for performance ratings in Minnesota was described earlier. Such arbitrary quotas may be unfair to groups that have an unusually high proportion of outstanding performers. Another potential problem is that supervisors may decide simply to rotate the top ratings (and the rewards) among their employees.

SUMMARY OF FINDINGS ON PERFORMANCE-BASED MERIT INCREASES

In general, there has been almost no systematic evaluation of the productivity impact of either traditional merit systems or the newer variations being used by state and local governments. Only slightly more information is available about their impact on employee job satisfaction. Such information as is available, however, indicates that reward systems that involve traditional merit increase procedures—appraisals based on subjective ratings of employee traits—generally appear to offer little incentive for improved performance.[25]

Given the foregoing concerns, it would seem that a comprehensive approach beginning with a complete overhaul of performance criteria (as in Dayton) offers a more promising way to provide performance-based merit increases. Such approaches have usually been characterized, however, by extensive initial efforts to develop service objectives and quantitative measures of service effectiveness (prior to their use as performance targets) and by careful training of managers in the meaning and use of these objectives and measures. Only then can an effort be made to use the measures as the basis of performance targets and wage increases. The entire process—as well as the performance measures used and the targets selected—needs to be carefully reviewed and coordinated by top management.

Performance-Based Wage Increases Through Productivity Bargaining

Productivity bargaining—the use of labor-management negotiations to link employee rewards to productivity increases—is

---

24. "New Method of Rating Goddard Employees," *The Washington Star*, February 7, 1977, p. F2.

25. For a discussion of further evidence on this issue, see Part Three.

a way to introduce performance-based wage increases (especially for nonmanagement employees) without depending on a merit system. Although this approach could become an important way to tie wage increases to performance, there are only a few verified cases in which it has actually been used by state or local governments. The apparent increase in the number of governments trying or planning to try productivity bargaining—from 5 percent in the 1973 UI/ICMA/NGC survey to 10 percent in the 1976 ICMA survey—must be approached with skepticism. Past experience shows that many jurisdictions tend to apply the term "productivity bargaining" to any formal negotiations between labor and management.

Although productivity bargaining has sometimes resulted in fixed wage increases in return for union agreement to certain work changes intended to improve productivity, such "buy-outs" are not generally aimed at motivating employees to increase their productivity.[26] Indeed, the existence of productivity bargaining is no guarantee that it will be used to introduce performance-based wage increases or any other kind of motivational program.

Where productivity bargaining has been used to introduce an incentive program, the program has usually involved shared savings bonuses rather than wage increases. A number of shared savings bonus systems involving productivity bargaining were described in Chapter 4. However, an important example of the use of productivity bargaining to introduce performance-based wage increases is the following.

Orange, California.[27] In July 1973, the city of Orange introduced a performance-based incentive plan for the 113 sworn and thirty-three nonsworn employees of its Police Department (only the chief and two captains were excluded). The plan was negotiated during productivity bargaining sessions between city officials and the City of Orange Police Association. Under the plan, across-the-

---

26. For instance, in the course of productivity bargaining, the Kansas City Fire Department recently agreed to exchange a salary increase for union adoption of a shorter, more flexible work schedule. See Institute for Local Self-Government, *Alternatives to Traditional Public Safety Delivery Systems: Public Safety Inspection Consolidation*, PSDS Report No. 3 (Berkeley, California, September 1977), p. 33. For other examples, see Greiner, Bell, and Hatry, *Employee Incentives*, pp. 79-86.

27. See John M. Greiner, *Tying City Pay to Performance: Early Reports on Orange, California and Flint, Michigan*, Labor-Management Relations Service (Washington, D.C., December 1974); and Greiner et al., *Monetary Incentives*, Chapter 6.

board wage increases were to be provided at certain times for all covered personnel if the total number of "repressible" crimes (namely, rape, robbery, burglary, and auto theft) reported over the next twenty months fell by specified percentages in comparison with the July 1, 1972, to June 30, 1973, base period, as shown in the table below:

Period of Concern	Change Required in Reported Crimes (or Crimes/1,000 Population)	Wage Increase	Date Increase Was to Be Effective
July 1, 1973-	To —3%	0%	—
Feb. 1, 1974	—3% to —6%	+1%	March 1, 1974
	—6% or more	+2%	March 1, 1974
July 1, 1973-	To —8%	0%	—
March 1, 1975	—8% to —10%	+1%	March 1, 1975
	—10% to —12%	+2%	March 1, 1975
	—12% or more	+3%	March 1, 1975

If the population increased by more than 1,500 during any period of concern, the number of reported crimes per 1,000 population was used. There was no penalty if crime rates rose. Note that the increases that could be earned in 1975 were in addition to any earned in 1974.

During the period of the program a number of departmental efforts were undertaken to prevent crimes, especially burglary (numerically the most important crime covered by the plan). A new position of "crime prevention officer" was created, an expanded crime prevention program was started, a crime prevention advisory committee was formed, a special enforcement team of four undercover officers and a sergeant was organized, and other police units—especially the narcotics division—intensified their efforts to prevent burglaries and related crimes. During the twenty months of the program, police employees reduced reported crime enough to qualify for the highest wage increases possible. The incentive plan was omitted from the next memorandum of understanding between the city and the association, however, in part because police officers felt that further crime reductions would be difficult. Other factors involved in the termination of the effort included external criticism of the plan and the desire of the association to turn to concerns other than wages.

The impact of the program was examined in 1975.[28] After corrections for inconsistencies between preprogram and postprogram reporting methods, it was found that the combined rate of the four crimes per 1,000 population fell 9.2 percent during the first seven months of the plan and 5.6 percent overall, relative to the baseline period. Despite many other department initiatives during this period, it was concluded that the incentive plan made a significant contribution to the reduction in reported crimes (indeed, many of the initiatives undertaken were stimulated by the incentive effort itself).

During the same period, the combined monthly rate (per 1,000 population) of all serious (Part I) crimes, including those not covered by incentives, rose 14.7 percent. Nevertheless, comparisons with five nearby cities indicated that the rate of increase in Part I crimes in Orange was among the lowest of the six cities during the period of the incentive program.

Over the course of the plan, the number of felony arrests per month rose 5.8 percent relative to the base year. The arrest rate for juveniles rose 33 percent, while that for adults decreased 4.6 percent. Many of the additional arrests were for burglaries and drug offenses.

Information on the quality of police services during the period of the incentive plan is ambiguous. The proportion of cases dismissed by the county district attorney rose from 3.3 percent (in FY 1973) to 4.1 percent during the incentive period. The proportion of adults arrested for felonies but later released also rose during the plan. However, the total number of citizen complaints per month filed against police officers in Orange fell during the plan, although the number and proportion of *valid* citizen complaints per month increased slightly. On the other hand, comparison with nearby cities indicated that the percentage of cases dismissed by the district attorney and the percentage of adults arrested for felonies and subsequently released were relatively low in Orange during the plan. There was, however, some evidence that the program may have contributed to somewhat harsher treatment of those suspected of crimes (i.e., persons with prior criminal records).

A survey of police employees found that the program appeared to increase the department's already high level of job satisfaction. It also found, however, that nearly half of

28. Greiner et al., *Monetary Incentives*, Chapter 6.

those interviewed reported an increase in pressure during the incentive period. Both management and labor reported that the program fostered increased cooperation and teamwork, greater sharing of information, and increased unity and cohesiveness. Although there were some increases in the rates of separations and disciplinary actions during the program, department officials did not feel they were due to the incentive effort. Although there was some initial resistance and apprehension among police employees regarding the program, this concern apparently dissipated after several months. The administrative cost of the entire program came to about $2,200. At the conclusion of the plan, the total added cost of the two wage increases amounted to approximately $82,400 per year, excluding fringe benefits.

There have been several other cases where productivity bargaining has been used to obtain performance-based wage increases for public employees. Examples include Plainfield, New Jersey (where firefighters agreed to the establishment of a safety patrol within the Fire Division to make better use of nonproductive time, in return for a wage increase) and Tacoma, Washington (where firefighters agreed to the establishment of a joint labor-management committee charged with finding ways to improve department productivity, on the condition that the savings identified be used to fund wage increases for firefighters).[29] New York City was heavily involved in productivity bargaining of this kind during the late years of the Lindsay administration.[30]

One development that may augur greater use of productivity bargaining should be mentioned. The public sector bargaining law passed by the Massachusetts legislature in 1973 explicitly allows employees to bargain over "standards of productivity and performance." [31] This law may ultimately encourage greater use of productivity bargaining in that state, although officials of the state municipal league report no such trend to date.

29. See Greiner, Bell, and Hatry, *Employee Incentives*, pp. 79-86.
30. Damon Stetson, "Productivity: More Work for a Day's Pay," Strengthening Local Government Through Better Labor Relations No. 13, Labor-Management Relations Service (Washington, D.C., November 1972).
31. Paul Somers and Daniel J. Sullivan, "Productivity Improvement a Must for Local Government," Personnel and Labor Relations Bulletin, Massachusetts League of Cities and Towns (Boston, December 1974), p. 8.

The various incentive plans utilizing productivity bargaining that were described in this and the previous chapter illustrate the difficulty of designing and implementing incentives during negotiations. The apparent success of several of these efforts, however, suggests that productivity bargaining, while difficult, is an approach well worth considering.

Chapter 6

SPECIAL CONCERNS ASSOCIATED WITH IMPLEMENTING MONETARY INCENTIVE PLANS

Jurisdictions considering the implementation of monetary incentive plans are likely to face a number of barriers to the introduction of such incentives. Most of these barriers also confront other motivational techniques, but the obstacles are usually more formidable when monetary incentives are involved.

Those obstacles that apply to several different types of motivational techniques are discussed in Part Five of this report. This chapter concentrates on barriers that are primarily associated with monetary incentives.

Legal Barriers

Three major types of legal barriers can affect the use of monetary incentives: statutory prohibitions against payment of monetary awards, special barriers to the use of shared savings programs, and appropriation laws.[1]

---

1. These are not the only possible legal barriers. Civil service rules and regulations and union contracts often have legal standing or are implemented by the passage of appropriate laws and ordinances (e.g., ordinances defining wage scales for the next fiscal year). These barriers are discussed later.

1. STATUTORY PROHIBITIONS AGAINST THE PAYMENT OF MONETARY INCENTIVES

Some state and local governments have laws or ordinances that prohibit them from giving employees any rewards except regular wages and salaries (including merit increases) or certain inexpensive rewards, such as service pins. Six states currently have such laws,[2] and many local governments (including King County, Washington; Kansas City, Missouri; Troy, Michigan; San Jose, California; and St. Paul, Minnesota) have felt it necessary to pass special ordinances to authorize monetary incentive plans. In New York state a senate task force concluded that "the legal framework of public employment may make monetary incentive for productive management inappropriate."[3] On the other hand, many jurisdictions have encountered no such obstacles, and in some instances (e.g., California, Colorado, Connecticut, Hawaii, Kansas, New Jersey, and Vermont) state law explicitly permits the use of monetary rewards for government employees.

A related problem is the belief, sometimes held by agency officials who are unfamiliar with the precise legal situation, that monetary rewards are illegal. Officials of one department in Virginia indicated to the authors their view that all monetary incentives were illegal under Virginia law. A review of the state's Personnel Act and discussions with officials of the state's Department of Personnel and Training uncovered no such legal prohibition (although monetary incentives had not been specifically authorized). Yet the existence of such beliefs can be as inhibiting as actual legal restrictions.

2. SPECIAL BARRIERS TO THE USE OF SHARED SAVINGS PROGRAMS

Because shared savings and suggestion awards do not represent wages paid for time worked, they sometimes come under legal restrictions on nonsalary awards to public employees. In the city of Hampton, Virginia, officials stopped considering suggestion awards when the use of tax dollars for employee

---

2. These states are Alaska, Georgia, Louisiana, New Mexico, North Carolina, and Washington. However, North Carolina's legislature recently authorized a one-year test of a shared savings plan involving monetary rewards for state employees in three organizational units.

3. John M. Flynn, "Productivity," Report by the Senate Task Force on Critical Problems, state of New York (Albany, October 1975), p. 42.

prizes was questioned. A ruling by Virginia's comptroller concerning the legality of suggestion awards for state employees held that using funds appropriated for state employee wages and salaries to pay for suggestion awards would represent an unauthorized use and hence was prohibited under the state Appropriation Act.[4] In San Jose, California, it was necessary to enact an ordinance to authorize a suggestion award program.

A related constraint is the requirement that unspent funds from federal grants be returned to the federal government. Depending on the interpretation of "unspent funds," this requirement can interfere with the distribution of bonuses as the employees' share of cost savings.

3. APPROPRIATION LAWS

Where monetary incentive plans require special appropriations, legal constraints built into the appropriation laws must be considered. Appropriation laws or ordinances sometimes prescribe in detail the pay rates for government employees. The introduction of monetary rewards in such circumstances can alter the effective rates of pay and violate the stipulation that the given rates be used.

Thus, changes in laws or ordinances may be needed to permit the introduction of monetary incentives. However, a number of jurisdictions have had little difficulty in passing the laws or ordinances necessary to authorize such incentive plans. Troy, Michigan, for example, authorized a plan for performance-based wage increases with a city council resolution of just one line. A number of other state and local government officials reported that they expected no legal difficulties in the implementation of monetary incentives; several noted that any legal authorizations necessary could be routinely incorporated in annual appropriation bills.

Civil Service Barriers

Three classes of civil service practices or stipulations are likely to pose special obstacles in connection with the introduction of monetary incentive plans. They include the following:

4. Commonwealth of Virginia, "A Study on Personnel Management Within the Commonwealth of Virginia," House Document No. 12 (Richmond, 1977), p. 86.

1. RESTRICTIVE PROCEDURES FOR GRANTING WAGE INCREASES

Civil service rules and practices often interfere with the flexibility necessary for granting incentive awards. Several kinds of constraints can be identified:

- Civil service regulations that prescribe or limit the frequency with which rewards can be granted (e.g., by limiting increases to no more than one a year, by requiring that an employee remain at a given step for a given amount of time, or by requiring that all employees be appraised at the same time).
- Prohibitions against temporary increases.
- Rules that make withdrawal of a wage increase difficult, if not impossible.
- Rules that make it impossible to provide financial rewards to employees who have reached the top step.

2. RESTRICTIONS ON PAY LEVELS

Civil service rules may make it necessary to compensate employees only at the levels specified under the civil service system for each job classification. The amount of the rewards may be tightly controlled and limited to fixed increases, no half steps or double steps being allowed. Furthermore, civil service rules and practices may require that certain pay differentials be maintained (e.g., between senior line employees and first-level supervisors). Such restrictions make it difficult to introduce monetary incentive plans in which rewards closely follow changes in performance (e.g., where rewards are based on a share of the savings) unless the awards are made compatible with the existing system of step increases.

3. REQUIREMENTS FOR JURISDICTION-WIDE UNIFORMITY

Civil service laws and regulations are usually written to emphasize uniformity in compensation: equal pay for equal responsibilities. But the need to maintain uniformity in a pay plan that covers all types of employees can serve as a major impediment to introducing a monetary incentive plan for employees in only one or two offices or departments. Several state personnel offi-

cials have indicated that the need to provide uniform and equitable compensation for all state employees would be a major
barrier to the introduction of any monetary incentive plan that
was not statewide. They interpreted the requirement for uniformity as implying that an incentive plan could not even be
tested in one agency unless it could be readily applied to all
agencies in the long run.

An additional set of equitability requirements applies to
state and local government employees funded under federal
grants and thus subject to federal merit system requirements.
Most states maintain that such personnel should have no more
(and no fewer) benefits than other state personnel. Federal
guidelines also require a certain degree of compensation comparability between federally funded employees and other employees.

Such uniformity requirements may restrict incentive programs that apply to only a few agencies unless special legislation is approved. An alternative, suggested by some state civil
service and personnel officials, is to make the incentive program
apply on a statewide basis only to certain job classes, at least
during the trial period. It has also been suggested that the job
classifications of employees in targeted agencies might be revised
to make them unique within the government, thus effectively
limiting the program to those agencies. However, such a revision
of classifications may be difficult to accomplish for some types
of group incentives, since the incentive group is likely to include
job classes which are common throughout the jurisdiction (for
instance, clerical positions).

Although many of the foregoing restrictions have legal
status, in practice their application is subject to considerable
interpretation. One state personnel official indicated that the
strictness with which the uniformity requirement was applied
depended on the governor and could be different under different
governors. Several state and federal officials observed that if a
state's civil service or personnel system is strong, it is likely to
emphasize uniform treatment (and hence the availability of
incentives) for *all* government employees. On the other hand, in
some cases special facilitating rules or policies can be issued
unilaterally by the governor, the civil service commission, or the
director of personnel, if they so desire. And in many jurisdictions, procedures exist for making "exceptional" awards and

wage increases; these procedures could serve as the mechanism for monetary incentive programs.

In general, however, it appears that the introduction of a monetary incentive plan will often require revisions in the state or local government's civil service or personnel rules. Philadelphia's bonus plans for employees of the Water Department's Meter Division, for example, are precisely defined in the city's civil service regulations.

Barriers Due to Employee Opposition

The attitudes of state and local government employees toward a proposed monetary incentive plan can be crucial to the plan's feasibility and effectiveness. As discussed in Chapter 2, there are numerous indications that public employees generally favor the idea of additional monetary rewards as a way to stimulate motivation. This apparently reflects a widespread feeling among public employees that they are neither adequately compensated nor given adequate recognition for excellence. Monetary incentives are often viewed as a way to address both problems.

Despite apparent approval of the *general* idea of monetary incentives, however, public employee reactions to specific plans have sometimes been quite negative. Indeed, the attitudes and perceptions of government employees can represent a serious obstacle to the introduction of certain types of monetary incentives.

The primary source of employee concern appears to be the perceived inequities associated with some monetary incentive plans. Employees often question whether it is possible to design a monetary incentive plan which is both fair and equitable (for employees not covered by the plan as well as for those who are). A second important source of employee resistance to monetary incentives is doubt concerning the adequacy and objectivity of the available performance measures. This issue is, of course, closely related to concerns over the fairness and equitability of the incentive plan.

Other concerns have also been raised by government employees from time to time. Some fear the impact of a monetary incentive plan on morale, interpersonal relations, or the work environment. They raise the spectre of dissension and competition within an office, increased bickering, and the stifling of cooperation. Another frequent criticism is that monetary incentives will have a perverse effect on work priorities, leading employees to play a "numbers game" while neglecting responsibilities not explicitly addressed or rewarded by the incentive plan.

Some government personnel (especially supervisors and managers) have resisted monetary incentives on the grounds that they are incompatible with the goals of public service. They feel that it is inappropriate to treat public employees like factory workers or salespersons, and they resist the idea of linking service to the public with cash awards to employees. Employees involved in providing social services and other direct help to the public seem especially concerned over the possibility that monetary incentives will lead to clients being viewed primarily in terms of how much they can contribute to an employee's earnings rather than in terms of addressing the client's own specific needs.

A number of government managers (as well as some employees) have resisted the introduction of monetary incentives on the grounds that government employees are already paid to be productive. They note that a government employee accepts the existing level of compensation when accepting the job in the first place, and they argue that no additional incentives should be needed to encourage someone to do the job for which he or she was originally hired.

The most intense employee opposition appears to be reserved for individual monetary incentive plans. The frequent problems such programs have exhibited with respect to equitability of rewards and adequacy of performance criteria coincide with the areas of most intense employee concern. For instance, with a few exceptions, individual performance measures for government employees tend to be neither comprehensive nor objective. Consequently, individual incentive programs are likely to cover only a limited number of employees or to rely at least partly on subjective performance assessments. Moreover, government employees often view such plans as likely to lead to "cutthroat" competition, interpersonal friction, and other problems detrimental to the morale of the work group and the quality of the work environment. Public employee opinions about these matters often appear to be colored by private sector experience —and problems—with individual incentives.

On the other hand, group incentives appear to provoke much less opposition among state and local government employees. Equity problems are reduced by providing equal incentive rewards to all members of the group, and there is less concern over performance criteria since, in contrast to individual performance, group performance can often be measured rather objectively. Where there are objections to group incentives, they tend to come from managers and high-performing employees who do not like the idea of rewards for persons who do not pull their own weight within the group.

The effectiveness of employee opposition in restricting the introduction of a monetary incentive plan was illustrated in 1972 by the fate of the proposed California job agent incentive system.[5] Resistance from the job agents (state employees whose function was to place unemployed, disadvantaged clients in continuing, self-sufficient jobs) was the primary factor leading to the abandonment of a plan that would have provided the agents with performance bonuses. Employee opposition to monetary incentives may also be translated into resistance by their employee organizations (see Chapter 26). In several instances (e.g., a proposed incentive plan for catchbasin cleaners in Philadelphia, a bonus plan for employment service personnel in the state of Pennsylvania), union opposition reflecting employee concerns was a key factor in decisions not to implement monetary incentives. Of course, once such a plan is implemented, employee and union criticism of the effort can still lead to its termination, as illustrated above by the fate of the shared savings plan for state employees in New York and the system of performance-based wage increases for police in Bloomington, Minnesota.

Political Barriers

The introduction of a monetary incentive plan can also generate political concerns which may lead to the demise of the program. Some of these concerns are discussed below.

---

5. See Greiner, Bell, and Hatry, *Employee Incentives,* pp. 60-62; and Greenberg, Lipson, and Rostker, "The Incentive Pay Plan."

1. LEGISLATIVE RELUCTANCE TO SURRENDER CONTROL OVER WAGE INCREASES

In one local government, a plan to give supervisors and the city manager wide discretion in awarding merit increases encountered opposition from the city council, which did not want to give up its control over wage increases for top management. The council's objections were overcome, however, and the program was implemented.

2. CONCERN OVER INCREASED COSTS

The budgetary impact of a monetary incentive program will naturally be of concern to state and local legislators. To the extent that a program requires additional funds or does not provide for a limit on the total additional funds that may be required for incentive payments, additional political resistance is likely. Under such circumstances, a shared savings plan (in which rewards are funded entirely out of savings) is likely to be the most feasible approach.

3. CITIZEN AND MEDIA RESPONSE

Unfavorable publicity (or anticipation of such publicity) can kill an incentive program. In the city of Orange, California, for instance, the police incentive program received considerable negative publicity on technical grounds. This publicity apparently contributed substantially to the decision to discontinue it after twenty months. Negative publicity regarding bonuses which appeared to be awarded to commissioners in the state of Minnesota for, among other things, the achievement of certain personal goals (e.g., curtailment of smoking or drinking) led to major modifications in that program.

Legislators sometimes worry that the public will see an incentive program as a "giveaway" of tax funds. In several jurisdictions, political concern over the high salaries paid to government managers has led to the restriction or abandonment of efforts to link merit increases to performance. The program changes in Los Angeles and Minnesota in response to the sensitivity of elected officials regarding the magnitude of the increases being earned under their incentive systems have already been described. In another city (whose officials asked that it remain unidentified), the city council reportedly was unhappy about a 1972 program that gave the city manager the authority to award performance increases, at his discretion, to the city's highest ranking managers. Each time the city manager made public the proposed recipients and their awards, there was a great deal of unfavorable publicity. As a result, few increases were authorized. In 1974 the plan was abandoned in favor of a system of automatic wage increases.

Barriers Due to Funding Restrictions

Unlike other types of motivational plans, monetary incentives by their very nature usually require that special funds be made available for rewarding employees under the plan. Even shared savings plans, designed to be "self-funding," may require start-up and administrative funds. The following funding problems reported by state and local officials may interfere with monetary incentive plans in some jurisdictions.

1. AVAILABILITY OF FUNDS

The wisdom of monetary incentive plans may be questionable where incentive payments are contingent upon the appropriation of funds or the largesse of external sources (e.g., the federal government). Legislative approval of cost-of-living and "merit" increases has become increasingly uncertain as state and local governments attempt to hold down personnel costs. Officials in several jurisdictions noted that recent cost-of-living adjustments had exhausted the money they had budgeted for salary increases. Consequently, merit and other performance increases have been suspended or sharply reduced in size.

2. RETURN OF SAVINGS TO THE GENERAL FUND

Unless special provision is made, success in improving productivity often results in all savings being returned to a jurisdiction's general fund, rather than at least part of them remaining available to the agency generating the savings. Encouragement of such savings means avoiding institutional "punishments" (such as major budget reductions) for productive agencies.

Comparison of Monetary and Nonmonetary Rewards

In general, monetary incentive plans face more implementation barriers than other types of incentive programs or other types of rewards. The heightened sensitivities associated with monetary rewards pose a fundamental question: to what extent should a government sacrifice motivational effectiveness for ease of implementation by using other rewards? Numerous state and local government officials have recommended the use of nonmonetary incentives (pins, citations, plaques, a feature story in the employee newspaper, or a visit from—and possibly lunch with—the head of the department or agency). These kinds of nonmonetary incentives face far fewer implementation barriers, but no systematic studies of the effectiveness of such programs have been found. Moreover, a number of programs involving nonmonetary rewards have been terminated as failures after a few months of operation. Additional investigation of this issue is clearly needed.

Chapter 7

SUMMARY OF FINDINGS AND RECOMMENDATIONS ON MONETARY INCENTIVES

Use and Impact of Monetary Incentives

With the exception of suggestion awards and merit increases, the use of monetary performance incentives by state and local governments is relatively rare. Although evaluative information is more readily available for monetary incentive plans than for other motivational techniques (in part because the operation of such plans often requires quantitative measurements of productivity), few evaluations of such plans have addressed the range of criteria needed to make a full assessment of their benefits and problems.

PERFORMANCE BONUSES

Monetary performance bonuses are still rare in state and local governments, but their use has expanded by nearly 50 percent since 1974, with most of the growth coming among local governments. At least twenty-three such bonus plans exist among state and local governments; another twelve were terminated after implementation or rejected at the planning stage. Half of the terminations were due at least partly to the absence of acceptable performance criteria; rejections prior to implementation were usually the result of union or city council opposition. Nine of the programs (including two of those terminated) involved

107

management personnel only. All but one of the bonus programs existing as March 1978 involved individual, rather than group, incentives. (Shared savings plans involving group bonuses are discussed later.)

Information on the impact of bonus plans is sparse. Of five jurisdictions where bonuses were based on objective performance criteria, productivity improvements at least partly attributable to the plans have been identified in four. Where performance criteria have not been objectively defined, the impact of the plans has been at best mixed and in four cases disappointing enough to contribute to termination of the plan.

In three of five jurisdictions where bonuses were based on objective performance criteria, the job satisfaction of employees covered by the plans generally increased. (No information was available on job satisfaction in the other two.) Where objective criteria were not used, the results were mixed but generally negative: job satisfaction was reported generally to have increased in two such jurisdictions and to have fallen in seven others.

PIECEWORK PLANS

The use of piecework incentive plans remains very low. Piecework (or measured day work, a related approach) was being used in nine local and two state governments, and three other governments were considering introducing such plans. The infrequent utilization of piecework plans is probably due to the limited applicability of the piecework approach to state and local government operations (such plans are usually most readily applied to routine jobs with well-defined, measurable outputs clearly attributable to an individual). None of the reported piecework incentives covered management personnel, although there have been plans to include first-line supervisors in piecework programs being developed by public housing authorities.

Two piecework plans have been extensively evaluated, and seven programs for public housing maintenance personnel will be evaluated in the near future. The available information indicates that, when applied in state and local governments, piecework plans have often contributed to major improvements in productivity. Significant improvements were identified in connection with each of the two piecework plans that have been extensively evaluated; in one case, those improvements have continued for nearly twenty-five years. Moreover, job satisfaction does not appear to have been damaged.

SHARED SAVINGS PLANS

These plans constitute an especially promising incentive technique, in view of statements by union leaders urging that the benefits of productivity improvements be shared with public employees.[1] Only six shared savings plans appear to have been used successfully by state and local governments. Three others were unsuccessful in providing rewards for employees, and a fourth was still in the planning stage. Most of the plans have involved a 50/50 split of productivity savings between employees and the government. One of the plans involved primarily management personnel. Of the ten plans (including the three unsuccessful efforts and the program still under development), all but one occurred in unionized jurisdictions; eight grew out of productivity bargaining or other labor negotiations. Five of the ten shared savings plans—including two of the six successful ones—involved the use of joint labor-management committees to devise ways to improve productivity and generate savings (and, in turn, rewards for employees). In two of these five cases, however, labor and management were unable to find mutually acceptable ways to generate substantial savings and productivity improvements. Consequently, these programs never produced any rewards for employees. In the other unsuccessful program involving joint labor-management committees, labor and management failed to include the plan in a new contract, largely because of political disagreements and union resistance to the use of the rewards as retirement benefits.

There is considerable information on the productivity impact of shared savings plans, since such data are usually needed for estimating and allocating the savings. Of the nine programs

---

1. Thus, in a 1972 statement, the American Federation of State, County, and Municipal Employees (AFSCME) said, "we insist that the fruits of increased productivity be shared with the workers who have contributed to a higher level of output or improved quality of service." (Resolution on the Productivity of the Public Service, adopted at AFSCME's 1972 Annual Convention) And AFSCME President Jerry Wurf has stated, "we have no problem with increasing productivity in local and state government services as long as the savings is proportionately shared with the workers involved and as long as the job rights of the employee are protected." ("Public Workers Put the Pressure On," *The American City*, January 1975, p. 8.)

that got past the planning stage, three were unable to produce any savings and a fourth generated only minimal savings (although it did help avert a walkout; shared savings plans have often been useful in helping to resolve disputes over wages). The other five plans have been credited with substantial productivity improvements, ranging from net savings of $38,000 over a two-year period in Flint, Michigan, to nearly $1 million of productivity savings in New York City. While the validity of some of the reported cost savings is questionable, other performance measures indicate that productivity improvements have occurred in a number of cases.

Less information is available on the impact of shared savings plans on employee job satisfaction. The data which do exist indicate mixed results—some instances of greater satisfaction and some of greater dissatisfaction.

The attractiveness of shared savings incentives may be somewhat dimmed during periods of high inflation. Under such conditions, it may be very difficult to generate enough savings to offset the spiraling cost of government operations.

SUGGESTION AWARD PLANS

These programs remain relatively common in state and local governments. Twenty-six states and more than 128 local governments have reported their use. Some have reportedly been responsible for substantial cost savings (e.g., $2.6 million in a single year for California, after deduction of awards paid). Although most suggestion award programs are similar in format, some innovations have been found. One city, for instance, offers a monthly prize ($50) for the best productivity improvement suggestion. Generally, suggestion award programs appear to involve only small awards. A number of jurisdictions place upper limits of $500 to $1,000 on the size of the rewards, thus possibly impairing their motivational effectiveness. The validity of the savings reported in conjunction with many suggestion award programs is questionable, and careful assessments of such reported savings appear to be needed.

PERFORMANCE-BASED WAGE INCREASES

The most common type of monetary incentive used by state and local governments is the provision of wage increases based, at least in principle, on performance, usually through a merit system. A number of general problems appear to limit the effectiveness of such merit increases. These include the absence of objective criteria focused on job performance, the lack of flexibility in the rewards available for outstanding performance, the difficulty (or impossibility) of rewarding employees who have reached the top step of their salary range, competition between cost-of-living increases and performance increases for the same funds, and resistance by managers to making the necessary personnel evaluations. As a result, there has often been little reward for "merit" under merit pay systems.

Some governments have introduced changes in their merit systems to tie pay more closely to performance. One of the most promising approaches is to link the annual performance appraisal process with (1) the development of service objectives and measures of effectiveness, and (2) the specification of employee performance targets based on those measures through the use of management-by-objectives (MBO) or appraisal-by-objectives (ABO) procedures.

On the whole, however, most efforts to focus merit rewards on job performance have been more limited, and the effectiveness of performance-based wage increases as monetary incentives remains to be demonstrated. Such programs suffer from the fact that rewards generally cannot be withdrawn if performance declines (in contrast with performance bonuses, under which rewards are given only for the periods of high performance). Some of the recent attempts to increase the emphasis on job performance in decisions on wage increases run the risk of reintroducing (under the guise of improving productivity) the political factors that characterized personnel decisions in earlier eras. For instance, granting managers greater discretion in evaluating and rewarding employees as they see fit (in an effort to focus appraisals more closely on performance) may be counterproductive—and invite union resistance—unless such a practice is coupled with extensive efforts (1) to identify service objectives and ways to measure progress toward those objectives, (2) to train managers in their use, and (3) to ensure that appraisals focus directly and objectively on job performance.

PRODUCTIVITY BARGAINING

Although not an incentive in itself, productivity bargaining has sometimes served as the means of introducing monetary incentive plans. The reported incidence of productivity bargaining is on the increase. The results in terms of the achievement of significant productivity improvements have been mixed, with some important successes and some equally impressive failures.

Overall Effectiveness of Monetary Incentives

Few public sector monetary incentive plans have been thoroughly evaluated in terms of their impact on productivity and job satisfaction. Most of the available information concerns productivity effects (primarily efficiency and cost savings), especially for shared savings plans, piecework plans, and suggestion award systems. All of these tend to generate such information as a by-product of their day-to-day operation. The results generally coincide with findings in the private sector: when the relationship between pay and performance has been made clear through the use of objective, results-oriented performance criteria that include quality controls, monetary incentives for government employees have contributed to significant cost savings and improvements in efficiency without sacrificing service quality. Piecework and shared savings plans have been associated most consistently with major savings and productivity improvements.

Fewer data exist on the effects of monetary incentive plans on the job satisfaction of public employees. The results that are available indicate that the programs have inflicted no long-term damage on job satisfaction and in some cases may have improved it.

Nevertheless, there is still considerable uncertainty as to the impact of certain public sector monetary incentive plans. A significant number of plans have been terminated or aborted during the planning stage. Although most suggestion award programs involve estimates of the projected first-year savings (and many have reported large savings and productivity improvements), there has yet to be a thorough review of actual benefits by outside evaluators. Until such a review is made, such savings remain suspect.

One of the most widely suggested alternatives to monetary incentives is the use of nonmonetary rewards and recognition—pins, plaques, testimonial dinners, and so on. No systematic assessments of their effectiveness have been found, however.

Barriers Inhibiting the Implementation of Monetary Incentives

Of the major approaches to improving employee motivation, monetary incentives face the most serious implementation barriers, despite indications that such programs are likely to be one of the most effective ways to encourage increased productivity. The major constraints on the use of monetary incentives appear to be legal restrictions, civil service and personnel rules and regulations, and—in some cases—public employee organizations and contracts involving them. (The role of the latter is explored in Part Five.) Employee opposition, stemming especially from concerns over equity and the absence of acceptable performance criteria, is also a major factor sometimes.

Recommendations for State and Local Governments

The limited information available suggests that monetary incentives for state and local government employees often lead to productivity improvements over and above their cost without causing lasting job dissatisfaction. The most promising types of monetary incentives appear to be shared savings plans and performance-based bonuses or wage increases tied to the achievement of performance targets and measures of service efficiency and effectiveness. Monetary incentive plans focusing on supervisory and management personnel may be especially attractive because fewer implementation obstacles are involved.

In view of these findings, we make the following recommendations:

1. State and local governments should give serious consideration to trying such monetary incentives as shared savings plans and performance bonuses, but these should probably be introduced only if the government takes the following steps:
    a. Makes an intensive effort to develop valid, comprehensive, and objective performance indicators.
    b. Obtains the participation of employees, employee organizations, and supervisors in developing the plan.

    c. Focuses—at least initially—on group incentives for non-managerial employees or individual incentives for managerial personnel.

    d. Prepares its plan thoroughly. Incentive formulas should be tested before being implemented, and supervisors should be adequately trained for their role in the plan.

    e. Provides periodically for a systematic, objective evaluation of the plan to determine whether it is productive or not.

2. Attempts to tinker with existing merit systems, without a prior effort to introduce appraisal techniques focusing clearly and objectively on job performance, seem ill-advised. Thus, efforts to improve the motivational effectiveness of merit increase procedures should:

    a. Begin with the development of objective, output-oriented performance appraisal criteria and techniques.

    b. Avoid giving managers increased discretion to award increases unless the criteria used and the decisions made are carefully coordinated by top management and focus on objective assessments of job performance.

    c. Emphasize one-time bonuses rather than permanent wage increases, so that performance in one year is rewarded only for that period.

    d. Provide for adequate training of supervisors in conducting performance appraisals and in discussing them with their employees (see Part Three for additional discussion of this issue).

    e. Recommendations 1b, 1d, and 1e above are also applicable.

Recommended Future Research

One of the purposes of our investigation was to identify the need for additional research that might be sponsored by the federal government or other interested parties (e.g., state governments). In our judgment, the following should have high priority:

TESTING AND EVALUATION OF SPECIFIC TYPES OF PROMISING MONETARY INCENTIVES

Several studies are needed before conclusive recommendations can be made concerning the feasibility and cost-effectiveness of the more promising options. The studies should include the following:

- A thorough examination of the shared savings plans that have been reported, to determine why some have failed and others have been successful.
- An evaluation of the impact of incentive programs involving performance targets and indicators of service effectiveness and efficiency, such as those in Dayton and Palo Alto, and the Huntsville-Madison County Mental Health Center.
- A pilot test and evaluation of both performance bonuses and performance-based wage increases (especially management incentives) in (a) jurisdictions that have already established service objectives and measures of effectiveness and efficiency, and (b) some that have not already developed such measures.
- An audit of a sample of suggestion award programs that have reported substantial savings, to determine the validity of those savings and the impact of the program on job satisfaction.
- For given types of incentive programs (e.g., performance bonuses, shared savings plans), an evaluation of the effects of substituting noncash rewards (extra vacation or sick leave, special job preferences, and perhaps nonmonetary rewards such as service pins, testimonial dinners, and so on).

EXPLORATION OF TECHNIQUES FOR LINKING PAY WITH PERFORMANCE THROUGH MERIT SYSTEMS

While the foregoing types of incentive programs appear promising, in many situations it will be considerably easier to work within the existing merit system. However, the present efforts to make relatively minor adjustments in existing merit increase procedures in order to tie them more closely to job performance do not appear to represent a fruitful approach. Instead, more basic changes and improvements are needed in the criteria and procedures used in connection with merit increments. The following efforts would address those needs:

- Development, testing, and evaluation of motivational techniques that utilize objective, results-oriented performance criteria and performance appraisal techniques (such as "appraisal by objectives") that can make ex-

tensive use of such criteria. Experience with such procedures should precede any effort to link appraisal targets
with incentive rewards.

- An exploration of the feasibility of providing *group* performance awards through merit systems; if feasible, the
  concept should be tested and evaluated in a state or
  local government setting.

Part Two:
PERFORMANCE TARGETING

Chapter 8

THE NATURE OF PERFORMANCE TARGETING

Performance targeting is the process of making explicit to employees, either individually or as a group, the level and type of work performance expected from them over a specific period of time. The provision of this explicit statement of the employer's expectations is believed to be a way of motivating improved performance (see the discussion of goal-setting theory in Chapter 1).

Performance targeting is customarily incorporated into larger systems for directing and judging employee performance, such as management by objectives (MBO), appraisal by objectives (ABO), work standards programs, or program budgeting. With respect to MBO programs, for example, targets are specific performance levels whose achievement marks progress toward more general objectives. For a police department whose objective is, say, to increase arrest rates, targets should specify how much arrest rates should increase, by what time, and perhaps, for which crimes. It is hypothesized that if such targets are communicated clearly and explicitly to employees, employee motivation will be affected.

Work standards are estimates of the time that should be needed to complete a specific activity. These standards become targets when employees are told about them and encouraged to meet or exceed them; thus, work standards used solely to schedule work or to estimate costs are not being used as performance targets.

Targets may also be associated with program or performance budgeting efforts. However, budgetary forecasts of employee efficiency and effectiveness levels based on past experience are not targets if management uses the forecasts solely to identify problems—that is, to identify areas in which performance falls seriously short of the forecast. To become a target, a budgetary forecast (of costs, for example) must be used in some way to guide employees in their work.

This chapter and the following ones focus on the motivational effects of performance targets in and of themselves, that is, targets with no linkage to a system of rewards. The reader, however, should be aware that many local and state governments link rewards and sanctions for employees to the achievement of goals or targets. Several examples of this were described in Chapters 4 and 5.

Throughout the remainder of this report, the terms "target" and "goal" will be used synonymously. Likewise, targeting, target setting, and goal setting are used interchangeably and refer to the same activity.

Basic Assumptions of Performance Targeting

Performance targeting is based on the idea that employees with specific aims or end results in mind—whether these end results are called targets, goals, objectives, quotas, or something else—work more effectively and efficiently than employees who lack them. One statement of the rationale for performance targeting is as follows:

> The basic motivational assumption of such goal-setting programs is that effort (and consequently performance) is increased by providing individuals with clear targets toward which to direct their energies. Thus, search behavior is theoretically reduced, allowing greater effort to be concentrated in a single direction ... the contribution of each member to organizational effectiveness is theoretically maximized.[1]

----

1. Richard M. Steers and Lyman W. Porter, "The Role of Task-Goal Attributes in Employee Performance," *Psychological Bulletin*, vol. 81 (1974), pp. 434-452.

A more elaborate explanation is provided in the following quotation:

> The basic premise . . . is that an individual's conscious intentions regulate his actions. A goal is defined simply as what the individual is consciously trying to do. . . . Hard goals result in a higher level of performance than do easy goals, and specific hard goals result in a higher level of performance than do no goals or a generalized goal of "do your best." In addition, . . . a person's goals mediate how performance is affected by monetary incentives, time limits, knowledge of results (i.e., performance feedback), participation in decisionmaking and competition. Goals that are assigned to a person (e.g., by a supervisor) have an effect on behavior only to the degree that they are consciously accepted by the person.[2]

Many articles and books describe the efforts of various companies and governmental agencies to implement performance targeting, particularly through the use of management-by-objectives programs. Exhibit 5 lists the factors which various authors have deemed important to successful implementation.

Exhibit 6 summarizes the links between target setting and its effects, as assumed or as reported to exist by various researchers, and Exhibit 7 lists the reasons given by some authors for the success of target setting. Most of the claims about the impact of targeting on worker productivity, however, remain unsubstantiated. Moreover, most studies of the effect of target setting present findings from private sector or laboratory tests. The extent to which these findings are applicable to the public sector is unclear, particularly since some authors argue that various constraints peculiar to the public sector complicate the achievement of targets appropriate for government services. Some of these constraints are listed in Exhibit 8. However, most of them are derived from studies that dealt with target setting at the federal level.

---

2. Gary P. Latham and Gary A. Yukl, "A Review of Research on the Application of Goal Setting in Organizations," *Academy of Management Journal*, vol. 18 (December 1975), pp. 824-845.

Exhibit 5
SIGNIFICANT FACTORS IN SUCCESSFUL IMPLEMENTATION OF PERFORMANCE TARGETING

Design Factors

Targets should be	*Programs should encompass*
— Clear	— Employee participation in goal/target setting
— Specific	— Flexibility to adjust targets if necessary
— Relevant	— Periodic review of progress
— Realistic	— Top management participation
— Consistent with authority delegated	— Feedback
— Suitable for periodic evaluation and adjustment	— Action plans written concurrently for accomplishing goals
— Compatible with higher-level goals	— Periodic progress reporting to higher-level manager
— Compatible with goals for interdependent functions	— Management communication of higher-level goals to provide context for lower-level target setting
— Quantifiable	
— Measurable	
— Priority-ranked	

Environmental Factors	*Implementation Factors*
Executive officer determination and capacity to manage	Training
Top management support	Organizational development work

Source: Compiled from references on performance targeting listed in the bibliography.

Exhibit 6
LINKAGES BETWEEN PERFORMANCE TARGETING AND VARIOUS TYPES OF IMPACTS

Target Setting → { Improved communication / Improved understanding of job / Improved goal orientation and focusing / Increased accountability, management control / Improved planning / Improved performance appraisal process } → { Improved productivity / Improved job satisfaction / Positive attitudes toward target setting }

Source: Synthesized from references on performance targeting listed in the bibliography.

Exhibit 7
SUGGESTED REASONS FOR THE MOTIVATIONAL IMPACT OF PERFORMANCE TARGETING

Raia	• Employees try to avoid "looking bad" and try to "look good" by meeting targets. • Participation in target setting fulfills nonmonetary job needs, e.g., for autonomy. • Target setting encourages two-way information flow. • Target setting gives workers a greater voice in defining job objectives.
Wikstrom	• The clearer the idea of what one wants to accomplish, the greater the chances of accomplishing it • Real progress can be measured only in relation to what one is trying to progress toward. • The process shifts emphasis from control over people to control over operations. • The process shifts emphasis from supervisory control to self-control. • The process reduces need for close supervision. • The process allows employee participation in goal setting. • In appraisal, managers have a better basis for talking with their employees about the work they plan to do, and the two play more equal roles, both having the same information about the results achieved. • The process creates team spirit.
Katzell and Yankelovich	• The process affects the pattern of control by giving workers greater voice in defining and revising job objectives and by affording workers greater freedom in devising ways of attaining those objectives.

Sources: A. P. Raia, "Goal Setting and Self-Control," *Journal of Management Studies,* vol. 2 (February 1965), pp. 34-53; Walter S. Wikstrom, *Managing By—and With—Objectives* (New York: National Industrial Conference Board, 1968); and Raymond A. Katzell and Daniel Yankelovich, *Work, Productivity, and Job Satisfaction: An Evaluation of Policy-Related Research* (New York: Psychological Corporation, 1975).

Exhibit 8
PUBLIC SECTOR CONSTRAINTS ON MBO IMPLEMENTATION

Brady	• There is no single return-on-investment objective to which subobjectives can be tied. • No overall agreement on objectives is generally possible. • Expertise in measuring costs and benefits is lacking. • Short operating cycle is likely to upset goals because of — the annual budgeting cycle and its unpredictability, — the high turnover rate of top-level decision makers, and — the frequent inadequacy of today's objectives for tomorrow's political setting. • There is a tendency to measure activities and not results, and to use the wrong criteria.
McConkey	• Many decision-making areas in the public sector are pre-empted by laws, rules, or regulations. • The public sector offers fewer opportunities to participate in setting objectives. • Many forms of rewards and recognition are set by law. • Emphasis is on seniority rather than merit. • Performance measures are often lacking—emphasis is on effort rather than output.
Malek	• Highest-priority items are often submerged by routine tasks. • Managers are frequently not held accountable for producing specific result(s). • Follow-through on major programs is often poor.

Sources: Rodney H. Brady, "MBO Goes to Work in the Public Sector," *Harvard Business Review,* vol. 51 (1973), pp. 65-74; Dale D. McConkey, "Applying Management By Objectives to Non-Profit Organizations," *SAM Advanced Management Journal*, vol. 38, no. 3 (January 1973), pp. 10-20; and Frederick V. Malek, "Managing for Results in the Federal Government," *Business Horizons*, vol. 17 (1974), pp. 23-28.

Chapter 9

LOCAL GOVERNMENT USE OF PERFORMANCE TARGETING[1]

The 1973 UI/ICMA/NGC survey found that of the forty cities with populations between 25,000 and 50,000 responding to the questionnaire, four (10 percent) had initiated programs that included the use of performance targets. Of the 315 cities with populations greater than 50,000 that responded, forty-one (13 percent) reported using programs incorporating performance targets, as did ten (7 percent) of the responding counties with populations over 100,000. Of the fifty-one programs reported by the larger cities and counties, however, eighteen were still in the planning stage.

The more recent surveys utilized for this study—namely, the 1976 ICMA survey and the 1976 IPMA survey—did not include direct questions about the use of targets. Instead, these two surveys sought to elicit information on specific types of managerial programs, such as appraisal by objectives (ABO), management by objectives (MBO), or work standards. Although such managerial programs often involve target setting, the results given below should not be interpreted as meaning that all of the reported programs included target setting or that these are the only jurisdictions using performance targeting.

---

1. Because of the widespread interest in performance targeting by local governments and the availability of recent information on local government use of such targets, we have chosen to focus here on local, rather than state, applications of targeting. An exception is the performance-targeting system used by New Jersey's Division of Employment Services, an especially sophisticated system that is described later in this chapter.

The 1976 IPMA survey found that 20 percent of the 402 responding cities and 17 percent of the eighty-one responding counties or parishes reported appraisal-by-objectives programs. The 1976 ICMA survey found that 156 cities (41 percent of the 377 responding) and thirty-two counties (40 percent of the eighty-one responding) reported using, or having used, management-by-objectives programs. The ICMA survey also found that 192 cities (51 percent of those responding) reported using, or having used, either work measurement or work standards programs.

One should, however, be cautious in accepting at face value the reportedly high incidence of performance targeting in state and local governments. Followup calls to governments reporting the use of such programs have frequently revealed the actual use of targets to be minimal. In some cases, "use" of MBO has meant nothing more than having some managers participate in several training sessions. Indeed, followup calls three years after the 1976 ICMA survey found that of forty-five cities that had reported using MBO in that survey, sixteen (36 percent) were no longer using or had never used the technique.

For this study we interviewed by telephone local government officials from twenty-three of the 118 cities and counties reporting use of MBO for twelve months or more in the 1976 ICMA survey. Also interviewed were officials from two of the twenty-five cities and counties that reported termination of MBO programs. In each case the selection was random. The telephone survey revealed that seventeen (74 percent) of the twenty-three communities were still using targets, either as part of an MBO program, an ABO program, a work standards program, or some combination of the three. Exhibit 9 shows the types of targets, their uses, and the programs in which they were incorporated.

As could be expected, performance-targeting efforts in the seventeen cities and counties varied considerably, both in scope and degree of sophistication. Most typically, targeting developed when MBO was introduced within the context of, or as an outgrowth of, program budgeting. The budget office, the chief executive, or the council generally monitored target achievement. Monitoring usually involved some form of recordkeeping or measurement system, with progress being reported periodically (generally monthly or quarterly). Most targets were set at the program or department level and were based on data from prior years' service levels.

Exhibit 9

TYPES OF PERFORMANCE TARGETS AND
THEIR USES

	MBO Pro-grams (N = 18)	*ABO Pro-grams (N = 10)*	*Work Stan-dards Pro-grams (N = 3)*	*Total Number (and Percent) of Jurisdictions*
TARGET TYPES				
Workload/level-of-effort	13	2	—	14 (56%)
Project completion	12	8[1]	—	13 (52%)
Project due date	8	3	—	8 (32%)
Effectiveness/quality	7		—	7 (28%)
Efficiency	1	—	2	2 (8%)
Cost	5	—	—	5 (20%)
TARGET USES				
Planning	2	2	1	5 (20%)
Communicating	1	3	—	3 (12%)
Motivating employees	2	1	—	3 (12%)
Appraising performance	5	10	1	13 (52%)
Compensating (providing increases)	4	8	—	10 (40%)
Selecting for promo-tion, firing, etc.	2	4	—	5 (20%)
Monitoring/problem identification	4	1	2	6 (24%)
Justifying budgets, allocating funds	4	—	2	4 (16%)
Scheduling work, allo-cating staff	—	—	2	2 (8%)
Training/staff development	—	3	—	3 (12%)

1. Five ABO programs used personal development objectives involving project or task completion; four programs used project completion targets not oriented toward personal development; and three programs used both.

Source: Telephone interviews with twenty-five local governments, conducted for this study. The sample was randomly drawn from governments reporting use of MBO programs in the 1976 ICMA survey. A total of eleven jurisdictions forwarded supporting materials that verified ten of the MBO programs, seven of the ABO programs, and two of the work standards programs.

Types of Targets

Targets of six general types were identified in the seventeen jurisdictions using target setting (see Exhibit 9):

1. Workload or Level-of-Effort Targets. Workload or level-of-effort targets specify the output or effort required for a particular task. Examples of such targets are the number of records reviewed, the number of persons interviewed, or the number of telephone calls answered. More jurisdictions (fourteen) reported the use of workload or level-of-effort targets in day-to-day operations than any other type of target. Such targets were found most frequently in governments that incorporated target setting within their budgeting process.

2. Project Completion Targets. These were found in thirteen of the seventeen jurisdictions using targets and were typically used more frequently by a given jurisdiction than any other type of target. Six of the appraisal-by-objectives programs relied heavily on project completion targets. Project completion targets often appeared to represent an intermediate stage in the development of a community's MBO program, before more sophisticated targets and measures were developed or required. Such targets tended to focus on special tasks or projects (rather than regular day-to-day responsibilities) and were relatively easy and inexpensive to specify and monitor. Progress reports typically entailed a simple statement that the entire project had been completed or that a given percentage had been completed. Progress monitoring usually involved a spot-check or an annual performance review.

Targets that focus on personal development constitute a special form of project completion target. Personal development targets specify training, educational, or other self-improvement efforts, such as participating in special courses on time management, attending a productivity conference, or writing an article for publication. At least five ABO efforts emphasized personal development targets along with—or in lieu of—targets addressing job-related projects or tasks.

3. Project Due-Date Targets. Project due-date targets involve the addition of explicit due dates to project completion targets. Communities that used due-date targets generally had initiated

MBO systems for management-level employees only and applied target setting as part of a management appraisal system. Typically, managers were required to turn in monthly or quarterly progress reports on the status of projects relative to the targeted completion dates. Alternatively, top-level management monitored project status informally or at the time of the manager's annual performance review. Seven of the eight communities with project due-date targets did not do any other type of targeting. Due dates were generally established through negotiation with the affected employee.

4. "Effectiveness" Targets. "Effectiveness" targets specify the quality or effectiveness of employee output. Examples include the number of citizen complaints received, the percentage of citizen requests answered within a specified time, the proportion of work exhibiting errors, or the percentage of "satisfied" or "highly satisfied" ratings in a survey of citizen experience. Only seven communities reported the use of "effectiveness" targets, and even these governments usually set relatively few of them.

5. "Efficiency" Targets. "Efficiency" targets specify a desired level of efficiency in terms of output per work-hour, cost per unit of output, etc. Examples include the number of interviews per hour or the average cost per interview. Only two governments reported using efficiency targets. Target levels were genrally based on a combination of observation, work measurement, engineered work standards, and the previous experiences of the particular community or of other communities. Note that several of the communities with "effectiveness" or "efficiency" targets had spent considerable time and money on the development of performance measures for a productivity improvement, work measurement, or work standards program.

6. Cost Targets. Cost targets specify the expected (or maximum allowable) cost of accomplishing a particular work effort, such as providing police service for the fiscal year at a cost of no more than $981,000. Cost targets are distinguished from efficiency targets by virtue of the fact that they generally involve only the establishment of the specific amount of money that may be spent on an activity rather than any particular level of output or effectiveness. Although any governmental budget can be viewed as a set of cost targets, budget figures are considered as targets here only if they were explicitly used as employee goals by a jurisdiction. Under this definition, only five of the jurisdictions surveyed used cost targets.

Types of Uses

The uses of performance targeting by the seventeen cities and counties varied considerably in scope and sophistication. Our survey found that targets had been used in carrying out the following operations (see Exhibit 9):

- Planning
- Communicating information, needs, and priorities
- Motivating improved performance in targeted areas
- Appraising performance
- Compensating employees—that is, determining pay increases
- Selecting employees for promotion, probation, or dismissal
- Performance monitoring and problem identification
- Justifying budget allocations and allocating budget funds
- Scheduling work and allocating staff
- Training staff members.

Information on target achievement was most frequently used for performance appraisal, pay increases, and other personnel decisions; for program monitoring and problem identification; and for planning, budget justification, and budget allocation. Efficiency targets specified in terms of work standards were most commonly used for planning, work scheduling, staff allocation, and budget justification.

Implementation of Targets

As Exhibit 9 indicates, targets in the public sector usually appear to be implemented as a part of MBO, ABO, or work standards programs.

MBO PROGRAMS[2]

Management by objectives has been defined as a system of management in which the superior and subordinate managers of an

---

2. MBO is discussed again in Part Three as an approach to performance appraisal.

organization jointly identify common goals, define each manager's major areas of responsibility in terms of expected results, and use these expectations as guides to managing the organization and assessing the contribution of each worker. Most of the MBO programs in the jurisdictions contacted in connection with this study had been started by a city manager or department head in connection with the introduction of program budgeting. MBO programs were usually initiated with the request that department managers establish objectives and measurement criteria for those objectives as part of their forthcoming budget submissions. Managers seldom received any training in establishing objectives or performance criteria, but examples of what was desired were usually included in instructions on how to prepare budget requests.

Objectives for the first year or two usually contained few, if any, specific targets, and progress reports were usually informal or made only at budget time. Typically, measures were not carefully linked to the stated objectives. Often, both objectives and measures were of the workload or level-of-effort type, or the objectives were project-oriented, with due dates as targets. Objectives were usually set with minimal participation by lower-level employees, and no subsequent use was made of the objectives or targets. MBO implementation was typically phased over an extended period of time, and little or no expense was incurred.

As experience with the concept increased, however, standards for the writing of objectives and selection of targets usually grew more rigorous. Most jurisdictions began to place increased emphasis on the requirement that objectives should be capable of being measured, and some began to include specific performance targets. Increased employee participation in target setting also began to occur. In addition, many jurisdictions began to install regular progress reporting procedures, such as quarterly or monthly reports. Performance review usually became a semiannual or quarterly event.

Today, MBO programs in communities with three or four years of implementation experience tend to include objectives with targets whose achievement is reported and reviewed on a regular basis and is tied to budget allocations, performance appraisals, or some similar use. Some communities also seem to be moving toward an emphasis on effectiveness targets accompanied by action planning (i.e., identifying the specific steps necessary to accomplish the proposed targets).

The following examples illustrate the use of MBO in connection with performance targeting:

Florence, South Carolina. In 1974 the city manager introduced an MBO program with performance targets as part of the city's annual budget preparation. The program was intended primarily as a management tool.

Each department was given an overall objective, such as this one for the Codes Enforcement Department: "to ensure the highest possible standard of health, safety, and general welfare through the enforcement of the city's non-criminal codes and ordinances." Each department was also given department-wide and project-related targets, in the form of either project due dates or performance standards based on existing or expected workload. The targets could be team- or unit-oriented. Examples of these targets were "to install radios in all vehicles used for inspection purposes by August, 1977" and "by April, 1978, to reduce by 50 percent the more than 400 cars abandoned in the city."

Once a year each department head prepared a revised set of targets and submitted them to the division manager on special forms stating their due dates. About half the department heads involved their employees in the process. After review by the division manager, the targets were sent to the city manager, who reviewed and sometimes revised them. The final list of targets was sent to the city council as part of the budget process. No weights were placed on particular targets, although due dates were likely to reflect council priorities.

Department managers recorded progress (e.g., percentage achievement) toward each target on a monthly basis. Due dates could be changed and obsolete goals could be eliminated, with the approval of the city manager. No particular rewards or sanctions were associated with the achievement or nonachievement of targets.

Although no formal assessments were made, productivity was reported by city personnel to have increased. City officials felt that the program had improved communication, both between the various levels of management and between management and employees, at least in those departments in which employees took part in setting targets. The program entailed no special costs.

Emphasis on the program decreased after 1976, when there was a change in city managers. The subsequent city manager reportedly placed less emphasis on the program, and departmental targets were no longer included as part of the budget request to the city council.

New Jersey.[3] New Jersey's Division of Employment Services developed a highly sophisticated MBO system that emphasized the negotiation of productivity targets. The program began in 1976 and covered about thirty local office managers in the state employment service. Each manager is sent a planning form and asked to set productivity targets for the coming year and to indicate the support services needed from the state to achieve those goals. Each manager then travels to Trenton to meet individually with the division director to negotiate the manager's targets. The manager's district supervisor and possibly the bureau chief also sit in on these negotiations. Completion of the negotiations for all managers is reported to require two to three weeks.

The negotiations focus on productivity (efficiency) targets—the number of individuals placed in jobs per staff-year worked and the total number of job placements per staff-year worked[4]—rather than on quantity of output, under the assumption that local office efficiency is more directly controllable by the manager than output (which depends greatly on staff size and economic conditions, among other things). The negotiations begin by comparing the manager's proposed target with an estimate of "potential productivity" developed by the division director's staff. This estimate is obtained from a statistical formula designed to estimate an office's potential productivity while taking account of local conditions, such as the demographic mix of applicants (proportion of minority applicants, proportion of unemployment insurance claimants, etc.) and local economic conditions (unemployment rate, size of labor force, per capita income, number of private job placement channels, etc.).[5] Separate estimates of the

---

3. Although the emphasis in this chapter is on local government target-setting programs, this state-level program is included to illustrate the sophistication possible in MBO systems involving efficiency and effectiveness targets.

4. The distinction between these two measures involves the way that placements are tallied. In the first measure, an individual is counted only once in a given year, even if placed in several jobs during that period. In the second measure, each time an individual is placed in a job is counted separately, so the measure emphasizes all job placements secured by local office staff during a year.

5. This formula was developed with the participation of local office managers. The division director instituted a Delphi process among the managers to identify the factors that they felt were most likely to influence local office performance. As a result, although the managers may not have completely understood the model, they felt that they had participated in its development and that, in effect, it was "their" model, quantifying their own intuitions regarding the factors which influence local office performance.

expected number of individuals to be placed per staff-year and the number of placements per staff-year are developed for each local office. The negotiations involve reconciling the manager's assessment of achievable productivity targets with the computer estimates. The division director will allow the final negotiated targets to lie anywhere within plus or minus one standard error of the estimated "potential productivity" (although this range is not communicated to the managers). In addition, an independent lower bound is sometimes imposed by federal requirements that the state show a certain overall improvement (e.g., 6 percent) in placement productivity.

When the negotiations are completed, the division director and each manager sign an agreement concerning the final performance targets and the commitments from the agency in terms of support services. Monthly printouts are provided to each local office manager showing how well the office is meeting its targets. The managers themselves developed a standard plan of diagnosis and action to be used when performance dropped more than 15 percent below the targeted level.

There has been no formal evaluation of the New Jersey effort. Management reports that when the plan was implemented the division experienced its best quarter in recent history with regard to meeting its overall placement goals. This increased performance was reported to have continued during the rest of the year. Because the state initiated many other programs to improve local office performance during the same time period, however, it is not clear what proportion of the improvements should be attributed to the MBO effort. Nonetheless, the division reports that local office managers have generally been quite positive toward the program.

ABO PROGRAMS[6]

Appraisal by objectives is the use of MBO procedures to carry out performance appraisals of management and nonmanagement employees. In the jurisdictions surveyed using ABO, the procedure was introduced either by managers seeking a more equitable basis for assessing employee performance or by managers who sought to make the procedure part of their employee devel-

---

6. ABO programs are also discussed in Part Three as an approach to performance appraisal.

opment effort. Objective achievement was usually only one facet of the employee evaluation process, and the programs typically included only management-level employees. The objectives usually involved project completion or personal development targets. If specific targets were set, they were usually due dates. Progress reporting was informal and typically involved monitoring by the manager or assistant manager to see if projects were being completed. Progress review occurred once a year, during the annual performance review. Due dates were typically flexible and used mainly as guidelines. Target accomplishment was ordinarily only one factor in determining an employee's compensation. Occasionally, the agreement on targets reached as part of the appraisal process was considered a kind of contract between the manager and the employee. Typically, no training was involved, no extra expense was incurred, and recordkeeping was minimal.

As time passed, managers usually became aware of the need to make a better assessment of their employees' day-to-day activities. Similarly, managers became increasingly aware of the problems associated with extending the appraisal procedure to line employees. Since such an extension generally was viewed as requiring some form of new or improved performance measurement system—and there was often management concern about possible union resistance to changing the existing appraisal process—the ABO process usually was not applied to line employees or to day-to-day operations.[7]

The typical effects of an ABO program were improved communication, improved employee satisfaction (with their jobs and with the appraisal process), increased likelihood that employees would become involved in accomplishing projects above and beyond their day-to-day work, and increased goal orientation.

The following example illustrates the use of MBO and ABO by the same department.

Pacifica, California. In 1972 the Pacifica Police Department initiated a management-by-objectives program to facilitate priority setting. An appraisal-by-objectives procedure was instituted soon thereafter for the department's thirty-eight sworn personnel.

---

7. Although the local governments interviewed in our random sample did not usually apply ABO to nonmanagement personnel, there have been a number of other governments—especially states—that have used ABO for both management and nonmanagement employees.

The MBO system is based on a set of general policy statements (e.g., "the preservation and maintenance of community health, safety, and assistance") and five-year goals (e.g., "to reduce vehicular accidents"). Each division chief consults with division employees and with the police chief to prepare annual division objectives incorporating targets (e.g., "to reduce personnel turnover by 25 percent per year," "to reduce the reported Part I crime rate by 1 percent for the calendar year"). The objectives are integrated into the annual budget. Quarterly information on progress toward meeting the objectives is included in the department's annual report.

The ABO procedure requires all employees and their supervisors to meet annually to set each employee's objectives. These must be tangible and achievable and must include measurable performance criteria. Objectives are set for a variety of areas, including routine duties, problem solving, staff projects, departmental programs, self-improvement, and career development. Employees are asked to state each objective (including a measurable target), describe how it is to be achieved and measured, and estimate the time needed for completion. Provision is made for revisions when the need arises. The employee signs the statement of objectives, and it functions as a performance "contract." Each employee also meets with the chief to review and discuss the objectives.

Employee performance is reviewed annually, although a special mid-year review may be requested. (Quarterly appraisals are held for new recruits or employees on probation.) The appraisal consists of two parts: an assessment of performance in terms of job-related performance standards, and an assessment of employee achievement of objectives. The overall rating then given to the employee is used to determine merit increases, promotions, and probationary decisions. Typically, each year 5 percent of the employees receive special merit increases (for outstanding achievements), and 5 percent are denied progression to the next step.

Department officials say the system has improved communication, forced problems to the surface, increased employee input and job satisfaction, brought the organization together, and provided a more objective method for evaluating employee performance. A survey of officers conducted after the introduction of ABO showed that more than 80 percent of them felt the new system was meeting their needs and was more objective than the previous performance appraisal system, which was based on subjective ratings of various personal traits.

The local police employee association was reported to have supported the program because it established a set of objective criteria for monitoring and evaluating the performance of each officer. The only problem reported was a tendency by officers to set their targets too high. Thus, during the first year or two of the program it was frequently necessary to amend targets. This problem diminished, however, as officers gained more experience in setting targets.

WORK STANDARDS PROGRAMS

Work standards are precise specifications of the work to be accomplished by individual employees or groups of employees, generally in terms of the amount and type of work to be accomplished, the time allotted for it, and so on. Two of the three work standards programs examined in the course of this study were initiated with the help of HUD funds used to hire consultants or special staff members to develop the measurement system. The departments involved included parks and recreation, streets, public works, and occasionally components of police or fire.

The program usually began with one department and involved a combination of on-site work measurement and the testing or adaptation of work standards from other jurisdictions. Generally, both department managers and line employees were involved in the measurement effort and the establishment of work standards. Standards tended to be set low initially and then were gradually tightened as further experience with them was gained. Output quality was indirectly addressed by providing time periods presumably adequate for doing the job at the desired level of quality. However, except for spot checks by supervisors, quality usually was not monitored subsequently. Generally, the standards were used for work scheduling, staff allocation, budget justification, and problem identification. They were rarely used for performance appraisal of line employees. However, managers tended to be held accountable for any excess costs incurred as a result of failing to achieve the efficiency levels implied by the standards.

Improvements in productivity arising from the use of work standards were frequently claimed but could not be verified. Auditing was infrequent or nonexistent. Among the problems cited were excessive amounts of paperwork, difficulty in getting workers to use required forms to request changes in work standards, and the cost and time involved in measurement and initial standard setting.

The following two examples illustrate the differing degree to which work standards have been used to motivate improved employee performance. In Riverside, California, work standards have been used as explicit performance targets for foremen; in Fremont, California, they have been applied informally.

Riverside, California.[8] In 1969 work standards were established for the 175 nonsupervisory employees in Riverside's Public Utilities Department to increase productivity and decrease labor costs. In 1973 the standards were extended to the nonsupervisory employees of four other departments: Street Maintenance, covering 120 people; Parks and Recreation, covering eighty-five people, primarily in parks maintenance; Sewers, covering thirty-two people (fifteen in field operations and seventeen in plant maintenance); and Equipment Maintenance, covering twenty-one mechanics.

To monitor and enforce the standards, six full-time technicians were chosen from about fifty applicants from within the city government. All six received a salary increase. Two consulting firms helped evaluate, select, and train the technicians. The private consultants also developed most of the standards, which specify the number of people and kinds of equipment to be used for each task.

At the beginning of a task, worksheets containing the standards for each subtask are given to employees. Supervisors record actual elapsed time, delay time, equipment used, and number of workers used. Foremen check the records and supervise and inspect the work. Standards technicians review these records to determine how well workers are adhering to the standards.

Crews are required to note special problems, any extra work done, and any additional time needed to complete

---

8. See Daniel E. Stone, "Work Measurement Applied to Municipal Service," Report No. 18651, Report Clearinghouse, Management Information Service, International City Management Association (Washington, D.C., December 1974); and Greiner, Bell, and Hatry, *Employee Incentives*, pp. 116-117.

the task beyond the time allowed in the standards. The technicians may revise a standard if they feel such a revision is warranted by special conditions.

The city has maintained a cumulative record of each crew's performance, and corrective actions have been taken when crew performance has fallen. For instance, the technicians found that water meter replacement crews were replacing about eight meters a day, half the standard number. Subsequent observation of the crews and enforcement of the standards caused production to rise to fifteen meters a day.

City officials report that the program led to improved efficiency and cost savings. Labor costs per hour decreased in both the water and electrical divisions. Water repair crews were reduced in size from three to two employees, with the extra personnel reassigned to new tasks. The number of employees in the electrical division was reduced 15 percent in five years. City officials report that the program resulted in net savings of $860,000 over the first five years, after deduction of $366,000 in program installation and operating costs. One-quarter of these savings were direct cost reductions due to reductions in the work force; the remainder represent estimated cost avoidance.

Neither the unions nor the employees themselves offered any resistance to the implementation of standards, although there was some grumbling about the creation of standards technicians. At first, some supervisors, especially foremen, felt that the standards formalized their work too much and eliminated or infringed upon some of their responsibilities. After further experience with the standards, however, foremen reportedly acknowledged that they were useful. Among other things, the standards made it possible for foremen to plan their jobs and material needs, to know where they would be working up to a week in advance, and (most important, in the foremen's view) to know exactly what was expected of them. No changes in turnover or absenteeism rates due to the implementation of the standards were reported.

Fremont, California. In 1974, with the help of a two-year $100,000 grant from HUD, Fremont initiated a work measurement program in its Parks and Recreation Department. The development of the standards involved a number of steps: deciding how much maintenance was required in each park and recreation area (e.g., the number of feet

of hedges to be trimmed), timing the individual maintenance activities, and developing time and frequency standards for each activity (e.g., X minutes for so many square
feet of weeding).

The time allowances were made large enough to permit
"quality" work. In some cases, standards used by other
jurisdictions were adopted with revisions to fit them to local
conditions. The resulting "Park Maintenance Management
System" included maintenance schedules and data on the
total time required annually for each activity and each park
and recreation area.

The standards were used as informal targets for managing and monitoring the performance of work crews. No
punitive actions resulted from lack of compliance with the
standards, and performance with respect to standards was
only a minor part of the performance appraisal process.
Supervisors collected performance data daily and weekly;
when standards were not met, the supervisors talked to
employees to find out why. In addition to departmental
monitoring, the city's Management Services Department
reviewed performance periodically.

City officials reported "considerable" cost savings from
the work standards program, particularly in terms of cost
avoidance, but no quantitative study had been conducted.
The program also was reported to have engendered greater
"results orientation" among workers and supervisors, as
well as increased communication between employees and
managers and somewhat greater competitiveness. The
program's effectiveness was attributed in part to the receptiveness of Park Department supervisors and the involvement of departmental employees in the initial development of the standards. No employee grievances had
been filed against the standards program.

A similar program was initiated in Fremont's Streets Department but proceeded at a slower pace, largely because
of the cessation of HUD funding and a lesser degree of
receptivity in the department. The city nonetheless anti-
cipates using work standards in other areas.

Summary of Findings on Use

Based on the evidence to date, target setting appears to be a
developing but not yet highly developed local government activity, particularly in terms of the use of effectiveness and efficiency

targets. It is difficult to know to what extent the trend toward increased targeting will continue, but targeting is a natural refinement of MBO and program budgeting, both of which have been increasing in past years. (Of the seventeen jurisdictions with targets that we contacted during the study, most had initiated their programs within the past three or four years.) Target setting's proliferation will hinge in part on the degree to which it helps local governments meet a series of increasingly felt needs: the need to increase accountability for both services performed and expenditures, the need to increase predictability and improve planning as part of a new emphasis on keeping costs in check, the need to evaluate and compensate employees more equitably, and the need to improve productivity.

Chapter 10
THE IMPACT OF PERFORMANCE TARGETING

As noted in the previous chapter, "self-reported" information on the perceived results of performance targeting has been obtained from several local governments. Unfortunately, however, the impact of performance targeting on the productivity and job satisfaction of government employees has seldom been systematically examined. In the course of this study, only three independent studies were found that had attempted to analyze the impact of performance targeting at the state or local government level.

One study, conducted in early 1974, attempted to examine a number of performance targeting programs uncovered by the 1973 UI/ICMA/NGC survey.[1] Few of these programs, however, had been in use long enough to adequately judge their effects on productivity or employee morale, and none of the jurisdictions were collecting information that would enable them to evaluate overall program effectiveness.

One community reported improved performance by managers whose previous performance had been rated low. A second community reported several good effects from the use of targets, including improved employee performance, more cohesive work efforts on the part of managers, the alleviation of crisis management practices, and a favorable reaction from members of the city council, who said they had encountered improved responsiveness to their requests for information and assistance. At the state level, a performance-targeting effort was credited with

1. Greiner, Bell, and Hatry, *Employee Incentives*, pp. 63-72.

143

having raised morale and improved productivity. As with the other programs, however, no firm data were available to substantiate these claims.

A second study, completed in 1975, examined the impact of work standards programs in Kansas City, Missouri; Harrisburg, Pennsylvania; and Philadelphia.[2] (In the latter program, the standards were linked to monetary rewards.) The study concluded that work standards had motivated employees to improve productivity only when the standards were coupled with bonuses. One of the three programs examined—the street maintenance work standards program in Kansas City—produced significant employee job dissatisfaction that had a negative impact on production during the first phase of the program.[3] This dissatisfaction was attributed to the work measurement analysts' practices of observing crews secretly (which crew members considered "spying"), of evaluating and comparing the performance of individual employees on the basis of work standards and related measures, and of unilaterally forcing changes in work methods. In the second phase of the Kansas City program, individual performance ratings and work crew comparisons were dropped, and the work standards were used primarily for work planning and scheduling, thus mollifying employees. No improvements in work quantity or quality that could be attributed to the use of standards were identified, however. The standards' motivational role appeared questionable, particularly after the performance appraisal component had been eliminated.

A third study was undertaken in 1976–1977 by the state of Utah's Division of Family Services. The division sponsored an experiment in which MBO was introduced for child welfare workers in one large office. The performance of these workers was compared to that of workers in a second office where MBO was not used. The researchers reported that MBO had a "significant and positive effect on performance as evaluated by supervisors over the period of the study . . . and on two of the four productivity measures used . . . ."[4] The measures which showed improvement were the proportion of foster care children with no

---

2. Greiner et al., *Monetary Incentives*, Chapters 2-4.
3. Ibid., pp. 19-20.
4. William J. Murray, "Management by Objectives: A Pilot Project for the Division of Family Services," Division of Family Services, State of Utah (Salt Lake City, December 1977).

more than one placement (which rose from 60 percent to 67 percent in the office using MBO while falling in the comparison office), and the number of protective service intervention cases closed per worker-month. The study also found that the use of MBO techniques had no impact on the workers' job satisfaction. The generalizability of these findings must, however, be tempered by noting that the evaluation criteria included no consideration of the quality of the outputs, and the time period of the trial was short—six months.

Impact of Performance Targets among Surveyed Jurisdictions

Exhibit 10 summarizes the impact which local government officials contacted for this study attributed to their MBO, ABO, and work standards programs.

Positive Impacts. The results reported by the jurisdictions, although subjective, were generally positive. Improved productivity, increased communication, and positive attitudes toward the program were the results most frequently mentioned. Several of those who mentioned increased communication indicated they meant communication between managers and employees, between different levels of management, and between management and the city council. One government reported increased communication among managers at the same level. The reasons for positive attitudes toward the programs ranged from managerial appreciation of MBO as a management tool to employee appreciation of participation in goal setting, more objective appraisals, and knowing where they stood and what was expected of them.

Four of the local government officials interviewed (three of which had appraisal-by-objectives programs) cited improved job satisfaction as an outcome of their efforts. There was, however, no objective verification of these opinions.

Only two jurisdictions had evaluated their programs in any formal way. Pacifica conducted a survey of police officer attitudes toward its ABO program, and Hampton, Virginia, obtained feedback during a weekend retreat of top managers to evaluate its MBO program. Neither evaluation provided specific informa-

Exhibit 10
IMPACTS OF TWENTY-EIGHT LOCAL
GOVERNMENT PROGRAMS INVOLVING
PERFORMANCE TARGETING

	MBO/ Program Budget- ing N = 15	Appraisal by Ob- jectives N =10	Work Stan- dards N = 3	Total Jurisdic- tions Reporting Impacts
POSITIVE EFFECTS				
Improved productivity	7	4	2	9
Improved management decisions	5	1	0	6
Increased job satisfaction	2	3	0	4
Improved communication	10	3	1	11
Positive attitude toward program	8	4	0	10
Improved focusing, sense of direction	2	2	1	4
NEGATIVE EFFECTS				
Increased costs	1	1	2	3
Employee dissatisfaction/ resistance	1	2	2	3
Harm to ongoing operations	1	0	1	2
Staff cuts	1	0	1	0
Excessive paperwork	2	1	1	4

Source: Telephone survey of twenty-five local governments conducted for this study.

tion on changes in productivity or job satisfaction. Twelve of
the fifteen officers responding in Pacifica felt that the new ABO
procedure was meeting their needs and was more objective than
the previous evaluation system. Only six, however, felt they had
a better understanding of the department's philosophy, goals,
and objectives because of the appraisal-by-objectives process. In
Hampton, the feedback about the program was said to be positive.

The jurisdictions cited a number of different reasons for
introducing programs involving target setting: to develop man-

agement skills, to improve communication and cooperation among departments, to improve accountability and management control, to give the city council a better understanding of the government's functions, to require the city council to set priorities so that it would stop making inconsistent demands on the administration, to determine the costs of services for budgeting purposes, to set up a management appraisal system emphasizing actual work performance, to find out what certain departments were doing before their department heads retired, and so on. Several jurisdictions seemed satisfied that their purposes had been accomplished, although a few failed to cite accomplishment of the initial purpose as an outcome of the program.[5]

Negative Impacts. Seven of the seventeen jurisdictions with ongoing targeting programs identified in our survey cited negative impacts, such as employee dissatisfaction, excessive emphasis on targeted activities to the detriment of other responsibilities, increased costs, and excessive paperwork. One community that reported employee dissatisfaction used its program to justify staff cuts. All three jurisdictions reporting increased costs used federal funds to support the development of work and performance measures, so the additional costs were not absorbed by the jurisdictions themselves. One of these, however, reported productivity savings in excess of the combined federal and local costs. Note that the jurisdictions with increased costs were the same ones that reported employee dissatisfaction with or resistance to the programs.

Of the four governments in which excessive paperwork was a problem, three attributed it to overly detailed program and activity breakdowns leading to an excessive reporting burden. The fourth attributed its paper overload to the frequency of appraisals. That program utilized quarterly performance appraisals, and all records had to be maintained by the personnel department.

Program Costs. Few of the jurisdictions surveyed had determined the cost of implementing and operating target-setting programs. The seven communities with MBO or ABO programs that included no special measurement efforts relied on existing

---

5. The individuals interviewed were not specifically asked whether their purposes had been accomplished, but merely what impact the target-setting activity had.

measures or used progress-reporting techniques requiring spot checks but no elaborate data collection. These seven communities generally indicated that costs were minimal and that the programs consumed only minor amounts of staff time.

The three jurisdictions that reported using federal funds to institute performance measurement as part of their targeting programs were able to pinpoint initial development costs more precisely and appear to have devoted considerably more staff time to program development and maintenance. One jurisdiction, for example, reported spending $10,000 for training and an additional $36,000 per year for a full-time manager for the program. A second community had spent $100,000 in federal grant money and $25,000 in matching funds over a two-year period to develop work measures and standards in one department and to begin such efforts in a second. Jurisdictions that had already implemented measurement systems prior to the introduction of the targeting activity generally did not count performance reporting as a program cost.

Programs Terminated. Of the twenty-five jurisdictions we examined, two had terminated MBO or program-budgeting activities, and a third reported that one program was in danger of termination. Termination had occurred (or was imminent) either because of council indifference (one jurisdiction) or employee resistance (two jurisdictions).

Information on Impact from Private Sector Trials

Extensive analysis of target setting has been undertaken in the private sector. These trials provide additional insights that appear potentially relevant to the public sector. However, as indicated in Chapter 8 and Exhibit 8, further research seems needed to establish whether the constraints peculiar to the public sector affect the applicability of private sector and laboratory findings.

Employee Performance and Productivity. Four reviews of findings from field studies and laboratory research have concluded that clear, specific, and challenging targets have a positive impact on the performance of individual workers in the private sector.[6] Other relevant findings from these studies are the following:

- More specific targets improve performance at a faster rate than do less specific targets.
- Increased specificity of targets is positively related to increased employee effort and better job performance.
- Difficult targets lead to better performance than easy targets as long as the employee accepts the validity of the targets and consciously attempts to achieve them.
- Difficult targets often stimulate employees, particularly supervisors, to analyze work problems more thoughtfully and deal with them in a more creative fashion.

Some of the private sector studies also revealed that special conditions often limited the effectiveness of target setting. One finding, for example, was that only supervisors with a high need to achieve put the same amount of effort into the rest of their work that they put into achieving specified targets or goals.[7] Another study, although less rigorous in design, found that target setting resulted in heightened motivation, improved communication, and improved concentration among employees.[8] This study also found that target setting with respect to quality control had a lasting effect only when supported by a system of rewards and sanctions. Other researchers have found that targets not linked with monetary incentives have a steadily smaller impact on productivity over time. In view of findings

---

6. Latham and Yukl, "Application of Goal Setting"; Denis D. Umstot, Cecil H. Bell, Jr. and Terence R. Mitchell, "Effects of Job Enrichment and Task Goals on Satisfaction and Productivity: Implications for Job Design," *Journal of Applied Psychology*, vol. 61 (1976), pp. 379-394; Steers and Porter, "Role of Task-Goal Attributes"; and Stephen J. Carroll, Jr. and Henry L. Tosi, Jr., *Management by Objectives: Applications and Research* (New York: Macmillan Publishing Company, 1973).

7. Richard M. Steers, "Task Goals, Individual Need Strengths, and Supervisory Performance" (Doctoral dissertation, University of California, Irvine, 1973). Others have reported similar results.

8. L. Miller, "The Use of Knowledge of Results in Improving the Performance of Hourly Operators" (Crotonville, N.Y.: Behavioral Research Service, General Electric Company, 1965). A case study of target setting in a local government's management-by-objectives program also concluded that MBO seemed to heighten managers' awareness of their responsibilities for service improvements and cost reductions. See National Center for Productivity and Quality of Working Life, *Improving Governmental Productivity: Selected Case Studies* (Washington, D.C., 1977), p. 28.

like these, closer analysis of the sustaining power of target setting appears to be in order.

Employee Job Satisfaction. In a review of research prior to 1976, one recent study concluded that "a conservative weighing of the evidence suggests that goal setting has . . . an unknown effect on job satisfaction." [9] From their own field examinations, however, these researchers found that target setting did have some impact on job satisfaction; indeed, the mere presence of targets made jobs more interesting and challenging, and therefore more satisfying. Job satisfaction, furthermore, increased significantly when target setting was combined with certain types of job enrichment, such as giving employees responsibility for identifying a task and the autonomy needed to devise their own way of doing it. [10]

Summary of Findings on Impact

The research reviewed, although mostly on private sector experiences, suggests that target-setting activities can improve productivity and job satisfaction. The research also appears to support the proposition that challenging goals are more effective than easy ones, and that more specific goals (e.g., targets) are more effective than general goals. No information seems to be available, however, on which types of targets have the greatest impact on productivity and job satisfaction, whether certain types of targets can lead to adverse results, or the relative effectiveness of group versus individual targets.

Most of the twenty-five local government officials interviewed had positive opinions about the general impact of their programs, although they lacked firm data to support those opinions. They had no data on the impact of different types of targets or different levels of target difficulty. However, nearly half of the seventeen jurisdictions with active target-setting programs had experienced some negative impacts, and 5.5 per-

---

9. Umstot et al., "Effects of Job Enrichment and Task Goals," p. 381. See also Stephen J. Carroll and Henry L. Tosi, "Goal Characteristics and Personality Factors in a Management by Objectives Program," *Administrative Science Quarterly*, vol. 15 (September 1970), pp. 295-305.
    10. Umstot et al., "Effects of Job Enrichment and Task Goals," p. 393.

cent of the 458 cities and counties responding to the 1976 ICMA survey reported terminating their MBO programs.

Nevertheless, given the results of laboratory and private sector field research, it seems reasonable to conclude that performance targeting can have a positive impact on productivity. Whether the results of performance-targeting programs in the private sector can be generally duplicated in the public sector is unknown at present. But despite the lack of supportive data, local governments in increasing numbers are initiating, maintaining, and refining MBO and other types of target-setting programs.

Chapter 11

FACTORS FACILITATING OR INHIBITING PERFORMANCE TARGETING

What factors contribute to the success or failure of performance-targeting programs? In general, the factors identified fall into three categories: design factors, implementation factors, and environmental factors. The following discussion summarizes both the findings of researchers, mostly in the private sector, and the views of local officials who responded to questions posed by the authors of this study. (Note that the terms "goal" and "target" are used interchangeably.)

Design Factors

1. Goal Clarity and Specificity. Research studies in the laboratory and in private sector MBO settings suggest that specific goals lead to better employee performance than do general goals or no goals.[1] MBO field studies also indicate, however, that even specific goals have limitations.[2]

Little evidence is available relating goal specificity (the existence of explicit targets) to better employee performance at the local government level. An important problem is that of getting managers to devise clear, specific, and measurable goals involving explicit targets. Officials of three governments cited

---

1. Latham and Yukl, "Application of Goal Setting," p. 830.
2. Ibid., p. 832.

this as an initial (and often continuing) problem; our own review of the actual objectives and targets used by local governments confirmed the difficulties. Although most of the governments we examined were attempting to move in the direction of increasing the specificity of their goals, it is only when quite specific targets are used that the impact of performance targeting can be assessed adequately.

2. Goal Difficulty. With but one exception, research studies lend support to the proposition that goals which are hard to achieve lead to better performance than do easy ones, as long as the goals are accepted by employees.[3] One study found that difficult goals can stimulate supervisors to undertake increased problem analysis (to discover the causes of poor performance) and can evoke creative behavior, both of which can result in performance improvements.[4] Challenging goals caused supervisors to act creatively rather than to push employees to work harder. This finding is in contrast to the fears expressed in two jurisdictions about line supervisors trying to compel their employees to work harder to obtain the reward offered managers for target accomplishment.

Another research finding (in a laboratory setting) was that difficult goals resulted in better performance only when they were established by the experimenter before the subjects set their own personal goals.[5] Subjects who set their own goals first tended to reject assigned goals as too difficult (or impossible) and failed to make a sincere effort. This finding suggests that higher group performance may result when supervisors take the initiative in setting forth their goals at the outset of discussions with employees.[6]

No local government research was discovered relative to optimum goal difficulty. The issue at the local level appears to be one of how goals should be set, and in particular, how to set them realistically (and how and when to alter them if conditions

---

3. Ibid., p. 835. The initial proposition and its strongest support stem from laboratory studies conducted by E. A. Locke and reported in "The Relationship of Intentions to Level of Performance," *Journal of Applied Psychology*, vol. 50 (1966), pp. 60-66. Subsequent studies have confirmed the finding.

4. A. C. Stedry and E. Kay, *The Effects of Goal Difficulty on Performance* (Crotonville, N.Y.: Behavioral Research Service, General Electric Company, 1964).

5. A. C. Stedry, *Budget Control and Cost Behavior* (Englewood Cliffs, N.J.: Prentice Hall, 1960).

6. Steers and Porter, "Role of Task-Goal Attributes," p. 442.

change). One government official mentioned that enthusiastic line employees had set target levels too high for the first year or two, leading to a great deal of anxiety on their part when it became clear that the targets could not be reached. An official of another community noted that when the city council began to set unrealistic goals, managers began trying to ensure their own participation in goal setting.

There was no reported tendency for employees to set easy targets for themselves (although such tendencies have been found in private sector studies where employees dominated the target-setting process). In one work standards program, however, the standards were intentionally introduced at fairly loose levels and gradually tightened as experience with them was acquired and more accurate levels could be set. Most jurisdictions reported having some procedure for adjusting targets when extraneous factors intervened to make goal attainment unrealistic. Some governments noted the need to set goals that were challenging and had built-in procedures allowing the budget officer or manager to add goals or raise goal levels.

3. Goal Priorities. Only one systematic study of this factor was identified. It found that subordinate managers' attitudes toward MBO and their relations with their supervisors improved where goal priorities were established.[7]

Some local communities reported setting priorities among goals, but most did not appear to do so. No evidence on the impact of this practice was available. One official contended that the city council's involvement in setting goals and goal priorities had ended the council's tendency to make contradictory demands on the executive. Most local governments, however, found that the goals they specified reflected their priorities simply because only a limited number of goals were being established for a given work period. One government official reported that the setting of goals only for special projects had led to some neglect of day-to-day operations.

4. Employee Participation. There is considerable research evidence on the positive impact of involving employees in the target-setting process. Organization theory holds that participation in decision making increases employee acceptance of the

---

7. Carroll and Tosi, "Goal Characteristics and Personality Factors."

decision and commitment to it.[8] However, three reviews of research findings concluded that although there is some evidence supporting the superiority of participatory goal setting, the importance of participation seems to depend on personality and other situational factors.[9] A fourth study found that participation was strongly and positively related to performance "only when subjects perceived a low level of threat and when they had a past history of high participation"; employees accustomed to little participation performed best when goals were set for them.[10] Subordinates who exhibited high levels of participation in the performance interview generally achieved a greater percentage of their improvement goals, had greater acceptance of their goals, and had better relationships with their supervisors.

This research, on the other hand, found that participation by managers was significantly related to performance only for managers whose need for achievement and affiliation was low.[11] Moreover, a survey of managers found that participation in goal setting tended to be positively correlated with an increase in effort by managers with high self-assurance but not by managers with low self-assurance.[12] These results should be treated with caution, however, because the performance measurement procedures used were subject to substantial uncertainty.

Another study, after surveying 198 administrators using MBO in a large state agency, concluded that favorable attitudes on the part of subordinates toward their bosses and toward MBO increased with increases in subordinate influence on goal setting up to the point where subordinate and boss had approximately equal influence.[13] When the subordinate's influence became much greater than the boss's, however, perceptions of the boss's effectiveness and attitudes toward MBO became more negative. (In 53 percent of the cases, goal setting was perceived to be

8. R. Likert, *The Human Organization* (New York: McGraw-Hill Book Company, 1967).

9. Steers and Porter, "Role of Task-Goal Attributes," p. 439; Latham and Yukl, "Application of Goal Setting"; and Robert A. Hollmann, "Applying MBO Research to Practice," *Human Resource Management*, vol. 15 (Winter 1976), pp. 28-36.

10. See J. R. French, E. Kay, and H. H. Meyer, "Participation and the Appraisal System," *Human Relations*, vol. 19 (1966), pp. 3-19.

11. Steers, "Task Goals."

12. Carroll and Tosi, "Goal Characteristics and Personality Factors."

13. John C. Aplin, Jr. and Peter P. Schoderbek, "MBO: Requisites for Success in the Public Sector," *Human Resource Management*, vol. 15 (Summer 1976), pp. 30-36.

subordinate-dominated.) There were also indications that when a subordinate had nearly complete freedom to establish goals, the subordinate expressed little concern about the consequences of failure to meet the goals. Thus, permitting the employee to set targets unilaterally or to dominate the target-setting process may lead to negative attitudes toward the supervisor (who may be viewed as "indifferent"), lack of interest in goal achievement, and the setting of lower targets than desired.

Considerable laboratory evidence supports the contention that goals affect behavior only to the extent that they are accepted.[14] "Goal acceptance" corresponds to "the degree to which an individual agrees with and develops a strong positive attitude toward his task goals . . . the degree to which there is a congruence between task goals and individual aspiration levels with respect to the goals."[15] Although it is commonly believed that greater participation leads to increased goal acceptance (goal "ownership"), this has yet to be conclusively demonstrated. No conclusive field research on the link between participation in goal setting and employee goal acceptance was identified, although the link has been inferred by some researchers.[16]

The local government officials we interviewed considered employee participation to be highly desirable. Participation was credited with increasing employee commitment and performance, increasing communication between supervisors and employees, and decreasing employee resistance. Lack of participation, on the other hand, was viewed as creating difficulties.

Eleven of the local governments reported employee participation in target setting to be characteristic of their programs. Several credited this participation with having contributed to successful program implementation. One official felt strongly that the participation of managers and other employees had given the employees a stake in the program outcome. An official of another community noted that the involvement of union stewards in target setting had precluded union opposition. Officials in two other jurisdictions believed that employees enjoyed taking part in the goal-setting process. On the other hand, another official expressed the belief that line employees were

---

14. Edwin A. Locke, Judith F. Bryan, and Lorne M. Kendell, "Goals and Intentions as Mediators of the Effects of Monetary Incentives on Behavior," *Journal of Applied Psychology*, vol. 52 (1968), pp. 104-121.

15. Steers and Porter, "Role of Task-Goal Attributes," p. 444.

16. Ibid., p. 445.

basically not interested in their work and thus had little to contribute to a goal-setting effort.

Failure to include department heads in the formulation of objectives was credited with causing the failure of one jurisdiction's MBO program. Employee unhappiness was also reported in a second jurisdiction, where a consultant developed goals without consulting department managers. In a third jurisdiction, the new city manager's coolness toward a goal-setting process initiated by his predecessor was held responsible for a slacking off of employee interest and effort.

5. Feedback or Knowledge of Results. Private sector research and laboratory evidence indicate the positive impact of providing frequent, relevant feedback to employees. According to Locke, feedback can lead to increased effort and performance by (1) inducing a person to set a goal to improve performance by a certain amount, (2) inducing a person to raise his goal level after attaining a previous goal, (3) informing a person that his present level of effort is insufficient for goal attainment and thus inducing him to increase his effort, or (4) informing a person of ways to improve his methods of performing a task.[17]

A 1968 study found feedback quality (e.g., timing, relevance, and manner of presentation) to be important to goal attainment.[18] A subsequent study found that the amount and frequency of feedback was positively correlated with self-rated goal attainment (though not with increases in self-rated effort).[19] Another study reported frequency and amount of feedback to be associated with greater self-reported motivation and better understanding of job requirements.[20] A fourth study, however, found the amount of feedback to be positively correlated with effort and overall performance ratings only for supervisors with high needs for achievement, affiliation, and independence.[21]

17. E. A. Locke, "Toward a Theory of Task Motivation and Incentives," *Organizational Behavior and Human Performance*, vol. 3 (1968), pp. 157-189.

18. D. A. Kolb, S. Winters, and D. Berlew, "Self-Directed Change: Two Studies," *Journal of Applied Behavioral Science*, vol. 4 (1968), pp. 453-473.

19. S. J. Carroll and H. L. Tosi, "Relationship of Characteristics of the Review Process to the Success of the MBO Approach," *Journal of Business*, vol. 44 (1971), pp. 299-305.

20. D. Duttagupta, "An Empirical Evaluation of Management by Objectives" (Master's Thesis, Baruch College, New York, 1975).

21. Steers, "Task Goals."

The conclusion from one review of the literature was that although study results support the need for frequent, relevant feedback in a goal-setting program, the evidence is limited and further research is needed.[22] A second reviewer of the same studies concluded that the effect of feedback in modifying performance depends on individual differences.[23]

These private sector findings were supported by the only public sector research identified on the subject. Feedback relevancy (i.e., how closely feedback was related to goals) was found to have a profound impact on public employee attitudes toward a state's MBO system. Managers who viewed feedback as closely goal-related tended to report (1) more positive attitudes toward their job, (2) greater effectiveness of their supervisors, (3) more concern with attaining goals, (4) greater organizational support for MBO, and (5) greater usefulness of MBO.[24]

Corporate researchers reported the content of feedback to be important in determining subsequent performance. Managers receiving more than an average amount of criticism in their review sessions showed less achievement than managers who received less criticism; moreover, managers improved considerably less in the areas criticized.[25]

Another reviewer of the research identified factors that should be considered when determining how often to hold feedback sessions.[26] These included:

- Extent of the subordinate's experience with MBO (more frequent sessions for less experienced employees).
- Length of time covered by the goals.
- Nature of a manager's job (more frequent sessions where jobs are more complex or changing).
- Subordinate's previous success in achieving objectives (more frequent sessions for less successful employees).
- Subordinate's need for independence (more frequent sessions if low level of need).
- Subordinate's desire for feedback.

Sixteen of the communities we contacted made some provision for feedback. Most of the local governments that used

22. Latham and Yukl, "Application of Goal Setting," p. 837.
23. Steers and Porter, "Role of Task-Goal Attributes," p. 440.
24. Aplin and Schoderbek, "MBO: Requisites for Success."
25. French, Kay, and Meyer, "Participation."
26. Hollmann, "Applying MBO Research," p. 33.

targets included performance review and reporting as an element of their program. The frequency of reporting and review varied. Some communities based their feedback on extensive collection and reporting of performance data on a daily, weekly, monthly, or quarterly basis. Others collected data only on a semiannual or annual basis. In ten jurisdictions the feedback was part of the annual employee performance appraisal. In several others the annual budget hearing was the main forum.

There was no local government evidence substantiating the importance of feedback or identifying more effective ways of conveying it. Local government officials made the following observations, however:

- Employees in one community expressed appreciation of the fact that they and the manager had the same information about the employee's performance for the annual performance review.
- The requirement that managers begin reporting their progress toward targets was credited by one official with having caused the managers to begin taking the process seriously.
- Inability to provide objective feedback or knowledge of results (because adequate measures did not exist) was the reason why one MBO program was not extended to line employees or day-to-day operations.

6. Association of Rewards or Sanctions with Goal Accomplishment.[27] One study of the link between monetary incentives and performance found that a *particular* goal level resulted in the same performance regardless of whether any monetary incentives were provided. The researcher concluded that "offering an individual money for output may motivate him to set his goals higher than he would otherwise, but this will depend on how much money he wishes to make and how much effort he wishes to expend to make it." [28] Although it was subsequently pointed out that the above study involved only small incentives and therefore might have demonstrated merely that small incentives did not increase performance, later laboratory studies have

---

27. See Part One for additional discussion of the use of monetary rewards in connection with target setting.
28. Locke, "Task Motivation and Incentives," p. 185.

shown that large incentives do result in higher performance.[29]

A study of 625 middle- and top-level managers in a large corporation found that 37 percent felt goal attainment should have some bearing on salary raises; 4 percent believed it should be almost the sole determinant.[30] Significant positive correlations were also found between managers' evaluations of MBO and the extent to which goal attainment was related to their merit compensation.

It is not the purpose of this chapter to investigate the links between goal or target attainment, any associated rewards or sanctions, and subsequent performance. Those links have been discussed in Part One. But the question of whether rewards or sanctions should be associated with goal or target accomplishment has been debated frequently in the MBO literature,[31] and was raised explicitly by some of the jurisdictions we contacted. One government had purposely not linked goals or targets with its reward/punishment system. This jurisdiction wanted to use MBO to clarify the work and purposes of government and not as an enforcement tool. Officials in a second jurisdiction expressed concern that a system of incentives might cause foremen to overwork their crews. Moreover, this jurisdiction did not want to institute a system in which poor performance was penalized.

7. Other Design Factors. Several other design factors were noted as potential problems by local officials. One official, for instance, felt that the target-setting program in his jurisdiction overemphasized workload or activity targets. Many other programs also tended to focus on workload rather than results.

In two jurisdictions where MBO was associated with program budgeting, officials cited overly detailed program and activity breakdowns leading to excessive paperwork as a major problem. Detailed measurement of progress toward targets and goals, in short, may not be cost-effective or useful for management control.

---

29. R. D. Pritchard and M. I. Curtis, "The Influence of Goal Setting and Financial Incentives on Task Performance," *Organizational Behavior and Human Performance,* vol. 10 (1973), pp. 175-183.

30. W. H. Mobley, "The Link Between MBO and Merit Compensation," *Personnel Journal,* vol. 53 (June 1974), pp. 423-427.

31. Mobley, "MBO and Merit Compensation"; Thomas H. Patten, Jr., "Linking Financial Rewards to Employee Performance: The Roles of OD and MBO," *Human Resource Management,* vol. 15 (1976), pp. 2-17.

Another problem cited was the setting of targets for inappropriate activities, leading to adverse results. One police department official, for instance, noted that targets might not be wise for certain types of departmental activities. A target which specified an increase in arrests, for example, might result in more false arrests of innocent persons.

One final design problem cited was the need to audit employees' reports of what they were doing. One official stated that employees in a work standards program soon learned to subvert the program simply by reporting what management wanted to hear, whether or not the work was actually accomplished.

Implementation Factors

Few systematic investigations have been conducted of the way in which target-setting programs have been implemented and the relation between implementation procedures and the program's degree of success.

1. Training. One author notes that "One of the biggest stumbling blocks is the fact that it all seems so clear-cut and obvious that most men believe that they already know what to do. They have to learn from experience that they still have something to learn about really managing with objectives." [32] While the importance of training has been discussed at great length in the literature, we found few studies that investigated training and its effect on performance or job satisfaction in MBO programs. One study of MBO in a private organization found that training which utilized top executives led to greater impact than training conducted solely by personnel staff. [33] Likewise, the disappearance of a program's positive effects was attributed to the lack of training reinforcement. [34] A more recent study found that MBO training and goal setting did not ensure goal use. If goal use is a necessary link to performance, but the goals are *not* being

32. Walter S. Wikstrom, *Managing by—and with—Objectives* (New York: National Industrial Conference Board, 1968), p. 2.
33. Bruce A. Kirchhoff, "A Diagnostic Tool for Management by Objectives," *Personnel Psychology*, vol. 28 (1975), p. 363.
34. John M. Ivancevich, James H. Donnelly, and Herbert L. Lyon, "A Study of the Impact of Management by Objectives on Perceived Need Satisfaction," *Personnel Psychology*, vol. 23 (Summer 1970), pp. 139-151.

used, neither MBO training nor goal setting itself may improve performance; they may, in fact, be dysfunctional.[35]

Five of the communities we contacted identified training as a significant factor in their program's success. One official noted that training was necessary because employees did not always understand the benefits of MBO or how to write objectives. A second jurisdiction felt that its prior organizational development work had increased management receptiveness to MBO. Two jurisdictions cited lack of training as a problem, resulting in confusion and anxiety as to what was wanted. Another jurisdiction cited the need to gradually educate departmental staff as the rationale for a four- to five-year program implementation process.

2. Other Implementation Factors. One study found that an employee starting a new job may accept specific goals as an integral part of the job, whereas an employee who has been working without specific goals may feel constrained when goals are added.[36] Officials of at least one local jurisdiction provided some support for this view, commenting that goals seemed to work well as motivators for new managers but not so well for others.

Although no further research on implementation factors was identified, several other considerations were mentioned as significant by local government representatives. The presence of good managers was cited as contributing significantly to program success in three jurisdictions. Two other communities deliberately selected only their best managers to participate in the program and viewed this practice as contributing greatly to the program's effectiveness. Conversely, lack of manager sophistication, resulting in poorly designed objectives, was viewed as a problem in three jurisdictions. One community noted that many managers still had not grasped the fundamental aspects of its two-year-old program.

Spokesmen for two other jurisdictions credited federal funds with enabling them to implement their programs, or at least to implement them at the pace they did. But a third jurisdiction noted that when it was required to divert HUD

---

35. John M. Ivancevich, "A Longitudinal Assessment of Management by Objectives," *Administrative Science Quarterly*, vol. 17 (March 1972), pp. 126-138.
36. Umstot et al., "Effects of Job Enrichment and Task Goals."

funds to a new activity, it was forced to eliminate the staff support necessary to extend its work standards program to another department.

Five jurisdictions reported that a phased implementation process that gave supervisors and employees the time to grasp the concept and operation of goal and target setting was a key factor. Four to five years were deemed an appropriate implementation period in one community.

Environmental Factors

Several studies have pointed out the need to consider various environmental factors in the design and implementation of an MBO program.[37] Similarly, several authors have stressed the differences between public and private sector environments and the need to adjust programs accordingly.[38]

1. Labor Relations and Superior-Subordinate Relationships. One study found that the greater a subordinate's satisfaction with his supervisor, (a) the more satisfied the subordinate was with MBO, (b) the greater the perceived goal success, and (c) the more improved the relationship with the supervisor.[39] Little other research on this factor was identified.

One of the jurisdictions contacted noted that a department head's excellent relations with his staff explained why the program was carried out without any particular problems. Good cooperation and communication among managers were cited as important to the success of the program in another jurisdiction.

Few of the governments contacted cited labor relations as a problem. However, few of those governments were required to bargain with unions, and few of the targeting programs affected line employees directly. Nevertheless, union opposition was viewed as an existing or potential problem in four commu-

---

37. Hollmann, "Applying MBO Research"; Steers and Porter, "Role of Task-Goal Attributes"; Latham and Yukl, "Application of Goal Setting"; and Fred Luthans, "How to Apply MBO," *Public Personnel Management*, vol. 5 (1976), pp. 83-87.

38. John C. Aplin, Jr. and Peter P. Schoderbek, "How to Measure MBO," *Public Personnel Journal*, vol. 5 (March/April 1976), pp. 88-95.

39. Henry L. Tosi and Stephen J. Carroll, "Some Factors Affecting the Success of Management by Objectives," *Journal of Management Studies*, vol. 7 (May 1970), pp. 209-223.

nities. A jurisdiction using work standards reported that if its program had not already been in full swing before a new union took over it might have been stopped, since the union disliked work standards. In a second jurisdiction, the union was reported to be resisting both the extension of performance measurement to the work of union employees and any new connection between performance and pay. In a third, because of union resistance to the performance appraisal concept, all classified employees *except* union members had been included in an appraisal-by-objectives program. In a fourth (with an apparently strong union), union members who complained to city council representatives about the increased recordkeeping requirements associated with MBO were reported to have "stalled the program."

Conversely, successful efforts by the city manager in one jurisdiction to engage union stewards in an ABO program were credited with having forestalled any opposition. Union officials in that jurisdiction were believed by the responding city official to like the program because of its relative objectivity.

2. Top Management Support. The importance of top management support to program success has been noted both in the research literature and by local governments. A survey of public administrators, for example, found that when top managers formulated objectives that were subsequently communicated to subordinates, the subordinates perceived that (a) the MBO program was important to the organization, (b) their goals were clearer and more specific, (c) their own job objectives were more important, and (d) MBO was more helpful and applicable to service-oriented organizations.[40] Similarly, introduction of a private sector MBO program was found to be more successful when it was initiated by the top management group than when it was initiated by the personnel department.[41]

Eleven of the twenty-five jurisdictions surveyed noted the importance of management support—either from the top elected or appointed official or from the head of the agency in which the program was being initiated. Indeed, management support was the environmental factor most frequently cited as significant to success (or lack of it). This was true whether the activity was MBO, ABO, or work standards.

---

40. Aplin and Schoderbek, "MBO: Requisites for Success," p. 33.
41. Ivancevich, Donnelly, and Lyon, "Impact of Management by Objectives."

City council support, or lack of it, was considered significant by nine jurisdictions and insignificant by one. Council support of the program budgeting and goal-setting process was seen as particularly significant to program success in one city, where the council began to orient its budget hearings toward programs and accomplishment of goals. In another jurisdiction, council lack of interest in the program budget (which had been provided explicitly for its use) was cited as the reason why an MBO/program-budgeting program was terminated, and council opposition stimulated by complaints from union employees was seen as having halted another MBO program. A fourth community found council support in priority setting to be crucial to program success. In a fifth community, however, a council's attempt to impose an MBO program developed by an outside consultant was thought to have caused considerable employee resistance. This suggests that council support is a desirable but not sufficient condition for success.

3. Job Complexity and Performance Measures. One laboratory study[42] found that setting specific goals for individuals facilitated performance when jobs were independent but inhibited performance when jobs were interdependent. These findings were attributed to coordination difficulties and employee preoccupation with individual goals at the expense of organizational effectiveness. It has also been found that interrelationships among jobs create problems in evaluating individual performance and goal attainment.[43]

One review of existing research noted that the feasibility of goal setting may be determined both by job complexity and measurement capability.[44] The reviewers also indicated that private sector goal-setting programs involving managers have encountered more problems and been less successful (due to job complexity) than has goal setting with nonmanagerial employees. In addition, a tendency to neglect aspects of a job that are not easily quantified has been noted.[45] The importance of

---

42. J. V. Baumler, "Defined Criteria of Performance in Organizational Control," *Administrative Science Quarterly,* vol. 16 (1971), pp. 340-350.

43. Latham and Yukl, "Application of Goal Setting," p. 842.

44. Ibid.

45. H. Levinson, "Management by Whose Objectives?" *Harvard Business Review*, vol. 48 (1970), pp. 125-134.

conducting an initial exploration of the way in which multiple goals direct behavior and the allocation of effort has been cited by others.[46]

Local government officials also mentioned some of these difficulties, most frequently in connection with setting objectives and measuring the performance of line employees. Lack of a measurement system was reported by one city as the major barrier to extending targeting programs to line employees or day-to-day operations. A second community encountered major difficulties in translating unit objectives into individual employee objectives. It ultimately dropped its system of performance appraisal for line employees. An official from another community expressed the belief that it is impossible to quantify the good performance of line employees on an individual basis and that accountability should begin at the first supervisory level. The jurisdictions that did develop work and performance measurement systems invested considerable time and effort in doing so; these jurisdictions were the ones that complained of excessive paperwork.

Numerous jurisdictions avoided the measurement problem by omitting line employees and day-to-day operations from their MBO and ABO programs. Objectives focused only on special projects or tasks, or on personal development activities. One jurisdiction noted that departments that traditionally had a project-oriented emphasis (e.g., engineering or public works) found the program considerably easier to implement than did other departments. Another jurisdiction, however, indicated that emphasis on special projects and the exclusion of daily operations from the goal-setting process caused managers to neglect daily operations to some extent.

An official in one jurisdiction noted the potential inequity of trying to measure and compare the efforts of workers doing apparently similar jobs because of differences in the job environment. It was, he said, extremely difficult to compare the performance of individual tree-trimmers, for example, because trees varied in size, accessibility, time required, and so on. As noted previously, complaints about inequities and employee dissatisfaction with being evaluated individually in terms of work standards led one community to discontinue the use of work standards to assess individual employee performance.[47]

---

46. Stedry and Kay, *Effects of Goal Difficulty.*
47. Greiner et al., *Monetary Incentives.*

4. Manager and Employee Attitudes. Employee attitudes stem-ming from their educational and cultural backgrounds have been cited as factors believed to influence the success of MBO pro-grams, but little systematic research on this subject appears to have been conducted. A survey of public administrators in MBO programs concluded that managers generally assume that social services cannot be measured; the researchers viewed this atti-tude as a constraint that can thwart efforts to develop and op-erate MBO programs.[48] A similar reaction was expressed during our survey by one local government official in reference to the difficulty of measuring the work of line employees.

The attitudes of local government managers toward line em-ployees and their perceptions of line employee attitudes were often cited as problems in implementing performance targeting. Lack of interest was cited by three jurisdictions as a reason why target setting could not succeed (or had not succeeded) with line employees. One official viewed line employees as uninter-ested in achieving goals and attributed this lack of interest to the employees' poor education. Another viewed line employees as basically uninterested in their work and thus as having little to contribute to an MBO effort.

5. Changes in Priorities. MBO administrators have cited the continual shifting of priorities in the public sector as a major constraint on successful MBO implementation.[49] In our own sur-vey, one government official with private sector experience con-firmed the problem. He noted that external factors, such as po-litical pressure, can make it impossible to control the flow or outcome of work in the public sector. Also, the episodic and project-oriented nature of much governmental activity made routine measurement of outcomes difficult. Another official re-ported political interference from council members in determin-ing merit increases for employees.

High turnover of top management personnel was cited as a problem in at least two communities. In one instance the pro-gram initiator left government service, while in the second in-stance an elected official supporting the program lost an election. These changes had a negative impact. Conversely, turnover in top level management was responsible for bringing in many of the key people who initiated target-setting programs.

---

48. Aplin and Schoderbek, "MBO: Requisites for Success," p. 34.
49. Ibid., p. 35.

6. Personnel System Characteristics. A jurisdiction's inability to reward good performance because of restricted pay scales was cited as a barrier to ABO programs in three communities. In one, only 30 to 40 percent of the employees had not already reached the top of their salary range. In a second, a rigid civil service system tying step increases to longevity prevented the tying of rewards to target accomplishment. These findings reinforce the conclusion of others that inability to reward different levels of performance can be a public sector MBO constraint.[50] Yet, as noted earlier, most jurisdictions appeared to have some flexibility to base management salary increases at least partly on target accomplishment.

7. Other Factors. No systematic research was identified on other factors believed to influence the success of MBO programs, although a number of such factors have been suggested in the literature, including the following:

- Lack of administrative power (e.g., dismissal authority) to enforce employee compliance in the public sector.[51] (This problem was not observed by the local officials contacted.)
- Inexperience with systems focusing on service-oriented objectives.[52]
- Past failures on the part of legislative bodies to articulate legislative intent, leading to misinterpretation of strategic goals and formulation of inappropriate operational goals.[53]
- Lack of local government capability to collect and process output or effectiveness data.[54]

The local government officials interviewed cited some additional problems. One jurisdiction attempting to set performance targets for individual employees noted that individuals whose targets did not fit their job descriptions could file grievances. Consequently, the kinds of targets that could be set were limited. A state requirement for line-item budgeting in Illinois was viewed as a problem in one jurisdiction where MBO had been introduced as part of a program-budgeting effort, since the council could not legitimately exclude line-item budgeting. And lack of staff resources to handle the required recordkeeping was cited as an additional difficulty.

---

50. Ibid., p. 34.
51. Ibid., p. 35.
52. Ibid.
53. Ibid.
54. Ibid.

Chapter 12

SUMMARY AND RECOMMENDATIONS ON PERFORMANCE TARGETING

Performance targeting is a way of motivating employees, either individually or as a group, by making explicit to them the work they are expected to accomplish over a specific period of time. A number of laboratory studies and field tests in the private sector indicate that the setting of specific goals, or targets, is positively related to improved employee performance. Some research also suggests that setting specific goals can increase employee job satisfaction.

In state and local governments, performance targeting is usually a part of management-by-objectives programs, appraisal-by-objectives programs, or work standards programs. Although many such programs link the achievement of targets with rewards or penalties, we have focused here on the use of targets as motivational factors in themselves.

Local Government Use of Performance Targeting

Although the 1976 ICMA and IPMA surveys of governmental operations did not ask specific questions about the use of performance targets, those surveys did show that among the responding jurisdictions MBO was used by 41 percent of the cities and 40 percent of the counties. Approximately 20 percent of both types of local governments reported using ABO systems,

171

while 51 percent of the cities and 46 percent of the counties reported using either work measurement or work standards programs.

To get an idea of how many of these programs incorporated performance targeting, we conducted a telephone survey of officials in twenty-five randomly selected jurisdictions. Twenty-three of these jurisdictions had reported using MBO for more than a year, while the other two had reportedly terminated their MBO programs. All the jurisdictions contacted had instituted their programs within the past seven years, a majority of them within the last three.

Only seventeen of the jurisdictions were actually using performance targets. In most of those communities, the specification of performance targets and the measurement of targeted performance were still in the early stages of development. The reported measures often did not appear to measure target accomplishment adequately. Most of the targets focused on workload or level-of-effort (e.g., number of records examined), or else they specified a particular task or project to be completed, often with due dates. Efficiency and effectiveness targets were relatively infrequent. Only seven of the communities had used effectiveness targets, and only two had employed efficiency targets.

Many of the governments, however, appeared to be refining their programs, in part by including more targets (particularly effectiveness and efficiency targets), in part by developing the measurement procedures necessary to determine whether goals and targets have actually been achieved.

The Impact of Performance Targeting

Only two systematic, quantitative studies of the impact of state or local government performance-targeting programs were found in the course of this study. The results were mixed. One study indicated some performance improvements when targets were used in connection with MBO; the other found that productivity improvements could be attributed to the use of work standards only when those standards were linked to monetary rewards. Several case studies of local government MBO programs are available, but these do not provide documentation of program effects.

Of the twenty-five jurisdictions contacted, only one had systematically gathered data on the effects of performance targeting, and this jurisdiction had focused only on employee attitudes, not on job efficiency or effectiveness. These data were collected through a survey of employee attitudes after one year of an ABO program. The survey showed positive attitudes toward the new appraisal procedure on the ground that it was more objective than the performance appraisal procedure previously used by the jurisdiction. The effects reported by other jurisdictions, although subjective and not supported by conclusive data, included improved productivity, improved management and decision making, increased job satisfaction, and positive attitudes toward the program. Few jurisdictions reported any increase in costs due to program implementation. However, nearly half of the governments using target-setting procedures reported at least some negative effects.

Factors Facilitating or Inhibiting Performance Targeting

Three types of factors were identified as significant to program success: design factors, implementation factors, and environmental factors.

Design Factors. The following factors generally enhanced a performance-targeting program's ability to improve employee performance:
- Goals that were specific, difficult to accomplish, and prioritized.
- Employee participation in target setting rather than supervisor assignment of goals, except when
  —there had been low employee participation in setting goals in the past;
  —employees saw the program as threatening their position;
  —employees had a high need for achievement or affiliation, and participation in goal setting was not necessary to ensure their commitment to goal achievement;
  —employees had low self-assurance; or
  —employees had too much influence in the setting of targets.

- Frequent, relevant, timely, and constructive (noncritical) feedback to employees about their progress toward targets.
- Setting of overall goals at the top level of the organization and communication of those goals to subordinates.
- Supervisor support for target setting.

Implementation Factors. Although little systematic research has been conducted in either private sector or public sector settings, a number of factors were cited as vital to successful implementation. These included the following:

- Involvement of top management in implementation.
- Adequate training of managers and employees.
- Gradual implementation over a four- to five-year period.
- Selection of good managers to introduce the program.
- Sufficient funding to develop performance measures.

Environmental Factors. Officials of local governments cited a number of environmental factors as important to success. In addition, four factors that tend to restrict success were identified. The positive factors included the following:

- Support from the mayor and city council.
- Support from unions and other employee organizations.
- Capable and sophisticated managers.
- The existence of a functioning measurement system and adequate performance measures.

The negative factors included the following:

- The attitudes and limited educational background of line employees, which tended to reduce their interest in helping to solve management problems.
- Restrictive pay scales or civil service system provisions that limited the tying of rewards to target accomplishment.
- Turnover among top management personnel. (In some instances, however, turnover was a positive factor.)
- Political pressures that resulted in changes in priorities.

Conclusions and Recommendations

1. Performance targeting has been implemented as a management and motivational technique in a number of local gov-

ernments. However, there seem to be some significant constraints on its widespread application in the public sector. These constraints warrant further investigation.

2. Little research has been conducted on the effectiveness of target setting in improving public employee productivity and job satisfaction. Psychological research and private sector findings are favorable, but the applicability of these findings to local government programs is uncertain. Thus, the impact of local (and state) government target-setting programs should be carefully evaluated, and there should be an examination of the conditions under which real productivity improvements occur (see Recommendation No. 6 also).

3. It has been argued—but not proved—that targets focusing on efficiency and effectiveness are more likely to result in higher productivity than targets focusing on workload. Since local government targeting programs tend to emphasize workload rather than effectiveness or efficiency targets, research is highly desirable to either verify or refute this contention.

4. There are some types of activities or services for which it may not be advisable to set performance targets because of the possibility of unwanted results. Targets should probably be avoided:

—when the employee has little control over the activity or the result;

—when realistic, measurable targets cannot be set because of the absence of adequate information;

—when information about target accomplishment cannot be verified; or

—when setting targets for some aspects of a job is likely to cause employees to overemphasize those aspects and neglect others of equal importance.

5. Little information is available on the motivational impact of group targets. Because group targets represent one possible solution to the problem of target setting for interdependent jobs (which complicate attempts to measure the contribution of any given individual), an examination of the effectiveness of group performance targets for public sector employees is recommended.

6. Lack of information about the duration of the impact of performance targeting on employee productivity is a serious weakness of existing research. Most field studies have been of short duration, and little information is available on whether the initial impact of these programs can be sustained. It is recommended that long-term research be conducted to fill the need.

7. Private sector studies have identified many factors in the way a performance-targeting program is designed and implemented, as well as factors in the program's environment, that appear to affect the effectiveness of targeting activities. Although our review suggests that similar findings are likely at the local government level, more systematic confirmation is desirable. It is recommended that such efforts be undertaken in conjunction with a general investigation of the effects of performance targeting in improving local government productivity. When better confirmation is obtained, guidelines should be prepared to assist local governments in determining when, whether, and how to implement performance-targeting programs.

Part Three:

PERFORMANCE APPRAISAL

Chapter 13

THE MAJOR APPROACHES TO EMPLOYEE PERFORMANCE APPRAISAL

There are several ways in which appraisals of employee performance could contribute to increased productivity. Performance appraisals could be used to determine which employees receive monetary or other incentives intended to reward improved productivity. Appraisals could serve as a means through which managers express their approval or disapproval of employee performance in an attempt to motivate employees to improve an already satisfactory record or overcome an unsatisfactory one. Appraisals could help employees and supervisors work together to find ways to improve performance. And appraisals could help managers to identify both productive and unproductive employees. The former could be retained and the latter replaced.

Despite these potential benefits, employee performance appraisal is a problem for government managers. No method of appraisal has proved its effectiveness decisively enough to be universally accepted, and existing methods have serious drawbacks.

This chapter briefly describes the appraisal techniques currently being used in state and local governments. They fall into three main groups: (1) supervisor rating of individual employees, (2) appraisal of individual employees based on their success in achieving preset performance targets (as in appraisal-by-objectives programs), and (3) group evaluation.

179

Supervisor Rating of Individual Employees

The most common approach to employee performance appraisal in state and local governments involves the periodic (usually annual) rating of employees by supervisors using standardized appraisal forms and procedures. While a few governments rely only on narrative appraisals, many use ratings from standardized instruments supplemented by narrative statements. Narrative appraisals and the most common types of standardized instruments for making ratings are discussed below.

Narrative appraisals require supervisors to use their own words to describe employee performance. Narratives may be written in essay or letter form or they may consist of specific paragraphs on such topics as "description of regular job assignment," "performance on regular job assignment," "attendance and punctuality," "supervision of other employees," "areas of exceptionally good or poor performance," and "overall appraisal."

Rating scales require the supervisor to compare the employee to a standard and decide the degree to which the employee meets the standard. These often take the form of a "multiple-step rating scale"—a scale on which only a few specific points or intervals have been defined. The rater must check one of those defined points. "Graphic rating scales" involve unbroken lines that the rater must mark at the point that best describes the employee. These lines are often divided into sections which, in practice, are frequently used like steps. In governments using these types of rating scales, employees are commonly rated on general traits, such as "dependability" and "quality of work." Exhibit 11 shows a multiple-step rating scale used by a state government, and Exhibit 12 shows a graphic scale used by a local government.

In "forced-choice rating scales," the supervisor is provided with four items and required to choose the one that is most characteristic of the employee as well as the one that is least characteristic. The four items are designed to include two which seem to describe poor performance and two which seem typical of good performance (e.g., "this employee is generally (1) uncooperative, (2) late, (3) accurate, (4) helpful"). Only one of the items relating to good performance and one of the items relating to poor performance can be counted in scoring, but the

Exhibit 11

EXAMPLE OF A MULTIPLE-STEP RATING SCALE

For each category please place a check (√) in the column which best describes the above employee.

Part I—To be completed for all employees	SUPERIOR	HIGHLY SATISFACTORY	MEETS REQUIREMENTS	NEEDS IMPROVEMENT	NOT SATISFACTORY
1. *Quantity of Work*—Consider amount of work generated in relation to amount of work expected for current job or position.					
2. *Quality of Work*—Consider overall knowledge of duties and responsibilities and completeness and accuracy of work.					
3. *Use of Time*—Consider attendance: is punctual reporting to work; accomplishes required work on or ahead of schedule.					
4. *Initiative*—Consider amount of direction or supervision required and concern for consistency in trying to do better.					

(Continued)

Exhibit 11 (Continued)

For each category please place a check (√) in the column which best describes the above employee.

	SUPERIOR	HIGHLY SATISFACTORY	MEETS REQUIREMENTS	NEEDS IMPROVEMENT	NOT SATISFACTORY
Part II—To be completed for employees who currently hold managerial, supervisory, professional, or technical positions.					
5. *Planning*—Sets realistic goals and objectives; anticipates and prepares for future requirements; establishes logical priorities.					
6. *Leadership*—Sets high standards; provides a good managerial example; delegates authority and responsibility effectively.					
7. *Subordinate Development*—Helps subordinates in job development; gives guidance and counseling.					
8. *Human Relations*—Establishes and maintains cordial work climate; promotes harmony; displays sincere interest in assisting employees.					

Comments or explanation of nonsatisfactory rating or of superior rating should be completed on the reverse side of this form.

Source: Performance Report Form, Personnel Division, State of Indiana. (Excerpt.)

Exhibit 12

EXAMPLE OF A GRAPHIC RATING SCALE

To the Supervisor

In the chart below, record your evaluation by placing an (X) at a point along the scale between (50) and (100) that best reflects this employee's work performance. Do this for each Performance Factor and write in the column to the right the numerical rating that is nearest to your (X).

PERFORMANCE FACTOR	100	95 SUPERIOR	90	85 GOOD	80	75 AVERAGE	70	65 FAIR	60	55 POOR	50	NUMERICAL RATING
Work Quality												
Work Quantity												
Dependability												
Attitude												
Attendance and Punctuality												

Source: Employee Performance Evaluation Form, Durham, N.C. (Excerpt.)

supervisor doing the rating does not know which items count and which do not. The scoring system is based on an analysis of the characteristics of good and poor performers in the specific job being appraised. Forced-choice scales are intended to lessen the possibility of supervisors intentionally distorting ratings.

Comparative ranking is a technique in which employees in a group are compared with each other rather than with a fixed standard. In "paired comparison," each employee is paired with every other employee and a score is computed from the total of all the pairings. In "rank-order comparison," employees are ranked in sequence from best to worst.

Behavior-based scales or checklists are appraisal instruments developed for specific classes of jobs.[1] They are based on surveys of knowledgeable persons who are asked to give specific examples of effective and ineffective work behavior they have observed. These "critical incidents" are analyzed statistically, and those on which there is the largest amount of agreement are grouped to form several performance dimensions or scales. Each dimension or scale contains a number of descriptions that characterize different levels of performance. A "behavior-based checklist" merely lists these statements (the critical incidents), and the supervisor checks whether (or to what extent) each

---

1. A behaviorally anchored rating scale and a conventional multiple-step or graphic rating scale with anchors may look quite similar. The difference lies in the method of development of the scales and the specificity of the behavior statements. Behaviorally anchored scales are systematically developed from "expert" assessments of job performance using statistical procedures, and the behavior statements are very specific in focusing on the particular behavior involved in specific jobs. The descriptive anchors used for conventional rating scales are usually quite broad and are designed to apply to many different types of jobs and employees. For more information on behavior-based evaluation procedures, see Donald P. Schwab, Herbert A. Heneman III, and Thomas A. DeCotiis, "Behaviorally Anchored Rating Scales: A Review of the Literature," *Personnel Psychology*, vol. 28 (1975), pp. 549-562. See also Wiley G. Hamby, *Development of Behaviorally Anchored Rating Scales—"BARS"—for Employee Evaluation*, U.S. Civil Service Commission, Atlanta Region. According to this manual, "A useful BARS (for one position) can be developed with approximately four days of professional time and approximately two days of clerical support," plus four half-day sessions with about six supervisors of the position being analyzed, who function as the "experts" on the position (pp. 5-6).

Exhibit 13
EXAMPLE OF A BEHAVIOR-BASED CHECKLIST

Agency Name: Department of Parks and Tourism

Job Title: Secretary I

Describe this employee's performance by responding to each statement below using the following scale.

+ Employee's performance is better than this statement

= Statement fits this employee's performance

— Employee's performance is not as good as this statement

For example, if you decide this employee's performance exceeds that described by the statement, "Would direct visitors to an office unannounced," you would blacken in the area under + like this: + = —

Do not omit any items. Use a soft pencil to mark your answers.

_____is the sort of employee who would

+ = —

1. Observe jobs that need to be done and do them in addition to what had been assigned.

+ = —

2. Notify supervisor of jobs that he/she has observed that need to be done.

+ = —

3. Willingly assist other employees thus promoting a cooperative atmosphere in the work unit.

+ = —

4. Verify that the materials being filed in a folder are related to the content of the file before filing.

+ = —

5. Proofread material for punctuation, typographical, and grammatical errors and make suggestions to clarify content.

+ = —

6. Keep a mailing list current for typing correspondence by changing addresses as they come in.

+ = —

7. Attach all pertinent information to correspondence to facilitate processing.

(Continued)

Exhibit 13 (Continued)

---

8. Send mail marked for regular postage through messenger service resulting in late delivery.   + = −

9. Reduce conflict between other employees by providing constructive suggestions to solve problems.   + = −

10. Turn in complete work products.   + = −

11. Perform duties as assigned when cutting corners could save time and not affect quality of end product.   + = −

12. Not reflect personal feelings in voice or manner when receiving callers.   + = −

13. Strictly observe mail marked personal.   + = −

14. Neglect to include referenced enclosures with a letter.   + = −

15. Withhold information about a way of doing something because it would require extra time and effort of him/her.   + = −

16. Occasionally create a hostile working atmosphere because of disagreement with coworkers.   + = −

17. Refer routine questions from callers that he/she should be able to answer.   + = −

18. Verify addresses before mass mailing.   + = −

19. Let a bad mood reflect in telephone conversations.   + = −

20. Be knowledgeable of agency operations so as to correctly answer questions and requests for unusual information if the need arises.

Source: Sample Performance Evaluation Rating Form, Office of Personnel Management, State of Arkansas. (Excerpt, slightly modified.)

statement applies to the employee being evaluated. Exhibit 13 shows the behavior-based checklist used by the Arkansas state government. A "behaviorally anchored rating scale" is similar to a behavior-based checklist, but the behavior statements are grouped into scales, with points on the scale calibrated ("anchored") by the behavior statements. The supervisor chooses the point on each scale that characterizes the employee.[1]

Appraisal Linked to Performance Targets [2]

Performance appraisal may consist of assessing the extent to which individual employees meet preset performance targets. The supervisor may prescribe standards or targets, or the supervisor and the employee may formulate them jointly. However they are set, the targets or standards are written down; in essence, the supervisor and the employee prepare a contract that spells out what the employee plans to accomplish to obtain a good appraisal. At the end of the work period the employee's accomplishments are compared with the preset targets. There may be periodic reviews between the initial setting of targets and the final appraisal, and targets may be modified in the event of extenuating circumstances.

A number of types of targets can be used. They may be (1) workload or level-of-effort targets, such as "review 100 case records"; (2) project completion or due-date targets, such as "complete efficiency study of ticket window operation by the end of the appraisal period"; (3) efficiency targets, such as "increase the average number of applications processed per week to thirty"; (4) cost targets, such as "maintain vehicle repair service at the same cost as in FY 1976-77"; or (5) effectiveness targets, such as "keep emergency response time below three minutes." Targets may be based on engineered work standards, on the experience of past years, or on a negotiated agreement between supervisor and employee regarding what the employee should be expected to accomplish.

Appraisal by objectives (ABO) is a form of employee performance appraisal based on the model of management by objec-

---

2. See Part Two for additional discussion of performance targeting.

Exhibit 14
EXAMPLE OF APPRAISAL BY OBJECTIVES

Part 1. APPRAISAL OF OBJECTIVES.

Supervisor is to list and evaluate all objectives for which the employee was held accountable during the last reporting period. Mark the appropriate column for each objective.

Responsi- bility	Indicator	Objectives	Objectives		
			Ex- ceeded	Met	Not met
Program development	New seminar program developed	By May 1, 1974, will have developed a four-hour seminar program on "Job Enrichment."			
Program implementation	Number of programs personally conducted	By Feb. 1, 1974, will have personally conducted sixteen (four-hour) management development programs for Agencies X and Y.			
Development and implementation of organization surveys	Attitude survey constructed	By Jan. 1, 1974, will have completed construction of an attitude survey for Agency B.			
	Attitude survey completed	By April 1, 1974, will have completed attitude survey for 200 employees of Agency B in-including the analysis of data and feedback.			

Source: Performance Appraisal Form, State of Illinois. (Excerpt, slightly modified.)

tives (MBO). Appraisal by objectives, like management by objectives, usually includes joint supervisor-employee target setting, periodic progress reviews, and joint final appraisal. ABO is commonly used to appraise managerial or professional employees. Exhibit 14 is an illustration of an appraisal-by-objectives form.

The performance targets most commonly used for line employees involve work standards. Although often based on historical performance or engineered time standards, in practice they are usually established by the supervisor or higher management, particularly when the standards have already been thoroughly tested elsewhere.

Group Appraisal

In some cases, individual appraisal may not be appropriate or feasible. When a group or team of employees is responsible for a task, as is often the case in government, the performance of individual employees may be difficult to ascertain. Therefore, a government may choose to assess the group as a whole on its performance of the group task and reward (or penalize) all members of the group equally.

Chapter 14

PERFORMANCE APPRAISAL TECHNIQUES USED IN STATE AND LOCAL GOVERNMENTS

Exhibit 15 summarizes the use of various types of performance appraisal systems by the fifty states, twenty-five counties, and twenty-five cities surveyed for this study. Fifty of the 100 governments used systems that involved supervisor ratings of individual employees, sixteen used systems in which employees were appraised on the basis of their achievement of performance targets, and the remaining thirty-four allowed individual departments to determine their own appraisal systems. One local government reported the use of group appraisals by one of its departments.

Supervisor Rating Systems

STATE GOVERNMENTS

Twenty-four state governments had appraisal systems in which supervisors rated employees. Two of these twenty-four states used only narrative appraisals. Twenty-one others used rating instruments with nonspecific performance factors (always including "quality" and "quantity" of work plus one or more personal traits, such as "attitude" or "knowledge"). The various

Exhibit 15
PERFORMANCE APPRAISAL SYSTEMS IN STATE AND LOCAL GOVERNMENTS

Type of Appraisal System	States	Counties	Cities	Total
Supervisor rating of individual employees	24 (48%)	13 (52%)	13 (52%)	50 (50%)
Appraisal based on preset performance targets	13 (26%)	1 (4%)	2 (8%)	16 (16%)
No formal government-wide procedures for conducting appraisal [1]	13[2] (26%)	11 (44%)	10 (40%)	34 (34%)
Total	50	25	25	100

1. Some individual departments within these governments had their own performance appraisal systems. One such department had the only group appraisal system reported.
2. Five of these states required an overall rating, such as "satisfactory" or "unsatisfactory," without specifying how the rating was to be determined.
Source: Our 1977 mail and telephone survey. The personnel departments of the fifty states were contacted by mail and requested to send copies of forms, instructions, laws, rules and regulations, and evaluative studies relating to their performance appraisal systems. Twenty-five city and twenty-five county governments, selected randomly from among cities over 50,000 population and counties over 100,000 population, were similarly contacted. The seven states, fifteen cities, and sixteen county governments that did not reply to the initial mail request or to a second mail request were interviewed by telephone.

factors were rated on three-point to seven-point scales. These scales often included definitions of the ratings but were not specifically tailored to individual jobs or employees, although a supplementary narrative statement was often suggested and sometimes required if performance was exceptionally good or exceptionally poor.

One state used behaviorally based checklists. It developed scales for a total of ninety-five different tasks and responsibilities, termed "functions."[1] From these ninety-five functions, the supervisor and the employee jointly selected the three to eight functions most important in the employee's own job. Based on their choice, a form was provided with anchored scales for each of the chosen job functions. For example, for a secretarial employee the supervisor might be required to decide whether the employee's performance was better than, worse than, or the same as the statement, "This is the sort of employee who would verify an individual's official title when typing correspondence." This rating, combined with ratings of two other statements regarding the same function, pinpointed the employee's rating on a seven-point scale for the given function.

This system involved an element of individual job analysis without requiring the development of separate rating scales for all the different jobs in the government. It provided some flexibility and some employee participation in choosing appraisal criteria. But it did not require actual performance data, and it relied on the judgment of the supervisor. Since the selection of job tasks might take place at the time of appraisal rather than at the beginning of the performance period, the employee might not know in advance what the appraisal criteria would be.

Three of the states that employed supervisor rating forms noted that they supplemented them with workload statistics or performance objectives, or that some individual departments used appraisal-by-objectives systems. One government exempted executives from the rating system and used management-by-objectives procedures with them. Another government used parts of the "process" of appraisal by objectives—namely, discussion of job descriptions between employees and supervisors, setting of objectives and standards, and semiannual progress reviews—in arriving at the scale ratings. One of the two governments using purely narrative appraisals encouraged a high degree of employee participation.

Face-to-face discussions of ratings were required in thirteen states. Seven states gave supervisors the option of not discussing ratings with employees, though they usually recommended such discussions. One other state left the decision on having a personal discussion up to the employee. Three states did not indicate whether a discussion was required or recommended.

---

1. Erich P. Prien, Mark A. Jones, and Louise M. Miller, "A Job-Related Performance Rating System" (Office of Personnel Management, State of Arkansas, 1976).

Although some states provided supervisors with manuals that contained extensive directions on how to conduct discussions of ratings with employees, several states provided only a one-page guide. Five states provided special training for supervisors.

LOCAL GOVERNMENTS

Of the fifty local governments in the sample, twenty-six used supervisor rating scales to make employee appraisals. In three of these twenty-six, however, some departments or employees were appraised using preset objectives or work standards. In one of these three governments, both group and individual appraisals were used in one department.

Twenty-two of these governments appraised employees annually, two appraised them semiannually, and two others appraised them semiannually until the top of the salary range was reached and annually thereafter. One government had a bonus program for managers that involved semiannual reviews.

Fifteen of the governments required supervisors to discuss ratings with employees, while four recommended it but left the decision up to the supervisor. One of these four, however, required it if an unsatisfactory rating was given. Seven other governments did not mention whether a meeting was required.

Appraisal Linked to Performance Targets

STATE GOVERNMENTS

Thirteen states appraised employee performance according to preset performance targets or goals. These ranged from vague goals incorporating no time, quality, or quantity targets to specific, measurable output targets and effectiveness criteria. "Process" targets, such as "conduct four orientation sessions per month," were more common than quality or outcome targets, and many of the goals were simply due dates for special projects. Objectives were not always measurable or clearly observable; many required that at least some subjective judgment be used in assessing the achievement of objectives.

To ensure that objectives were of consistently good quality and covered all aspects of a given job, seven states provided detailed manuals and sample forms that took supervisors and employees through the objective-setting and evaluation process step by step. In one of these states, for example, employees participated in writing specific descriptions of a number of basic performance factors, such as "quality of work." These factors were required to include measurable objectives, such as due dates for projects and other quantitative performance targets. At the end of the performance period a score was assigned to each performance factor. This score was based on achievement of the corresponding objective. When the scores for the factors were added together, the total score fell into one of five performance score categories. This category was used to guide personnel actions.

The weight assigned to the achievement of targets or goals varied from state to state. Three states (including the state discussed above) based an employee's overall performance rating entirely on target achievement. Seven other states used an overall rating for personnel decisions, but there were no specific guidelines for deriving this rating from the achievement of targets nor for designating how large a role quantitative results should play. Four of the thirteen states with appraisal-by-objectives systems also used traditional performance rating scales, on which employee traits were determined subjectively.

All of the thirteen states using targeting systems required annual appraisal. In addition, one state required quarterly appraisals, one required quarterly performance reviews if performance was unsatisfactory, one required either quarterly or semiannual performance reviews, and one recommended at least quarterly reviews. Two required semiannual performance reviews, and two others recommended frequent feedback on performance. In all of these states, meetings between the supervisor and the employee were required for target setting, for performance reviews, and for the annual appraisal.

There appears to be a trend toward greater use of performance targeting systems. Of the seventeen states which indicated that their current appraisal systems had been installed since 1970, eleven used performance targets, one had a behaviorally based rating system, and five had traditional performance-rating forms, although they advised managers to encourage as much employee participation as possible. In addition to these seventeen states with relatively new systems, twelve other states were reportedly planning to install new systems. Four of these definitely planned to use a performance target system, and six others were considering such a system as one possibility. Two states were developing behavior scales tailored to specific jobs.

LOCAL GOVERNMENTS

Two cities and one county in the random sample of fifty local governments reported using appraisal-by-objectives systems for managerial employees only. Two of the governments wanted to use performance standards and objectives for line employees as well as managers but anticipated that it would take a long time to develop standards and train supervisors and employees.

As reported in Part Two, we conducted telephone interviews of twenty-five additional local governments, all of which had previously indicated that they had used management by objectives. Of these twenty-five, thirteen reported that they also used appraisal by objectives. Ten of these thirteen used a formal appraisal-by-objectives model, in which supervisors and employees jointly set individual objectives and decided how well objectives were met. In the other three, department or unit objectives were set as a part of the management or budgeting process, and managers were to some extent held accountable for achievement of those objectives. Line employees were generally excluded from the appraisal-by-objectives systems.

The objectives used were mainly project or personal development goals, typically with due dates as the only targets and with little recordkeeping. Several of the thirteen governments also used a traditional performance-rating scale, and only one of the thirteen based its appraisals exclusively on the meeting of objectives. Five others included an "overall rating" in which the weight assigned to the objectives ranged from one-quarter to one-half. One government did not base its appraisal on achievement of the objectives but on the degree of effort shown by the employee in trying to reach the goals.

How Appraisals Are Used

STATE 'GOVERNMENTS

Exhibit 16 shows, for each type of performance appraisal, the extent to which it is used by the states, and the ways in which it is used. In many states the reported uses of performance appraisals were primarily punitive. Often, an outstanding appraisal did not guarantee a pay or promotional reward, while an unsatisfactory rating increased the risk of layoff or required the withholding of a step increase, demotion, or even dismissal. While twenty-seven state governments said they were permitted to give pay increases to reward superior performance, only three of these states guaranteed an extra merit increase for a superior appraisal in the same way that they guaranteed a pay cut or denial of a step increase for an unsatisfactory appraisal.

Most states did not provide figures on how often employees were penalized as a result of poor appraisal scores. One state, however, provided figures on the frequency of poor appraisals.[2] In one year, 6.5 percent of its probationary employees received unacceptable appraisals; fewer than one-sixth of these were fired. Among its permanent employees, less than one-half of 1 percent of the appraisals were unsatisfactory. (This state's regulations provided that a poor appraisal could lead to the loss of step increases and contribute toward demotion, layoff, or dismissal.) Another state reported that fewer than 1 percent of its employees were denied merit increases each year on the basis of unsatisfactory appraisals.[3]

Interviews with personnel department and civil service officials in eight other states provided additional information on how often annual step increments were denied because of unsatisfactory performance ratings. One state reported less than 5 percent, one less than 2 percent, three less than 1 percent, one "1 or 2 percent," one "seldom," and one "never."

One state official remarked that "due to the questionable accuracy of resultant ratings from our present forms, we do not have any regulations requiring that they be used in conjunction with promotions, increases, etc." (This state was considering switching to appraisal by objectives.) Two states had recently discarded traditional rating systems because they were not thought to be worthwhile. Instead, these two states "certified by exception" for annual increases—that is, almost all employees were deemed satisfactory and were recommended for increases.

---

2. State of New Jersey, Office of Fiscal Affairs, "Administration of the New Jersey State Civil Service System" (Trenton, January 1975), pp. 159-160 and 163.

3. Commonwealth of Virginia, "A Study on Personnel Management," p. 69.

Exhibit 16

STATE GOVERNMENT USES OF PERFORMANCE APPRAISAL

Uses	States with No Formal Statewide Systems N = 13 [1]	States Using Supervisor Performance Ratings and/or Narratives N = 24 [1]	States Using Preset Targets in Appraisals N = 13 [1]	Total Number of States with Each Type of Use N = 50 [1]	Total Percentage of States with Each Type of Use N = 50 [1]
"REWARDS"					
Pay: superior appraisal *guarantees* special raise or bonus (in addition to regular step)	0	1	2	27	54%
Pay: superior appraisal *may influence* special raise or bonus (in addition to regular step)	4	7	13		
Promotion: superior appraisal *guarantees* improved chance for promotion (e.g., additional "points")	0	4	3	31	62%
Promotion: superior appraisal *may influence* chances for promotion	4	12	8		
"PUNISHMENTS"					
Pay: regular annual step increase *must be* withheld for poor appraisal	4	10	5	40	80%
Pay: regular annual step increase *may be* withheld for poor appraisal	4	7	10		

(Continued)

Exhibit 16 (Continued)

Application					
Pay: salary decrease *may be influenced by* poor appraisal	2	8	3		13	26%
Promotion: poor appraisal *guarantees* ineligibility for promotion	2	6	2		34	68%
Promotion: poor appraisal *may decrease* chances for promotion	4	12	8	⎫	32	64%
Demotion: poor appraisal *guarantees* demotion	0	2	0	⎭		
Demotion: poor appraisal *influences* demotion	5	16	9	⎫	26	52%
Layoff: retention priorities include appraisal results	4	13	9	⎭		
Firing of probational employee *required* if appraisal is poor[2]	2	8	1	⎫	36	72%
Firing of probational employee *influenced by* poor appraisal(s)	2	11	12	⎭		
Firing of permanent employee *required* if appraisal is poor[2]	1	5	0	⎫	32	64%
Firing of permanent employee *influenced by* poor appraisal	3	12	11	⎭		

1. Figures include only governments that made explicit mention of the applications in question.

2. These governments specified that a poor appraisal, or a series of two or three poor appraisals, requires dismissal.

Source: In 1977, we contacted the personnel departments of the fifty states by mail and requested copies of forms, instructions, laws, rules and regulations, and evaluative studies relating to their performance appraisal systems. The seven states that did not reply to the initial mail request or to a second mail request were interviewed by telephone.

The unsatisfactory performance of those few employees denied an increase had to be documented. A majority of the states required special written documentation of the reasons for punitive action instead of, or in addition to, regular performance appraisals. One state with an appraisal-by-objectives system reported that it had used its appraisals in grievance cases, with good results when the appraisal objectives were of "good quality."

Two of the states using appraisal-by-objectives systems had professional counseling programs for employees whose work or personal problems affected their performance. Both states reported that identification of employees needing help was one of their program's explicit purposes.

Four state governments reported using performance appraisal systems mainly for employee development. Two of these states had no other uses for appraisals; the other two allowed an optional, special merit increase for superior performance. A fifth state government had two parallel systems: a rating system for personnel actions and an appraisal system for employee development. All four of the states that used performance appraisal primarily for employee development utilized individual job analyses and reported a relatively high degree of employee involvement in the appraisal process. The legislature in another state had recently passed a bill requiring the development of a statewide appraisal system, but it chose not to tie the system to pay because a pilot study in one department suggested that merit pay would not increase productivity enough to offset the costs of the merit pay program.

Most of the other state governments mentioned employee development as one purpose of performance appraisal but also listed a number of "negative" applications, as noted in Exhibit 16.

LOCAL GOVERNMENTS

Exhibit 17 details the uses of performance appraisal among the fifty local governments contacted. As with the states, punitive applications outnumbered rewards.

Among the additional twenty-five governments interviewed in connection with the performance targeting portion of this study (Part Two), four had purposely avoided using target achievement in connection with appraisals that affected personnel decisions. One of the four feared that managers would use the targets punitively. This local government indicated it might eventually link appraisals with target achievement but did not intend to tie target achievement to monetary incentives. Two others planned to proceed slowly in formalizing accountability for target achievement. They were concerned that by introducing rewards and punishments too soon, they would put pressure on their managers and create negative feelings that could damage the development of their management-by-objectives programs. The fourth government—in the process of discarding a personnel management system that emphasized negative reinforcement—planned to avoid tying pay to target achievement except at the department head level because it did not want to re-emphasize penalties for poor performance. This government was also concerned with the possibility that supervisors might overwork crews to obtain monetary incentives for themselves.

One of these twenty-five governments, which had a traditional performance rating system that allowed for the withholding of step increases, reported that the employees' union had challenged the right of the government to withhold increases on the basis of appraisals. There was widespread discontent with the rating system among this government's employees, and even the personnel manager thought that the system was unreliable, since it failed to eliminate personal bias.

Exhibit 17
LOCAL GOVERNMENT USES OF PERFORMANCE APPRAISAL

Uses	Local Governments with No Formal Government-wide Systems N = 21 [1]	Local Governments with Traditional Performance Ratings and/or Narratives N = 27 [1]	Local Governments with Appraisal by Objectives N = 2 [1]	Total Number of Local Governments with Each Type of Use N = 50 [1]	Total Percentage of Local Governments with Each Type of Use N = 50 [1]
"REWARDS"					
Pay: superior appraisal *guarantees* special raise or bonus (in addition to regular step)	0	0	0	} 24	48%
Pay: superior appraisal *may influence* special raise or bonus (in addition to regular step)	4	18	2		
Promotion: superior appraisal *guarantees* improved chance for promotion (e.g., additional "points")	0	5	0	} 22	44%
Promotion: superior appraisal *may influence* chances for promotion	3	12	2		
"PUNISHMENTS"					
Pay: step increase *must be withheld* for poor appraisal	0	16	0	} 30	60%
Pay: step increase *may be withheld* for poor appraisal	6	6	2		

(Continued)

Exhibit 17 (Continued)

Pay: salary decrease *may be influenced by* poor appraisal	0	11	0	11	22%
Promotion: poor appraisal *guarantees* ineligibility for promotion	0	3	0	22	44%
Promotion: poor appraisal *may decrease* chances for promotion	3	14	2		
Demotion: poor appraisal *guarantees* demotion	0	1	0	19	38%
Demotion: poor appraisal *influences* demotion	0	17	1		
Layoff: retention priorities include appraisal results	0	8	0	8	16%
Firing of probational employee *required* if appraisal is poor[2]	0	6	0	23	46%
Firing of probational employee *influenced* by poor appraisal	1	15	1		
Firing of permanent employee *required* if appraisal is poor[2]	0	3	0	21	42%
Firing of permanent employee *influenced* by poor appraisal	1	16	1		

1. The figures include only governments that made explicit mention of the applications.

2. These governments have rules that specify that a poor appraisal, or a series of two or three poor appraisals, requires dismissal.

Source: In 1977, we contacted by mail twenty-five city and twenty-five county governments, selected randomly from among cities over 50,000 population and counties over 100,000 population, and requested copies of forms, instructions, laws, rules and regulations, and evaluative studies relating to their performance appraisal systems. The fifteen cities and sixteen counties that did not reply to the initial mail request or to a second mail request were interviewed by telephone.

Chapter 15

THE QUALITY AND IMPACT OF EMPLOYEE APPRAISAL SYSTEMS

Two issues must be considered in any attempt to determine the general effectiveness of employee appraisal as a motivational device: (1) the accuracy and fairness of the appraisal, and (2) the impact of the appraisal process on employee performance.

Accuracy and Fairness of Appraisal

Most research on performance appraisal has focused not on the impact of the process on employee performance but on whether various instruments and procedures provide "valid" measures of performance. The question of whether an appraisal method is valid—that is, whether it produces fair and accurate assessments—is especially important when the assessments are used to determine pay raises or other personnel actions.[1]

---

1. "Validity" is the extent to which a test or appraisal method measures what it is supposed to measure. "Content validity" is the extent to which the test is a representative sample of an area of knowledge, skill, or performance. "Predictive validity" is the extent to which inferences can be made from the test regarding an individual's standing on some other variable at some later point in time. "Reliability" is the consistency with which a test or appraisal method measures something—the degree to which repeated measurement of the same individual by the same or different raters would tend to produce the same results. See Grace H. Wright, ed., *Public Sector Employment Selection: A Manual for the Personnel Generalist* (Chicago: International Personnel Management Association, 1974).

ACCURACY AND FAIRNESS OF RATINGS BY SUPERVISORS

Each type of standardized rating instrument has drawbacks.[2] Graphic rating scales are subject to personal bias, halo effects (situations where one particularly good or poor aspect of performance distorts the perception of overall performance), lack of interrater reliability, and other problems. Such scales often involve personal traits that cannot be rated objectively and are not job-specific. Checklists can have low validity unless they deal with specific job behavior and are prepared separately for each job. Even then, they are subject to the personal bias of raters. Forced-choice rating scales are unpopular with supervisors (who frequently regard such scales as arbitrary) and must be prepared separately for different jobs. Comparative ranking techniques are subject to personal bias and are unfair to groups of employees with many outstanding performers. Critical incident records are time-consuming for supervisors, may focus on exceptional incidents while neglecting day-to-day performance, and are subject to bias. Narrative evaluations are subject to personal bias and do not facilitate comparisons of employees.

There have been several studies of the effects of different types of raters on the validity of the ratings. Ratings by the immediate supervisor have been found to be more valid than ratings by persons who do not observe much of the day-to-day work of the employee. However, there is evidence that the validity of an immediate supervisor's rating is diminished in situations where important decisions (such as promotion and salary) depend on the rating.

Behaviorally anchored scales and behavior checklists developed specifically for particular jobs have higher validity than do the more common trait-rating scales that are not job-tailored. But they do not provide detailed documentation of actual performance; if documentation to support personnel actions is desired, narrative formats are needed. Furthermore, behavior scales

---

2. This overview of the validity of selected rating procedures is drawn mainly from: Public Services Laboratory, Georgetown University, *Do Productivity Measures Pay Off for Employee Performance?* Staffing Services to People in the Cities No. 9 (Washington, D.C., 1975), pp. 53-69. For a summary of procedures for instrument development and validity testing, and an annotated bibliography on performance appraisal, see L. L. Cummings and Donald P. Schwab, *Performance in Organizations: Determinants and Appraisal* (Glenview, Ill.: Scott, Foresman and Company, 1973).

do not measure outcomes; behavior is connected with results only through the judgments of "experts" (those persons knowledgeable about the job who contributed to the preparation of the scale) as to what behavior produces good results. Finally, it is costly and time-consuming to develop different behavior scales for each type of job in a government.[3]

Two states reported formal studies of the accuracy and fairness of their supervisor performance ratings. The state that used behaviorally based scales analyzed the internal consistency of the scales and also checked for rating patterns among supervisors that might indicate bias (e.g., uniformly high ratings for all employees). However, the ratings were not compared against objective performance data.[4]

The second state, which used multiple-step rating scales, studied a sample of its supervisors' performance ratings and found several problems, including halo effects and interrater unreliability. The philosophy in one department was "always room for improvement," and this department's supervisors gave consistently lower ratings than did supervisors in most other departments. Supervisors in another department, however, consistently rated employees highly because they thought employees would be angry with low ratings. There was a high positive correlation between seniority, salary level, and rating scores, a correlation that did not seem to be accounted for by truly superior performance. This government also reported that performance appraisals had not provided adequate documentary support for personnel actions; a high proportion of disciplinary actions based on appraisals had been successfully challenged by employees. (The personnel department of this state was proposing a switch to appraisal by objectives.)

Several other states that used standardized performance ratings expressed little confidence in them, although they had done no formal evaluations. Among the problems mentioned were perfunctory ratings (three states), interrater or interde-

---

3. One local government with a small (one professional) personnel unit reported that behaviorally anchored rating scale development had averaged two to three months per position. After receiving a grant under the Intergovernmental Personnel Act in 1975, the unit had developed checklists for four positions. One state, which was conducting job analysis and other research for content validation, estimated that it took six months to one year to complete validation of its ratings for one class of jobs.

4. Prien, Jones, and Miller, "Performance Rating System."

partment inconsistency (three states), and "grade escalation" (one state). One state, which was analyzing jobs prior to installing multiple behavior-based checklists, was concerned that the state's traditional rating system was legally indefensible, although it had not yet been challenged.

In another state which had used a traditional rating scale, some supervisors had declared that the rating was meaningless. One supervisor admitted that he merely copied the previous year's ratings for each employee. At the same time, there were many complaints by employees who contended that appraisals were used punitively. This government subsequently discarded the traditional type of appraisal and planned to install a performance-based system. Meanwhile, all employees who were certified as satisfactory received merit raises. If a manager wanted to deny a raise, the manager wrote the employee a letter of documentation that had to be approved by the personnel department. In 1977 (the most recent year for which information was available), "unsatisfactory" letters were submitted to the personnel department on about 1 percent of the employees, and slightly over half were allowed to stand; the remainder were overruled on the ground that the proposed denial of a raise was insufficiently related to performance.

No local governments in our sample had conducted formal studies of their rating systems, but a few had some information regarding quality. At the request of the local civil service commission, one local government had tested a forced-choice rating instrument. Both supervisors and employees disliked its arbitrariness, and it was discarded. This government had a traditional supervisor rating system, and an analysis of samples of completed forms had indicated halo effects to be common. An attempt was made to correlate ratings with other performance factors. However, there was only a narrow spread in rating scores (they clustered between 90 and 100), and correlations with other performance indicators were weak. Because most employees received about the same score, ratings had not been an effective way of determining promotions. (This jurisdiction planned to test a critical incident system next.)

A number of other local governments reported problems with rating systems, including interdepartment and interrater inconsistencies (four governments), inaccuracy due to supervisors' being insufficiently familiar with employees' performance (one government), insufficient documentation for personnel actions (two governments), and halo effects (one government). In one county, the county board discontinued the merit pay system because the traditional performance rating, which was used to determine eligibility for increases, was unevenly applied in different departments. Another government had changed its system frequently, but with little success. The personnel manager said he would prefer a system in which employees were merely rated "satisfactory" or "unsatisfactory," with documentation required for an unsatisfactory rating and with an employee right to appeal. This approach appeared preferable to continuing to use an invalid system. The supervisors in another government expressed a similar wish.[5]

On the other hand, several local governments with traditional performance-rating systems reported no challenges to their systems. These governments had no plans to change the approaches they were using.

ACCURACY AND FAIRNESS OF APPRAISALS USING PERFORMANCE TARGETS

The validity of the appraisal in an appraisal-by-objectives system depends on the quality of the targets—the extent to which they are measurable, realistic, challenging, and reflective of all the important aspects of performance. Targets or goals that are vague and unmeasurable will not contribute to the appraisal's validity. Developing objective, measurable performance targets is difficult, however, particularly in governments that do not already have performance measures in place. (See Part Two of

---

5. One researcher who has studied performance appraisal extensively recommends such an approach. Specifically, he urges that step increases be automatic except for clearly unsatisfactory performers, who must be warned in advance. Otherwise, step increases would follow schedules negotiated at the time of hiring. Performance appraisals would only be used for work planning, improving performance, and employee development. See Herbert H. Meyer, "The Pay-for-Performance Dilemma," *Organizational Dynamics*, vol. 3, no. 3 (Winter 1975), pp. 39-50; also Herbert H. Meyer, Emanuel Kay, and John R. P. French, Jr., "Split Roles in Performance Appraisal," *Harvard Business Review*, vol. 43 (January-February 1965), pp. 123-129; and French, Kay, and Meyer, "Participation." This recommendation is consistent with the theory that pay is not a "motivator" but a "hygiene factor" (see Chapter 1). Under this theory, a performance-pay link will not contribute to productivity and is likely to lead to dissatisfaction if the pay awarded for performance is less than the employee expects.

this report for additional discussion of the issues and problems involved in performance targeting.)

A major drawback to appraisal by objectives is that important areas of employee performance, such as a supervisor's contributions to the morale or development of subordinates, do not lend themselves to objective measurement. Less easily measured areas tend to be neglected.[6] Another problem is that targets or goals may depend on factors beyond the individual employee's control, such as availability of equipment. Comparability among different jobs and employees with different goals or targets is also a difficult issue. Moreover, appraisal-by-objectives programs focus on results. Since learning to improve results requires an understanding of the process leading to the results, focusing only on objectives may restrict improvement. Thus, the setting of targets or goals should be supplemented by an effort on the part of the supervisor and the employee to identify the process necessary to achieve them. A final difficulty in using appraisal by objectives is that training supervisors and employees to formulate and use targets or goals is time-consuming and difficult.

As noted in the preceding chapter and in Part Two of this volume, the quality of the objectives and performance measures used by governments in connection with appraisal by objectives has varied considerably. A common problem has been that objectives were not always measurable.

One state, which appeared to have a successful appraisal-by-objectives program, reported that the quality of its objectives had improved steadily since inauguration of the system in 1974 but was still uneven. Departments that had used quantitative measurements in the past (e.g., engineering) tended to use measurable outcome-oriented objectives more often than did depart-

---

6. One private sector study found that objective measures of performance used in one company's MBO program did not correspond well with subjective judgments of overall performance made by upper management. Twelve field units in one department were ranked by nine central headquarters managers associated with that department, and twenty units of another department were ranked by six managers. Thirteen objective measures were examined for the first department's units, twenty-five measures for the others. Using factor analysis, the author found that "the objective performance data . . . apparently have little consistent relationship to subsequent evaluations of relative performance made at corporate headquarters." One possible explanation for such a finding is that the objective measures omitted important areas of performance. See Ronald C. Bishop, "The Relationship Between Objective Criteria and Subjective Judgments in Performance Appraisal," *Academy of Management Journal*, vol. 17, no. 3 (September 1974), pp. 558-563.

ments (such as social services) that traditionally relied on "process" measures. This state monitored the quality of the objectives established by employees in an effort to maintain the quality of its appraisals.

Another state with a performance target system required supervisors to maintain "critical incident" logs (records of actual incidents of good or poor performance) in an effort to improve the objectivity of judgments on hard-to-define objectives. A third state reported that there have been "few cases in which quantitative workload standards have been developed." Several state and local governments reported the development of such standards to be a difficult, time-consuming process, requiring extensive training and monitoring.

Five states reported difficulties in writing standards specific enough to be measurable. One state reported time and paperwork problems. One local government which started an appraisal-by-objectives system in 1974 under an IPA grant reported that after three years the system had been implemented in only half the government, due largely to the extensive cost and training required. A state government had a problem because the scale used to calculate a numerical score from the objectives was based on 100 points, with 50 being "meets standards"; the supervisors, perhaps accustomed to an academic grade scale on which 70 is "pass," had been reluctant to rate average performers at 50. (The state planned to change the scale.)

Several other governments using appraisal-by-objectives systems also reported problems. Nevertheless, all believed their systems to be superior to the traditional supervisor ratings they had used previously.

Impact of Appraisal on Employee Performance

The second issue that must be addressed in connection with the effectiveness of appraisals is the impact of the appraisal process on employee performance. Before reviewing the evidence about the impact of the different types of appraisals used by state and local governments, it is helpful to consider the factors that influence the general linkage between the appraisal process and performance.

FACTORS POTENTIALLY AFFECTING THE IMPACT OF APPRAISALS ON EMPLOYEE PERFORMANCE

Chapter 1 reviewed the major theories of employee motivation. Regardless of which motivational theory is adopted, the evidence from private sector and laboratory research suggests that if an organization wants to tie performance to rewards through appraisal, the appraisal method should possess the following attributes:

- *Be Meaningful and Dependable:* The consequences of appraisal should be clear, dependable, and specified in advance, so that employees can be confident that performance at a given level will lead to the consequences promised beforehand. In addition, any incentives should be meaningful to employees—i.e., valued rewards or real punishment. The supervisory approval or disapproval conveyed in an appraisal may in itself be a valued reward or an important punishment.

- *Have Ascertainable Content:* Appraisal should be based on observed behavior or measured results. Employees should know in advance which behavior and results are desirable and which are not.

- *Have Proper Timing:* Appraisals should occur frequently enough to allow for timely feedback to employees; there should be a close connection in time between performance and reward or punishment.

Although private sector findings may not be fully applicable to governments,[7] many of the lessons learned from those experiences appear relevant to the public sector. Indeed, until there is more systematic research on the impact of appraisal on the performance of state and local government employees, private sector and laboratory research offers virtually the only guidance available in designing a suitable appraisal procedure.

Considerable private sector and laboratory research points to the crucial role of the employee-supervisor interview and its effect on employee performance. For instance, in a series of studies done by the General Electric Company in the 1960s, ninety-two employees completed questionnaires before and after performance rating interviews with their supervisors to measure, among other things, changes in attitudes and self-appraisal. Em-

---

7. For instance, one study found that various rewards are valued differently by employees in the two sectors. See J. R. Schuster, "Management-Compensation Policy and the Public Interest," *Public Personnel Management*, vol. 3 (November-December 1974), pp. 510-523.

ployee performance ten to twelve weeks after the appraisal interview was measured by asking managers to estimate on a percentage scale the extent of changes they had observed in
employees. Among the influencing factors examined were degree
of employee participation in the interview, separation of salary
reviews from interviews, and amount of negative criticism by
the supervisor. Although the findings were weakened by the confounding effects of the several variables and supervisor subjec-
tivity in assessing performance, the report found the following:

- Interviews to discuss ratings were generally frustrating
  for both parties—for the subordinates because the appraisals and salary increases were lower than their own
  self-appraisals, and for the supervisors because they felt
  that employees did not respond adequately to praise.
- "Criticism has a negative effect on achievement of goals."
- "Praise has little effect one way or the other."
- "Defensiveness resulting from critical appraisal produces
  inferior performance."
- "Interviews designed primarily to improve a person's performance should not at the same time weigh salary or
  promotion in the balance."[8]

Thus, although better performance, improved supervisor-
employee communication, and greater employee development are
often cited as benefits of appraisal, in practice they may be difficult to realize. For instance, the employee is almost always in a
subordinate position during the appraisal and therefore is vul-
nerable to supervisory disapproval. As noted above, there is evidence that criticism can actually produce poorer performance.[9]

Moreover, effective interviewing requires skill, and training
is necessary to enable even well-meaning supervisors to conduct
appraisal interviews well. If the interview is to be more than a
one-way conference, with the supervisor "telling" the employee,
the supervisor must have learned how to "listen." Research has
demonstrated that the ability of people to help others often depends on personal characteristics (warmth, genuineness, and
empathy) rather than on techniques that can be taught easily.[10]
Although a manager appraising an employee is not a therapist

8. Meyer, Kay, and French, "Split Roles in Performance Appraisal."
9. See also Public Services Laboratory, *What Determines City Employees Compensation?*, pp. 24-26.
10. C. Truax and K. Mitchell, "Research on Certain Therapist Interpersonal Skills in Relation to Process and Outcome," in *Handbook of
Psychotherapy and Behavior Change*, eds. A. Bergin and S. Garfield
(New York: John Wiley and Sons, 1971), pp. 199-344.

giving personal counseling, the two types of interaction have important features in common. In fact, employee-supervisor sessions may often be more difficult than counseling, since employees frequently tend to resist advice from supervisors, who may or may not be trusted to have the employee's best interests in mind. If a supervisor feels negatively toward an employee, the employee may detect this and resist attempts to examine or change job behavior.

If the appraisal is not based on observable or measurable performance and clear criteria agreed on beforehand by supervisor and employee, there is a good possibility that supervisor and employee will disagree in their assessment of the employee's performance.[11] The employee may view the appraisal (and the supervisor) as unfair, and as a result become angry, work less well, or even quit.

If employees stand to lose pay, promotion, or job security, they may be less likely to engage in frank mutual discussion of their weaknesses. Such reticence can prevent the identification of training and development needs. There is evidence that such reticence does indeed occur when appraisals are linked to personnel actions.

If supervisors or employees are uncomfortable with appraisal, or do not believe it is fair or meaningful, they may handle it in a perfunctory way, doing the minimum necessary to produce a "rating." Such perfunctory appraisal is not likely to assist employee development.[12]

Good instrument and procedure design is only part of what is needed to avoid the pitfalls listed above. The organizational environment (overall morale, goal orientation, etc.) and the training given to supervisors and employees greatly influence the quality and effectiveness of appraisal.

---

11. In the General Electric study described above, ninety-two employees rated their performance on a percentile ranking scale, and their supervisors also rated them. Eighty-five percent of the employees were rated lower by their managers than they rated themselves. See Meyer, "The Pay-for-Performance Dilemma"; and Meyer, Kay, and French, "Split Roles in Performance Appraisal."

12. Perfunctory handling of appraisal has been a problem in the federal civil service, which has used a traditional supervisor appraisal method (supervisors assign a rating). See Husain Mustafa, "Performance Rating Revisited," *Civil Service Journal*, vol. 9, no. 4 (April-June 1969), pp. 29-31.

THE IMPACT OF EMPLOYEE PERFORMANCE RATINGS BY SUPERVISORS USING STANDARDIZED FORMS

Little research has been conducted on the effects of supervisor ratings on the performance of government employees. None of the states or localities surveyed as part of this study had any hard evidence that supervisor rating systems had led to improved employee performance.

One local government, which for the past two years had used a rating scale supplemented by special training for supervisors and a requirement for ongoing documentation of unusual incidents and day-to-day performance, reported that productivity had been enhanced by the appraisals. Officials there believed that from seventy-five to eighty employees had resigned because of poor appraisals and withholding of merit pay. They also thought that the successors of those employees had helped to increase productivity.

On the other hand, in one state a report on personnel management criticized the state's traditional rating system in these words:

> The most prevalent observation made by agency heads and personnel administrators [in a survey conducted by the state] is that the present system is ineffective . . . the system is one dedicated to form over substance. It provides no basis for the establishment of a meaningful relationship between the job responsibilities of employees and the performance factors upon which they are judged. . . . Performance appraisal, as it now exists, is often applied by supervisors only as a tool of negative discipline to deny salary adjustments and to terminate employees whose performance fails to meet benchmarks set by the performance levels of their peers. No reasonable evidence is discernible to indicate that the system is accomplishing the progressive objectives set forth in the rules when it was designed.[13]

The report recommended conversion to a system of performance targets but acknowledged that conversion was likely to require significant educational effort, would be hampered by a lack of up-to-date position descriptions, and would be likely to take as

---

13. Commonweath of Virginia, "A Study on Personnel Management," pp. 68-69.

long as three years. The report recommended that in the meantime the state should improve the old system. Improvements should include augmenting the definitions of the rating factors, requiring narrative descriptions of employee strengths and weaknesses, and requiring employee-supervisor discussion of appraisals.

In another state, an official reported that traditional performance ratings had at times hampered efforts to dismiss poor employees. Supervisors tended to give satisfactory ratings until problems in performance became quite serious, with the result that the employee could often point to a long history of "documented" satisfactory performance.

There appears to be no research evidence—or theoretical basis—to support the hope that increases in employee motivation and improvements in performance will result from the standard merit pay system. Under such a system, an employee receives a regular annual step increase if performance is rated as average and loses the step increase if performance is rated unsatisfactory. However, the employee is not guaranteed an extra increase if performance is superior. Moreover, performance assessments for merit increases are usually based on vague, subjective criteria. Thus, traditional merit pay systems lack many of the attributes which have been found to be important for effectively tying pay to performance through appraisals:

- Merit appraisals are not based on observed behavior or objective results;
- They do not provide meaningful, dependable rewards for superior performance; and
- They do not provide timely feedback and a close connection in time between performance and reward or punishment.

Such annual increases, it is true, may function as a "hygiene factor" to keep employees from feeling dissatisfied with pay, and they may contribute to keeping up with inflation and maintaining comparability with the private sector as an employee's seniority and experience increase. These purposes, however, could probably be accomplished by nonperformance-related raises, such as fully automatic seniority or longevity raises, across-the-board cost-of-living raises, or periodic salary adjustments based on wage and classification reviews.

Tying traditional merit increases to performance may actually cause dissatisfaction that would not occur were there no such linkage. If superior performers are given the same increase as average performers, the former may feel they are unfairly treated, decide that extra effort will not be rewarded, and decrease their effort. (See the discussion of "equity theory" in Chapter 1.) But if a government tries to discriminate between superior and average performers by, for example, awarding two steps to superior performers, average performers may in turn feel dissatisfied with their single-step increases.

THE IMPACT OF APPRAISALS BASED ON PERFORMANCE TARGETS

Performance appraisal using preset performance targets appears to meet, to some extent, the requirements for motivational effectiveness that were summarized above, provided it includes the following:

- Joint supervisor-employee job analysis and setting of targets, or at least joint discussion of targets set by management.
- Specification of what actions (for example, pay increases) will follow if targets are or are not met.[14]
- Regular progress reviews (biweekly, monthly, or quarterly).
- Annual or semiannual appraisals of whether targets were met and setting of new targets for the coming period.

There is virtually no empirical evidence, however, on the impact of target-based appraisals used by governments on employee performance or productivity. In one state government, personnel department officials in various agencies were asked for their opinion of the existing MBO system, which included quarterly progress reviews. The general response was that the overall concept was good because it required managers to work with employees in establishing performance descriptions and performance standards. But a majority of the officials also said that the actual procedures were unnecessarily complex and time-consuming, and not properly and uniformly utilized

---

14. As noted in Chapter 1 and Part Two of this volume, there is evidence that goal setting in itself improves productivity. Setting conscious, specific, and ambitious goals appears to increase productivity. The expectation of rewards may affect productivity by influencing employees to set higher goals.

throughout the state. This situation was believed to stem from a lack of uniform, established performance descriptions and standards.[15]

None of the states contacted had any firm evidence that their ABO systems had led to improved productivity. All of the state representatives with an opinion thought their appraisal systems had encouraged employees to plan and undertake more projects than they otherwise would have. One state thought that appraisal by objectives improved supervisor-employee communication (although many supervisors thought the process too time-consuming). Two states reported that the absence of a link between performance and pay increases was causing morale problems.

One local government had surveyed a group of employees covered by its appraisal-by-objectives system. About three-quarters of the respondents said they thought appraisals were more "objective" than they had been under the previous numerical rating system and that the new program "met their needs." But some thought the system did not work well for clerks and dispatchers (although the reason was not noted).

One city with an ABO system for top management cited the lack of a tie to pay as having a negative effect on productivity. Management pay superiority was reportedly being eroded by union salary increases, and there were morale problems.

This city used a traditional rating system for nonsupervisors, but ratings in some functional areas were based on performance standards and workload data. Special training had been given to supervisors to improve documentation and appraisal. At first, some supervisors were unhappy with the added time and work involved in the augmented appraisals, but later feedback showed greater satisfaction. Supervisors felt that the improved documentation put them in a better position in grievance cases, which in some instances had been lost through lack of documentation. Moreover, although no exact figures were

---

15. State of New Jersey, "Administration of the New Jersey State Civil Service System." In addition, the U.S. General Accounting Office's two-year study of federal employee performance appraisal systems recommended that federal agencies develop collaborative appraisal systems, such as appraisal by objectives. GAO conducted a survey of employee attitudes toward appraisal and interviewed managers in a sample of federal agencies. (See "Federal Employee Performance Rating Systems.") However, reviewers of this study have pointed out that collaborative appraisals are costly, require extensive training to install and to maintain, and may be difficult to use for personnel actions.

available, this city reported that there was some improvement in employee retention and performance. The city planned to extend its appraisal-by-objectives system to line employees.

Generally, officials in local communities with appraisal-by-objectives systems believed the systems were good and said that they improved communications while encouraging people to plan better and undertake more new projects. It was also noted, however, that these systems called for considerable training. (One program used two eight-hour training sessions separated by two months of drafting objectives, followed by a six-month trial period.) Once implemented, these systems also demanded more time from supervisors—typically, preparation and interview time for three sessions per employee each year (a work-planning session, a progress review, and the appraisal session). Indeed, most of the complaints from supervisors concerned the heavy demands of the system on their time.

These findings generally mirror the evidence from the private sector on the impact of appraisals linked to performance targets.[16] One company started an MBO program that included performance reviews at frequencies ranging from biweekly to semiannually. Production levels improved significantly following installation of the program. It is not clear, however, what role performance reviews played in this gain. While biweekly performance reviews were planned for supervisors and foremen, they actually occurred on the average of one every three to six months. Seven of thirty-four supervisors (and no foremen) said there were "not enough performance reviews." Upper-level managers and supervisors reported high degrees of participation in goal setting, but fourteen out of thirty-three foremen reported no participation.[17]

The General Electric studies which were described previously included an examination of a "work-planning-and-review" system (with emphasis on mutual goal planning and frequent discussions of performance). A group of employees who chose to

16. See Part Two for additional information concerning public and private sector experiences with performance targets.

17. Anthony P. Raia, "A Second Look at Management Goals and Controls," *California Management Review*, vol. 8 (Summer 1966), pp. 49-58. There are several other studies on the effectiveness of management by objectives, but they do not distinguish the effect of the appraisal from the effects of the entire MBO process. For an evaluation of research on the effectiveness of MBO itself, see Wayne A. Kimmel, William R. Dougan, and John R. Hall, *Municipal Management and Budget Methods* (Washington, D.C.: The Urban Institute, 1974).

remain in the conventional supervisory rating system was compared with a group of employees in the work-planning-and-review program. The study found that "participation by the employee in the goal setting procedure helped produce favorable results" and that "performance improves most when specific goals are established." [18] (The "self-selection" of employees into the groups may mean that the groups were dissimilar in important ways, so the results must be viewed cautiously.)

In another private sector study, information was obtained on employee satisfaction through a questionnaire administered to employees in two companies. Eighty-three percent of seventy-five employees in the company with appraisal by objectives "liked" to be appraised, contrasted with 65 percent of ninety-four respondents in the company with traditional appraisals.[19]

A number of other private sector studies report favorable employee attitudes toward appraisal by objectives. However, these studies provide no comparative data and do not link attitudes toward appraisal with changes in productivity.

---

18. Meyer, Kay, and French, "Split Roles in Performance Appraisal."

19. Thomas A. Stone, "An Examination of Six Prevalent Assumptions Concerning Performance Appraisal," *Public Personnel Management*, vol. 2, no. 6 (November-December 1973), pp. 408-414.

Chapter 16

PRESSURES ON EMPLOYEE APPRAISAL SYSTEMS AND OBSTACLES TO IMPROVING THEM

The use of performance appraisal to determine personnel actions is increasingly being subjected to judicial scrutiny.[1] Recent court decisions suggest that unless performance appraisals, whether formal or informal, have demonstrated validity, personnel actions based on them will not be upheld. The standards for validity commonly referred to in court decisions are the federal Equal Employment Opportunity Commission's guidelines for selection procedures, which note that "whatever criteria are used, they must represent major or critical work behaviors as revealed by careful job analyses."[2] At a minimum, appraisal

---

1. For a summary of legal activity regarding performance appraisal, see William H. Holley and Hubert S. Feild, "Performance Appraisal and the Law," *Labor Law Journal*, vol. 26, no. 7 (July 1975), pp. 423-430.

2. Equal Employment Opportunity Commission's Guidelines on Employee Selection Procedures, Title 29, Chapter XIV, Sec. 1607.5, Code of Federal Regulations. Although the title of the EEOC Guidelines refers to "selection," the guidelines also cover other personnel actions: "For the purpose of the guidelines in this part, the term 'test' is defined as any paper-and-pencil or performance measure used as a basis for any employment decision." (EEOC Guidelines on Employee Selection Procedures, Sec. 1607.2.) "Job analysis" involves a study of work performed to determine what is to be done on a job, the procedures followed in doing it, and the knowledge, skill, and employee behavior necessary to carry out the work. A test or appraisal is "job related" if it samples knowledge, abilities, skills, or other characteristics shown through a careful job analysis to be necessary or important for successful performance of a job.

systems must include thorough job analysis, assessment of the principal factors identified in the job analysis as necessary for satisfactory performance, standardized administration sufficient to provide an equitable review, and a design that provides statistical reliability.[3] One state government agency lost a case involving a pattern of lower appraisal scores for a group of minority employees because "no data were presented to demonstrate that the evaluation instrument was a valid predictor of employee job performance." [4]

Punitive actions, of course, are more likely to be challenged in court than actions that reward. And as noted previously, traditional standardized performance ratings designed to cover a wide range of jobs appear to have questionable validity. Thus, the prevalence of potentially punitive applications of performance appraisal in governments using these rating systems of questionable validity presents a high potential for legal problems.

The careful job analyses and validity tests required by the EEOC guidelines are time-consuming and expensive. Estimates of the total annual cost of a full program of test validation among all state and local governments (assuming that tests can be constructed for all jobs) range from $100 million to several billion dollars.[5] Appraisal by objectives, in which job analysis is done jointly by supervisor and employee, may be cheaper than developing government-wide standardized job analyses, although the training costs to implement performance target systems can be substantial. The elements of consensus between supervisor and employee and objectivity of performance criteria may provide an appraisal that is legally defensible. This is conjectural, however, since no court tests of appraisal-by-objectives systems

3. For a discussion of content validity, see Stephen J. Mussio and Mary K. Smith, "Content Validity: A Procedural Manual" (Minneapolis: Civil Service Commission, Division of Personnel Research, City of Minneapolis, n.d.). See also C. H. Lawshe, "A Quantitative Approach to Content Validity," *Personnel Psychology*, vol. 28 (1975), pp. 563-575.

4. Holley and Feild, "Performance Appraisal," p. 427.

5. Neal R. Peirce, "Civil Service Systems Experience Quiet Revolution," *National Journal*, vol. 7, no. 48 (November 29, 1975), pp. 1643-1648. One state gave us an estimate of six months to one year to perform job analyses and other research required for content validation of one class of jobs—in a government which has 1,100 different classes! For a discussion of procedures for job analysis, see U.S. Civil Service Commission, Bureau of Intergovernmental Personnel Programs, *Job Analysis: Developing and Documenting Data*, BIPP 152-35 (Washington, D.C., December 1973).

were found during this study. If jurisdictions must develop job analyses for selection purposes anyway, the possible cost advantages of target systems over job-tailored rating scales may be diminished.

Employee unions have also criticized performance appraisal systems. Unions are especially concerned about appraisal systems that give supervisors too much arbitrary power, that is, appraisals based primarily on subjective judgments. In some cases, collective bargaining has included negotiations over performance appraisal procedures. At least two state government contracts with employee unions—in Pennsylvania and Wisconsin—provided explicitly for step increases without reference to employee performance.[6] New Jersey's agreement with its administrative and clerical employees specified the style of the appraisal (appraisal by objectives) and the frequency of appraisal conferences. It also specified that "no changes shall be made as to the elements of the Performance Evaluation System as incorporated herein without negotiating with the Association."[7] A recent collective bargaining agreement in Connecticut called for the development of separate rating forms to meet the needs of different bargaining units.[8] Note that three states with performance target systems reported that their unions preferred the target systems to the supervisor rating systems used previously.

Laws and civil service commission rules specifying appraisal methods also may serve as barriers to changes in appraisal systems, although there is a trend at all levels of government toward giving the executive branch more control over personnel management while reducing the authority of independent civil

6. The Pennsylvania agreement stated that "An employee's performance rating shall not be used in determining his entitlement to [an annual service] increment." See "Agreement Between Commonwealth of Pennsylvania and American Federation of State, County, and Municipal Employees, AFL-CIO" (July 1, 1973 to June 30, 1976), p. 35. Wisconsin's contract provision was reported in *AFSCME Public Employee*, vol. 42, no. 7 (August 1977). Pennsylvania's social service and employment security employee unions have negotiated the content of performance evaluations (the agreement required four adjectival rating levels to replace the three levels formerly used) and their application to layoffs (from the lowest quartile of evaluations in order of seniority).

7. "Agreement: The State of New Jersey, New Jersey Civil Service Association, and New Jersey State Employees Association—Administrative and Clerical Services Unit" (July 1, 1974, to June 30, 1977), pp. 21-22.

8. Labor Relations Coordinator, state of Connecticut, personal communication, July 20, 1977.

service commissions. There is often political opposition to proposals to change appraisal systems, and managers and employees are understandably cautious about changes in methods,
particularly when pay or promotion may be affected.

The content and procedures of appraisal systems were not
fixed by law in any of the forty-four states whose officials
replied to our inquiry on legal constraints, although in four
states the procedure to be used was specified in civil service
rules. Four other states had civil service regulations specifying
appraisal content but not in a potentially constraining amount
of detail. There thus appeared to be no serious legal barriers to
modifying appraisal forms and procedures within these states.

Forty-two of the fifty states indicated that they had either
laws or regulations that required or allowed the application of
performance appraisal to decisions on pay, promotions, firing,
and the like. Civil service law in one state, however, specified
that appraisals could not be used to determine disciplinary
actions, pay, or layoff priorities; seniority was the only allowable characteristic. Nineteen states had civil service regulations
stating that merit increases were to be given automatically and
periodically to all employees except those who received unsatisfactory ratings.

Performance appraisal procedures are addressed by the
guidelines issued pursuant to the federal Intergovernmental
Personnel Act. These guidelines suggest that "employees [in
governmental units receiving federal funds] need to be evaluated periodically on a systematic job related basis to provide needed information . . . as a basis for personnel actions
including promotion, recognizing or rewarding superior performance, and correcting inadequate performance or separating
employees in cases where inadequate performance cannot be
corrected." [9]

Appraisal did not appear to be fixed by law among local
governments. In five, however, the procedures were spelled out
in civil service rules. One local government indicated that civil
service regulations limited the use of performance appraisals in
pay and promotion decisions; the rest of those with formal appraisal systems had regulations requiring or allowing such
applications.

9. "Standards for a Merit System of Personnel Administration," *Federal Register*, vol. 44, no. 34 (February 16, 1979), pp. 10238-10263, especially p. 10244.

Of the twenty-one local governments without formal appraisal systems, eight mentioned that union agreements called for automatic step increases or negotiated, annual, across-the-board raises, although none said that contracts explicitly ruled out merit pay. In one government with an appraisal system, denial of a step increase for poor performance had to be negotiated with the union. In two jurisdictions the unions were opposed to the local government's desire to install appraisal systems and merit pay. In another jurisdiction, however, the unions requested a merit system but management opposed it as an attempt to escalate pay. Two governments without formal systems reported that they had independent department heads (some of them elected), and installation of a government-wide appraisal and merit pay system would be extremely difficult.

Finally, we note that the most significant barrier to better appraisal systems is probably lack of knowledge about the effects of employee appraisal and the absence of any clearly superior appraisal method.

Chapter 17

CONCLUSIONS AND RECOMMENDATIONS ON PERFORMANCE APPRAISAL

Performance appraisal in state and local governments has the potential ability to influence employee productivity by linking performance to rewards or punishment. Supervisory approval or disapproval expressed during appraisal also can serve as an incentive. In addition, appraisal can improve communication between supervisors and employees, and help identify the training and self-development needs of employees. Moreover, federal as well as state and local laws and regulations often compel appraisals to be made by requiring or recommending that personnel actions be based on performance. On the other hand, performance appraisal may be counterproductive if it is unfair, causes hostility, or has other adverse effects on those being appraised.

The evidence currently available indicates that systems utilizing supervisor ratings of personal traits and focusing on nonspecific aspects of performance are not valid or effective enough to be worthwhile. Governments using such rating systems have failed to meet the burden of proof in court cases in which the validity of their systems has been challenged. Performance appraisal and its connection with pay and promotion are also under attack by unions in some jurisdictions. Yet despite these pressures and the questionable validity of rating instruments and procedures, many governments continue to use such supervisor ratings to justify personnel actions.

There are indications that appraisal systems using preset performance targets are more effective in motivating improved performance than are supervisor ratings, and that using preset performance targets avoids the problem of developing separate rating instruments for each job. Nonetheless, the evidence for the effectiveness of such systems is weak, and they have important drawbacks. Moreover, appraisal-by-objectives systems and appraisals based on work standards are not easy—or inexpensive—to develop and use.

Group appraisal appears to be worth trying, particularly in government units where task performance requires a team effort. However, little experience has accumulated to indicate how workable, or how effective, group appraisal might be in the public sector.

Further Investigations Needed

If state and local governments are to develop performance appraisal systems that are effective in improving performance and serving as guides to personnel actions, investigation of the impact of promising systems on employee performance is a necessity. Techniques such as the following need more systematic evaluation:

- Appraisal by objectives.
- Appraisal by objectives supplemented by behavioral rating scales or checklists.
- Group appraisal, based either on objectives or on some combination of objectives and rating scales.
- Peer appraisal and self-appraisal as supplements to supervisor appraisal.

The studies should compare various appraisal techniques when applied with differing frequencies, with different types of employees (line employees, managers), and in various work situations. Governments trying new systems should (a) interview both supervisors and employees regarding their opinions of the old and new systems; (b) keep track of patterns of ratings— that is, the frequency of high and low ratings—in order to compare the old system to the new and compare various raters' and departments' ratings; (c) collect data over time to allow for a longitudinal study of the predictive validity of the appraisals; and (d) attempt to measure the effects of various types of appraisals on productivity.

In addition, the process of implementing new appraisal systems should be examined, with particular attention to training for those who participate in appraisals, the cost of developing new systems, the problems of formulating performance measures that can be used in appraisal, and employee perceptions of the appraisal process. If possible, evaluations should be conducted by persons other than those who design and implement the appraisal system.

The lack of evidence regarding the effectiveness of various appraisal systems is a major barrier to state and local governments attempting to improve their appraisal systems. Since both behavior-based rating instruments and appraisal-by-objectives systems are costly, difficult, and time-consuming to implement, federal or other technical assistance and funding support are probably needed, both to enable state and local governments to implement new systems and to assure that evaluative studies of the systems' effectiveness are carried out and disseminated.

Interim Solutions

The efforts suggested above will take time. Meanwhile, governments are faced with the problem of what to do. Since there is no method that is simple to install and demonstrably effective, a government wanting to try a new system should test its plan in one or two units or agencies before installing it throughout the government. The recommendations outlined above for monitoring the effectiveness of the new system should be followed, if possible.

Many governments have appraisal systems that are clearly inadequate. Rather than tinkering with them, governments may find it preferable to discard them and rely on "appraisal by exception." Under this arrangement, exceptionally good or bad employee performance is carefully documented and personnel actions are based on the "facts in the case." Performance by all other employees is assumed to be satisfactory, and such employees receive regular merit increases, standard promotions, or other automatic rewards.

Over the long run, we hope that appraisal techniques can be developed that, based on field tests, demonstrate substantially greater effectiveness in encouraging improved employee performance while being more satisfying to both employees and management. Meanwhile, governments should be cautious, recognizing that they may waste resources by committing themselves too quickly to unproven appraisal systems.

Part Four:
JOB ENRICHMENT

Chapter 18

THE NATURE OF JOB ENRICHMENT

Like monetary incentives, performance targeting, and performance appraisal, job enrichment is an attempt to improve productivity while at the same time making employees more satisfied with their jobs. Job enrichment differs from the techniques discussed earlier, however, in its emphasis on altering the content of the tasks performed, and in its explicit attention to improving employee job satisfaction.

The theoretical basis for the various approaches to job enrichment was sketched in Chapter 1. Job enrichment theory holds that if a job is to provide substantial intrinsic satisfaction and motivation to an employee, it should exceed certain "critical levels" in each of four "core dimensions." These four dimensions are:

1. Autonomy, meaning the worker's degree of freedom in deciding upon and carrying out tasks;
2. Diversity, or the performance of separate tasks that involve a number of skills;
3. Wholeness, meaning carrying out a task from beginning to end rather than merely performing fragmented parts of tasks; and
4. Feedback, meaning providing employees with clear and timely information about their job performance.[1]

In general, job enrichment programs seek to improve jobs by changing one or more of these dimensions. It should be noted, however, that these dimensions sometimes overlap. A change in

---

1. Hackman and Lawler, "Employee Reactions."

the "wholeness" of a job, for example, may also increase its "diversity."

Another important concept in job enrichment is the distinction between "vertically loaded" and "horizontally loaded" jobs. "Vertically loaded" jobs—that is, jobs that involve greater responsibility, greater difficulty, and greater self-fulfillment—are believed to motivate employees to a greater extent than so-called "horizontally loaded" jobs, jobs that only provide increased diversity and interpersonal relations.[2]

Underlying both these concepts is the fundamental hypothesis that motivating employees by enriching their jobs will lead to greater productivity while simultaneously improving their job satisfaction. Katzell and Yankelovich, for example, found in a survey that both labor and management officials generally agreed that "if workers were more satisfied with their jobs, there would be greater productivity."[3]

After examining some forty reports on the impact of job enrichment programs in the private sector, however, Katzell and Yankelovich concluded that the positive results often reported were of questionable validity. Much of this private sector literature, they found, was testimonial in nature and therefore of uncertain objectivity and accuracy. Moreover, job enrichment has often been accompanied by other changes, such as revision of pay scales, that make it difficult to determine how much of any measured change in employee performance or satisfaction is due to the enrichment effort itself. Katzell and Yankelovich concluded that the connection between job enrichment and improved productivity or greater job satisfaction has not been proven:

> Efforts to redesign jobs have not produced results that
> are generally persuasive in validity or consistent in di-
> rection, although there are tantalizing bits of evidence,
> including the results of four prototype experiments,
> which suggest the potential value of the approach to
> better the quality of working life and economic per-
> formance.[4]

---

2. Frederick Herzberg, *Work and the Nature of Man* (Cleveland: World Publishing Company, 1966). An attempt to enrich a job by increasing the diversity of the tasks performed without substantially altering the other dimensions is often termed "job enlargement."

3. Katzell and Yankelovich, *Work, Productivity, and Job Satisfaction*, p. 17. They also found that three out of four policy makers agreed that job enrichment was a promising strategy for improving productivity (ibid., p. 18).

4. Katzell and Yankelovich, *Work, Productivity, and Job Satisfaction*, p. 184.

The rest of the literature on the impact of job enrichment in the private sector also appears to be inconclusive.[5] Moreover, the effects of certain intervening variables, such as the psychological readiness of workers for "enriched" jobs and the advanced technology of many production processes, are not yet completely understood.

Whether the results of private sector studies are equally applicable to the public sector is hard to tell. Several studies of job enrichment stress the fact that its value often depends on such variables as the type of worker and the type of job. Compared with private sector jobs, such as work in a manufacturing plant, many public sector jobs provide employees with considerable freedom of action. Police officers and sanitation workers, for example, perform most of their work without any direct supervision. Differences such as these between private and public sector jobs, plus the small number of in-depth studies of job enrichment in the public sector, make it difficult to know to what extent the results of job enrichment in the private sector apply to job enrichment in the public sector.

Types of Job Enrichment Used in the Public Sector

Job enrichment programs used by state and local governments, while quite numerous and diverse, can be grouped into four major classes. To some extent, these four classes overlap.

TEAM EFFORTS

Team efforts are designed to bring employees performing diverse functions or working in different units together to work as a group. The establishment of teams can enrich the jobs of team members by increasing the variety of tasks to be performed, encouraging greater worker cooperation, and enhancing employee autonomy. Team efforts also can provide team members with a better idea of the outcome of their work. The use of teams has

---

5. See, for instance, the reviews by Srivastva et al., *Job Satisfaction and Productivity*; and Katherine Janka, *People, Performance . . . Results* (Washington, D.C.: National Training and Development Service Press, 1977).

often been combined with other types of job enrichment, such as participative management or job restructuring. Of the various kinds of teams, three are particularly significant:

1. *Operating teams* are groups of employees who perform their normal day-to-day tasks as a team.

2. *Problem-oriented teams* (often termed "task forces") are groups of employees brought together to discuss and recommend solutions to specific problems. Ordinarily, these teams do not possess the authority to implement solutions. Problem-oriented teams can be either temporary or permanent, and may meet regularly or sporadically. In any case, participation on the team is not considered part of an employee's regular job but an addition to the regular job.

3. *Management teams* are groups of supervisory and management personnel who work together regularly to deal with operational problems, make daily decisions, or address objectives that fall between (or transcend) existing organizational boundaries.

INCREASED PARTICIPATION

There are a number of techniques whose primary contribution to job enrichment lies in giving employees increased opportunities to contribute to the decision-making and problem-solving responsibilities customarily reserved for management. These techniques enrich the job by giving the employee some degree of influence over plans, production methods, schedules, task allocations, and similar matters.

One technique for increasing participation is to establish joint labor-management committees that give a formal but non-adversary role to employee unions or associations in dealing with such noncontractual items as productivity, working conditions, and safety. Although the employee participants often consist of union officials and shop stewards, joint labor-management committees frequently include rank-and-file members as well. The latter type of joint committee potentially contributes more to increasing employee participation and is of special interest here.

There are a number of other techniques for giving employees an opportunity to influence managerial decisions and promote participative decision making, ranging from giving employees an advisory role (in informal meetings or opinion surveys) to giving them the opportunity to vote on—or even to veto—managerial decisions. In some cases, line employees have been made a temporary—or permanent—part of an organization's policy-making body. In others, managers have asked all employees to work as a group to solve certain specific problems or issues, such as safety problems or compliance with equal employment opportunity guidelines.

JOB ROTATION

Job rotation provides employees with periodic experience in different jobs. By increasing the variety of an employee's work, job rotation can reduce boredom and widen horizons, thus potentially improving job satisfaction. At the same time, it can enlarge the capabilities and work experience of employees, thereby improving their effectiveness. Rotation of line employees into supervisory positions can have another benefit—that of giving line employees a perspective on how organizational and work problems appear from management's vantage point. Job rotation may occur within a department, between departments, or even between different jurisdictions.

JOB REDESIGN

Although the term "job redesign" has sometimes been used as a synonym for job enrichment, its use in this study is restricted to efforts to redefine the jobs of individual employees in a comprehensive, systematic way. Job redesign, in other words, means redefining a job to give the employee the following:
1. Responsibility for completing an entire task rather than a fragment of a task;
2. Greater control over how and when work is done;
3. Frequent feedback on performance;
4. More varied job responsibilities.

Of the various kinds of job redesign, two are particularly important from the standpoint of improving productivity. *Job enlargement*, also known as "horizontal loading," involves increasing the number of tasks assigned to an employee without making a commensurate increase in the employee's autonomy, decision-making authority, or skill level. Since these new tasks usually are not closely related to the employee's previous tasks, job enlargement tends to broaden the job rather than deepen the employee's responsibility for it.

Job restructuring, on the other hand, means systematically redesigning a job by assigning to it greater skill requirements, greater autonomy, and greater responsibility for planning and performance. Job restructuring is an attempt to raise the level of a job and is therefore often referred to as "vertical loading."

The Limits of This Study

Because job enrichment programs in state and local governments are so numerous and diverse, it was found necessary to impose the following constraints on this part of the study:

1. Job enrichment programs were not studied if they were primarily for managerial or supervisory personnel.[6]

2. Joint labor-management committees were not examined in depth if their labor membership included only shop stewards and other union officials, while omitting rank-and-file members.

3. "Preenrichment" efforts—employee job satisfaction surveys, organizational development, and team building—are excluded for the most part.[7]

4. Programs that contribute to job enrichment only indirectly, such as flexitime, career development, job sharing, and training programs, are excluded.

5. Management-by-objectives and appraisal-by-objectives programs, which include certain aspects of job enrichment, are excluded here. They have already been discussed in Part Two.

The emphasis of the study has been on programs with the greatest likelihood of directly and significantly improving productivity. These include operating teams, increased participation, and job redesign programs. Less emphasis has been placed on job rotation.

---

6. Consequently, team management was not a major focus of study.

7. Although such efforts do exhibit elements of job enrichment in and of themselves (e.g., increased employee participation), they have usually been used by governments to prepare their employees for other job enrichment efforts, such as problem-solving teams, increased participation, etc.

Chapter 19

THE EXTENT OF JOB ENRICHMENT USE IN THE PUBLIC SECTOR

Although public sector use of job enrichment programs appears to have lagged behind use in the private sector, the number of public sector job enrichment efforts has expanded considerably in recent years. In a 1973 survey of state and local (both city and county) governments, eighty-one (15 percent) of the 550 respondents reported the use of job enrichment techniques.[1] By March 1978 a total of 217 state and local governments were reported to be using such techniques, an increase of more than 165 percent over 1973 (see Exhibit 18).

Local governments account for most of this growth. Since 1973 the number of local government users has risen almost 180 percent, with efforts by city governments constituting over 85 percent of all reported programs.

Public sector job enrichment efforts have been more common on the West Coast. Fifty-five (23 percent) of the 244 state and local governments reported to have tried job enrichment are located there. California, where job enrichment programs have been tried by at least forty-eight local governments as well as by the state government, has had by far the greatest number. Other states where job enrichment programs have been more frequent include New York with seventeen, Illinois with fifteen, Michigan with fourteen, New Jersey with eleven, and Florida with ten.

---

1. Greiner, Bell, and Hatry, *Employee Incentives*, pp. 5, 7.

Exhibit 18
OVERALL REPORTED USE OF JOB ENRICHMENT
(As of March 1978)

	Cities	Counties	States	Total
Number of Different Programs in Use [1]	267	24	18	309
Total Number of Jurisdictions Using Job Enrichment	184	20	13	217
Total Number of Jurisdictions That Have Tried Job Enrichment [2]	206	23	15	244

1. "In Use" implies that we have no information to indicate discontinuance of the program. However, in some cases our information is up to four years old. Programs designed to be "one-shot"—e.g., a task force addressing a single, finite problem—are also counted here as being "in use."
2. This includes jurisdictions that have terminated their job enrichment efforts, as well as those that appear to be continuing with their programs.
Source: Information obtained from the 1973 UI/ICMA/NGC survey of incentives, the 1976 ICMA survey of productivity improvement techniques, interviews by project staff, and a review of the relevant literature. Many of the programs included in these tallies were included on the basis of self-reports by the jurisdictions involved. For a discussion of the uncertainty concerning the actual number of existing, substantive programs, see text.

Fifty-six public sector job enrichment programs (excluding programs *designed* to last for only a short time—e.g., task forces to deal with a particular issue) had reportedly been terminated. The greatest number of terminated programs (twenty) involved efforts to combine the responsibilities of fire and police personnel into the single position of "public safety officer." Ten other terminated programs involved team policing. The reasons for the various terminations ranged from union or employee association opposition to management's belief that the program was not achieving its goals.

Exhibit 18 shows the reported incidence of job enrichment programs in state and local governments as of March 1978. These figures must be viewed with caution, however. In a number of cases, programs reported in surveys have turned out to be nothing more than a glint in the eye of a government official. Telephone interviews conducted for this study, for example, showed that 11 percent of twenty-two reported programs were nonexistent. On the other hand, it is likely that some job enrichment programs were not identified, inasmuch as not all governments responded to the surveys, and some of the newer enrichment programs probably passed unnoticed.

Exhibit 19 shows the reported incidence of the various types of job enrichment programs in state and local governments. Overall, team efforts and job redesign have been the most popular approaches, and police jobs have been the most frequent targets of enrichment efforts: 52 percent of the enrichment programs which had been tried involved police personnel. The next most popular target was the firefighter: 21 percent of all reported job enrichment programs involved firefighting personnel.

Each major type of job enrichment program will be discussed in turn in the next four chapters, both as to the extent of use by state and local governments and the information currently available on the impact of the program on productivity (efficiency and effectiveness), employee job satisfaction, and labor-management relations.

Exhibit 19
REPORTED JOB ENRICHMENT PROGRAMS, BY TYPE
(As of March 1978)

Type of Job Enrichment	Cities	Counties	States	Total
TEAM EFFORTS				
Operating Teams				
Team Policing	67	4	0	71
Other Operating Teams	7	2	2	11
Problem-Oriented Teams				
and Task Forces	23	3	3	29
Team Management	17	1	0	18
TOTAL TEAM EFFORTS	114	10	5	129
INCREASED PARTICIPATION				
Joint Labor-Management				
Committees	28	6	6	40
Miscellaneous Increased				
Participation	14	1	1	16
TOTAL PARTICIPATION	42	7	7	56
JOB ROTATION				
Within a Department	16	2	0	18
Between Departments	9	0	0	9
Between Cities	4[1]	0	0	4
TOTAL JOB ROTATION	29	2	0	31

(Continued)

Exhibit 19 (Continued)

Type of Job Enrichment	Cities	Counties	States	Total
JOB REDESIGN				
Job Enlargement				
Public Safety Officers	36	0	0	36
Expansion of Duties of				
Firefighters [2]	5	0	0	5
Generalist Building				
Inspectors	12	0	0	12
Miscellaneous Enlargement	5	2	0	7
TOTAL ENLARGEMENT	58	2	0	60
Job Restructuring				
Redesign of Police Jobs [3]	14	1	0	15
Career Executive Programs	0	0	6	6
Miscellaneous Restructuring	10	2	0	12
TOTAL RESTRUCTURING	24	3	6	33
TOTAL JOB REDESIGN	82	5	6	93
TOTAL NUMBER OF REPORTED JOB ENRICHMENT PROGRAMS	267	24	18	309

1. This is the number of distinct programs; over six different cities are involved.
2. Excludes efforts to give firefighters additional responsibilities for conducting fire code inspections, an approach used by many jurisdictions.
3. Excludes use of civilian paraprofessionals to free police officers from routine duties, a practice which is widespread.
Source: Sources noted in Exhibit 18.

Chapter 20

TEAM EFFORTS

Team efforts have been reported by 124 local governments and five state governments. Most of these efforts have involved either operating teams or problem-oriented teams ("task forces").

Operating Teams

Operating teams are found most often in police departments, where they take the form of team policing efforts. These programs are discussed first, followed by a review of the use of operating teams by other agencies.

TEAM POLICING

Team policing was recommended in the final report of the President's Commission on Law Enforcement and the Administration of Justice in 1967 as an alternative to the centralized direction and task specialization characteristic of most police departments. Team policing, it was hoped, would result in better service to the community and improved working conditions for patrol officers.

In the years since then, a large number of team policing efforts have been undertaken. As of March 1978, programs were reported to exist in sixty-seven cities and four counties; ten other team policing programs had been terminated (see Exhibit 20). Team policing apparently has been adopted by large, medium, and small cities in approximately equal numbers.

In traditional police operations, patrol officers are rotated periodically from one geographical area to another. They fre-

Exhibit 20
TEAM POLICING PROGRAMS
(As of March 1978)

Jurisdictions Reporting Use	Existing (E), Rejected (R), or Terminated (T)[1]	Comments/Notes
Albany, N.Y.	E	Uses blazers. Jobs redesigned.
Albuquerque, N.M.	T	Squad policing. Some redesign of jobs.
Arlington County, Va.	E	
Baltimore, Md.	E	
Bellevue, Wash.	E	
Berkeley, Calif.	E	
Bethlehem, Pa.	E	
Bloomington, Minn.	E	Squad policing. Some redesign of jobs.
Boise, Idaho	E	Includes 4-10 plan[2] and some redesign of jobs.
Boulder, Colo.	E	City also uses public safety officers.
Bristol, Conn.	E	
Burbank, Calif.	E	Includes 4-10 plan.
Burnsville, Minn.	E	
Carol Stream, Ill.	E	
Charlotte, N.C.	E	Includes increased decision participation.
Cincinnati, Ohio	E	Includes use of task forces, increased participation.
Culver City, Calif.	E	
Cypress, Calif.	E	
Dallas, Tex.	R	
Dayton, Ohio	T	Included blazers, increased participation, job redesign.
Dearborn, Mich.	E	
Detroit, Mich.	T	
Durham, N.C.	E	City also uses public safety officers.
East Hartford, Conn.	E	Includes 4-10 plan.
El Dorado, Kan.	E	Neighborhood police/fire teams handle patrol, traffic, and fires.

(Continued)

Exhibit 20 (Continued)

Jurisdictions Reporting Use	Existing (E), Rejected (R), or Terminated (T)[1]	Comments/Notes
Elizabeth, N.J.	E	Some redesign of jobs.
Fremont, Calif.	E	
Golden Valley, Minn.	E	
Hartford, Conn.	E	Includes increased participation, job redesign.
Holyoke, Mass.	T	Included blazers, increased participation, job redesign.
Huntington Beach, Calif.	E	Squad policing. Includes 4-10 plan.
Jacksonville, Fla.	E	
Kansas City, Mo.	E	Department also uses task forces extensively.
Kenosha, Wis.	E	
Lakewood, Colo.	T	
Los Angeles, Calif.	E	Two programs. Includes increased participation.
Louisville, Ky.	E	
Madison, Wis.	E	Included use of implementation task force.
Menlo Park, Calif.	E	Squad policing. Includes use of organizational development (OD), blazers, increased participation, job redesign.
Monterey Park, Calif.	E	
Mt. Lebanon, Pa.	E	
Multnomah County, Oreg.	E	Includes use of MBO.
Newark, N.J.	E	
New Brunswick, N.J.	E	
Newburgh, N.Y.	E	
New Orleans, La.	E	
New Rochelle, N.Y.	E	Includes job redesign.
New York, N.Y.	T	Included increased participation, job redesign.
North Charleston, S.C.	E	Squad policing. Includes 4-10 plan.
Oak Park, Ill.	E	
Omaha, Neb.	E	
Orem, Utah	E	

(Continued)

Exhibit 20 (Continued)

Jurisdictions Reporting Use	Existing (E), Rejected (R), or Terminated (T) [1]	Comments/Notes
Oxnard, Calif.	E	
Pacifica, Calif.	E	Includes job redesign.
Palo Alto, Calif.	T	Squad policing. Included 4-10 plan, increased participation.
Pawtucket, R.I.	E	
Phoenix, Ariz.	E	
Pittsburg, Calif.	E	
Pueblo, Colo.	E	
Racine, Wis.	E	
Richmond, Calif.	E	Squad policing. Includes increased participation.
Rochester, N.Y.	E	Some redesign of jobs.
Sacramento, Calif.	E	
St. Paul, Minn.	E	Some redesign of jobs.
St. Petersburg, Fla.	T	Included MBO, use of blazers, some increased participation.
San Bruno, Calif.	E	Squad policing. Includes 4-10 plan.
San Diego, Calif.	E	Squad policing. Includes increased participation, job redesign.
San Diego County, Calif.	E	
San Joaquin County, Calif.	E	
Santa Ana, Calif.	E	
Scottsdale, Ariz.	E	
Simi Valley, Calif.	R	Included use of blazers, increased participation,
Stockton, Calif.	E	extensive job redesign,
Syracuse, N.Y.	E	organizational redesign.
Tacoma, Wash.	E	
Tampa, Fla.	E	
Tucson, Ariz.	E	
Tulsa, Okla.	E	
Victoria, Tex.	E	
Winston-Salem, N.C.	E	City also uses public safety officers
Yonkers, N.Y.	E	

Exhibit 20 (Footnotes)

1. "Existing" indicates that the program appears to still be functioning, according to our latest information. However, in some cases that information is up to four years old. "Rejected" means that the program was planned but never implemented. "Terminated" means it was implemented and subsequently disbanded.

2. Under a "4-10" plan, a police department schedules three ten-hour shifts per day, and officers work four days a week. This scheduling gives police officers a three-day weekend, and allows police departments to put more officers on the street during high crime periods by scheduling the overlaps between adjacent shifts for those periods.

---

quently go outside their beats in response to requests for service and are isolated organizationally from investigative personnel. In contrast, team policing involves the permanent deployment of "teams" of police officers to a particular geographical area or neighborhood, where they become responsible for virtually all police activities in the area, including criminal investigations.

Police teams have ranged in size from as few as fifteen to as many as sixty members. The number of officers allocated to a team usually depends on neighborhood population, crime rate, patrol workload, the extent of the team's responsibility, and the like. Some police teams are known as "area teams" because they are responsible for providing police services in their area twenty-four hours a day. Other teams are called "shift teams" because their team responsibility lasts only during their eight-hour shift.

The responsibilities assigned to police teams vary from place to place. In some communities, for example, teams simply carry out the basic duties of patrol officers, including conducting preventive patrol, responding to calls for service relayed by radio dispatchers, and enforcing traffic laws. Such teams have been used in the California cities of Richmond and San Bruno, and in North Charleston, South Carolina.

In other communities, police teams conduct criminal investigations as well as basic patrol activities.[1] They may have the responsibility for investigating all crimes, or for all but a few selected crimes, such as murder. The Rochester, New York,

---

1. The delegation of investigative responsibilities to patrol officers constitutes a form of job redesign and is discussed in more detail in Chapter 23.

police department is an example of a department which utilizes patrol-investigative teams.

Still another kind of police team combines the performance of basic patrol services with the performance of community relations work. Such teams are usually found where relations between the police department and certain neighborhoods are clearly in need of improvement. Communities that have used such teams include Albuquerque, Hartford, New York City, and San Diego.

A fourth kind of police team is the so-called "full-service team," which is responsible for basic patrol, investigations, and community relations. Such teams have been used in Albany, Charlotte, Cincinnati, Detroit, and Los Angeles, among other cities.

Team policing is often found in conjunction with some degree of participative management. For instance, first-line supervisors and patrol officers often plan and carry out patrol and other strategies together. This, however, is not an essential part of team policing.

The Impact of Team Policing. Team policing has been studied far more thoroughly than any other public sector job enrichment effort. A recent survey of the literature on team policing conducted by the National Sheriffs' Association (NSA) concluded that although the evidence is limited, team policing does result in more efficient use of police personnel. Among other things, the NSA study cited an improved ability to coordinate personnel with service demands (reported by the police department of Richmond, California) and an increase in patrol mileage (reported by the San Bruno, California, police department).[2]

Team policing has rarely been introduced as a means of reducing costs, and no reports of reduced costs occurred. Where team policing has been accompanied by substantial increases in expenditures, however, the reason has usually been a concurrent increase in the size of the department. Nevertheless, an Urban Institute study of six team policing efforts found that such programs "need not involve substantial, continuing budgetary outlays."[3]

---

2. William G. Gay et al., *Issues in Team Policing: A Review of the Literature*, National Institute of Law Enforcement and Criminal Justice, Law Enforcement Assistance Administration (Washington, D.C., September 1977), p. 7.

3. Thomas White et al., "Evaluation of LEAA's Full Service Neighborhood Team Policing Demonstration: A Summary Report" (Washington, D.C.: The Urban Institute, December 1977), p. 94.

Evidence on the effectiveness of team policing in providing police services, although voluminous, presents a mixed picture. Most police departments assess the effectiveness of police patrol by examining the rise and fall of crime rates. The NSA study of the literature on team policing found that crime rates had fallen in three communities that had experimented with team policing—Los Angeles; New Brunswick, New Jersey; and Albuquerque.[4] The NSA's own assessment of nineteen team policing projects, however, presented a more uncertain picture. In three communities (Rochester, New York; Holyoke, Massachusetts; and Los Angeles) crime rates in team-policed areas decreased in comparison to areas with traditional policing. In New York City and St. Petersburg, Florida, on the other hand, there was little difference in the crime rates in team and nonteam areas.[5]

Several recent evaluations of team policing efforts cite positive effects on reported crime rates. In Bellevue, Washington, residential burglaries fell over 17 percent in the first eighteen months of the program, relative to the year preceding the introduction of police teams.[6] (Prior to that time, residential burglaries had been increasing at a rate of nearly 50 percent a year.) Orem, Utah, reported that the number of serious (Part I) crimes per thousand population fell from fifty-one in 1975 to thirty-seven in 1977, after the introduction of neighborhood police teams in conjunction with other crime prevention measures.[7] The Urban Institute/Police Foundation evaluation of the Cincinnati team policing experiment (COMSEC) found that "For burglary there appeared to be compelling evidence that COMSEC was more successful than traditional policing in reducing that crime type." [8]

Another way to judge the effectiveness of team policing is to examine clearance rates and the number of cases that are handled well enough to be prosecuted. Clearance rates seemed

---

4. Gay et al., *Issues in Team Policing*, pp. 6-7.

5. William G. Gay, H. Talmadge Day, and Jane P. Woodward, *Neighborhood Team Policing*, Phase I Summary Report, National Institute of Law Enforcement and Criminal Justice, Law Enforcement Assistance Administration (Washington, D.C., February 1977), pp. 28-29.

6. William G. Ellis, "Neighborhood Team Policing," *The Police Chief*, vol. 44, no. 5 (May 1977), pp. 38-40.

7. International City Management Association, *The Guide to Management Improvement Projects in Local Government*, vol. 1, no. 1 (Washington, D.C., January-February 1977), item no. 24.

8. A. I. Schwartz and S. N. Clarren, *The Cincinnati Team Policing Experiment: A Summary Report* (Washington, D.C.: The Police Foundation, 1977), p. 25.

to improve in some of the communities that used team policing. Examples include Albuquerque (where clearance rates for serious crimes were reported to have doubled), Los Angeles, Cincinnati, Dayton, and Rochester. The Albany, New York, team policing effort, however, produced no significant change in the number of clearances. With respect to the number of cases handled well enough to permit prosecution, the evidence is unclear, although the NSA report concluded that police teams have performed as well as, and sometimes better than, traditional police units in terms of investigative effectiveness.[9]

Still another way to measure the effectiveness of team policing is to see what effects it has had on the relationship between the police and the citizens they serve. Here again, the results are mixed. A general survey of public attitudes toward the police department in Bellevue, Washington, indicated no significant change in public perceptions twelve months after the introduction of team policing. However, surveys of citizens who had reported burglaries showed significant improvements in satisfaction with service following the introduction of Bellevue's team policing program.[10] The NSA study concluded that team policing resulted in more positive citizen attitudes toward the police in Albany, Los Angeles, and San Diego, had no effect on citizen attitudes in Holyoke and Cincinnati, and apparently increased negative citizen attitudes in New York City and Dayton, Ohio.[11]

The NSA report, however, also points out that various problems interfered with the implementation of team policing in all four communities where the results were neutral or negative.[12] In Dayton, Holyoke, and New York City, team policing was introduced at times of unusual stress within the police department, sometimes with little planning. In Holyoke, furthermore, the attitude of citizens toward the police became more positive in the early stages of team policing and only became less so after funds for community relations activities ran out. And although public attitudes in general did not change in Cincinnati, citizens

---

9. Gay, Day, and Woodward, *Neighborhood Team Policing*, pp. 25-27.
10. Battelle Memorial Institute, "An Evaluation of the Bellevue Police Department's Experiment in Team Policing" (Seattle, Washington, December 1976), pp. 18-21.
11. Gay, Day, and Woodward, *Neighborhood Team Policing*, p. 37.
12. Ibid.

there reported that they felt safer walking in areas patrolled by teams and that team officers were more responsive to calls for service.[13]

Team policing also seems to have had a positive effect on police officer attitudes toward the community. Data from five jurisdictions (San Diego, Cincinnati, Albany, Albuquerque, and Los Angeles) indicate that team officers received greater cooperation and support from the community than did officers in traditional units.[14]

Attempts to determine the effect of team policing on the job satisfaction felt by team members show no consistent pattern. None of these studies separated the satisfaction felt as a result of being a team member from the satisfaction that stemmed from increased responsibilities and increased participation in the decision-making process. It should also be remembered that many teams were staffed with officers who volunteered to serve on them; hence, those officers may have been particularly unhappy in their previous situation or especially inclined toward the team policing approach.

Nevertheless, members of police teams in San Bruno, Detroit, and Dayton reported high levels of satisfaction with the program, and Carol Stream, Illinois, police officials reported that team policing improved department morale and created a competitive spirit among the teams.[15] The NSA review found that, of four efforts to measure changes in job satisfaction among team members, only one (Charlotte, North Carolina) indicated greater satisfaction after the police teams were initiated.[16] Job satisfaction in San Diego and Cincinnati did not change, but satisfaction among Cincinnati's police officers was quite high even before the team policing effort began. In New York, however, 80 percent of the team officers felt their jobs got worse after the introduction of team policing. On the other hand, reductions in turnover and sick leave, which may indicate increased job satisfaction, were found among team members in San Bruno, California, and there were reductions in sick leave among team members in Cincinnati and New York.[17]

---

13. Schwartz and Clarren, *Cincinnati Team Policing*, p. 6.
14. Gay, Day, and Woodward, *Neighborhood Team Policing*, p. 36.
15. Gay et al., *Issues in Team Policing*, p. 10; and *Guide to Management Improvement Projects*, vol. 1, no. 1, item no. 24.
16. Gay, Day, and Woodward, *Neighborhood Team Policing*, p. 17.
17. Ibid., p. 16; Gay et al., *Issues in Team Policing*, p. 10.

An evaluation of the team policing effort in Bellevue, Washington, found no increase in job satisfaction among team members and suggested that the reason was that team membership offered no obvious rewards.[18] In Albany, on the other hand, the attitude of team members in the high-crime areas where teams had been introduced was originally quite positive; however, interest in the program began to subside as crime rates—and the corresponding challenge of the job—were reduced.

There is some evidence that team policing has improved relations among police personnel, as shown by better communication between the various units and increased socialization between supervisors and patrol officers after hours.[19] However, one of the two police teams in Bellevue, Washington, reported decreased satisfaction with supervision. In some cities, detectives have become dissatisfied upon being assigned to a neighborhood police team, viewing it as a diminution of their status.

Finally, the impact of team policing on labor-management relations appears to have been nil. Neither problems nor improvements between management and employee associations or unions have been reported.

Overall, team policing seems to have had mixed but mostly favorable effects. While a number of programs have resulted in little change, only in rare instances have significant negative effects been identified.

OPERATING TEAMS IN OTHER DEPARTMENTS

The use of operating teams in agencies other than police departments appears to be relatively infrequent. Exhibit 21 shows eleven such teams, two in states and the rest in local governments.

Several of these have involved attempts to coordinate the daily activities of persons from different departments by having them work together on a regular basis. Inspection teams com-

18. Battelle, "Bellevue Experiment," p. 65.
19. See, for instance, J. A. Zurcher, "The Team Management/Team Policing Organizational Concept," *The Police Chief*, vol. 38, no. 4 (April 1971), pp. 54-56; L. G. Phelps and L. Harmon, "Team Policing—Four Years Later," *FBI Law Enforcement Bulletin*, vol. 41, no. 12 (December 1972), pp. 2-5f; P. M. Sears and S. Wilson, *Crime Reduction in Albuquerque: Evaluation of Three Police Projects*, New Mexico University (University Park, 1973); and L. W. Sherman, C. H. Milton, and T. V. Kelly, *Team Policing: Seven Case Studies* (Washington, D.C.: The Police Foundation, 1973).

Exhibit 21
OPERATING TEAMS, EXCLUDING TEAM POLICING
(As of March 1978)

Jurisdictions Reporting Use	Comments/Notes
Baltimore, Md.	Housing and health inspection teams; nursing teams.
Baltimore County, Md.	Arson teams involving personnel from police, fire, and county attorney's office.
Cincinnati, Ohio	Health care teams.
Fort Lauderdale, Fla.	Public safety inspection teams composed of police and fire personnel.
Hempstead, N.Y.	Custodial teams.
Minneapolis, Minn.	Clerical team in selection section of Personnol Department.
New York, N.Y.	Housing inspection teams.
Riverside County, Calif.	Community resources teams for probation services.[1]
Springfield, Ill.	Inspection teams comprised of a building inspector and a fire safety specialist.
State of Nevada	Unemployment insurance claimant placement teams comprised of employment service and unemployment insurance specialists.
State of Oregon	Mental hospital teams.

1. Similar teams are reported to have been tried in sixteen other jurisdictions in the west and midwest. See Charles McNamara, "Community Resources Management Approach Reports Success With New Team Concept," *American Journal of Correction,* vol. 39, no. 4 (July-August 1977), pp. 32-36f.

posed of fire, police, and sometimes other personnel have been used by several governments, including Baltimore County, Maryland; Fort Lauderdale, Florida; and Springfield, Illinois.

Baltimore, Maryland. The city of Baltimore set up teams of inspectors composed of employees from the departments of housing and health. Each team was composed of four or five specialists in different types of inspections who worked together to inspect a given building. This procedure differs significantly from the traditional one, in which the various types of inspectors (building, fire, health, and so on) work independently of each other and with little knowledge of each other's work.

Another kind of operating team was created in the town of Hempstead, New York.

Hempstead, New York. In 1975, Hempstead established a single operating team consisting of all of the approximately thirty employees in the custodial division of the General Services Department. To complete their nightly task of cleaning the town's public buildings, all members of the team worked together at cleaning one floor before moving down to the next floor. In addition, the various tasks—trash collection, mopping, and so on—were rotated among the workers. Prior to 1975, employees working in groups of two had been assigned to clean each floor.

Another type of operating team is the health care team composed of doctors and nurses. Varieties of these teams have been used in Baltimore, Cincinnati, and Oregon.

Cincinnati, Ohio. The teams in Cincinnati included a pediatrics team, an obstetrics-gynecology team, and an adult medical care team. Participation in such teams has often resulted in greater responsibility and variety for team members. Nurses on Cincinnati's health care teams, for example, were given the tasks of screening and referring patients.

The Impact of Operating Teams in Other Departments. Because there have been few formal evaluations of the impact of operating teams in nonpolice agencies, we conducted telephone interviews with persons associated with the custodial team in Hempstead and the various health teams in Cincinnati. Thus, much of the following information on impact is subjective and impressionistic.[20]

The use of arson teams combining fire and police personnel was widely reported to have been successful. For instance, Bal-

---

20. One of the few programs which was carefully evaluated—the clerical team in the Minneapolis Department of Personnel—also involved a considerable amount of job restructuring. The results are discussed with job restructuring in Chapter 23. A federal effort to create operating teams to handle citizen complaints produced major improvements in productivity and job satisfaction. See Tim McNamar, "White Collar Job Enrichment: The Pay Board Experience," *Public Administration Review*, vol. 33, no. 6 (November-December 1973), pp. 563-568.

timore County's arson investigation team was credited with contributing to a significant increase in solutions to known arsons. Before the team was created, only 12 percent of the county's arsons were solved; during the first three months of the team program, 45 percent were solved.[21] For most team programs, however, it was difficult to isolate the effects of the operating teams from those of other innovations occurring at the same time.

In Hempstead the introduction of the custodial team resulted in some apparent improvements in efficiency and building cleanliness, although these improvements did not include a reduction in the number of employees required to carry out custodial tasks.[22] An unexpected benefit of the Hempstead operation was smaller electric bills; instead of lights being on throughout the building as custodians did their work, lights were turned off as the team moved from floor to floor. The amount saved, however, was not known. More efficient use of materials was also reported: a decrease of about 10 to 12 percent in the overall cost of materials was calculated eight months after the team was initiated. A slight initial increase in the number of desks cleaned was not sustained.

Improvements in efficiency due to the creation of operating teams in Cincinnati's public health center were difficult to pinpoint because of an accompanying change from the traditional episodic type of medical care to a form of comprehensive, prevention-oriented family medical care. Although the introduction of teams required an increase in the number of clinic personnel (and thus in personnel costs), it is hard to say how much of the increase was attributable to team care and how much to the preventive, family care concept. The increase in personnel costs was matched by an increase (of an unstated amount) in other clinic costs as well. The clinic representative contacted in the course of this study attributed the increases to the new comprehensive approach to health care and the decentralized administration of the clinic rather than to the introduction of teams.

---

21. James K. Lathrop, "Public Safety Inspectors Program a Success," *Fire Command*, vol. 45, no. 9 (September 1978), p. 34; and International City Management Association, *The Guide to Management Improvement Projects in Local Government*, vol. 1, no. 2 (Washington, D.C., March-April 1977), item no. 95.
22. Hayes, *Productivity*, p. 77.

The use of health care teams in Cincinnati was reported to have had various beneficial effects on patient care. More patients were cared for on a continuing basis, patients kept appointments more faithfully, and there was greater patient adherence to the instructions of physicians than had occurred earlier. The team approach also appears to have contributed to improved scheduling (all members of a family could be seen at the same time, reducing the number of trips to the clinic and thus reducing the number of cancelled appointments), less red tape for new patients who sought treatment without an appointment, and better understanding by clinicians of the needs of each family. However, no information was available on various common indicators of health care quality, such as changes in the number of patient-days at the clinic or changes in the number of days during which patients were unable to carry on their daily activities. The clinic representative did report, however, that its hospitalization rate was lower than that of hospitals where patients were treated more traditionally.

There are indications that employee job satisfaction increased, at least temporarily, in both Hempstead and Cincinnati subsequent to the introduction of operating teams. Employee surveys in Hempstead indicated improved satisfaction with pay after the introduction of team cleaning, although there was less satisfaction with supervision.[23] Absenteeism dropped 7.3 percent after the new procedure was introduced, but agency management in Hempstead reported that the reduction did not last. In Cincinnati the turnover rate among health care teams was only 3 percent, compared to 30 to 40 percent in the rest of the city health department. In both cities, department officials reported that understanding, respect, and cooperativeness increased among employees and between employees and supervisors. And in both jurisdictions team members seemed to express greater interest in their work, as reflected in the increased number of suggestions about how to improve various procedures.

The team concept in Cincinnati, however, also caused a certain amount of employee dissatisfaction. Some physicians not chosen as team leaders by team members were unhappy at this lack of formal deference to their authority, and some were annoyed at having their work evaluated by the nurses who had been elected team leaders. Since team leaders were also respon-

---

23. Ibid.

sible for administrative matters, however, some of the physicians viewed the relief from administrative responsibility as compensation for not being selected as team leader.

The team concept appears to have had little effect on labor-management relations in either Cincinnati or Hempstead. In the latter case, this may be due partly to the fact that representatives of the union representing the custodians were invited to participate in the program's implementation and were assured that the team concept was not an attempt to make employees work harder or longer.

Problem-Oriented Teams

Problem-oriented teams are groups of employees assigned the task of providing advice on—and in some cases resolving—a specific problem of a local or state government. Twenty-nine of these teams (sometimes called task forces) were identified—twenty-three in cities and towns, three in counties, and three in state governments. Another two programs had been terminated. (See Exhibit 22.)

Problem-oriented teams vary considerably, particularly in terms of the problems they address. Some consider only a particular issue and then disband; others operate on a continuing basis, dealing with whatever problems arise. In some respects, however, problem-oriented teams are similar to each other. Many, for example, have been deliberate efforts to encourage lower-level employees to work together to solve problems, as in the following examples.

In Austin, Texas, an employee task force was created to help in developing performance appraisal procedures. In Little Rock, Arkansas, employee task forces were established to design and implement a survey of employees and to respond to the problems it revealed. In Kansas City, Missouri, police department task forces developed experiments and provided advice on various policing problems, such as the effectiveness of alternate patrol strategies. In Forsyth County, North Carolina, three problem-oriented teams have been used, including a "Resource Identification Committee" whose task was to identify sources of federal funding to help in achieving the county's objectives. In New Jersey, the state Department of Labor and Industry

Exhibit 22
PROBLEM-ORIENTED TEAMS AND TASK FORCES
(As of March 1978)

Jurisdictions Reporting Use	Comments/Notes
Arlington County, Va.	
Austin, Tex.	Performance evaluation task force.
Bellevue, Wash.	Reclassification task force.
Cincinnati, Ohio	Task force to plan and implement team policing.
Dallas, Tex.	Task force in Water Utilities Department to implement findings of employee survey.
Dayton, Ohio	Top management task forces for interdisciplinary problems: 60 managers involved.
Eugene, Oreg.	
Forsyth County, N.C.	Five task forces focusing on various problems (government organization, obtaining federal grants, etc.).
Fort Worth, Tex.	
Garden Grove, Calif.	
Kansas City, Mo.	Police task forces to study various problems.
Leavenworth, Kan.	Task forces and committees on personnel issues and internal research (to examine survey results).
Liberty, Mo.	Management task force to make budget cuts.
Little Rock, Ark.	Research and implementation task forces (to design, implement, and respond to employee survey).
Madison, Wis.	Police task forces to investigate team policing, crime prevention, patrol strategies.
Milwaukee, Wis.	Teams and task forces to consider plans and operational alternatives.
Montgomery County, Md.	OD task forces in personnel, environmental protection areas.
Mountain View, Calif.	Problem-oriented teams appointed by management advisory group.
Oakland, Calif.	

(Continued)

Exhibit 22 (Continued)

Jurisdictions Reporting Use	Comments/Notes
Phoenix, Ariz.	Multilevel OD task force.
Pomona, Calif.	
Pueblo, Colo.	Multidepartment, project-oriented teams (mostly supervisors).
Reading, Pa.	Management "corps" of supervisors and line personnel trained to serve as a continuing resource for examining broad problems (terminated).
Rockville, Md.	Public works, parks and recreation task forces on absenteeism, refuse collection.
Seattle, Wash.	Arson task force.
Sioux City, Iowa	Employee problem-solving groups.
Tacoma, Wash.	Numerous employee teams and task forces, e.g., to implement and act on results of employee survey, to divide revenue-sharing funds, to develop an inner-city plaza, and to resolve various special problems (fireboat purchase, police recruitment, etc.).
State of New Jersey	Two separate efforts in Department of Labor and Industry: —Ten employee task forces on general problems (terminated). —Participative problem-solving teams within work groups.
State of North Carolina	Productivity team (of supervisors) in Highway Division.
State of Washington	Problem-solving teams throughout the Department of Agriculture.

has utilized twenty-three problem-oriented teams of from seven to fourteen employees for "participative problem-solving." They have dealt with such issues as erroneous data in claims reports, problems of motivating employees, confusing civil service procedures, and delays in the receipt of payroll checks. This New Jersey department also created a problem-oriented "Committee of 100" whose ten subcommittees dealt with various personnel issues, ranging from employee incentives to career development and equal employment opportunity. Reading, Pennsylvania, created a so-called "Municipal Management Corps" to serve as a continuing source of ideas and help concerning the city's management problems. This group, which included both supervisory and nonsupervisory employees, dealt with problems in interdepartmental relations, personnel administration, and financial administration. And Tacoma, Washington, has used numerous problem-oriented teams to help resolve problems brought to light by employee surveys.

The Impact of Problem-Oriented Teams. No formal, systematic evaluations of problem-oriented teams were found in the course of this study, although accounts of some of the accomplishments of such teams have been published. Information on the Forsyth County program was obtained from a county description of the effort, and information on the teams in New Jersey and in Reading, Pennsylvania, was obtained through telephone interviews with program representatives. No firm data on changes in effectiveness, efficiency, or employee job satisfaction had been collected for the teams in these three jurisdictions. In all three cases, however, the problem-oriented teams made some recommendations that later were implemented.

In Reading, the "Municipal Management Corps" suggested the elimination of two positions it found to be unnecessary, prepared personnel discipline and personnel evaluation systems (both now inoperable as a result of new contractual restrictions), and demonstrated an improved budgetary system. This last effort resulted in a reorganization of the city's accounting office and inclusion of the city's capital improvements program as a regular part of the budget.

In New Jersey, the Department of Labor and Industry's problem-oriented teams made several suggestions that produced "probable" cost savings. In the Division of Planning and Research, for example, an examination of overdue and inaccurate reports from local unemployment compensation offices led to a suggestion by the employee problem-solving team that local office personnel be given additional training. The result was an estimated 50 percent reduction in the number of overdue reports and a 70 percent reduction in time spent checking the reports. Another team's examination of the department's problems in getting the payroll out on time resulted in suggestions that led to elimination of overtime and annual savings of about $3,600.

The department's Committee of 100 made 123 recommendations, of which eighteen were implemented, sixty-six were to be implemented as soon as feasible, twenty-four were rejected, and fifteen were determined to be outside the department's control. Many of those outside the department's control involved suggestions to introduce monetary incentives for department employees; such suggestions were sent to the governor's office for consideration.

In Forsyth County, an in-depth analysis of the county government by employee task forces led to the creation of two county departments. The task forces also prepared forty applications for federal grants. No examples of net savings or improved services were identified, however.

Several other jurisdictions provided some information on the impact of their problem-oriented teams. Seattle, Washington's arson task force was credited with contributing to a 13 percent reduction in arson incidents, a 35 percent reduction in dollar loss due to arson, and a 40 percent increase in the monthly rate of arson arrests during its first year of operation.[24] Rockville, Maryland, reported that its task force on sick leave abuse and absenteeism was instrumental in achieving a 23.5 percent decrease in absenteeism and the abuse of sick leave by blue-collar workers over the twelve months following implementation of the task force's suggestions. This translated into a savings of nearly $22,000.[25] And Washington's State Department of Agriculture reported that among the benefits of its many problem-oriented teams were the resolution of a long-standing agency problem on the use of state vehicles (which led to the return of 100 vehicles to general state use) and improved commodity inspections (which led to annual cost savings of $185,000 for producers of those commodities).[26]

Overall, most teams have focused on problems related to internal administrative matters or small-scale service issues. There appear to have been few significant attempts, thus far, to apply problem-oriented teams to major service delivery issues.

24. International City Management Association, *The Guide to Management Improvement Projects in Local Government*, vol. 1, no. 4 (Washington, D.C., July-August 1977), item no. 190.

25. Daniel G. Hobbs, "Productivity in Rockville, Maryland," City of Rockville (December 6, 1977).

26. Raymond M. Ryan, "Employee Relations Key in Washington State Productivity," *LMRS Newsletter*, vol. 7, no. 7 (July 1976), pp. 3-5.

The limited data available suggest that setting up and training problem-oriented teams can be expensive. In Reading, Pennsylvania, the consultant fees associated with setting up the Municipal Management Corps and the in-kind services underwritten by the government (such as the time spent by members of the team) came to nearly $40,000. Program officials in New Jersey estimated that the total cost of their problem-solving teams was about a quarter of a million dollars, including consultant fees, trainer time, training materials, and the lost production of participating employees.

Information about the effect of problem-oriented teams on employee job satisfaction is, at best, impressionistic. In general, the teams seem to have stimulated employee innovation and greater cooperation among individual employees and among the departments represented by team members. Some participants reportedly felt that management had become more responsive. However, in Reading, all line employees eventually resigned from the Municipal Management Corps on grounds that the team's tasks were too difficult for them to handle.

The impact of problem-oriented teams on labor-management relations in Forsyth County and New Jersey has been negligible. However, city officials in Reading reported that union leaders questioned the advisability of having employees and first-line supervisors participate in a "management" corps; union pressure was viewed as contributing to the city's decision to terminate the program.

Chapter 21
INCREASED PARTICIPATION

At least fifty-six jurisdictions—including forty-two cities, seven counties, and seven state governments—have used joint labor-management committees or other techniques to give employees the opportunity to participate in decisions that affect them. Fifteen other programs designed in whole or in part to increase employee participation have been used but are known to have been terminated. In many instances, participatory programs have served as the vehicle for introducing other motivational approaches, such as monetary incentives and job redesign.

Joint Labor-Management Committees

The objective of a joint labor-management committee is to create an atmosphere in which labor and management can discuss problems of mutual concern in a casual, nonadversary setting, in contrast to that which customarily prevails at the bargaining table. Frequently, establishment of the committee is stipulated by contract or in a memorandum of understanding between management and labor that defines the scope, power, and composition of the committee. In many cases, joint labor-management committees have come into existence following a period of conflict between labor and management.

The committees usually are composed of equal numbers of management and labor representatives. The labor participants often consist primarily of union officials, shop stewards, and the like. However, in a number of instances the committees have included participation by line employees and other members of

the rank-and-file. The latter are usually selected by union officials or are elected by their fellow employees.

Joint labor-management committees have been set up in
forty-eight jurisdictions, including eight where the program was
subsequently abandoned (see Exhibit 23).[1] Seven of the committees were at the state level, eight were created by counties,
thirty-two were formed in city governments, and one involved
a joint effort by a county and three of its towns. Several of these
jurisdictions have had more than one committee.

In addition, a number of governments have provided for
such committees in their labor agreements. In an analysis of 400
public sector labor agreements, the Bureau of Labor Statistics
found that seventy-six (19 percent) included provisions for joint
safety committees, twenty-four (6 percent) contained provisions
for joint committees to discuss labor relations issues (e.g., working conditions, job evaluations), and seven (2 percent) called
for the formation of productivity committees.[2] It is not known
how often these stipulations resulted in the actual establishment
of labor-management committees.

Of the eight terminated committees, four were at the city
level, three were at the county level, one was at the state level,
and one was a joint committee including both county and
town representatives. Two of these committees were dissolved
because of disagreement between labor and management, while
a third was ended after a year of discussions resulted in agreement on only two small productivity improvement efforts. Most
of the others apparently died because of lack of interest.

The following paragraphs describe some examples of public
sector labor-management committees and the kinds of issues
they consider.[3] As the examples indicate, the powers of labor-

---

1. The emphasis here is on "in-house" committees focusing on the
concerns of government employees. Although some governments (such as
Jamestown, New York, and Chicago, Illinois) participate actively in joint
labor-management committees involving *private sector* unions and management, such committees are not relevant to this discussion.

2. U.S. Department of Labor, Bureau of Labor Statistics, *Characteristics of Agreements in State and Local Governments January 1, 1974*,
Bulletin 1861 (Washington, D.C., 1975), p. 18.

3. For a description of other public and private sector joint labor-
management committees, see National Center for Productivity and Quality of Working Life, *Directory of Labor-Management Committees* (Washington, D.C.), Edition 1 (October 1976) and Edition 2 (Spring 1978);
also, National Commission on Productivity and Work Quality, *Labor-
Management Committees in the Public Sector* (Washington, D.C., November 1975).

Exhibit 23
PUBLIC SECTOR LABOR-MANAGEMENT COMMITTEES
(As of March 1978)

Jurisdictions Reporting Use	Existing (E) or Terminated (T)	Comments/Notes
Ann Arbor, Mich.	T	Involved transit authority and transit workers.
Champaign, Ill.	E	Four committees: fire, police, plumbers, other workers.
Chatauqua County, N.Y.	E	Committees for public works, social services, county home, buildings and grounds, and health services departments.
Cincinnati, Ohio	E	Highway maintenance. Explicit focus on improving productivity.
Columbus, Ohio	E	Citywide. Explicit focus on productivity, incentives, and quality of working life.
Cumberland, Md.	E	Public works.
Dade County, Fla.	T	Police.
Dayton, Ohio	E	Public works. Productivity focus.
Decatur, Ill.	E	Two committees—police, all others. Productivity focus.
Del City, Okla.	E	Firefighters. Emphasis on health, safety, and training.
Denver, Colo.	E	Public school teachers, staff, and administrators.
Detroit, Mich.	E	Citywide, at discretion of each union local or city department.
District of Columbia	E	Committees for sanitation, maintenance, and water services. Explicit productivity focus in several.

(Continued)

Exhibit 23 (Continued)

Jurisdictions Reporting Use	Existing (E) or Terminated (T)	Comments/Notes
Dunkirk, N.Y.	E	Committees for public works, fire, and police.
Flint, Mich.	E	Hospital-wide committee in Hurley Medical Center. Has examined use of employee incentives.
Jamestown, N.Y.	E	Committees for public utilities, public works, Jamestown General Hospital, public school system. Explicit focus on quality of service and quality of working life.
Kansas City, Mo.	E	Citywide.
Memphis, Tenn.	E	Committees for sanitation and public works have been terminated. Another committee continues at the City of Memphis Hospital.
Milwaukee, Wis.	E	
Nassau County, Hempstead, North Hempstead, and Oyster Bay, N.Y.	T	Part of Multi-Municipality Productivity Project. Explicit focus on productivity and employee incentives.
New York, N.Y.	E	Citywide joint productivity council; committees in most departments, transit authority, housing authority, etc. Includes explicit emphasis on incentives and productivity improvement.
Niagara County, N.Y.	E	Two committees. Emphasis on safety and similar issues.
Ocean County, N.J.	T	Involved 12 unions. Explicit productivity focus.

(Continued)

Exhibit 23 (Continued)

Jurisdictions Reporting Use	Existing (E) or Terminated (T)	Comments/Notes
Oklahoma City, Okla.	E	Fire department. Emphasis on training.
Orange County, N.Y.	E	
Pima County, Ariz.	E	Countywide. Emphasis on training, job enrichment, and employee incentives.
Prince George's County, Md.	E	Licenses and permits department. Examined job redesign for building inspectors.
Rochester, N.Y.	E	Three committees: fire, police, and one covering most other employees.
Rockville, Md.	T	Parks and recreation, public works. Explicit productivity focus (to implement shared savings bonus plan).
San Diego, Calif.	E	Sanitation, vehicle maintenance. Focus on productivity and improving the quality of working life.
Savannah, Ga.	E	
Seattle, Wash.	E	Fire and police.
Seattle and Other Cities in State of Washington	E	Nursing practices committees focus on effectiveness of service in over 18 area hospitals.
Shelby County, Tenn.	E	Shelby County Hospital and five unions.
Springfield, Ohio	E	Five committees (police, fire, etc.). Focus on productivity, job redesign, and improving the quality of working life.

(Continued)

Exhibit 23 (Continued)

Jurisdictions Reporting Use	Existing (E) or Terminated (T)	Comments/Notes
Tacoma, Wash.	E	Committee in Electrical Division since 1962. Explicit focus on productivity. Another committee covers most city departments and their employees.
Troy, Mich.	E	Public works. Explicit focus on work methods, safety training, job enrichment, productivity, and quality of working life.
Tucson, Ariz.	T	Covered 300 of 4,000 city employees.
Urbana, Ill.	T	Expired after a few meetings.
Wahiawa, Hawaii	E	Wahiawa General Hospital.
Wichita, Kan.	E	Committee involves one union representing one-third of the city's employees. Explicit focus on productivity, employee incentives, training, and performance appraisal.
State of Alaska	E	Teaching staff at University of Alaska.
State of Connecticut	E	Statewide. Explicit focus on training, safety, employee incentives, and quality of working life.
State of Florida	E	Human Services Unit (state hospitals and correctional facilities).
State of Nevada	E	Statewide. Explicit focus on productivity, performance standards and appraisals, and performance-based incentives.

(Continued)

Exhibit 23 (Continued)

Jurisdictions Reporting Use	Existing (E) or Terminated (T)	Comments/Notes
State of New York	T	Part of shared savings effort.
State of Washington	E	Two distinct efforts: — 22 labor-management committees involving state government employees (since 1953). — Committees involving transit workers and the Metropolitan Seattle Transit and Wastewater Facility (a regional, state-run agency).
State of Wisconsin	E	Statewide. Includes shared savings effort.

management committees vary considerably from one jurisdiction to the next.

Tacoma, Washington. In Tacoma, Washington, management and labor in the electrical division of the Department of Public Utilities have used a joint committee to examine such subjects as safety, employee examinations, job training, and employee health and welfare. Labor representatives of the committee were elected from each job classification (e.g., lineman, dispatcher). The committee was given the power to implement the recommendations of its subcommittees upon approval of the full committee.

Seattle, Washington. In Seattle and other cities in the state of Washington, two kinds of labor-management committees involving hospital management and nurses have dealt with various work-related matters. In conference committees, nurses and management have explored ways to give the nurses a greater voice in hospital administrative matters. Nursing practice committees have concentrated on such issues as limiting the legal liability of nurses and improving the quality of patient care. These joint committees usually have had advisory powers only.

In Memphis, Tennessee, the city government and the local public employee union formed joint labor-management committees to examine operating problems (e.g., equipment maintenance), health, safety, and sanitary matters. In Denver, joint committees of administrators and teachers have met to consider and resolve various professional issues, such as changes in school curricula. And in Decatur, Illinois, joint "productivity workshops" have been held. A workshop with members of the police union, for instance, dealt with abuses of sick leave and how to provide police services during a shortage of police personnel.

A number of labor-management committees have looked into the possibility of improving employee motivation. Committees in Columbus, Ohio; Flint, Michigan; Nassau County, New York, and three of its towns; New York City; Pima County, Arizona; Rockville, Maryland; Troy, Michigan; Wichita, Kansas and the states of Connecticut, Nevada, New York, and Wisconsin have examined ways to provide employee incentives based on performance. In Wichita and the state of Nevada, committees have looked into employee performance appraisal procedures; and in Pima County, Arizona, Prince George's County, Maryland, and Springfield, Ohio, joint labor-management committees have looked into ways to redesign jobs. Indeed, many joint labor-management committees are committed to the general goal of improving the quality of working life for employees.

The Impact of Joint Labor-Management Committees. As with most of the job enrichment approaches discussed here, systematic and objective evaluations of the impact of joint labor-management committees on effectiveness, efficiency, and job satisfaction are hard to come by.[4] The following discussion relies heavily on interviews with representatives of joint committees in Decatur, Illinois, and Tacoma, Washington, as well as some published materials, in particular a report by the National Commission on Productivity and Work Quality.[5]

---

4. Some evaluative information should be forthcoming from an examination of nine public sector labor-management committees being conducted by the University of Pennsylvania and jointly sponsored by the National Center for Productivity and Quality of Working Life, the U.S. Department of Housing and Urban Development, and the U.S. Department of Labor. See "Improving Productivity and Quality of Worklife in the Public Sector: Pioneering Initiatives in Labor-Management Cooperation," second report on Project Network, Management and Behavioral Science Center, University of Pennsylvania (Philadelphia, Pennsylvania, July 15, 1978).

5. *Labor-Management Committees in the Public Sector.*

One of the subjects often addressed by labor-management committees is safety and its relationship to work practices. In Memphis, Tennessee, for example, the attention given to safety by labor-management committees in the various departments of the city government has reportedly resulted in the purchasing of safer equipment, better maintenance of existing equipment, and investigation of accidents to determine ways to prevent them in the future. Such attention to safety can be expected to have a positive effect on overall efficiency.

The District of Columbia's Department of General Services reported productivity improvements following establishment of a joint labor-management committee. Committee discussions were said to have resulted in the gradual acquisition of newer, safer, and more efficient equipment and gradual reductions in injury and accident rates.

Productivity improvements were also reported from the efforts of a joint committee in the New York City Transit Authority to improve bus and subway car maintenance, scheduling, and availability, as well as driver courtesy. Specific projects included changing certain maintenance and inspection procedures for buses and subway cars, installing more effective attendance and sick leave controls, revising work standards through the use of union-management teams, and encouraging improved driver courtesy. Among the improvements reported were a 66 percent increase in the efficiency of the subway car "wheel-trueing" operation, a 58 percent reduction in road failures for buses, and a 63 percent reduction in the need for maintenance personnel.[6]

In Cincinnati, a joint labor-management committee was credited with rescheduling highway maintenance crews, substituting labor-saving trucks, and increasing work output, despite reductions in personnel.[7]

In Prince George's County, Maryland, committee discussions prompted the Department of Licenses and Permits to consolidate inspections (a form of job redesign). Inspectors were given responsibility for handling a variety of building inspections, and their fears about job security were allayed with the aid of the committee.[8]

---

6. Ibid., pp. 14-19.
7. "Bill Donaldson Shakes Up Cincinnati," *LRMS Newsletter*, vol. 9, no. 11 (November 1978), p. 6.
8. Sam Zagoria, "Labor-Management Committees," in *Productivity—A Positive Route*, Labor-Management Relations Service (Washington, D.C., January 1978).

The effect of joint labor-management committees on employee job satisfaction is similarly undocumented, although informal reports suggest that some committees have made a significant impact. In Decatur, for example, a joint labor-management effort successfully curtailed sick leave abuse by persuading the union to urge members to be more careful regarding use of sick leave. In Springfield, Ohio, discussions by a joint committee impelled the Sanitation Department to experiment with job redesign—allowing members of two-person waste collection teams to alternate between driving and collecting trash. The result was said to have been increased cooperation among employees, as well as reduced absenteeism and tardiness.

On the other hand, a survey of participants from New York City's joint labor-management committees indicated considerable dissatisfaction with the effort, especially on the part of labor. Forty-four percent of the respondents felt that the program was inequitable, and two-thirds of the labor representatives responding felt that the committees would disband after the current contract expired.[9] Much of this dissatisfaction can probably be traced to the role forced upon the committees by the city's financial problems and the state and federal governments. The committees were seen by labor primarily as a way of identifying and authorizing changes that would save money, not for soliciting worker input or contributing to improved job satisfaction.[10]

Many joint labor-management committees, however, appear to have had a distinctly positive effect on the relationship between employee associations or unions and management. Committees in Tacoma, Washington, and the District of Columbia were among several reporting that their creation led to greater trust, diminished antagonism, and greater understanding of the need for mutual efforts to achieve goals. Joint committees have also been credited with allowing both sides to deal with troublesome issues early, before they could lead to confrontation. For instance, joint labor-management committees in Cincinnati and Kansas City have been credited with producing a significant reduction in the number and seriousness of formal grievances. Joint committees also seem to have eased the job of some union

---

9. Anna C. Goldoff and David C. Tatage, "Union-Management Cooperation in New York," *Public Productivity Review*, vol. 3, no. 2 (Summer/Fall 1978), pp. 35-47.
10. Gotbaum and Handman, "A Conversation."

officials. In Tacoma, for example, the joint committee in the Department of Public Utilities is reported to have made the job of the business manager of the electrical employees union a little easier. Union members were reported to be more content knowing that they had a representative who participated in decision making, even when the actual decision was not to their liking.

At the same time, however, it should be noted that in at least three instances joint committees were not able to temper relations between labor and management. The problems which arose in connection with New York City's joint labor-management committees have already been described. In Wisconsin and New York State, joint committees established to identify potential productivity improvements for shared savings plans were unable to agree on any potential improvements. In New York State, in fact, the union used the contract's productivity clause as a means of preventing any change in employee assignments or work procedures. The union contended that such changes could be made only through the joint committee because they were possible sources of productivity savings that could lead to bonuses for employees.[11]

Participative Decision Making

In addition to joint labor-management committees, which give employee associations or unions a formal role in management decision making, there are a variety of other techniques that give employees a way to influence the work process. These range from informal efforts to solicit employees' ideas to giving employees partial or total responsibility for decisions about their own work, or even appointing employees to policy-making bodies. Thus, participation can take many forms, ranging from a purely advisory role to shared or full responsibility for making decisions.[12]

In all, sixteen such programs have been identified, fourteen of them in cities and one each in a county and a state government (see Exhibit 24). Seven others have been terminated. Four of the terminated efforts were designed to address specific prob-

---

11. Osterman, "Productivity Bargaining."
12. For a discussion of the various forms of participation, see Sherry R. Arnstein, "A Ladder of Citizen Participation," *Journal of the American Institute of Planners*, vol. 35, no. 4 (July 1969), pp. 216-224.

Exhibit 24
MISCELLANEOUS EFFORTS TO INCREASE PARTICIPATION
(As of March 1978)

Jurisdictions Reporting Use	Existing (E) or Terminated (T)	Comments/Notes [1]
Altamont Springs, Fla.	E	Personnel Administration Board includes three elected employee representatives.
Boston, Mass.	E	Management Council composed of 13 middle managers, elected by their peers to address the problems of middle management.
Dallas, Tex.	T	Participative management in Police Department.
Greensboro, N.C.	E	Employee "personnel" committee in public works, with elected representatives.
Lakewood, Colo.	T	Participative management in Police Department.
Kansas City, Mo.	T	Two programs: — Employees in Sanitation Department given task of developing effective safety incentive plan. — Department heads, analysts, and line employees involved in developing street maintenance work standards.
Little Rock, Ark.	E	Increased participation in Sanitation Department via meetings, surveys, etc.
Maitland, Fla.	E	Police review board includes line employees.

(Continued)

Exhibit 24 (Continued)

Jurisdictions Reporting Use	Existing (E) or Terminated (T)	Comments/Notes [1]
Orange (city), Calif.	E	Wide variety of efforts to involve police in decision making, sharing responsibilities, etc.
Portsmouth, Va.	E	Police employees organized groups to explore alternate patrol strategies.
Redondo Beach, Calif.	T	Police chief solicited and tested ideas from patrolmen on ways to reduce crime.
Scottsdale, Ariz.	T	Recreation department employees invited to participate in design of park facilities.
Simi Valley, Calif.	E	Top management team expanded to include line employees. Police designed own 4–10 plan. Line employees contributed to budget preparation and budget decisions.
Sunnyvale, Calif.	E	Line employees added to Manager's Advisory Council.
Tacoma, Wash.	E	Formal feedback sessions on employee survey results; employee ideas on problems are encouraged.
Vancouver, Wash.	E	Management "invites" employee participation.
Vigo County, Ind.	E	Participative management in library via employee "orbits."
Waco, Tex.	E	

(Continued)

Exhibit 24 (Continued)

Jurisdictions Reporting Use	Existing (E) or Terminated (T)	Comments/Notes[1]
Westminster, Calif.	E	Police "policy discussion teams"—employees select representatives, consensus required to act.
Wheaton, Ill.	E	Police sergeants and a patrolman included on committee to implement results of management study.
State of California	E	Highway patrol involves line personnel in planning, execution, and review of decisions.
State of Ohio	T	Experiment to increase participation in work decisions by maintenance crews in the Department of Highways.

1. Many other programs include at least some increased participation, e.g., the performance bonus plan developed in Helena, Mont. (see Chapter 4), and the employee task forces in Leavenworth, Kan., and the Kansas City, Mo. Police Department (see Chapter 20). This exhibit does not include management-by-objectives programs, although these too may significantly increase participation.

lems and were phased out when the problems were resolved. A fifth effort died after the agency director retired. The other two (both in police departments) encountered a number of problems and were abandoned when new police chiefs took over. As the following examples show, several jurisdictions have tried some rather innovative ways of giving employees a greater role in decisions hitherto reserved for management.

Scottsdale, Arizona. In Scottsdale, a team of employees was established to advise the architect designing a new Park Department building. The team consisted of all those who would work in the building, from the recreation superintendent to the janitor. The Scottsdale Police Department also has involved employees in the decision-making process: patrol officers have participated in interviewing applicants and choosing new recruits.[13]

California. Another law enforcement organization that has used participative decision making is the California Highway Patrol. In that organization, management established three categories of decision making. Category 1 included "autocratic" decisions made by management alone, Category 2 included "consultative" decisions made by management after obtaining employees' opinions, and Category 3 consisted of "democratic" decisions made by an informal vote of all employees. An example of a "Category 3" decision was the determination of whether officers should be required to wear hats in public (the employees voted no).

Little Rock, Arkansas. Little Rock's Sanitation Department introduced a form of participativo decision making to ease the tensions caused by a strike in 1974. Employees were given the opportunity to meet weekly with the department director to offer suggestions, register complaints, and provide advice on such matters as the purchase of new equipment.

Vigo County, Indiana. In 1969, the Vigo County Public Library in Terre Haute established an "orbital organization" for its librarians, clerks, and supervisory personnel. Every full-time employee was assigned to one of ten groups or "orbits," each of which usually covered an entire service unit. Each member of the department's executive committee served as a regular member of at least one orbit. However, within an orbit, all decisions had to be reached by consensus.[14]

Lakewood, Colorado. Participatory management was introduced in Lakewood's newly organized police department in 1970 as one of several innovations. All police employees in Lakewood were allowed to attend staff meetings at which important department issues were debated, and each employee in attendance had an equal vote. At one point, patrol officers actually elected their own watch commanders. The use of participatory management

13. William V. Donaldson, "Participatory Management—Employees Are Creative!" Strengthening Local Government Through Better Labor Relations No. 16, Labor-Management Relations Service (Washington, D.C., June 1973).

14. See Greiner, Bell, and Hatry, *Employee Incentives*, pp. 42-43; and Edward N. Howard, "The Orbital Organization," *Library Journal*, vol. 95, no. 9 (May 1, 1970), pp. 1712-1715.

declined, however, as officers from traditional departments joined Lakewood's department, and the approach was abandoned after the arrival of a new chief of police in 1971.[15]

Dallas, Texas. Dallas appears to have had an experience similar to that of Lakewood. In early 1972, the chief of the Dallas Police Department tried to introduce a form of participatory management. The objective was to have assistant chiefs jointly make decisions which traditionally had been reserved for the chief. However, the assistant chiefs had not been prepared for their new roles or for the process of making group decisions, and the overall decision-making process began to bog down. In fact, because the assistant chiefs were often unwilling to delegate responsibility where necessary, decision making actually became more centralized than it had been before. The use of participatory management was discontinued following the chief's resignation in October 1973.[16]

Other governments have tried to encourage employee involvement by presenting problems or issues directly to employees as a group for resolution.

Kansas City, Missouri. After many unsuccessful programs to reduce accidents, the Department of Public Works in Kansas City asked its employees to try to find a solution themselves. The result was an employee-designed safety incentive plan which incorporated competition plus individual and group incentive awards.[17]

Orange, California. In the city of Orange, police officers were given collective responsibility for handling numerous matters, ranging from the purchase of new patrol cars to the design of a protective console for the special equipment installed in those cars and the development of a training program for new officers. (The training program was developed not by supervisors, as is usual in police departments, but by patrol officers, on the assumption that the latter would be best equipped to prepare new recruits for what to expect on the beat.)

---

15. Gerald W. Garner, "Lakewood, Colorado: Evolution of an Innovative Police Agency," *The Police Chief*, vol. 45, no. 11 (November 1978), pp. 57-65.

16. Mary Ann Wycoff and George L. Kelling, *The Dallas Experience: Organizational Reform* (Washington, D.C.: The Police Foundation, 1978).

17. Myron D. Calkins, "A Municipal Safety Program That Works," *The American City* (August 1971), pp. 67-68.

A number of governments have established advisory committees of employees or employee representatives that meet regularly to discuss various issues.

> *Greensboro, North Carolina.* The Department of Public Works in Greensboro established six such committees, one in each of its divisions. The participating employees were elected by their peers. The committees discussed and made recommendations on a variety of issues, ranging from work uniforms and vacation schedules to the introduction of a four-day work week. However, personnel matters, such as terminations and promotions, were excluded on the grounds that they represented management prerogatives.

Other governments have used less formal approaches to obtain greater employee involvement. The police chief of Redondo Beach, California, circulated a memo asking employees for ideas on ways to reduce crime.[18] Kansas City's Streets Division introduced a series of regular "information meetings" between management and field employees to provide for the exchange of ideas, concerns, and suggestions, especially regarding the issue of reintroducing work standards.[19] And Tacoma, Washington, used an employee attitude survey to solicit employee input, both through the survey responses and during meetings with small groups of workers to discuss the survey results.

The Impact of Participative Decision Making. Formal evaluations of three participative decision-making programs—those of Little Rock, Arkansas, the state of Ohio, and Kansas City, Missouri—were found in the course of this study.[20] In addition, information on the programs in Greensboro, North Carolina, and the state of California was sought through telephone interviews.

Although the data were far from complete, there were indications that some of these programs had a positive impact on

---

18. Edward M. Glaser, *Productivity Gains Through Worklife Improvements* (New York: Harcourt, Brace, and Jovanovich, 1976), pp. 30-32.

19. Greiner et al., *Monetary Incentives*, p. 15.

20. Evaluations of two federal efforts to increase employee participation have also been published. See Arthur A. Thompson, "Employee Participation in Decision Making: The TVA Experience," in *A New World: Readings in Modern Public Personnel Management,* ed. Jay M. Shafritz (Chicago, Illinois: International Personnel Management Association, 1975), pp. 80-86; and Jane Presley and Sally Keen, "Better Meetings Lead to Increased Productivity: A Case Study," *Management Review,* vol. 64, no. 4 (April 1975), pp. 16-22.

employee efficiency. In Kansas City—where employees in the Public Works Department were asked to devise a safety program —the resulting system of monetary incentives helped, in the first year, to reduce vehicular accidents by 49 percent, bodily injuries by 41 percent, lost work-hours by 72 percent, and the cost of vehicle repairs by 23 percent. Savings of about $5,800 were reported, compared to costs of about $1,900 in bonuses and extra vacation time.[21]

But in the Ohio experiment it was found that varying the amount of decision-making responsibility given to six highway construction and maintenance crews produced no statistically significant improvements in productivity.[22] Two of the two-man crews were given complete responsibility for their work schedule, while the other four crews in the experiment were given lesser degrees of responsibility. The crews with the most responsibility, however, consistently performed poorly. Although the findings cannot be considered conclusive, given the brevity of the experiment ($5\frac{1}{2}$ months) and the small number of employees involved (twelve), those who conducted the experiment surmised that increased responsibility without monetary incentives may not be enough to improve productivity.

Data were not available on the efficiency impact of the California Highway Patrol's program, but a representative of the agency reported that the number of patrol officer accidents had declined since the start of the effort to increase employee involvement in decision making. Another efficiency improvement resulted from the suggestion of some officers that traffic cones instead of flares be used during daytime hours. This resulted in reported savings of about $16,000 a year. Highway patrol officers also reported a quadrupling of services to motorists and an increase in the level of highway law enforcement, despite attrition that had reduced the number of uniformed officers by about 300 during the three years preceding the program.

In Little Rock the average number of citizen complaints about trash collection fell from a high of forty-three per day in the second quarter of 1974 to 5.5 in the first quarter of 1975 and 1.5 in the second quarter. The decline followed the introduction of weekly meetings between the department director

21. Calkins, "Municipal Safety Program," p. 68.
22. Reed M. Powell and John L. Schlacter, "Participative Management—A Panacea?" *Academy of Management Journal*, vol. 14 (June 1971), pp. 165-171. Significance was measured at the 5 percent level.

and sanitation employees. In the meantime, the percentage of routes completed on time increased from 50 percent to 98 percent.[23]

The impact of increased participation on employee job satisfaction was mixed. In Little Rock, a survey taken before the program showed that job satisfaction among sanitation workers was lower than in any other department for twenty-three of twenty-six job satisfaction categories; a survey two years later showed a notable increase in satisfaction. The mean job satisfaction score for fourteen survey respondents increased from 2.48 to 3.83, on a scale on which "1" was "very dissatisfied" and "5" was "very satisfied." Following introduction of the program, Little Rock also reported an 81 percent decline in the number of unauthorized absences among sanitation employees. (However, it should be noted that Little Rock's participative decision-making program was introduced after, and as a result of, the tensions caused by a strike. Thus, it is not clear how many of these improvements would have occurred even without the new program.)

In the Ohio experiment the researchers found that morale improved significantly among the two crews given the greatest degree of responsibility but not among crews given less responsibility. For five of the six crews, however, absenteeism increased during the experiment. (The researchers did not indicate which group showed no increase in absenteeism.)

Several other governments have provided subjective assessments of the impact of increased participation on employee attitudes, and the results are quite similar. For instance, increased inventiveness and initiative on the part of employees was reported in connection with the programs in California, Greensboro, and Little Rock. (In the latter case, an increase in the number of employee suggestions was noted.) Greensboro also reported improvements in employee enthusiasm and cooperation.

Some of those who participated in Greensboro's employee advisory committees, however, felt the committees did not have enough authority, although management did implement a committee suggestion for a four-day-a-week, ten-hour-a-day, work

---

23. Howard F. Day, "Job Satisfaction, Motivation, and Job Performance: A Case Study," Department of Personnel, City of Little Rock, Arkansas (February 1976).

schedule. In the long run, however, an official of the department felt the committees had improved job satisfaction.

One problem in the California Highway Patrol program was that some supervisors viewed participative decision making as a reduction of their importance, and they began to worry about their job security. Supervisors also were concerned that they would be judged on the degree of participation among those they supervised. In addition, a few Highway Patrol employees reportedly were unhappy because some of their suggestions were rejected. The extent to which these concerns affected overall job satisfaction could not be determined, however.

Very little information is available regarding the effect of these participative decision-making programs on relations between labor and management. In Greensboro, where the employee committees were created one year after a strike of sanitation workers, relations appeared to have generally improved. In Little Rock, where the program was also begun after a strike, no further problems were reported. But it is difficult to say to what extent the peaceful relations between labor and management in both places were attributable to increasing employee access to the decision-making process. The California Highway Patrol program apparently had no impact on labor-management relations, although the various associations representing department employees endorsed participative management as a good idea.

Chapter 22
JOB ROTATION

Job rotation enriches work by adding to its variety. In some cases it also provides employees with new skills. This study concentrated on job rotation programs conducted on a regular, systematic basis. Thus, the statistics and discussion presented below exclude ad hoc rotation (i.o., the assignment of an employee to take care of the duties of another employee temporarily absent because of vacation, illness, or some other reason). Also excluded are rotational programs for training purposes, such as programs in which management interns are rotated through a variety of posts before being given a permanent assignment.

State and Local Government Job Rotation Programs

A total of thirty-one systematic job rotation programs were identified, twenty-nine of them in cities and two in county governments (see Exhibit 25). No examples of job rotation at the state level were found. One additional program is known to have been terminated (because grant funds ran out). It involved the rotation of police officers among six city police departments in California.

Of the thirty-one programs, eighteen involved job rotation within departments, nine provided for rotation between departments within the jurisdiction, and four rotated employees between separate jurisdictions. In all, over twelve governments (including the six in the terminated California program for police officers) were involved in the interjurisdictional rotation programs.

Exhibit 25
JOB ROTATION PROGRAMS
(As of March 1978)

Scope	Jurisdictions Reporting Use [1]	Comments/Notes
Within a Department	Claremont, Calif.	Police, fire, parks, administrative services.
	Elmhurst, Ill.	Police: detectives, juvenile officers.
	Eureka, Calif.	Police.
	Fayetteville, N.C.	Police, fire, clerks (finance department), sanitation, streets.
	Greenville, S.C.	Police: detectives.
	Jersey City, N.J.	Finance Department.
	Los Angeles County, Calif.	Several departments.
	Miami, Fla.	Parks, other departments.
	Ogden, Utah	Police.
	Pacifica, Calif.	Police.
	Pueblo, Colo.	Police and several other departments.
	Richland County, S.C.	Finance, personnel, public works, clerk of courts.
	San Jose, Calif.	Police; combined with job redesign.
	Santa Ana, Calif.	Police, fire—mostly for training purposes.
	Simi Valley, Calif.	Police.
	Tyler, Tex.	Clerks, keypunch personnel.
	Whittier, Calif.	Police.
	Woodbridge, N.J.	Clerks (in all departments).
Between Departments	Cincinnati, Ohio	Middle managers rotated into city manager's office for two-month periods.
	Eugene, Oreg.	Employees serve as temporary community relations officers.
	Fort Wayne, Ind.	Top 20 department heads rotate for one week.
	Glendale, Ariz.	Employees rotate into Personnel Department from other departments.

(Continued)

Exhibit 25 (Continued)

Scope	Jurisdictions Reporting Use [1]	Comments/Notes
	Jersey City, N.J.	Laborers and truck drivers from public works rotate into Director's Office as analysts.
	Long Beach, Calif.	Managers and supervisors rotate between departments.
	Simi Valley, Calif.	Department heads rotated; lower level managers rotate into city manager's office.
	Sunnyvale, Calif.	Supervisors and project directors rotate between departments. Public safety officers alternate in fire and police duties.
	Tacoma, Wash.	Middle managers rotate into city manager's office.
Between Cities [2]	Costa Mesa and Santa Ana, Calif.	Exchange parks and recreation supervisors.
	Farmer's Branch, Tex. and nearby towns	Employees work for other jurisdictions under contract, as needed.
	Fremont, Hollywood, Menlo Park, Oakland, Palo Alto, and San Jose, Calif.	Rotation of police officers between departments. (Program terminated.)
	Normal and Bloomington, Ill.	Cities share city manager and some staff.
	Placentia, Calif., and nearby cities.	Secretaries visit counterparts in other cities.

1. Cities where rotation is on an "as-needed" basis to cover for absentees or is part of an informal cross-training effort are excluded.
2. Note also that internships sponsored by the Labor-Management Relations Service and through other Intergovernmental Personnel Act grants provide rotational assignments at the federal, state, and local levels. In addition, many states have programs involving traveling city managers and other administrators ("circuit riders") who serve several small towns.

Police departments have used rotation programs more often than any other type of agency. Thirteen of the thirty-one programs (plus the terminated California experiment) involved police agencies. Other leading candidates for rotation were managers (seven programs), firefighters (four programs), and clerks (four programs). Of the nine programs that involved rotation between departments, six involved rotation of management personnel.

The job rotation programs involved as few as ten, and as many as seventy-seven, employees. The time spent by rotated employees in a given job ranged from a single month to as long as three years, and the criteria for selecting employees for rotation also varied. Some departments rotated employees automatically, according to a prescribed arrangement, while others chose the participants on the basis of such characteristics as adaptability, willingness to assume responsibility, and quality of work. In one police department the selection was made from among employees who ranked highest on the eligibility list for sergeant.

In some cases employees returned to their original jobs before being rotated to a different job. In others, employees moved through several jobs before returning to their original positions. Most of the time, job rotation involved moving to a job that ranked about the same as the employee's original one, but there were some cases in which rotation moved an employee to a job with increased responsibilities.

The following examples illustrate the great variety found among rotation programs in local governments.

Pacifica, California. The Police Department in Pacifica has regularly rotated all of its uniformed personnel (forty-three out of a total of fifty-three employees) since 1970. Captains rotate every two years among the department's three divisions, and sergeants also rotate every two years among such positions as watch commander, training sergeant, reserve commander, traffic sergeant, and detective sergeant. Patrol officers rotate about every six months among such assignments as detective, court officer, traffic officer, and crime prevention officer. In addition, patrol officers assigned to the city's police teams are encouraged to change beats every six months.

Sunnyvale, California. Sunnyvale has conducted an extensive rotation program focused primarily on management and supervisory personnel.[1] In 1973 the city's eight department directors were all assigned to other departments for a two-month period. The Fire Commander, for example, became the Building Inspection Superintendent, the Purchasing Agent became the Principal Librarian, and the Director of Public Works became Chief of the Public Safety Department. A year later, fifteen other managers (most of them division heads) also were given new assignments for a two-month period, and in 1975 the program was completed with the rotation of supervisors and administrative assistants for a period of six weeks.

In still another rotation program in Sunnyvale, employees of the city's Public Safety Department alternated annually between police and firefighter duties.[2]

Glendale, Arizona. Under this program, begun in 1971, firefighters, waste collection employees, and other line personnel In various departments were shifted into the personnel department for a period of three months. There, they were assigned increasingly complex tasks in personnel selection, such as analyzing employee examinations, designing personnel forms, and writing job specifications.

Claremont, California. The city of Claremont has introduced several types of job rotation into four of its departments. Employees in the parks division, for example, have rotated between mowing and other groundskeeping assignments; patrol officers and patrol sergeants have served as detectives for one- or two-month periods; fire-fighting personnel are rotated to different stations every two years, and many have served temporarily in higher posts. Rotation has also touched other positions, ranging from account clerk to planning director and deputy city manager.[3]

The terminated police officer rotation program already mentioned involved the six neighboring California police departments of Fremont, Hayward, Menlo Park, Oakland, Palo Alto, and

---

1. "Sunnyvale Rotates Supervisors for 'Total City' Approach," *LMRS Newsletter*, vol. 7, no. 3 (March 1976), p. 4.

2. Robert A. Platty, "Local Government Structure and Organization," a discussion paper published jointly by the National League of Cities, the International City Management Association, and the National Association of Counties (Washington, D.C., n.d.), p. 15.

3. See "Coast Cities Try Job Rotation," *LMRS Newsletter*, vol. 4, no. 7 (July 1973), p. 5.

San Jose.[4] During 1975 an officer from each department served as staff assistant to a police chief in a neighboring department. In their temporary assignments they dealt with issues ranging from budgetary procedures and performance appraisal to crime prevention and deployment of personnel.

The Impact of Job Rotation

Formal evaluations of the impact of job rotation on employee efficiency, effectiveness, and job satisfaction in the public sector are rare. In the course of this study, only one (inconclusive) effort at formal evaluation was found. We have also drawn on information available from published articles and from a series of interviews we undertook in 1974 with city officials associated with job rotation programs. In addition, we conducted one new interview on job rotation (with officials from Pacifica, California).

Evaluations of job rotation in the private sector are almost as rare as evaluations in the public sector, and they suggest some of the problems in determining the value of rotation. A recent study of job rotation in two clothing pattern plants, for example, showed that an increase in output was largely due to the so-called "Hawthorne effect"—the improvement that comes when employees realize they are the subjects of special attention.[5] Other private sector studies have shown that numerous factors impinge on the effects of job rotation and thus make it difficult to determine the specific impact of rotation itself.

Another recent study of some interest involved an assessment of job rotation among 155 infantry squad leaders in the Army. This study suggests that the success of rotation of supervisors in improving performance depends on the experience and psychological makeup of the supervisors.[6]

Among local governments, representatives of several jurisdictions could suggest only that job rotation may have con-

---

4. Victor Cizanckas et al., "Increased Regional Cooperation in Policing: The Bay Area Middle Management Exchange," *The Police Chief*, vol. 42, no. 11 (November 1975), pp. 22-23f.

5. Albert S. King, "Expectation Effects in Organization Change," *Administrative Science Quarterly*, vol. 19, no. 12 (June 1974), pp. 221-230.

6. Paul M. Bons and Fred E. Fiedler, "Changes in Organizational Leadership and the Behavior of Relationship- and Task-Motivated Leaders," *Administrative Science Quarterly*, vol. 21 (September 1976), pp. 453-473.

tributed to improved operations; the rationale was that rotating employees had taught them to do a greater variety of tasks and thereby facilitated flexibility in scheduling and contributed to smoother overall operations. Although officials in the Pacifica Police Department were able to point to statistics indicating higher productivity for the seven years since job rotation had been introduced there, they also noted that the department had undertaken several innovative programs in addition to job rotation. In fact, they suggested that there might even have been a temporary loss in productivity each time an employee was rotated to a new and unfamiliar position, but they had conducted no formal studies to find out how true this supposition might be.

Exchange of information and ideas was the major benefit most jurisdictions reported in connection with job rotation, but the effect of these exchanges on employee effectiveness and efficiency has not been objectively determined. Most jurisdictions using job rotation reported an increase in the innovativeness and creativity of the employees involved in those plans, especially when the rotation was between departments or jurisdictions. In Sunnyvale, California, the rotation of managers between departments reportedly encouraged a citywide rather than a departmental approach to problem solving. Rotation between jurisdictions appears to be an especially promising way for employees to learn new techniques while infusing new ideas into the department to which they are temporarily assigned. The largest program involving rotation between jurisdictions, that affecting six police departments in California, was said to have been particularly beneficial in terms of the exchange of ideas. The San Jose police officer who served in Fremont, for example, subsequently arranged meetings involving city planners and police officials from both cities at which Fremont officials explained their "Crime Prevention Through Physical Planning" program.

The impact of public sector job rotation on employee job satisfaction has not been formally evaluated. Subjective assessments by administrators in several cities, however, indicated that employees liked job rotation. In Pacifica, for example, officials reported that patrol officers often arrived at work earlier, stayed later, and sometimes worked on their days off after the introduction of job rotation—which was, as noted earlier, combined with other changes in departmental operations. Rotation also appeared to reduce the traditional barriers beween detectives, patrol officers, and traffic officers.

Officials of the Elmhurst, Illinois, Police Department reported that turnover and absenteeism were lower after the introduction of job rotation than they had been before. Here again, however, job rotation had not been the only change made. Elmhurst officials also reported that some employees developed a great liking for their new posts and disliked further rotation. A few employees and their immediate supervisors complained that the rotational periods were too short; as a result, the periods were increased from two years to three years.

Woodbridge, New Jersey, reported that younger employees generally liked job rotation more than older employees did. And an official of Fayetteville, North Carolina, indicated that employees felt job rotation gave them increased opportunities to broaden their experience and thus qualify for higher-level jobs. In Glendale, Arizona, conversely, it was reported that rotated employees had no greater success in obtaining higher posts than did employees who had not rotated.

The impact of job rotation on labor-management relations appears to have been quite limited in the public sector. The only place in which such a program was reported to have had an effect was Pacifica, where the police association argued during bargaining sessions that police officers should be paid more because they were doing more kinds of tasks following the introduction of job rotation. Management reported, however, that this argument had no overall impact on the outcome of the negotiations.

Chapter 23
JOB REDESIGN

Job redesign is essentially an effort to redefine the tasks assigned to the individual employee. In many instances, however, the distinction between job redesign and other types of enrichment is only one of degree, and the classification of any given program may sometimes appear arbitrary. This is especially true of programs that incorporate more than one approach to job enrichment. The establishment of police teams, for example, is one approach to enriching jobs, as discussed under Team Efforts (Chapter 20). It may or may not be combined with job redesign, for instance by giving patrol officers responsibility for conducting criminal investigations.

As of March 1978 a total of ninety-three state and local government programs, including eighty-two in cities, five in counties, and six in states, were reported to involve the two principal forms of job redesign, namely, job enlargement and job restructuring (see Exhibit 19). Twelve other programs were reported to be in the planning stage. Of the twenty-eight job redesign programs reported terminated, twenty involved attempts to establish the broadened position of "public safety officer" (which includes both police and fire responsibilities), while seven more involved other attempts to restructure police jobs. Police jobs have been involved in more than half of the state and local government job redesign efforts. Indeed, the creation of public safety officer positions was the single most popular type of job redesign.

These figures, however, should be viewed with caution. In many cases they are based on unverified reports by the jurisdictions themselves, and more reported examples of job redesign proved to be unfounded than did any other type of job enrichment examined in this study. Attempts to gain additional information on twenty-four reported job redesign efforts in the course of this study revealed that eight did not exist at all.

Job Enlargement

Job enlargement ("horizontal loading") is one of the two types of job redesign most frequently encountered in the public sector. It involves an increase in the *number* of tasks, responsibilities, or operations performed by a worker, but with little corresponding increase in the skill levels, autonomy, or decision-making scope associated with the work. Job enlargement thus does not tend to deepen an employee's responsibility for his work but instead widens the number of tasks for which he is held responsible.

Closely related to job enlargement is the practice of cross-training employees to perform a number of diverse tasks. This is often the first step in enlarging an employee's job.

Some sixty job enlargement programs were reported to be in operation, fifty-eight in cities and two in counties (see Exhibit 26). Two other programs were reported to be in the planning stage, and twenty—all involving the use of public safety officers—had been terminated.

Of the sixty job enlargement programs, thirty-six involved the creation of public safety officers. Under these programs, police officers are trained to provide certain fire suppression services necessary at the scene of a fire while firefighters are trained to provide certain police patrol and support functions when they are not needed for fighting fires.

There have been numerious variations in public safety officer programs.[1] In Center Line, Michigan, for instance, police

---

1. See, for instance, Esai Berenbaum, *Police-Fire Consolidation: A Case Study*, Management Information Service Report, vol. 6, no. 3-A, International City Management Association (Washington, D.C., March 1974); Marie Hayman, *Public Safety Departments: Combining the Police and Fire Functions*, Management Information Service Report, vol. 8, no. 7, International City Management Association (Washington, D.C., July 1976); City of Flagstaff, Arizona, "Police/Fire Specialists," Report no. 19232, Report Clearinghouse, Management Information Service, International City Management Association (Washington, D.C., circa 1975); James H. Barnett, "A Study of Police and Fire Department Integration in Selected Cities of North America," Special Report No. 35, Bureau of Governmental Affairs, University of North Dakota (Grand Forks, Janu-

officers could volunteer to be firefighters, and the fire department operated the night desk for the police department. In El Dorado, Kansas, public safety officers handled all crime patrol, firefighting, and traffic control functions. And in Plainfield, New Jersey, fire safety patrols comprised of public safety officers handled fire inspection and fire prevention as well as firefighting, crime surveillance, and police patrol duties.

A number of other job enlargement programs have involved expansion of the duties of firefighters.[2] In general, these efforts have focused on giving firefighters additional tasks to make more productive use of their time when they are not fighting fires. In Glenview, Illinois, firefighters operated the municipal print shop. In Mesa, Arizona, firefighters patroled their areas in distinctively marked vehicles to provide assistance to stranded motorists and others in need of help. In Seattle, Washington, and Shorewood, Wisconsin, firefighting personnel served on so-called "neighborhood fire patrols," conducting a variety of fire prevention activities. And in Springfield, Illinois, firefighters conducted fire safety and building code inspections.

Indeed, it is now common practice to expand the tasks of firefighters to include regular fire code inspections of businesses, schools, and apartment buildings (single-family homes are usually excluded from regular inspection). A 1977 survey of fire departments serving populations of 25,000 or more found that among the responding departments that conducted regular inspections, 460 (65 percent) used firefighters to supplement their full-time inspection personnel. Forty-three departments (6 percent of those responding) reported that firefighters made all of the department's inspections.[3]

---

ary 1973); Gordon K. Zenk, "Police-Fire Consolidation," *Nation's Cities*, vol. 10, no. 6 (June 1972), pp. 27-29f; David H. Olson, "Integrated Police and Fire Service: Gladstone Experience," *Missouri Municipal Review*, vol. 39, no. 4 (April 1974), pp. 9-11; Citizens Research Council of Michigan, *Saving Taxpayer Dollars Through Consolidated Police and Fire Services*, Memorandum No. 227 (Detroit, Michigan, October 1975); and "Police and Fire Consolidation: In the Interest of Public Safety," *Uptown*, Municipal Association of South Carolina (February 1978).

2. For an extensive list of additional duties that might be assigned to firefighters, see Institute for Local Self-Government, *Public Safety Inspection Consolidation*, p. 27.

3. John R. Hall, Jr., et al., "Fire Code Inspection Practices: Results of a 1977 Survey," project report to the National Fire Prevention and Control Administration (Washington, D.C.: The Urban Institute, March 1978).

Exhibit 26

JOB ENLARGEMENT PROGRAMS
(As of March 1978)

Type of Program	Jurisdictions Reporting Use	Existing (E) or Terminated (T)	Comments/Notes
Public Safety Officers [1]	Aiken, S.C.	E	
	Bayonne, N.J.	T	Dropped before implementing.
	Beverly Hills, Mich.	E	
	Boulder, Colo.	E	
	Brown Deer, Wis.	E	
	Buena Park, Calif.	T	
	Cayce, S.C.	E	
	Center Line, Mich.	E	Police volunteer as firefighters; firefighters operate police night desk.
	Champaign, Ill.	T	
	Chesapeake, Va.	E	Primarily cross-training.
	Claremont, Calif.	E	
	Clifton, N.J.	E	
	Dearborn, Mich.	E	
	Des Peres, Mo.	E	
	Durham, N.C.	E	Extensive evaluation.
	El Dorado, Kan.	E	Public safety officers perform all crime patrol, fire, and traffic control functions.
	Evanston, Ill.	E	Cross-training and police-fire cooperation.
	Farmington, Mich.	E	
	Fayetteville, N.C.	E	Public safety personnel work only at airport.

Exhibit 26 (Continued)

Public Safety Officers (continued)	Flagstaff, Ariz.	E	
	Fort Lauderdale, Fla.	E	Public safety inspection teams cross-trained in crime and fire prevention.
	Fox Point, Wis.	E	
	Fraser, Mich.	E	
	Fremont, Calif.	T	
	Gladstone, Mo.	E	
	Glencoe, Ill.	E	
	Grosse Point Woods, Mich.	E	
	Grosse Point Shores, Mich.	E	First public safety officer program in U.S.
	Hawthorne, Calif.	T	Now involves management only.
	Hollywood, Fla.	T	
	Huntington Woods, Mich.	E	
	Lincoln, Neb.	T	
	Maryville, Mo.	E	
	Melvindale, Mich.	T	
	Mexico, Mo.	E	
	Monterey Park, Calif.	T	
	North Augusta, S.C.	E	
	Oak Park, Mich.	E	
	Oakwood, Ohio	E	
	Oregon City, Oreg.	T	
	Park Forest, Ill.	T	
	Peoria, Ill.	T	

(Continued)

Exhibit 26 (Continued)

Type of Program	Jurisdictions Reporting Use	Existing (E) or Terminated (T)	Comments/Notes
Public Safety Officers (Continued)	Plainfield, N.J.	E	
	Port Royal, S.C.	E	
	St. Petersburg, Fla.	T	
	San Diego, Calif.	T	Dropped before implementation.
	Sanger, Calif.	T	
	San Marino, Calif.	T	
	Sewickley Heights, Pa.	E	
	Shorewood, Wis.	T	Six-month experiment in which firefighters performed certain police auxiliary duties.
	South Bend, Ind.	T	Injunction obtained by firefighters and upheld in court.
	Spartanburg, S.C.	T	
	Sunnyvale, Calif.	E	
	Waukegan, Ill.	T	
	Winston-Salem, N.C.	E	
	Wisconsin Rapids, Wis.	E	
	Glenview, Ill.	E	Firefighters operate municipal printing press.
	Mesa, Ariz.	E	Firefighters staff mobile units to help motorists.
Expansion of Duties of Firefighters[2]	Plainfield, N.J.	Planned	Firefighters would conduct fire and building code inspection.
	San Jose, Calif.	Planned	Firefighters would conduct neighborhood preservation and rehabilitation inspections.

Exhibit 26 (Continued)

Seattle, Wash.	E	Firefighters staff neighborhood fire prevention patrol.
Shorewood, Wis.	E	Roving firefighter patrols check for fires, false alarms, and fire code violations.
Springfield, Ill.	E	Firefighters conduct fire safety and building code inspections.
Generalist Building Inspectors		
Berkeley, Calif.	E	
Dallas, Tex.	E	Involves several departments, including consumer affairs.
Detroit, Mich.	E	
Los Angeles, Calif.	E	
Milwaukee, Wis.	E	
Normal, Ill.	E	
Phoenix, Ariz.	E	
Raleigh, N.C.	E	
Rocky Mount, N.C.	E	
Scottsdale, Ariz.	E	
Tyler, Tex.	E	Combined code inspections, pollution control, and public health inspections.
Westminster, Calif.	E	Cross-training.
Clay County, Mo.	E	Cross-training via limited rotation in many departments.
Miscellaneous Programs [3]		
Cottage Grove, Oreg.	E	Public works employees trained to support firefighters.

(Continued)

Exhibit 26 (Continued)

Type of Program	Jurisdictions Reporting Use	Existing (E) or Terminated (T)	Comments/Notes
Miscellaneous Programs (Continued)	Cuyahoga Falls, Ohio	E	Job consolidation.
	Fox Point, Wis.	E	Public works employees volunteer for training to help with firefighting duties.
	Little Rock, Ark.	E	Expansion of park maintenance supervisor jobs.
	Montgomery County, Md.	E	Secretarial jobs upgraded to that of administrative assistant.
	Scottsdale, Ariz.	E	Persons from various departments trained as "fire wranglers."

1. In addition, the following seventeen cities have reported the presence of partly or completely consolidated police and fire departments: Alamogordo, N.M.; Bayside, Wis.; Birmingham, Mich.; Chapel Hill, N.C.; East Grand Rapids, Mich.; Escanaba, Mich.; Essexville, Mich.; Hearne, Tex.; La Peer, Mich.; Loma Linda, Calif.; Manistique, Mich.; North Palm Beach, Fla.; Parsons, Kan.; Rohnert Park, Calif.; Royal Oak, Mich.; South Lyon, Mich.; and Westmont, Pa. Two additional cities report discontinuing consolidated police and fire departments: Boyne City, Mich., and Blue Ash, Ohio. Consolidated police and fire departments are likely to be (but are not always) associated with the use of public safety officers. See Institute for Local Self-Government, *Alternatives to Traditional Public Safety Delivery Systems: Public Safety Inspection Consolidation*, PSDS Report No. 3 (Berkeley, California, September 1977), pp. 91–92.

2. There are also many cities in which firefighters have been given some degree of responsibility for conducting fire code inspections. In a recent survey of fire departments serving 25,000 or more persons, 503 departments (72 percent of the responding departments which had code inspection programs) reported that firefighters were responsible for conducting at least some fire code inspections. See John R. Hall, Jr., et al., "Fire Code Inspection Practices: Results of a 1977 Survey," project report to the National Fire Prevention and Control Administration (Washington, D.C.: The Urban Institute, March 1978).

3. Programs where cross-training has been conducted but was never clearly put to use are excluded.

Another relatively popular form of job enlargement is to train building inspectors to carry out a variety of inspections that have traditionally been carried out by several different persons, each of whom performed only one kind of inspection (plumbing, heating, electrical, fire, public health, etc.). This kind of job enlargement program has been predicated on the belief that consolidated inspections require less travel and less total inspection time while making greater use of employee skills, thus increasing employee productivity while improving job satisfaction. Although reportedly common in small and some medium-sized cities, consolidation of building inspections is reported to be rare in large cities.[4] In the course of this study, twelve generalized building inspector programs were uncovered.

Los Angeles, California. Los Angeles was the first large municipal government to use generalized inspectors, and its example influenced many other large cities, including Detroit and Phoenix.[5] The Los Angeles program began in 1968, when the city's Department of Building and Safety consolidated its structural, electrical, plumbing, and heating inspections under a single housing code compliance program. This program's goal was the inspection of all dwelling units in the city over a period of fifteen years.

Detroit, Michigan. Detroit's consolidated inspection program began in 1973, after the city agreed to conduct building inspections for an HUD program to insure homes purchased by low-income families. When the city's Building Department found itself swamped by the large number of investigations needed within a short period of time, a special unit composed of thirty-five generalized inspectors was created. Each of the thirty-five was trained to perform structural, electrical, plumbing, and heating inspections, but specialized inspectors were available when needed to assist the generalized inspectors. In 1976, a city ordinance mandated comprehensive inspections for all dwellings offered for sale and not just those insured by HUD.

---

4. Institute for Local Self-Government, *Public Safety Inspection Consolidation*, p. 15.

5. Robert J. Williams, "The Housing Code: Flexibility, Public Relations, Combined Inspections Are Keys to Successes," *The Building Official and Code Administrator*, vol. 2, no. 1 (January 1977), pp. 16-20; and "Detroit, Phoenix and Los Angeles Try New Inspections," *LMRS Newsletter*, vol. 8, no. 6 (June 1977), pp. 3-4.

Similar consolidated inspection efforts have been established in Dallas and Tyler, Texas, and in Rocky Mount, North Carolina. In Tyler and in Rocky Mount, inspectors were trained not only to conduct the four major types of building inspections but also to handle health, sanitation, and pollution control inspections. In Dallas, generalized inspectors handled zoning, health, and litter inspections, as well as the usual types of building inspections.

Other programs designed to enlarge jobs have been relatively infrequent. In several communities (such as Scottsdale, Arizona; Cottage Grove, Oregon; and Fox Point, Wisconsin) employees from other departments have been trained to serve as, or to provide support to, firefighters.[6] In 1973, Montgomery County, Maryland, converted 250 secretarial jobs into positions as "administrative aides," with increased responsibilities and higher salaries. Little Rock recently enlarged the jobs of its park maintenance supervisors by giving them increased responsibilities for obtaining and replacing equipment, assigning and monitoring work crews, and inspecting finished work. This action came about after line employees and their unions complained that the supervisors were not doing their fair share of the work.

The Impact of Job Enlargement. Most of the information on the impact of job enlargement in the public sector comes from published evaluations of public safety officer programs.[7] In addition, some information on the impact of consolidated inspection programs was obtained through a telephone interview with building department officials in one city and several published reports. Virtually no information was found on the impact of other state and local government job enlargement efforts.

Several cities reported net savings in costs due to the creation of public safety officer programs, the savings being primarily due to reductions in staff size. In Durham, Dearborn, and Peoria, the establishment of public safety officer programs allowed reductions of 15 to 25 percent in the number of em-

6. For a description of Scottsdale's "fire wrangler" program—a group of twenty-five city employees drawn from thirteen departments and cross-trained as firefighters—see Institute for Local Self-Government, *Public Safety Inspection Consolidation*, pp. 69-74.

7. See, in particular, Berenbaum, *Police-Fire Consolidation*; Hayman, *Public Safety Departments*; and Barnett, "Police and Fire Department Integration."

ployees hired to provide police and fire services. Although the programs in some other cities (such as Glencoe, Illinois) led to an increase in the number of personnel hired to provide police and fire services, the increases were less than what would have been required if the cities had hired additional police officers and firefighters rather than assigning both tasks to public safety officers.[8]

Winston-Salem, North Carolina, reported first-year implementation costs of $84,500, and an estimated net saving of nearly $200,000. Flagstaff, Arizona, which did not report its implementation costs, estimated that it saved $196,000 in salaries the first year by using the same employees to perform both police and firefighting tasks. Spartanburg, South Carolina, estimated savings of $10,000 a year from its combined program. Similarly, Peoria concluded in 1970 that its public safety officer program had saved $2.9 million in salaries during the preceding eight years. This saving was offset by increased operating costs of about $2 million, leaving a net saving of about $900,000. The savings in these cities occurred even though public safety officers were often paid from 5 to 25 percent more than employees performing only police or fire tasks.[9]

Public safety officer programs have had a varied impact on service effectiveness. Some cities, such as Durham and Winston-Salem, reported reductions in property losses due to fire following the introduction of public safety officers. In Peoria, however, it was estimated that property losses were $4.5 million more than what would otherwise have been expected by projecting preprogram fire rates.[10] Thus, even though Peoria had a net saving of $900,000, the increases in property losses potentially attributable to the absence of full-time firefighters resulted in an overall cost to the public of about $3.6 million. For this and other reasons (including operational conflicts, animosity between public safety officers and regular firefighters, and a change of administration), Peoria terminated its public safety officer program in 1969.

Public safety officer programs have had mixed effects on fire insurance ratings in cities that have used such programs. In Spartanburg, South Carolina, and Oregon City, Oregon, the

8. Hayman, *Public Safety Departments*, p. 12.
9. Ibid., pp. 4, 10, 13, 14.
10. Ibid., p. 13.

ratings suffered as a result of the programs. Yet in Sunnyvale, California, and Oak Park, Michigan, ratings improved after the introduction of public safety officers.

Other improvements in service effectiveness have reportedly coincided with the introduction of public safety officers. Both Durham, North Carolina, and St. Petersburg, Florida, noted decreases of between 8 and 9 percent in the number of reported crimes in areas served by public safety officers. Moreover, Sunnyvale, while employing public safety officers, has had one of the lowest crime rates of any city its size. Many cities reported that the use of public safety officers had reduced the response time on fire calls. Some cities also noted that such programs had resulted in more officers being on the streets, thus providing a more visible police presence. The assumption—an untested but possibly reasonable one—was that a more visible police presence enhanced crime prevention and gave citizens a greater feeling of security.

Three cities, however, ultimately judged their public safety officer programs to be ineffective and discontinued them. These were Peoria, already discussed; Lincoln, Nebraska; and Champaign, Illinois. In Champaign, the program failed largely because of operational problems. In Lincoln the demise of the program can be traced largely to firefighter dissatisfaction. Firefighters in Lincoln were especially unhappy about taking on additional police duties without a corresponding increase in pay (their work week was seventy-two hours compared to forty hours for police personnel, but the latter earned twenty dollars per month more than firefighters).[11]

The impact of another typical job enlargement effort—the consolidation of building inspections—seems to have been generally positive, although quantitative evidence on the extent of service improvement is rare. Los Angeles' Building and Safety Department estimated that its generalized inspectors were nearly six times as efficient as the specialized inspectors used previously,[12] and Detroit officials reported a threefold increase in inspector productivity. The Budget Research Department in Phoenix estimated that the use of generalized inspectors for single-family dwellings meant an annual savings of about

---

11. Hayman, *Public Safety Departments*, p. 13; Barnett, "Police and Fire Department Integration," p. 8.
12. "Detroit, Phoenix and Los Angeles," *LMRS Newsletter*.

$750,000.[13] In these cities and others where costs are reported to have been reduced by consolidated inspections (including Normal, Illinois; Tyler, Texas; and Rocky Mount, North Carolina), the savings have resulted chiefly from more efficient use of inspectors' time. In particular, the amount of time spent traveling to inspection sites has decreased, while the amount of time spent actually performing inspections has increased. These changes have also resulted in reported savings in travel costs, chiefly gasoline and vehicle maintenance.

On occasion, however, the use of generalized inspectors has raised costs. In Detroit, for example, the program resulted in the transfer of thirty-five inspectors from the Health Department to the Building Department, where their salaries had to be raised an average of $6,000 to equal the salaries of other building inspectors. And the Detroit program did not eliminate the need for specialized inspectors, who were the only ones authorized to make industrial, commercial, and apartment building inspections as well as reinspections to certify the elimination of problems identified by the generalized inspectors. Phoenix also found it necessary to limit the types of inspections conducted by its generalized inspectors.

There have been a few indications that the use of consolidated inspections has improved the quality and effectiveness of inspection services. Both Tyler and Rocky Mount reported that they received fewer citizen complaints about code violations and uninspected buildings after the program was instituted. Rocky Mount, Dallas, Detroit, and Los Angeles reported that more inspections were conducted and more buildings brought into compliance with local codes after they began using generalized inspectors. In Detroit, the introduction of generalized inspectors led to the elimination of a large backlog that had produced delays of eight weeks in responding to a request for an inspection. And several cities also noted that the inspection process had become more convenient for contractors, since the latter could deal with one inspector rather than having to meet with four different inspectors.

Job enlargement programs have demonstrated mixed success in improving employees' satisfaction with their work. In some cities (Clifton, New Jersey; Dearborn, Michigan; Glencoe,

---

13. National Center for Productivity and Quality of Working Life, *Managing Inspections for Greater Productivity* (Washington, D.C., 1977), p. 19. This estimate includes salaries, fringe benefits, and vehicle costs.

Illinois; Durham and Winston-Salem, North Carolina), officials
reported that the introduction of public safety officer programs
had had no lasting adverse effects on job satisfaction and sometimes had increased morale.[14] This positive impact can be traced
to the greater challenge of the work itself, the elite image that
some cities have tried to create for such jobs, and, last but not
least, the higher pay. In Glencoe, for example, public safety
officers received a 15 percent premium, while those in Durham
received 10 percent.

There are, however, numerous reports of instances in which
the creation of public safety officers lowered morale among police
officers, firefighters, or both. In Peoria, for example, the switch
to public safety officers was accompanied by a layoff of twenty
firefighters and the elimination of nineteen other fire department
positions. The remaining work force in Peoria subsequently
showed considerable hostility to the program. In several other
cities, employee displeasure was aroused by public safety officer
programs which seemed to be designed more for the purpose of
saving money than for enriching jobs. In Buena Park, California,
and St. Petersburg, Florida, morale plunged as a result of the
great increase in workload when an employee became a public
safety officer; and there was resentment in Lincoln and Oregon
City when police and firefighter jobs were broadened without
extra compensation.[15]

In Lincoln and Buena Park, as well as Fremont, California,
and Melvindale, Michigan, employees were reported to be particularly disturbed at losing their identities as police officers or
firefighters. In these and other cities, police officers often expressed little or no interest in performing fire suppression duties,
while firefighters were equally unenthusiastic about doing police
work. Many employees, in short, preferred their existing job
specialization to job enlargement, and in places like Spartanburg
employee unhappiness actually resulted in termination of the
program.

Durham, Winston-Salem, Dearborn, and Glencoe helped
themselves to avoid problems like these (as did such cities as

---

14. For a discussion of the impact of the Durham, North Carolina,
public safety officer program on job satisfaction, see Berenbaum, *Police-
Fire Consolidation*, p. 4; and "A Review of Durham's Public Safety Officer
Program After the First Three Years," City of Durham, North Carolina
(November 5, 1973), p. 19.

15. See Hayman, *Public Safety Departments*; Barnett, "Police and
Fire Department Integration"; and Zenk, "Police-Fire Consolidation."

Flagstaff, Arizona; Fox Point, Wisconsin; Gladstone, Missouri; and Oakwood, Ohio) by filling public safety officer positions with volunteers and newly recruited personnel. These cities retained some traditional firefighter and police officer positions and used public safety officers to supplement—or partly replace—the existing forces.

Unlike the public safety officer programs, the consolidated inspection programs generally seem to have improved job satisfaction. Although no systematic evaluations have been conducted, city officials in Detroit, Phoenix, Rocky Mount, Tyler, and Los Angeles all said that the morale of their generalist inspectors had risen following consolidation. Rocky Mount officials particularly mentioned that inspectors liked their increased responsibility and independence (they no longer had to coordinate their work with that of the specialized inspectors). In Los Angeles nearly all of the department's specialized inspectors chose to take the examination that qualified them for the consolidated inspection training program during the first year of consolidation. In Detroit, however, it is difficult to say whether the improved job satisfaction of the generalized inspectors resulted from their greater status and independence or from their substantially enhanced salaries and job security. All thirty-five generalized inspectors, in fact, had been in danger of losing their prior jobs as health inspectors through cutbacks in personnel; the fact that they got new city jobs, and at notably higher salaries, may have had more to do with their job satisfaction than the actual design of their job.

Unlike most other kinds of job enrichment, job enlargement appears to have had a considerable—and often negative—effect on labor-management relations, particularly in cities that have implemented public safety officer programs. In many cities the programs aroused intense opposition from the unions representing police officers and firefighters. An extreme example of this occurred in Wisconsin Rapids, Wisconsin, where the firefighters' union sought a court injunction to prevent the city council from instituting a public safety officer program. The court denied the request and held that the council had a legal right to institute such job changes; the reported outcome was an atmosphere of bitterness and hostility between labor and management.[16]

_____

16. Zenk, "Police-Fire Consolidation," pp. 29f.

Job enlargement efforts have also had the effect of prompting unions to seek increases in pay where management has not voluntarily raised wages. Pressure for increased pay occurred both in Oregon City in connection with a public safety officer program, and in Detroit in connection with the generalized inspector program. So intense was the feeling in Detroit, in fact, that the union threatened to strike. While wages were one issue—and were, as mentioned earlier, eventually brought into parity with those of other inspectors—another issue was union opposition to the use of special tools and test equipment by the generalized inspectors. Management willingness to limit use of the tools and equipment, and to negotiate salary increases, apparently averted the strike. Although the union is reported to have ultimately recognized the benefits that the program provides to employees and to have cooperated in setting inspection standards, the department has played down the savings associated with the program in order to avoid additional problems.

Not all reports about the effect of job enlargement on labor-management relations indicate worsened relations, however. In Little Rock, for instance, enlargement of the jobs of park maintenance supervisors reportedly eliminated a substantial part of the friction between management and the unions representing maintenance employees. Labor-management relations were also reported to have improved in Cottage Grove, Oregon, where public employee unions enthusiastically supported a program of training public works employees to assist the city's firefighters.[17]

Job Restructuring

Job restructuring ("vertical loading") usually involves a systematic effort to make major, studied changes in jobs to achieve many or all of the basic objectives of job redesign:

- Responsibility for completing an entire piece of work rather than performing a fragmented task;
- Greater employee autonomy in deciding how and when work is done;
- More varied job responsibilities; and
- Frequent, direct feedback to the employee on job performance.

---

17. International City Management Association, *The Guide to Management Improvement Projects in Local Government*, vol. 1, no. 4 (Washington, D.C., July/August 1977), item no. 191.

This means increasing the "depth" of a job by building into it higher knowledge and skill requirements, greater autonomy, and increased responsibility for planning, directing, and controlling the work done.

Job restructuring can be achieved in at least two ways. One way is to eliminate the routine aspects of a job, thus allowing the employee to concentrate on the job's more complex and demanding responsibilities. A second way is to redefine the tasks associated with the job and assign it new responsibilities of a totally different magnitude.

Thirty-three state and local government job-restructuring programs were found in the course of this study. (See Exhibit 27.) Twenty-four of these were in cities, three were in counties, and six were in state governments. Ten other programs were in the planning stage, and eight were reported to have been terminated.

The first of the two approaches to restructuring described above (elimination of routine duties) has been widely used by police departments. In police agencies, this type of restructuring usually involves the use of civilian paraprofessional workers to handle standard tasks associated with communications, identification, detention, and responding to calls for service that do not involve crime. Some departments have also used police cadets to handle routine chores. The use of civilian paraprofessionals by police departments is widespread. A 1970 report of the Federal Bureau of Investigation indicated that 35,565 civilians were then working for local and state police agencies.[18] It is likely that many of them were performing routine, nonprofessional tasks that had once been done by police officers.

The second major type of restructuring—provision of redefined tasks and new responsibilities of a different magnitude—was also found frequently in police departments. Fifteen police job restructuring programs were reported, fourteen in cities and one in a county government. All but five of the existing programs were combined with team policing efforts; however, this type of police job restructuring does not require the use of team policing. Another five restructuring programs of this type were reported to be in the planning stage, while seven others had been terminated.

The restructuring of police officer jobs through the assignment of additional investigative responsibilities—the most com-

---

18. Alfred I. Schwartz et al., *Employing Civilians for Police Work*, Paper No. 5012-03-1 (Washington, D.C.: The Urban Institute, 1975), p. 3.

Exhibit 27

JOB RESTRUCTURING PROGRAMS
(As of March 1978)

Type of Program	Jurisdictions Reporting Use	Existing (E), Planned (P), or Terminated (T)	Comments/Notes
Redesign of Police Jobs[1,2]	Albany, N.Y.	E	Generalist officers: conduct follow-up investigations, crime prevention efforts. Wear blazers.
	Albuquerque, N.M.	T	Officers had extra community relations responsibilities.
	Arlington County, Va.	P	Plan to give patrol officers responsibility for follow-up investigations of some crimes.
	Berkeley, Calif.	E	Patrol officers have complete responsibility for investigation of crimes they encounter.
	Birmingham, Ala.	P	Plan to have officers do more investigations.
	Bloomington, Minn.	E	Patrolmen responsible for investigative follow-up.
	Boise, Idaho	E	Patrolmen follow through on investigations.
	Dallas, Tex.	T	Planned to use generalist/specialist patrol officers with responsibility for follow-up investigations, but program was never implemented. Efforts to flatten and demilitarize the organization also failed.

Exhibit 27 (Continued)

Redesign of Police Jobs (continued)		
Dayton, Ohio	T	Generalist officers: conducted follow-up investigations, crime prevention. Wore blazers.
District of Columbia	E	Limited demilitarization of department.
Elizabeth, N.J.	P	Greater officer involvement in public relations, crime prevention.
Hartford, Conn.	E	More officer responsibility for community relations.
Holyoke, Mass.	T	Generalist officers: conducted follow-up investigations, crime prevention efforts. Wore blazers.
Lakewood, Colo.	T	Tried generalist officers responsible for follow-up investigations, blazers, nonmilitary ranks. All but use of blazers ultimately abandoned.
Menlo Park, Calif.	E	Generalist officers: handle follow-up investigations, crime prevention efforts. Wear blazers. Demilitarized ranks. Participative management.
Montgomery County, Md.	E	Patrol officers do some detective work.
New Rochelle, N.Y.	E	Patrolmen conduct preliminary investigations.
New York, N.Y.	T	Officers had extra community relations responsibilities.
Pacifica, Calif.	E	Patrolmen follow through on initial contact.

(Continued)

Exhibit 27 (Continued)

Type of Program	Jurisdictions Reporting Use	Existing (E), Planned (P), or Terminated (T)	Comments/Notes
Redesign of Police Jobs (continued)	Portsmouth, Va.	E	Generalist officers: handle follow-up investigations for felonies and other special cases.
	Rochester, N.Y.	E	Patrolmen conduct limited preliminary investigations.
	St. Paul, Minn.	P	Restructuring detective's job.
	St. Petersburg, Fla.	T	Used blazers.
	San Diego, Calif.	E	Also responsible for crime prevention.
	San Jose, Calif.	E	Use preference list to select duty options.
	Santa Monica, Calif.	P	Plan to have patrol officers conduct preliminary investigations.
	Simi Valley, Calif.	E	Redesigned job (became "community safety officers," follow through on certain initial contacts; at one time wore blazers and used demilitarized organization.
Career Executive Programs	State of California	E	Experimented with bonuses (abandoned them).
	State of Georgia	E	Certified Public Managers Program.
	State of Indiana	E	Certified Public Executive Program.
	State of Massachusetts	P	Will tie step increases to performance.
	State of Michigan	P	
	State of Minnesota	E	Includes pay tied to performance.
	State of New Jersey	P	

Exhibit 27 (Continued)

Career Executive Programs (continued)	State of New York	P	Executive service and pay for performance. Previous proposals rejected by legislature.
	State of Oregon	E	Executive service.
	State of Washington	P	General managers' classification.
	State of Wisconsin	E	
Miscellaneous Examples of Job Restructuring [3]	Arapahoe County, Colo.	E	Redesign of license and permit jobs.
	Cambridge, Mass.	E	Redesign of paramedical jobs in Cambridge Hospital.
	District of Columbia	T	Job redesign for blue-collar workers in two divisions of Office of General Services—rejected as infeasible.
	Liberty, Mo.	E	Clerical employees assigned integrated tasks.
	King County, Wash.	E	General job redesign effort.
	Minneapolis, Minn.	E	Redesign of clerical positions in employee selection division of personnel department.
	New York, N.Y.	E	Clerks handle routine paper work for social workers so the latter can concentrate on professional duties.
		E	Redesigned jobs of park supervisors, planners (due to joint labor-management committee).
		E	Redesigned ("broadbanded") highway repair, parks maintenance, electronic data processing, and clerical job classifications.

(Continued)

Exhibit 27 (Continued)

Type of Program	Jurisdictions Reporting Use	Existing (E), Planned (P), or Terminated (T)	Comments/Notes
Miscellaneous Examples of Job Restructuring (continued)	Rocky Mount, N.C.	E	Increased the responsibilities of sanitation workers.
	Salem, Oreg.	E	Redesigned jobs of staff handling permit applications to provide complete responsibility for all types of permits.
	Springfield, Ohio	E	Sanitation crews given more autonomy (outgrowth of joint labor-management committee).
	Tacoma, Wash.	E	Personnel Department staff responsible for all dealings with given agency rather than specialized functions.

1. For all except Birmingham, Dallas, District of Columbia, Montgomery County, Portsmouth, San Jose, Santa Monica, and Simi Valley, these changes were associated with the use of team policing.

2. Another approach to restructuring police jobs—the use of paraprofessionals to free police officers from routine, nonprofessional duties—is reported to be widespread. See Alfred I. Schwartz et al., *Employing Civilians for Police Work*, Report No. 5012-03-1 (Washington, D.C.: The Urban Institute, May 1975). Cadet programs (such as those in Jackson, Mich.; Worcester, Mass.; and many western cities) can also relieve police of routine duties.

3. Other examples which include elements of job restructuring include the introduction of custodial teams by Hempstead, N.Y.; efforts by Santa Ana, Calif., to restructure jobs and consolidate functions into new positions; and the Ohio Department of Highways experiment with increasing employee autonomy and participation. Continuous reclassification efforts such as that in Anoka County, Minn., have some elements of job restructuring. And some jurisdictions have completed task analyses for certain types of jobs (for instance, library jobs in the state of Illinois, police jobs in Fremont, Calif.). Such analyses can serve as the basis for future efforts to restructure jobs.

mon form of restructuring—represents a distinct change from the traditional conception of the job, in which officers are assigned to car or foot patrol to respond to calls for service. Under the traditional model, patrol officers provide only the assistance immediately needed and then turn the case or situation over to a specialist or someone of higher rank. A number of police departments, however, have sought to restructure the police officer's job by giving the officer the responsibility of doing whatever is needed to deal with the situation responded to, from carrying out preliminary investigations (in criminal cases) to referring citizens to other public service agencies. Those who fill these restructured positions are often called "generalist officers."

In a 1974 survey of police departments, 58 percent of the 153 responding agencies reported that they gave their patrol officers virtually no role in investigations. The other 42 percent gave them at least some investigative responsibilities, and 7 percent of the cities and 17 percent of the counties responding relied fully on generalist officers, with no specialized detective units.[19]

This restructuring of police officer jobs has sometimes been associated with a movement away from the traditional military model for police departments to a more "professional" model. In such a model, professional decision making is substituted for hierarchical decision making, uniforms and military rankings are eliminated, weapons are concealed in order to minimize the authoritarianism that might be felt by citizens, and the police department role is integrated with that of other public agencies. Several examples of both kinds of police job restructuring—generalist officers and the use of the "professional" organizational model—are given below.

Albany, New York. In 1971 the Police Department of Albany instituted team policing in a section of the city where relations between the department and citizens were tense. A year later a second team was established in another trouble-ridden area in response to a citizen peti-

19. Questionnaires were sent to 300 jurisdictions (those with 150 or more full-time law enforcement employees or that served a population of over 100,000); the response rate was 51 percent. See Peter W. Greenwood et al., *The Criminal Investigation Process, Volume III: Observations and Analysis*, Report no. R-1778-DOJ (Santa Monica, California: The Rand Corporation, October 1975), p. 8.

tion. The ninety-four members of the two teams wore slacks and blazers instead of uniforms and were made responsible for providing any police services necessary in response to any specific call for aid. The chain of command was also relaxed.

Pacifica, California. In Pacifica, the establishment of team policing and job rotation around 1970 was accompanied by the restructuring of police officer jobs. The officers were made responsible for handling all aspects of cases and were given considerable freedom to experiment with new ways of performing their tasks, within certain budgetary, ethical, and legal guidelines. Detectives functioned as support staff for patrol officers.

Simi Valley, California. In 1971 the city of Simi Valley established a Community Safety Agency staffed by community safety officers, youth coordinators, investigation coordinators, counseling coordinators, and supervisors. In this nonhierarchical organization the community safety officers served as generalists: they were responsible for handling each case, although the various kinds of coordinators were available to assist when necessary. Investigation coordinators assisted community safety officers on difficult crime cases, youth coordinators provided aid on problems related to young people, and counseling coordinators helped to resolve particularly sensitive family situations. The nontraditional image of the agency was enhanced by the absence of uniforms and military ranks, and the concealment of weapons.

As the agency increased in size, however, its nontraditional structure made it increasingly difficult to manage, and in 1974 the agency was reorganized along more traditional lines. The customary rankings were created, uniforms were adopted, and weapons were no longer concealed. The latter changes were largely in response to criticisms about the appearance of the officers and the public's inability to identify them. Although the concept of the generalist officer was retained, it was modified to allow officers to transfer certain cases (especially those that tended to divert them from their regular assignments) to a major investigations unit.[20]

---

20. Bruce Altman, "A New City, Unfettered by Tradition, Breaks New Ground in Management," *Nation's Cities* (June 1973), p. 37; Bruce Altman, "A 'New Image' Police Department," *The American City* (March 1972), pp. 89-90; and Bruce Altman, "Simi Valley—The City of the Seventies," *Public Management*, vol. 55, no. 5 (May 1973), pp. 5-6.

Lakewood, Colorado. Lakewood's Department of Public Safety evolved along a path quite similar to that of Simi Valley. When founded in 1970, Lakewood's Department of Public Safety introduced a number of innovations, including participatory management (see Chapter 21), team policing, and the generalist officer approach. Police officers wore blazers and kept their weapons concealed. The department avoided a military rank structure, opting instead for an organizational hierarchy modeled after that used by the FBI: Director, Assistant Director, Agent in Charge, and Agent (the generalist officer).

Although citizen surveys in Lakewood from 1971 through 1973 testified to the public's general approval (90 percent of the respondents agreed with the department's approach to law enforcement and 82 percent were satisfied with its performance), there was some public criticism, especially of the use of blazers instead of traditional uniforms. With the influx of officers from traditional police departments and a new police chief in 1974, the department gradually abandoned the use of generalist officers and the nonmilitary rank structure in favor of more traditional approaches. However, the use of blazers and the concealment of weapons continued.[21]

Another type of job restructuring has occurred at the senior executive level. Six states (but no city or county governments) have established programs in which senior executives become part of a pool of high-level employees who can be transferred quickly from one department or job to another, depending on the need for their skills and their demonstrated performance.[22] Five other states are reported to be considering similar programs.

Apart from the restructuring of executive and police officer jobs, twelve other restructuring efforts have been reported—ten city and two county. One other program was terminated before implementation. The following examples illustrate some of the diversity to be found in these efforts.

Cambridge, Massachusetts. In 1971 the jobs of registered nurses at the municipal hospital in Cambridge were re-

---

21. Garner, "Lakewood, Colorado: Evolution."

22. For descriptions and discussions of several career executive programs at the state level, see Birkenstock, Kurtz, and Phillips, "Career Executive Assignments"; State of New Jersey, Department of Civil Service, Division of Administration, "Improving Managerial Competence: The Recognition and Selection of Government Executives" (Trenton, April 1976); and State of Minnesota, "Department of Personnel."

structured to eliminate routine and easy tasks and thus permit nurses to concentrate more on medical care. The eliminated tasks, in turn, were assigned to nurses' aides, who were upgraded to nurses' assistants.[23]

Minneapolis, Minnesota. In Minneapolis the employment division of the Personnel Department created the position of paraprofessional in 1972 in an effort to combat low morale among their clerical workers. The eight employees holding these paraprofessional positions were given several tasks with greater responsibilities than their earlier clerical duties, including setting up oral examinations for job applicants, conducting classification surveys, and preparing rating forms. In addition, teams composed of one professional employee, one paraprofessional employee, and two clerks were formed and given complete responsibility for providing personnel services to specific municipal departments.[24]

Arapahoe County, Colorado. In 1973 Arapahoe County restructured the jobs in its licensing and documents section. Instead of performing fragmented tasks in connection with the issuance of licenses, birth certificates, and other legal documents, clerks were made fully responsible for the complete processing of specific kinds of documents.[25] Salem, Oregon, recently adopted a similar approach for employees handling permits.[26]

Tacoma, Washington. The jobs of personnel analysts in Tacoma were recently restructured to make each analyst responsible for all personnel matters in a given department. Prior to the restructuring, personnel analysts handled specific types of duties, such as recruiting, compensation, or pensions, for all departments. One advantage of this restructuring has been that officials of the various departments need to deal with fewer people about personnel matters.

---

23. Harold M. Goldstein and Morris A. Horowitz, *Restructuring Paramedical Occupations: A Case Study,* Northeastern University (Boston, Massachusetts, January 1972); Harold M. Goldstein and Morris A. Horowitz, "Paramedical Manpower: A Restructuring of Occupations," Northeastern University (Boston, October 1971); and "Restructuring Paramedical Jobs," *Manpower,* vol. 5, no. 3 (March 1973), pp. 3-7.

24. Luis R. Gomez and Stephen J. Mussio, "An Application of Job Enrichment in a Civil Service Setting: A Demonstration Study," *Public Personnel Management,* vol. 4 (January-February 1975), pp. 49-54.

25. Greiner, Bell, and Hatry, *Employee Incentives,* p. 37.

26. Greg Longhini, "How Three Cities Fared in One-Stop Permitting," *Planning,* vol. 44, no. 9 (October 1978), p. 31.

Washington, D.C. The District of Columbia provides an example of a restructuring plan that was ultimately rejected. In 1971 the District government considered but eventually dropped a plan to restructure blue-collar jobs in the Division of Printing and Reproduction and the Bureau of Building Management. The proposed restructuring was seen as a way to prepare employees for higher-level positions, but the low turnover among high-ranking employees, as well as the amount of training that lower-level employees would have needed to fill higher positions, led to the proposal's demise.[27]

New York City. New York has undertaken several job restructuring efforts in recent years. Through productivity bargaining the city negotiated a change in the jobs of social workers that amounted to restructuring. Routine tasks such as paperwork were assigned to clerks, and social workers were allowed to spend more time on professional duties.[28] New York has also begun to "broadband" a number of job classifications. "Broadbanding" involves grouping together positions of similar complexity, responsibility, supervisory relationships, background, and experience requirements, but with duties in different areas of activity (so that they are initially in different classifications). This process rearranges highly specialized job classifications to allow more flexible assignments for workers. After an extensive study of city jobs and job classifications, New York merged ("broadbanded") eleven highway repair titles into three new titles, twenty-three parks maintenance titles into six new titles, forty-three electronic data processing titles into thirteen new titles, and fifty-eight clerical titles into eight new titles. The new titles allow employees to perform any—or all—aspects of a job rather than only a particular phase of the operation. Thus, broadbanding can potentially lead to more satisfying jobs for employees and improved productivity for the city (because of the possibility of utilizing employees more efficiently).[29]

---

27. Michael Wilson, *Job Analysis for Human Resource Management: A Review of Selected Research and Development*, Manpower Research Monograph No. 36, U.S. Department of Labor (Washington, D.C., 1974), p. 21.

28. Stetson, "Productivity," p. 6.

29. See W. K. Williams and Company, "Job Restructuring Study," Report to the Department of Personnel, City of New York (March 1974); and Peter Allan and Stephen Rosenberg, "New York City's Approach to Civil Service Reform: Implications for State and Local Governments," *Public Administration Review*, vol. 38, no. 6 (November-December 1978), pp. 579-584.

The Impact of Job Restructuring. As noted earlier, job restructuring can be achieved in two ways. One way is to revise and upgrade a job's tasks and responsibilities, while a second way is to eliminate a job's routine tasks, thus permitting the employee to concentrate on the job's more challenging aspects.

Formal evaluations of the impact of either kind of restructuring on the effectiveness, efficiency, and job satisfaction of state or local government employees are rare.[30] One of the most systematic assessments involved the upgrading of the jobs of eight clerks in the Minneapolis Personnel Department.[31] Under this program, the eight became paraprofessional employees with more responsible tasks. To assess the impact of this change, supervisors not only gave these employees an overall job effectiveness rating but also graded them on qualities such as "dealing with the public," "dealing with other employees," "paying attention to detail," and "cooperation." Preexperiment and postexperiment scores showed significant improvements in the supervisors' assessments of these employees. The largest increase came in the category of "showing responsibility." The employees also showed improvement in the other six characteristics on which they were judged, with the smallest increase occurring in "paying attention to detail." In addition, supervisors made favorable comments about the quality of the work of the employees.

The restructuring initially meant greater efficiency, since the department was able to handle the same workload with two fewer employees, a saving of about $20,000 annually. In the long run, however, salary increases for the eight paraprofessionals offset the savings.

Some evaluative information is available on one of the commonest types of job restructuring, in which police officers are given greater investigative responsibilities as "generalist" officers. However, although several jurisdictions using generalist police officers have evaluated these programs, the results were not clearcut because in each case the restructuring was accompanied by the creation of police teams. In Albany, for example, police officials reported greater efficiency and effectiveness but were unable to say how much of the improvement was due to

---

30. Two evaluations of job redesign efforts for federal employees should be noted: McNamar, "White Collar Job Enrichment"; and Harold M. F. Rush, *Job Design for Motivation* (New York: The Conference Board, 1971), pp. 46-55.
31. Gomez and Mussio, "Job Enrichment."

the generalist approach and how much to the creation of teams, which greatly increased the concentration of police officers in the two neighborhoods where they were used. Portsmouth, Virginia, reported a 17 percent decrease in reported crime subsequent to the implementation of a program that included the use of generalist officers as well as several other new efforts.[32]

A recent evaluation of "crime control teams" (police teams that focus only on crime control, with complete responsibility for disposing of criminal incidents) in Syracuse, New York, also suffers from the difficulty of distinguishing the cause of the improvement. The study found that these teams of generalist officers had significantly greater crime clearance rates than police in areas of the city using conventional police methods; it attributed these differences in part to the use of teams of generalists.[33] Whether these results were primarily due to the use of teams, the use of generalist officers, or the use of both approaches together could not be determined.

A recent study of police investigation procedures conducted by the Rand Corporation provides a somewhat negative assessment of the effectiveness of generalist officers. On the basis of a nationwide survey coupled with intensive on-site investigations of more than twenty-five agencies, the Rand team concluded that *"The method by which police investigators are organized (i.e., team policing, specialists vs. generalists, patrolmen-investigators) cannot be related to variations in crime, arrest, and clearance rates."*[34] Instead, the study suggested that the most important determinant of whether or not a case will be solved is the information the victim is able to supply to the responding officer. These findings would indicate that, at least in terms of changes in crime, arrest, and clearance rates, generalist officers are no more (or less) effective than traditional officers.

Other restructuring efforts generally receive good marks from city and state officials. Highway Department officials in New York City report that the broadbanding of jobs has pro-

---

32. International City Management Association, *The Guide to Management Improvement Projects in Local Government*, vol. 2, no. 4 (Washington, D.C., July-August 1978), item no. 163.

33. J. F Elliott, "Crime Control Teams: An Alternative to the Conventional Operational Procedure of Investigating Crimes," *Journal of Criminal Justice*, vol. 6 (1978), pp. 11-23.

34. Peter W. Greenwood and Joan Petersilia, *The Criminal Investigation Process, Volume I: Summary and Policy Implications*, Report no. R-1776-DOJ (Santa Monica, California: The Rand Corporation, October 1975), p. vi.

duced "substantial gains" in the productivity of their crews, largely because of management's increased flexibility in reassigning personnel.[35] In Arapahoe County, Colorado, where clerks were given full responsibility for processing specific types of legal documents, officials reported that the number of records processed per employee increased, while the time required for processing any given document decreased. A similar effort in Salem, Oregon, was reported to have halved the staff needed to process applications and cut operating costs by $2,000 during the first year despite an 18 percent increase in workload.[36] Rocky Mount, North Carolina, officials said that the number of citizen complaints decreased after the drivers of sanitation trucks were given direct responsibility for deciding how to provide service and deal with complaints. King County, Washington, officials said that the job restructuring program there had turned "marginal" workers into "better than average" ones because the program made them feel worthwhile and made them appreciate the importance of their work.

Where jobs have been restructured through elimination of routine tasks, evaluations of the impact on efficiency and effectiveness have usually concentrated on the efficiency and effectiveness of those hired to perform the routine tasks, that is, civilian paraprofessional employees.

A study of thirteen police departments that used paraprofessionals found that police managers who supervised these civilians generally gave them good ratings.[37] Sixty-three percent of the thirty supervisors who responded to one survey felt that the civilians were doing a "very good" job, while the rest thought the civilians were doing a "good" job. In evaluating the performance of the civilian paraprofessionals with respect to each task carried out, these supervisors gave ratings of "very well" on 75 percent of the tasks undertaken and "fairly well" on 22 percent.

No quantitative information (e.g., error rates) was given on the quality of the service provided by the paraprofessionals nor on the effect that the use of paraprofessionals had on regular police services, such as the amount of officer time available for patrol.

---

35. Allan and Rosenberg, "New York City's Approach," p. 582.
36. Longhini, "How Three Cities Fared."
37. Schwartz et al., *Employing Civilians for Police Work*, p. 63.

It should be noted, however, that only 16 percent of the police managers surveyed said that improved service or increases in manpower (e.g., patrol time) were the chief objectives of using paraprofessionals.[38] Nineteen percent of the twenty-three respondents said that cost savings were the major objective of the program; 58 percent said that cost savings had been achieved.[39] In the thirteen cities examined in the study, the savings in salaries and benefits from using civilians in place of uniformed officers averaged 29 percent of the average total cost of a regular patrol officer (salary plus overhead). In addition, the average cost of training and equipping a civilian was $289, compared to an average cost of $7,000 for training and equipping a uniformed officer.[40]

Fort Lauderdale, Florida, provides an illustration of the increased efficiency that can result from the use of paraprofessionals. There, approximately $50,000 per year was saved by training fifteen civilians to perform traffic accident investigations that had been performed by fifteen police officers. The latter were assigned to a new police unit with responsibility for reducing traffic accidents at hazardous locations.[41]

Cost reduction was also the primary reason for restructuring the jobs of social workers in New York City by assigning routine paperwork to clerks. The difference between the average annual salary for social workers and for clerks was $3,500.[42]

The impact of job restructuring on employee job satisfaction seems to have been generally positive, although (as has been noted earlier) determining the impact of restructuring in police departments is particularly difficult because restructuring is often coupled with the introduction of team policing. Police officials in both Pacifica and Albany reported increased dedication, creativity, and morale among their "generalist" officers, while evaluators in Dayton, Ohio, said that generalist officers

---

38. Ibid., p. 61.
39. Ibid., p. 15.
40. Ibid., p. 16.
41. International City Management Association, *The Guide to Management Improvement Projects in Local Government*, vol. 1, no. 3 (May-June 1977), item no. 135.
42. Stetson, "Productivity," p. 6. Under the provisions of a contract negotiated with New York's social service workers, the restructuring of caseworker jobs was combined with revisions in caseload limitations and a $340 a year increase. According to New York's Deputy Director for Labor Relations, this agreement ultimately saved the city $120,000,000 a year through improved efficiency and better operating procedures.

there took special pride in their jobs. In all three communities, of course, job restructuring in the police department was combined with the introduction of team policing.

Both Pacifica and Albany, it must be noted, also reported some negative effects from their restructuring. In Pacifica—where police officers were given increased responsibility for handling various situations—the officers sometimes became more aware of their inability to prevent crimes, especially those arising out of domestic conflicts. At times this inability was viewed as a personal failure. In Albany, where the combined generalist-police team approach resulted in a notable drop in criminal activity, some police officers experienced considerable boredom.

Job restructuring has also had mixed results in other police departments. In both Menlo Park and Simi Valley, California, for example, weapon concealment and the change from standard uniforms to blazers and slacks caused considerable unhappiness. In Menlo Park, in fact, it was reported that half the force resigned within six months after adoption of the new "uniform." [43]

Simi Valley reverted to using the traditional uniform after about three years, but Menlo Park did not. Formal studies of the program in the latter city showed that the introduction of blazers was associated with a 50 percent reduction in the number of assaults on police officers, even though arrests of adults were increasing substantially at the same time.[44] The wearing of blazers was also accompanied by several changes in the attitudes of Menlo Park police officers—more tolerance, greater flexibility and less resistance to change, and greater egalitarianism.[45]

Job restructuring in civilian departments seems to have had a generally good effect on employee job satisfaction. In Minneapolis, for example, the personnel clerks whose jobs had been restructured expressed "substantially" higher levels of satisfaction on a questionnaire they completed six months after the change occurred. Furthermore, postexperiment interviews with participants revealed a nearly unanimous preference for the restructured jobs. Absenteeism rates for twelve months before

43. "Blazers on the Beat Bring New Attitudes," *Washington Post*, July 1, 1973, p. E8.
44. Victor Cizanckas, "Experiment in Police Uniforms: An Interim Report," *The Police Chief*, vol. 37, no. 4 (April 1970), pp. 28-29.
45. "Blazers on the Beat," p. E8.
46. Gomez and Mussio, "Job Enrichment," p. 52.

and six months after the restructuring, however, showed no significant change.[46]

Officials in other local jurisdictions reported similar effects on employee satisfaction after job restructuring. Personnel officials in King County, Washington, said that restructuring efforts in several departments there had improved morale and decreased the rate of turnover. They also reported that the restructuring had helped them recruit new employees, and that employees in departments not involved in restructuring had sought restructuring for their own jobs.

In Rocky Mount, officials said that sanitation crews with increased responsibility for servicing their routes had shown a decrease in turnover. In Montgomery County, Maryland, personnel officials said restructuring of secretarial jobs into administrative aide positions had increased the morale of the affected employees and the respect they received from others. Management in Arapahoe County, Colorado, said clerical employees whose jobs were restructured like the changes, found their jobs more stimulating, and seemed more interested in their work.

Although there are no systematic studies of the effect that civilian paraprofessionals have on the job satisfaction of uniformed police officers, the impact does not appear to be great. The chief concern expressed by police officers was that their job security might be affected through the use of civilians for so-called "light duty" jobs previously reserved for physically disabled officers.

Of greater significance was the effect of restructuring on the job satisfaction of civilian paraprofessionals themselves. In some jurisdictions the annual rate of paraprofessional turnover ranged from 40 percent to 160 percent, compared with an overall rate of 5 percent for metropolitan police departments as a whole.[47] Much of this turnover seems to have been the result of low pay. Interviews of forty-six civilians employed in police departments showed that nearly one-third of the problems they cited involved compensation.[48] Other problems included personality conflicts with police officers, limited opportunities for advancement, excessive workloads, and—for jail personnel—lack of physical safety.

Job restructuring efforts have sometimes appeared to damage—at least temporarily—the morale of persons not included

---

47. Schwartz et al., *Employing Civilians for Police Work*, p. 17n.
48. Ibid., p. 71.

in the effort. In Albany, for example, some animosity was reported between the generalist officers and the rest of the Police Department concerning the work flexibility enjoyed by the generalists and the fact that the latter reported only to their commanding team officers instead of having to go through the regular hierarchy. Supervisory personnel in the Pacifica Police Department expressed fears over the security of their jobs in connection with the introduction of generalist officers. And in King County, Washington, some of the older employees with longer tenure reportedly expressed resentment toward job restructuring efforts.

The impact of job restructuring on labor-management relations appears to be slight, but information on this is quite limited. A number of the cities contacted for this study (Albany, Minneapolis, Pacifica, Simi Valley) reported that their job-restructuring efforts had had no effects on formal labor-management relations. There were indications, however, that job restructuring sometimes had a positive effect on day-to-day interaction between employees and supervisors.

Chapter 24

OBSTACLES TO JOB ENRICHMENT PROGRAMS

Each type of job enrichment program is subject to various obstacles that may either prevent a program from getting started or weaken one that is already under way. This chapter summarizes the obstacles identified in the course of this study.

The substantial literature on team policing shows that although there are few obstacles to the establishment of this kind of program, there are many that can prevent a program from achieving maximum impact. One of the most common obstacles relates to the fact that police teams are often deliberately established in neighborhoods where crime is high and relations between police and citizens are poor. What police administrators hope to gain by establishing teams in these neighborhoods is both a more concerted attack on crime and greater attention to police-community relations. Many police officers, however, see their role as primarily that of "crime fighter" and dislike being responsible for easing the tension between the police department and the public. Their lack of interest in performing what they often refer to disparagingly as "social work" may make them uncomfortable and less than totally effective in their team role.

Another common problem in the creation of police teams involves detectives. In most police departments, detectives are stationed in a central detective bureau and have considerable status and independence. Team policing, however, often involves the assignment of detectives to a team in a specific neighborhood. Furthermore, team policing often gives patrol officers greater responsibility for tasks which detectives normally handle, such as the preliminary stages of criminal investigations.

On both counts, then, detectives may see their assignment to a team as a loss of status and react unhappily.

The many other changes entailed in moving from the traditional centralized police department to team policing may also make the latter difficult to implement. Major management responsibilities once handled in centralized bureaus are shifted to sergeants and lieutenants who often lack management experience. Novel communications and coordination problems often arise within teams, between teams, and between teams and other parts of the department still operating within the standard structure.

Many other obstacles can arise to hamper team policing. In Boulder, Colorado, for example, patrol officers on the teams generally were opposed to making criminal investigations ordinarily conducted by detectives. In Cincinnati a somewhat similar problem occurred: investigations remained the preserve of a few officers who had previously established their expertise in handling investigations; consequently, the so-called "generalist" approach was never fully realized. And in Elizabeth, New Jersey, team members had a sense of being ostracized by other members of the department. This situation may have stemmed from envy of what was believed to be the greater freedom granted to team members.

Much less is known about the obstacles to other types of operating teams, which have been used far less often than police teams. One specific problem mentioned by those associated with the health care teams in public clinics in Cincinnati was that some nurses and clerks were unhappy because, even though they had been given additional responsibilities, civil service regulations prevented an increase in their salaries. Another obstacle to fully effective teams in Cincinnati—one that has already been alluded to—was the unhappiness that some physicians felt at not being chosen as team leaders.

The operation of problem-oriented teams can be hampered by several obstacles, all of which were mentioned by officials interviewed in the course of this study. One was the simple matter of scheduling. Because problem-oriented teams usually meet on a periodic basis, it is often difficult to establish a meeting time that is convenient for everyone.

A more significant obstacle was the effect that problem-oriented teams sometimes had on team members, supervisors, and coworkers. Coworkers occasionally resented the fact that team members were able to leave their regular tasks to attend team meetings, and supervisors sometimes complained because team members were at meetings and not performing their regular tasks. Supervisors who belonged to teams sometimes felt threatened by the notion of solving problems in conjunction with lower-level employees.

Management fears of a more institutional nature have sometimes hampered the creation or operation of joint labor-management committees. In the state of Washington, for example, some hospital managers opposed the establishment of joint labor-management committees involving hospital administrators and nurses, on the ground that the committees would infringe upon management's prerogatives. Similarly, in Denver some school principals were dubious about the creation of joint committees of school administrators and teachers.

While management has sometimes feared that its power was threatened by these committees, labor has sometimes been apprehensive that giving employees a voice in management decisions might make employees begin to think more like managers. In addition, union leaders and members have sometimes expressed concern that productivity improvements stemming from joint committee discussions would lead to the layoff of workers.

Like joint labor-management committees, other forms of participative decision making may encounter obstacles in the planning or implementation stage as a result of the fears of one side or the other. Some evidence on this score came from the California Highway Patrol's participation program, in which some supervisors were concerned about a potential loss of their authority, and ultimately, their jobs.

Fears like these can hamper a program, as can labor's apprehension that programs giving workers a voice in management will dilute employee allegiance to the union. There was evidence that in at least one state the officials of a public employee union gave only reluctant support to a participation program. They seemed to think that programs like this might ultimately make the union superfluous. Neither the literature on job enrichment nor the interviews conducted for this study, however, provided very much evidence that would support these largely hypothetical fears on the part of both labor and management.

Employee resistance is one of several obstacles that may be encountered in programs involving job rotation. Some employees may resent being shifted from a job which they feel confident about handling to one in which they may encounter the unexpected. Others may be uncooperative if rotation involves a drop in status, salary, or rank. Another form of resistance may be found among regular employees who find a new, temporary employee from some other department, agency, or jurisdiction in their midst.

These constraints on the use of job rotation are much less significant than the problems that may be encountered in union contracts. A recent analysis of 504 police and firefighter contracts by the Labor Department's Bureau of Labor Statistics (BLS) found that forty-eight gave employees the right to choose assignments (usually on the basis of seniority), while one-third of them contained provisions that regulated temporary out-of-rank assignments, usually with respect to the pay to be received in a higher classification.[1] Some limitations on the methods for selecting employees for temporary transfers also were found, including the need to consider seniority or to select only from an existing list of eligible employees.[2]

Another BLS study of 318 contracts involving civilian employees in state and local governments identified other constraints that might affect the use of job rotation. Limitations on temporary promotions were found in 139 of the contracts, twenty-five limited the period of a temporary promotional assignment, eighty-three contained provisions on pay for a temporary promotional assignment, and thirty-one addressed both time and pay.[3] Temporary assignments to jobs in lower classifications and criteria for selecting persons for temporary assignments were also the subject of contract provisions, although the BLS study provides no figures for either one. These various constraints, particularly those requiring higher pay, can dampen a local or state government's enthusiasm for job rotation.

Civil service rules also can be an obstacle to job rotation, although the jurisdictions contacted in connection with this study did not provide enough examples to confirm the recent assertion that "in the public sector, civil service rules often make

---

1. U.S. Department of Labor, Bureau of Labor Statistics, *Collective Bargaining Agreements for Police and Firefighters*, Bulletin 1885 (Washington, D.C., 1976), pp. 77, 78.
2. Ibid., p. 73.
3. U.S. Department of Labor, Bureau of Labor Statistics, *Collective Bargaining Agreements for State and County Government Employees*, Bulletin 1920 (Washington, D.C., 1976), p. 22.

. . . job rotation impossible."[4] In Pacifica, civilian personnel could not rotate into jobs filled by sworn officers. In a few other cases narrowly defined job classifications sometimes seriously limited the use of rotation.

Employee and union resistance constitutes by far the greatest obstacle to job redesign, particularly job enlargement. In well over half of the twenty jurisdictions that terminated public safety officer programs, union or employee opposition was the chief cause. And in a number of jurisdictions, employees made it clear that they would refuse to participate in such enlargement programs if they did not receive additional pay.

Public safety officer programs also encountered political obstacles—that is, opposition by elected politicians or the public. In two jurisdictions, in fact, the public voted to terminate such programs. In part, however, this lack of public acceptance probably derived from the opposition of the employee organizations. In Fremont, California, voters elected two city council candidates who had pledged to introduce traditional fire and police operations.[5] And in Buena Park, California, dissatisfied public safety officers circulated a petition calling for a public vote on the continuation of the consolidated police and fire department. Meanwhile, the city's fire insurance rating had been changed, raising insurance rates in the area. Not surprisingly, the voters opted for a traditional police and fire organization.[6]

In addition to these more common obstacles to the use of public safety officers, there were a variety of less frequent ones, such as state laws that specified how a firefighter's time on the job should be used, the threat of poor insurance ratings attributable to the program, and problems in coordinating the program.

---

4. James S. Larson, "Participative Management: Why Has It Failed?" *IPMA News*, International Personnel Management Association (July 1977), pp. 2-4.

5. Barnett, "Police and Fire Department Integration," p. 9.

6. Ibid., p. 14.

Chapter 25

SUMMARY OF FINDINGS AND RECOMMENDATIONS ON JOB ENRICHMENT

Team Efforts

Of the various kinds of job enrichment discussed in Part Four, the use of teams has clearly been the most popular approach among state and local governments. The widespread use of team policing accounts for this preeminent position: team policing programs constituted 55 percent of the 129 reported team efforts in state and local governments. Team policing is also the most extensively evaluated form of public sector job enrichment.

Unfortunately, the available information does not give a clear indication of the overall usefulness of team policing as a job enrichment technique. The impact of police teams on the quality of service has generally been mixed, although mostly on the positive side. While such teams have often been credited with more efficient use of police personnel, in no case have they been associated with cost savings.

Job satisfaction is probably the most critical indicator of whether job enrichment has occurred. A job enrichment program which does not increase employee job satisfaction cannot truly be said to have enriched the job, at least from the employee's perspective. The impact of team policing on job satisfaction has not been consistent: some police teams are reported to have improved job satisfaction, some have reduced it, and a considerable number have had no effect at all. Hence, the degree to which team policing actually has enriched the job of the police officer is still open to question.

At the same time, however, team policing offers a distinctive alternative to the traditional operation of police departments. Many jurisdictions in recent years have found that the traditional mode has not proven effective, either as a means of dealing with crime and providing other services to citizens or as a means of providing police officers themselves with stimulating daily challenges. The prospect for continued experiments in team policing may therefore be substantial, particularly in view of the fact that team policing comes in so many sizes and shapes that it can usually be adapted to any local situation.

Team policing exemplifies a class of team efforts termed "operating teams"—employees brought together to conduct as a group the day-to-day tasks they once did separately. The use of operating teams in agencies other than the police is rare: only eleven examples were identified. There is little evaluative information on these programs, and their diversity makes it unlikely that the results of team policing evaluations can be applied to them. There have been a few reports of improved effectiveness or greater job satisfaction in connection with the use of nonpolice operating teams, but it is usually difficult to isolate the effect of using such teams from the effects of other innovations introduced at the same time.

In principle, the use of operating teams appears to be a promising way to motivate public employees to improve their productivity. Such teams emphasize and strengthen the tendency of many public sector jobs to depend on the efforts of a variety of individuals, and the use of teams can easily be combined with other types of job enrichment, such as increased participation or job redesign. While both police teams and other types of operating teams have generally been associated with an increase in the quality of the services delivered, their impact on costs and job satisfaction is still uncertain.

Problem-oriented teams, which constituted about a quarter of the team efforts identified, appear to be easier to implement than operating teams. While there have been virtually no formal evaluations of problem-oriented teams, in general they do seem to have been successful in proposing solutions that have been both useful and acceptable to management. But the question remains—do such efforts enrich jobs, or is participation on such teams often regarded as just another burden to be borne? Such teams can potentially add interest to an employee's daily routine while helping to eliminate some of the normal insularity of people in different ranks, positions, or organizational units. However, there is virtually no information about the impact of problem-oriented teams on the job satisfaction of participants or about whether participating in a team leads team members to improve their work in their regular jobs. While there have been reports that problem-oriented teams tend to stimulate the innovativeness and creativity of participants, there is still a suspicion that such programs are, at best, a superficial form of job enrichment. Indeed, the usually limited scope and ad hoc nature of problem-oriented teams suggest that they are not likely to make major continuing improvements in productivity and employee job satisfaction.

Increased Participation

Efforts to give employees greater opportunities to participate in deciding matters related to work and the workplace constitute the third most popular type of job enrichment being used by state and local governments. The use of joint labor-management committees has been the single most common approach to enhancing employee participation: over 70 percent of the known efforts to increase employee involvement have incorporated such committees. This may reflect a number of factors: the increasing unionization of public employees, an emerging awareness on the part of management of the need to deal cooperatively and constructively with public employee organizations, and a corresponding realization on the part of the leaders of such organizations that their cooperation will be needed if their members are to continue to enjoy higher wages in a period of tight government budgets.

With few exceptions, it would appear that the introduction of joint labor-management committees has improved labor-management relations in the jurisdictions using them. In many instances, such committees have emerged from a period of labor conflict. They have served as a way to cool passions and put labor-management relations on a more cooperative basis.

The *potential* value of such committees for improving productivity appears high. Nearly one-third of the forty governments reported to be using joint labor-management committees indicated that those committees were looking into ways to enhance employee motivation—through the use of employee incentives, job enrichment, or both. Indeed, most of these committees apparently see their primary role to be improving the quality of worklife.

Despite these worthy objectives, the impact of joint labor-management committees on employee productivity and job satisfaction has yet to be clearly established. There have been virtually no systematic evaluations of the effectiveness of such programs, although an assessment of nine committees is now underway. While there have been reports of substantial savings and productivity increases in connection with the work of some committees, in other cases the productivity benefits seem relatively small or nonexistent.

The effects of such committees on employee job satisfaction are generally unknown, although some significant improvements have been claimed. There is evidence that when labor and management are compelled to cooperate—as in the case of the joint committees introduced in New York City under the terms of the plan for assisting that city during its financial crisis—the result will be unsatisfying to employees and union officials alike. But until more systematic evidence is obtained, one cannot determine the extent to which joint labor-management committees actually succeed in enriching the jobs of participants. Although shop stewards and other union officials usually constitute the principal labor representatives, line employees would probably be more likely to view participation on a committee as an enriching experience. However, the inclusion of line employees on joint labor-management committees appears to be limited.

In general, many joint labor-management committees seem fragile. Although they show promise, they cannot be expected to be feasible everywhere. Indeed, such problems as the fears of management and the wariness of labor indicate that the establishment and operation of successful joint labor-management committees are likely to continue to require a considerable measure of mutual good faith and trust and—if they are to contribute significantly to increased participation—broader involvement by line employees.

There have been a number of other, less formal efforts by state and local governments to increase employee involvement. These have exhibited a great deal of diversity, including varying degrees of employee impact on the decision process itself. Although there is little systematic information on the effectiveness of these programs, the few existing evaluations provide grounds for cautious optimism. A number of these efforts have been associated—if tenuously—with improved efficiency and effectiveness, and in the two cases for which systematic information on job satisfaction was available, significant improvements were found. Most of the programs appear to have contributed to increased enthusiasm, inventiveness, and initiative among employees, demonstrating that efforts to encourage employee involvement can help tap the reservoir of employee talents that, in the view of many observers, often lie unused.

Although it would appear, on the basis of job satisfaction results, that efforts to increase employee participation are viewed an enriching by the employees themselves, there are still some questions about their impact on productivity. It is frequently hard to attribute specific productivity improvements directly to the use of increased participation; even when an experimental approach was tried in an effort to isolate the effects of participation, the results were inconclusive. Moreover, there are indications that such programs are hard to sustain and are very dependent on the presence of a few key management individuals. Three of the seven terminated participation efforts succumbed when the originator of the program (in each case, a police chief) left the department. Apparently there are some important intervening variables whose role must still be understood before increased participation can be counted on as a reliable, long-term strategy for improving productivity and employee job satisfaction.

Taken together, joint labor-management committees and other approaches to increase employee participation appear to represent a promising way to improve productivity and job satisfaction, on the basis of the limited documentary evidence available. They also appear to be particularly useful as a vehicle for introducing other motivational approaches, such as monetary incentives or job redesign. Indeed, to a large extent efforts to increase employee participation merely represent good management practice in a time of increasing activism among employees and their organizations.

On the other hand, such programs are not likely to be easy. Evaluations of participative decision making in the public sector make it clear that such programs may encounter resistance from supervisors fearful about loss of authority. Indeed, participative decision making requires a management style that may be quite alien to some supervisors and managers.

Job Rotation

Of the four major approaches to job enrichment—team efforts, increased participation, job rotation, and job redesign—job rotation appears to have been the one used least frequently by state and local governments. The most frequent users of rotation have been police departments, but a surprising number of programs involving rotation of managers have also been reported.

The impact of job rotation efforts is hard to discern and equally hard to predict. These problems arise from the difficulty of differentiating the effects of rotation from the effects of concurrent programs and from the fact that the impact of rotation appears to depend quite heavily on a number of intervening variables. In view of these uncertainties, the usefulness of job rotation as a way to improve employee motivation and productivity appears to be questionable. The greatest benefit of a job rotation program may lie in the exchange of new ideas and new operating methods which it promotes. This process of cross-fertilization is probably most effective when rotation occurs between different departments or different jurisdictions. Employees participating in rotation programs have also been reported to have shown greater innovativeness and creativity as well as improved skills.

The effects of rotation on job satisfaction have not been documented systematically. A number of improvements have been reported anecdotally, but so have instances of employee dissatisfaction.

Job Redesign

Although a relatively large number of state and local governments reported job redesign efforts, public administrators who seek to introduce similar programs in their own jurisdictions should be prepared for a number of technical, personnel, and institutional problems, such as civil service and labor contract restrictions. No other type of job enrichment seems likely to encounter so many obstacles.

The most widespread and serious obstacles to job redesign have occurred when public safety officer programs have been introduced. Such programs have confronted nearly every conceivable type of obstacle, from legal barriers and intense employee opposition to political and financial problems. Despite these obstacles, the creation of public safety officer positions appears to be the single most popular form of job redesign. This popularity may indicate either that the seriousness of the reported obstacles has been exaggerated or that administrators have been especially persistent in their efforts to introduce such programs, probably because of their cost-saving potential.

The information that is available suggests that job redesign has had no consistent effect one way or the other on productivity, job satisfaction, or labor-management relations. While some programs have generated improvements, others have been ineffective. This generalization holds true for both types of job redesign—job enlargement and job restructuring.

As with other kinds of job enrichment programs, little information is available on the total cost of job redesign efforts and their net savings (public safety officer programs are an exception). Although some examples of improved productivity have been traced to the use of job redesign, the savings appear at times to have been at least partly offset by associated increases in wages and other costs.

Since improved employee satisfaction is expected to be the hallmark of job enrichment programs, the mixed impacts of job redesign on satisfaction would appear to be a cause for concern. The most intense dissatisfaction has been associated with the use of job enlargement, especially public safety officer programs. Because enlargement tends to place more emphasis on increasing the number of tasks than on increasing the autonomy and skills of employees, enlargement efforts seem especially likely to be seen as simply an excuse for assigning more work rather than as enrichment. Where an enlargement program has been associated with greater job satisfaction, substantial salary increases have usually accompanied the enlargement.

In jurisdictions where the emphasis of the program has been on systematic restructuring of jobs, the effect on job satisfaction appears to have been positive even when pay remained unchanged. Thus, unsurprisingly, jobs that require greater knowledge and skill, greater autonomy, and increased responsibility are more likely to be seen as enrichment by the persons involved than are jobs that merely require that a greater number of tasks be performed.

Public administrators considering job redesign programs (or any other job enrichment approach) should also take into account the potential effect of a program on other employees, those whose jobs are not redesigned. These employees have sometimes shown a decrease in job satisfaction when the jobs of others were upgraded. Effects like these can offset whatever benefits are gained by redesign.

Despite numerous unresolved questions, however, job redesign still appears to be a promising strategy for improving government productivity and employee satisfaction. In many ways this approach—especially when it stresses job restructuring—appears to correspond to a modern version of the "methods improvements" long used by industrial engineers to improve efficiency. Nonetheless, the distinguishing characteristic of job redesign, and job restructuring in particular, is its emphasis on humanistic treatment of employees as well as job efficiency. As human values and the nature of the public work force evolve, the need for explicitly and systematically considering both elements of the performance equation appears to be increasingly important.

Overall Findings and Conclusions on Job Enrichment

For many, job enrichment is a very attractive idea. It is an attempt to improve the lot of government employees yet does not, at least on the surface, involve major expenditures.

Various forms of job enrichment have been tried by a number of state and local governments. A total of 365 distinct enrichment efforts were reported; of these, fifty-six had been terminated. The most common general approach was the use of teams (39 percent of the reported programs), followed by job redesign (33 percent) and increased participation (19 percent). Team policing was the most common specific example of enrichment, with eighty-one cases reported (ten of which had been terminated). Joint labor-management committees (forty-eight examples) and public safety officers (fifty-six examples) were also relatively common. Two other programs involving elements of job redesign—the use of civilian paraprofessionals to relieve police officers of routine, nonprofessional duties, and the assignment of fire code inspection responsibilities to firefighters—also appeared to be common.

Police jobs have been the favorite target of state and local government job enrichment efforts: 52 percent of all reported programs (including those known to have been terminated) involved police personnel. Three types of programs—team policing, public safety officers, and generalist officers—accounted for over 80 percent of the police job enrichment efforts reported, but no major enrichment approach has been ignored by police officials.

No single factor appears to account for the frequent use of job enrichment by police departments. The 1967 recommendations of the President's Commission on Law Enforcement and Administration of Justice (which urged the use of team policing and the integration of patrol and investigative functions), as well as demonstration funds provided by the Law Enforcement Assistance Administration, have clearly been influential. Other police job enrichment programs, however, appear to have been isolated innovations begun solely on the initiative of individual police officials.

The second most common target of state and local government job enrichment efforts has been the firefighter: nearly 20 percent of all reported enrichment programs involved fire department personnel. However, in this case the primary goal appears to have been more productive use of the firefighter's time when the latter was not needed to combat fires. It is likely that enrichment of jobs and improvement of job satisfaction in connection with these changes in assignments (nearly three-quarters of which involved job enlargement) were secondary to the objective of saving dollars or otherwise improving firefighter productivity.

Job enrichment appears to involve a not insignificant risk of failure for state and local governments. Fifteen percent of the reported programs had been terminated, primarily those involving job redesign and increased participation. The reasons for termination ranged from the normal turnover of key personnel to active opposition by labor, management, or the public. Programs with especially high failure rates included those involving public safety officers (36 percent were terminated), generalist police officers (32 percent), and efforts to increase participation without the use of a joint labor-management committee (30 percent). In the latter case, the high rate of failure is probably indicative of the difficulty that many managers experience in adapting to a more open, participative style. Enrichment efforts appear to have been especially painful for the uniformed services: one in four programs involving firefighters, and one in five involving police personnel, were terminated.

Despite the relatively large number of job enrichment efforts, there appear to have been few *substantive* examples in state and local governments. Instead, many of the programs seemed highly limited in the number of employees affected and in the changes wrought on employee jobs. Exceptions were team policing, public safety officers, and generalist officer programs, plus a few other instances of job redesign (e.g., the use of generalist building inspectors). But where enrichment programs have made substantial changes in employee jobs, their rate of failure has often been especially high. For instance, although about one out of six of *all* reported job enrichment programs have been discontinued, the rate was one out of three for public safety officers and for generalist officers, both of which involved substantial job changes.

As to the key questions of whether state and local government job enrichment efforts improve productivity or employee job satisfaction, there is little documentary evidence, with the exception of team policing and a few efforts to redesign jobs or increase participation.

On the basis of the limited information available, it appears that state and local government job enrichment efforts have often been associated with modest improvements in effectiveness or efficiency. However, these improvements have not usually been very large, and no one type of approach appears to have been consistently effective. This may reflect the relatively insubstantial nature of many of the job enrichment programs encountered. The scope of such programs often appeared to be too limited to provide much opportunity for significant productivity improvements.

Where specific productivity improvements were found, they were usually associated with enrichment programs that involved the redesign of the employee's day-to-day job or increased participation by workers in decisions affecting them. On the other hand, most job enrichment efforts were reported to have led to increased cooperation and mutual respect among employees, as well as greater employee innovativeness and creativity. And a number of job enrichment programs (especially those involving increased participation) appear to have been successful in improving labor-management relations. While the foregoing may, in fact, lead to increased productivity, there is little concrete evidence of it as yet.

In most cases, information on the costs associated with these programs was almost totally lacking. It is known, however, that the costs of implementing certain team and job redesign programs were quite high. Moreover, such programs sometimes led to pressures from employees for higher pay to match their increased responsibilities. Although job rotation and increased participation generally involved few out-of-pocket expenses, both kinds of programs may be responsible for a number of hidden costs, such as (in the case of job rotation) lost time, temporary inefficiencies, and disruption of the work force.

A critical question is the impact of these programs on employee job satisfaction. Increased satisfaction is often regarded as the hallmark—and principal benefit—of job enrichment. One would expect that if such a program did not improve employee job satisfaction, it probably would not be perceived by the employee as truly enriching. Since the impact of most state and local government job enrichment efforts on productivity appears to have been limited, their attractiveness is likely to be seriously diminished if they cannot at least promote greater job satisfaction.

Overall, the results seem mixed. A number of programs appear to have had little or no impact on job satisfaction. Indeed, the potential for enriching jobs (and thereby improving job satisfaction) often does not seem to have been fully utilized. Joint labor-management committees, problem-solving teams, and public safety officer programs have rarely been designed with the explicit goal of enriching the jobs of participating line employees. Only programs designed to restructure jobs or enhance employee involvement in decision making appeared to have produced fairly consistent improvements in job satisfaction. But these and other enrichment efforts sometimes also produced instances of dissatisfaction, especially among detectives and first-line supervisors, who often viewed job enrichment as reducing their authority, diminishing their status, and—in the long run—threatening their jobs.

The latter problems point to the difficulty of implementing job enrichment programs in state and local governments, especially programs involving job redesign, operating teams, or increased participation. Of the motivational approaches discussed in this book, only monetary incentives appear to have faced more serious obstacles. Job enrichment programs have encountered opposition from public employee organizations, contractual constraints, and restrictive civil service regulations. Furthermore, such programs often require a management style that is quite different from that usually encountered in state and local governments. Where management has not been sincerely interested in improving jobs and employee satisfaction but has merely paid lip service to the goals of job enrichment while using it as an excuse for giving employees more work, such efforts have generally had little impact on—and have occasionally damaged—employee productivity and job satisfaction.

It remains to be seen whether job enrichment can be effective on a large scale in state and local governments. To date, most applications have been relatively circumscribed efforts carefully tailored to specific jobs or groups. To some extent, this is required by the nature of the approach, which demands that close attention be paid to the unique features of the work itself and the given work environment. However, such limited efforts do not usually lend themselves to rapid, large-scale increases in productivity, although they may provide modest improvements in specific situations. To date there have been too few substantive, comprehensive enrichment efforts in state and local governments to be able to judge whether large-scale productivity increases are possible through job enrichment.

Recommendations

A substantial amount of additional testing is necessary before job enrichment can be accepted as a reliable, effective tool for improving employee motivation and productivity. Such tests should focus on more substantive enrichment efforts, longer periods of observation, and more careful evaluations than have been the norm in the recent past.

Although most local governments and most states cannot afford the thorough evaluative efforts recommended below, they still have an obligation to themselves and to their citizens to assess in a systematic way the impact of any programs they try. At minimum, a separate record of program costs should be maintained, and data on the cost and quality of services and employee job satisfaction should be obtained before and after implementation (allowing a sufficient period of time for the identification of long-term effects). A simple questionnaire can be used to assess job satisfaction and to determine how the program has actually affected the way employees do their work. A small effort such as this can provide a more objective, meaningful picture of the value of the approach.

The other major recommendations pertaining to job enrichment are directed toward the federal government and other organizations able to support substantial efforts aimed at advancing the knowledge available to state and local governments. They are urged to support the following:

1. *Evaluations of the effectiveness of major existing job enrichment programs in state and local governments.* With the exception of police teams and public safety officer programs, there have been few systematic assessments of the impact of job enrichment on productivity and employee job satisfaction in state and local governments. Careful evaluations of substantive state and local government enrichment efforts are needed, including information on service efficiency and quality, employee job satisfaction, and direct and indirect costs (including the value of the time spent on the program by employees, the cost of training, consultant fees, and any expenditures for higher wages). Efforts should be made to assess the influence of any relevant intervening variables, concurrent motivational efforts, or external events in order to distinguish the effect of the job enrichment effort itself. Evaluations should probably focus on enrichment programs that are especially likely to have a direct (and therefore readily detectable) impact on government productivity—that is, those that involve redesign of the employee's day-to-day job or increased participation in decision making for line employees (especially concerning activities related to their own work).

2. *New experiments in state and local governments to test and evaluate substantive job enrichment efforts.* Many questions concerning the benefits and costs of job enrichment in the public sector can best be answered through the design and implementation of new experiments involving substantive job enrichment efforts. Such experiments should cover a long enough period (at least eighteen to twenty-four months) to ensure that longer-term impacts can be detected and to give Hawthorne effects a chance to subside.

Planning for the evaluation of these programs should be undertaken before implementation to ensure that adequate baseline data are obtained and that provision is made for the subsequent collection of data on costs, service efficiency, service quality, and employee job satisfaction (for the employees whose jobs are enriched as well as for their supervisors and coworkers). Efforts should be made to control for the many intervening variables and other confounding factors commonly associated with job enrichment in order to identify the effects of the job enrichment effort itself. Factors hampering or facilitating the introduction of such programs should also be identified, and the experiments should attempt to determine the conditions under which particular approaches appear to be successful.

The approaches to be tested should emphasize, at least initially, those types of enrichment programs most likely to affect productivity—i.e., programs that involve the redesign of the employee's day-to-day job or increased decision participation for line employees, especially concerning their own work. Programs combining job enrichment with other motivational techniques, such as monetary incentives or performance targeting, should also be explored. While such programs (e.g., a public sector Scanlon plan) do not appear to have been used by state and local governments, they might compensate for the weaknesses of using a single enrichment approach.

Part Five:

SOME FACTORS THAT MIGHT AFFECT THE IMPLEMENTATION OF PUBLIC SECTOR MOTIVATIONAL PROGRAMS

Chapter 26

CONCERNS OF PUBLIC EMPLOYEES AND PUBLIC EMPLOYEE ORGANIZATIONS

The introduction of motivational techniques to improve employee productivity can be hampered by a number of factors, including resistance from employees and employee organizations, legal and civil service barriers, technical problems, and political and financial considerations. These factors frequently interact. Consequently, characterizing particular constraints as arising from legal, union, civil service, or other sources is often somewhat arbitrary.

This chapter examines employee concerns regarding certain motivational techniques as well as the kinds of pressure that employee organizations may seek to exert on implementation.

Employee Concerns

Employee fears about speedups, loss of jobs, and related concerns can be a potent obstacle to the use of motivational techniques. Sometimes such fears are based on personal experience or on second-hand information about similar techniques in the private sector. In other cases, employees resist motivational efforts because they see them as opposed to the demands of professionalism or as emphasizing undesirable aspects of the job. Some police officers trained as "generalists," for example, have been reluctant to divert their efforts away from traditional law enforcement activities.

One of the major concerns expressed by employees is that rewards should be provided in a fair and equitable manner. This involves not only the use of objective criteria and procedures but also the inclusion of techniques to compensate for external factors over which employees have no control. In some cases it can be quite difficult to satisfy the latter requirement. A related concern is the exclusion of certain employees from the plan, especially those with whom the covered employees work or associate closely. This can create pressures on the covered employees as well as complaints (and possibly grievances) from those not covered.

Another important concern of employees is that the performance criteria used as the basis of awards accurately reflect their jobs. Overemphasis of a single aspect of a job (e.g., efficiency) to the exclusion of other important elements (e.g., service quality, effectiveness) is often viewed as likely to divert employees from the major purposes of their work (especially employees in "human resources" agencies).

Widespread employee resistance to incentive plans based on individual (as opposed to group) performance has also been encountered, as noted in Chapter 6. Such plans have been criticized as being divisive and bad for morale, stimulating younger employees to compete against older ones, and producing a tendency to cut corners. Such problems are particularly evident when monetary rewards are at stake.

Employees have also resisted certain types of job redesign. For instance, when local governments have sought to create a public safety officer position, many employees have preferred to retain their separate identities as police officers or firefighters. Firefighters have often been especially unwilling to perform police functions. Police departments have sometimes encountered resistance from police officers to proposals for eliminating traditional ranks, on the grounds that rank serves as an effective way to recognize performance (through promotions) and hence is an important incentive.

The support of first-line supervisors is often crucial to the success of motivational programs. Nevertheless, a number of instances of supervisor resistance to motivational programs have been identified. These include reluctance to make distinctions between employees, opposition to monetary rewards and work standards, resistance to the paperwork associated with some motivational efforts, unwillingness to devote the time necessary to make the plans work, and in some cases a feeling that they are threatened by efforts to give line employees more autonomy and a greater role in decision making.

Concerns of Public Employee Organizations

The absence of a federal law requiring collective bargaining for state and local government employees has led to great diversity. As of 1976, collective bargaining with state employees was mandatory in twenty-six states; collective bargaining with local government workers was mandatory in twenty-three states. In addition, state employees in six states and local government employees in nine states were explicitly "permitted" to bargain. Bargaining with public employees was clearly prohibited in only four states—North Carolina, Texas, Utah (state employees only), and Virginia.[1] In other states the legal status of collective bargaining tended to lie between the above extremes and often was somewhat ambiguous. (Note that this is an area where the legal situation is changing rapidly.)

The provisions and distinctions found in collective bargaining laws are sometimes rather complex. For instance, although collective bargaining with local government employees is mandatory in Michigan, state employees have only the right to "meet and confer." In the state of Washington, state employees are forbidden to negotiate over wages but not over benefits, working conditions, or promotional policies. Because of differences like these, as well as local variations in the strength of public employee organizations and other conditions, the role of such organizations in the introduction of motivational plans varies considerably from jurisdiction to jurisdiction.[2]

Despite such variations, however, the presence of public employee organizations and unions is a fact of life in most state and local governments, one that must be dealt with constructively by governments seeking ways to improve productivity by enhancing employee motivation. Unfortunately, there appears to

---

1. See U.S. Department of Labor, Labor-Management Services Administration, *Summary of Public Sector Labor Relations Policies* (Washington, D.C., 1976).

2. See also Raymond D. Horton, David Lewin, and James W. Kuhn, "Some Impacts of Collective Bargaining on Local Government: A Diversity Thesis," *Administration and Society*, vol. 7, no. 4 (February 1976), pp. 497-514.

have been very little systematic research into the impact of public employee organizations on motivational efforts.[3] Only five studies that look systematically at the nature of that impact were found in the course of this project.[4] Consequently, most of the impacts discussed here must be considered potential rather than actual ones. Whether public employee organizations impede or facilitate the introduction of motivational programs cannot usually be answered with confidence on the basis of the information available so far. What is clear is that management—and labor—must often anticipate union-related impacts and be ready to deal with them if motivational plans are to be effective.

The concern that employee organizations feel about motivational programs appears to focus primarily on the use of monetary incentives. Employee organizations are often concerned over the possibility that employees will lose their jobs or be forced to speed up the pace of their work if incentive programs are introduced. Moreover, they often perceive incentives as being misdirected—that is, as being directed at employees when it is management that is actually responsible for low productivity.

In some cases, union resistance has prevented the introduction of monetary incentive plans. In one state a union was able to hamstring a shared savings plan by claiming that the contract clause providing for the sharing of productivity increases with employees meant that all changes in operating practices, no matter how minor, had to go through the joint labor-management committee so that their potential savings could be assessed and added to the bonus pool.[5] In other jurisdictions, efforts to increase supervisor discretion in selecting performance criteria and specifying the size of wage increases have been widely opposed by unions concerned over the lack of objectivity and the favori-

3. See, for instance, Ralph T. Jones, *Public Sector Labor Relations: An Evaluation of Policy-Related Research*, Contract Research Corporation (Belmont, Massachusetts, 1975), pp. xv, xxix; Stanley D. Nollen, *The Effect of Collective Bargaining on Municipal Personnel Systems: A Research Review*, Georgetown University (Washington, D.C., 1975); and David Lewin, Peter Feuille, and Thomas A. Kochan, *Public Sector Labor Relations: Analysis and Readings* (New York: Thomas Horton and Daughters, 1977).

4. Osterman, "Productivity Bargaining"; Greenberg, Lipson, and Rostker, "Technical Success, Political Failure"; Greiner et al., *Monetary Incentives*; Hayes, *Productivity*; and Greiner and Wright, "Employee Incentives."

5. Osterman, "Productivity Bargaining," p. 23.

tism that may be associated with such a procedure. (Indeed, most of the jurisdictions we contacted that had granted such discretion to supervisors had avoided applying it to unionized employees.)

Unions are likely to be especially wary of programs that may produce competition and conflict between their members or generate numerous grievances. Obviously, it can be difficult for union leaders to explain why they have negotiated a bonus or wage increase for some union members but not others.[6] One way for them to minimize such problems is to demand uniform treatment under a given monetary incentive plan for all employees in the bargaining unit. Consequently, union approval of such a plan may be conditioned on citywide or statewide application.

The concern of employee organizations has not been directed solely toward monetary incentives and similar reward systems. They have also opposed certain job redesign efforts. The following types of problems, although extracted from private sector experiences, appear relevant to public sector job redesign efforts as well:[7]

- Disputes have sometimes arisen over what constitutes equitable compensation for workers whose jobs have been redesigned.
- Job redesign of tasks that cross union jurisdictional lines has sometimes met with resistance.
- Union leaders have sometimes expressed concern that increased productivity resulting from job redesign would reduce the number of jobs.
- Occasionally, job redesign has been perceived by union officials as an attempt to divert worker loyalty away from the union—e.g., by giving employees a taste of manage-

6. This equity issue arose in two of the three monetary incentive programs we studied in past work. See the discussions of Philadelphia and Flint in Greiner et al., *Monetary Incentives*. The two programs were each limited to a single group of employees within a larger bargaining unit.

7. See, for instance, Rush, *Job Design*; Robert M. Monczka and William E. Reif, "A Contingency Approach to Job Enrichment Design," *Human Resource Management*, vol. 12, no. 4 (Winter 1973), pp. 9–17; Ted Mills, "Human Resources—Why the New Concern?" *Harvard Business Review*, vol. 53, no. 2 (March/April 1975), pp. 120–134; Glaser, *Productivity Gains*; and Leonard A. Schlesinger and Richard E. Walton, "The Process of Work Restructuring, and Its Impact on Collective Bargaining," *Monthly Labor Review*, vol. 100, no. 4 (April 1977), pp. 52–55.

ment responsibilities, or by reducing the number of potential members.[8]

- In some cases where redesign was initiated by management, unions have made it clear that they thought the program was unnecessary.
- And occasionally union officials have been alienated by intellectuals who attempted to sell job redesign with evangelical fervor while exhibiting what was interpreted as an implicit antiunion bias.

On several occasions, public employee organizations have resisted the integration of previously independent functions. City officials in Detroit reported that careful negotiations with the unions representing specialized inspectors were needed to introduce generalist inspector positions. Probably the most consistent and intense opposition to job redesign has focused on the use of public safety officers. Unions have argued that such programs may compromise the safety of employees (because their training may not be adequate to allow them to perform both jobs well), harm morale, create administrative problems, reduce efficiency, and damage service effectiveness.[9] One researcher found that in nine cities "the opposition of firefighters has been sufficient to inhibit serious consideration of the plan."[10] A number of other cities have also reported union opposition so intense as to have prevented the introduction of public safety officers. On the other hand, several cities (Flagstaff, Arizona; Durham and Winston-Salem, North Carolina; and Lincoln, Nebraska) have implemented such programs despite the objections of employee organizations. Ultimately, the employee organizations in these cities agreed to cooperate with the program.

Unions have been fairly supportive of some job enrichment programs, especially efforts that include joint labor-management committees and attempts to improve the quality of working life. In Cambridge, Massachusetts; Clifton, New Jersey; Cottage Grove, Oregon; and Detroit, Michigan, public employee unions and associations have been helpful in connection with job rede-

---

8. In New York State, the Civil Service Employees Association reportedly opposed the creation of a career executive corps in part because of fear that the association would lose members and that a management corps might be more resistant to Association demands. See Flynn, "Productivity," p. 4.

9. These and other arguments against the use of public safety officers are reviewed in Hayman, *Public Safety Departments*.

10. Zenk, "Police-Fire Consolidation," p. 43.

sign. In New York City and Springfield, Ohio, job redesign programs have emerged from the cooperative efforts of joint labor-management committees.

Public employee unions have also helped in the establishment and operation of several monetary incentive plans. Considerable cooperation existed in connection with the plans undertaken in Orange, California (police department); Flint, Michigan (solid waste collection); and Detroit (solid waste collection). In these cities the plans were established through productivity bargaining. The productivity project undertaken by Nassau County and three of its towns also involved considerable union cooperation. Other unions and employee associations have expressed interest in certain types of monetary incentive plans and a desire to be involved early in any planning for such programs.[11]

In some states, public employee bargaining laws increase the need for consultation or negotiation between labor and management regarding proposed motivational programs. For example, some laws require that no changes be made in working conditions without giving the union an opportunity to bargain over them, whether or not they are covered in existing agreements.[12] And as discussed in Chapter 27, motivational plans often impinge on contract stipulations. Under such circumstances, securing the participation and cooperation of unions and employee associations can be crucial to program acceptance.

Whether required to or not, however, many state and local governments inform their employees and employee organizations about a contemplated motivational program as a matter of courtesy and good labor relations. Indeed, good labor-management relations appear to be an important prerequisite to the introduction of many types of motivational programs.

While employee organizations have occasionally been criticized for obstructing certain types of motivational plans, sometimes the real obstacle is management's *perception* of the

---

11. "Public Workers Put the Pressure On," *The American City*, January 1975, p. 8.

12. ". . . under many laws governing labor-management relations, no changes in working conditions can be made without affording the union an opportunity to bargain, whether or not the particular policy is contained in an agreement." ("Reducing the Effects of Layoffs on Your Affirmative Action Program," EEO for State and Local Governments, Issue No. 15, U.S. Civil Service Commission [Washington, D.C., n.d.], p. 5.)

difficulty of devising a plan acceptable to public employee organizations and management's corresponding reluctance to discuss such motivational programs with the union. Some managers (especially in jurisdictions that have only recently begun to bargain collectively) have expressed fears that if they try to introduce an incentive or other motivational plan they will set a precedent that could become an issue in future negotiations. There are also indications that management may sometimes be reluctant to inject consideration of a motivational program into negotiations because it is not the type of issue over which management is prepared to make concessions.

Yet in view of the obvious relevance of many motivational programs to employee wages, hours, and working conditions, early and meaningful participation by employees and their organizations in the planning and implementation of such programs seems vital. Union officials have consistently urged that management consult with them early in the planning process and invite the participation of employee organizations in the design and implementation of such plans. And many employee organization officials have been relatively optimistic over the likelihood of working out a mutually satisfactory approach when this is done. This does not mean, however, that public employee organizations will inevitably accept such an invitation. In some cases they have preferred to stand aside from the planning of motivational programs. One union official stated that if a motivational program seemed likely to cause divisions within the union's membership, the union would be unlikely to participate in the planning.

Two recent studies of the role of public employee unions in employee-centered productivity improvement efforts found little or no initial resistance to such efforts. One, a study of motivational programs in five cities, found that resistance developed only after the programs were implemented and problems developed over inequities, speedups, and the need for better supervision and equipment.[13] The other study found no significant union opposition in three out of five cities with well-developed productivity programs, leading the author to conclude that "there are few situations where the unions constitute the critical factor in productivity improvement."[14]

---

13. Greiner et al., *Monetary Incentives*, p. 7.
14. Hayes, *Productivity*, p. 241.

Assessments of the likelihood of cooperation by employee organizations in monetary incentive plans for state employment service personnel, provided by regional staff of the U.S. Civil Service Commission, indicated that in fourteen states the likelihood of resistance to such incentives by state employee organizations would be slight; in five states it would be moderate; and in one state there was great likelihood of resistance. (Estimates for the other thirty states were not provided.) Moreover, in six states the likelihood of cooperation by employee organizations was viewed as great, while in ten others it was deemed moderately likely. Such support was viewed as especially likely in states where employee associations, rather than state affiliates of national unions, were the major organizations.

There appears to be a high degree of support among public employee organizations for shared savings plans, quality-of-worklife experiments, and joint labor-management committees. The latter may be an especially promising mechanism for bringing together labor and management in an informal, noncombative atmosphere. The use of such committees may go a long way toward ameliorating management reluctance to work with public employee organizations to improve employee motivation.

Chapter 27

THE POTENTIAL EFFECT OF CONTRACT STIPULATIONS ON MOTIVATIONAL PROGRAMS

Public employee contracts and memoranda of understanding may include any of a number of stipulations that can affect the introduction of motivational programs.[1] For instance, an examination of 121 contracts between local governments and the International Association of Fire Fighters identified provisions affecting the following items, each of which is potentially relevant to one or more types of motivational programs:[2]

- merit raises
- wage parity
- length of work week
- longevity pay
- use of unused sick leave
- hours of vacation and holiday leave
- priorities of established work rules (vs. contract stipulations)
- filling of vacancies
- assignment of out-of-class work
- management rights
- promotions.

1. For the sake of convenience, the term "contract" will be assumed to include memoranda of understanding for the remainder of this volume.
2. Thomas A. Kochan and Hoyt N. Wheeler, "Municipal Collective Bargaining: A Model and Analysis of Bargaining Outcomes," *Industrial and Labor Relations Review*, vol. 29, no. 1 (October 1975), pp. 44-66.

Similar clauses are found in collective bargaining agreements for other state and local government employees.[3] Depending on the type of motivational program being considered, the presence of such clauses may necessitate discussion—and possibly negotiation—between labor and management about the proposed plans. The likely need to identify and resolve such issues emphasizes once again the importance of a good labor-management atmosphere and early, meaningful participation by employees and labor organizations in the development of motivational programs.

It should be emphasized that while the contract stipulations discussed in this chapter are likely to affect the implementation of motivational programs in jurisdictions with formal labor agreements, there is little evidence on the frequency and degree to which such stipulations have actually affected such programs. Clearly, there are many jurisdictions where contracts and public employee organizations are weak or nonexistent and where stipulations such as these will have little or no impact. Until a systematic assessment has been made, they must be viewed only as potential issues. Nevertheless, government officials contemplating motivational plans should be aware of these potential constraints.

Stipulations on Employee Compensation

Although the wages of over half of all public employees are not established by collective bargaining agreements,[4] a number of contracts do specify or otherwise address compensation levels. Such stipulations can seriously affect the introduction of certain types of monetary incentives. Under the requirements of New Jersey's state employee contracts, for instance, any major changes in compensation must be negotiated. Three types of contractual stipulations are likely to be especially important in connection with the introduction of monetary incentives—provisions for wage increases, wage scales, and parity and wage differential requirements.

---

3. See, for instance, the previously cited Bureau of Labor Statistics (BLS) Bulletins 1885 and 1920.

4. Horton, Lewin, and Kuhn, "Impacts of Collective Bargaining," p. 514.

PROVISIONS FOR WAGE INCREASES

There are several ways in which contract stipulations on wage increases can constrain motivational programs. First, contracts may require all wage increases to be automatic, with little or no consideration of performance or merit. As noted in Chapter 16, contracts covering state employees in Pennsylvania and Wisconsin have eliminated any consideration of merit criteria in connection with step increases. The Pennsylvania contract reads:

> An employee's performance rating shall not be used in determining his entitlement to such [step] increment. The annual increment shall be granted solely on the basis of service on the employee's anniversary date.[5]

A recent Bureau of Labor Statistics (BLS) study of 624 state and local government collective bargaining agreements effective on or after July 1, 1975, found that 288 (46 percent) provided for automatic wage increases at fixed intervals without consideration of merit.[6] One-third of the sixty-nine agreements covering state employees included such provisions; the corresponding figures were 47 percent of the 281 agreements covering county employees, and 50 percent of the 234 agreements covering municipal employees. (Another forty agreements applied to employees in special multijurisdictional districts.) Public employee unions in Orlando, Florida, and the state of New Jersey recently negotiated contracts that eliminated step increases based on merit in favor of across-the-board increases.

A much smaller percentage of the contracts explicitly accepted the concept of raises based on merit. Fifty-two (8 percent) of the 624 agreements included provisions stating that increases would be granted or withheld on the basis of employee performance appraisals.[7] Ten percent (seven) of the sixty-nine agreements covering state employees included such provisions, as did 10 percent of the 281 agreements covering county em-

---

5. Article XIX, Section 3, "Agreement Between the Commonwealth of Pennsylvania and American Federation of State, County, and Municipal Employees" (July 1, 1973—June 30, 1976). An almost identical clause is included in the contract between the Service Employees International Union and the state of Pennsylvania for the period August 14, 1975, to June 30, 1977. Union officials explain that these clauses merely formalize explicitly the procedure that had, in practice, been used to grant step increments prior to the introduction of collective bargaining.

6. U.S. Department of Labor, Bureau of Labor Statistics, *Characteristics of Agreements in State and Local Governments July 1, 1975*, Bulletin 1947 (Washington, D.C., 1977), p. 21.

7. Ibid.

ployees and 5 percent of the 234 agreements covering municipal workers. Another seventeen (3 percent of the total) provided for both automatic and merit increases.

A critical issue here is whether the absence of explicit performance incentives leads to significantly lower efficiency or work quality. Are there enough inherent motivators in the work environment to assure that significant degradations of performance will not occur? Or are the kinds of incentives precluded by contract stipulations actually ineffective and therefore of little concern? The research on this issue as it pertains to the public sector is slight. Studies in the private sector, however, lend considerable credence to the view that the absence of such incentives means lower productivity.[8]

WAGE SCALES

In many jurisdictions, wage levels for specific job classifications are established by the civil service commission, personnel department, or similar agency. In such cases the union or employee association generally has only limited influence on wage levels through its lobbying activities and through contract provisions concerning seniority (longevity pay), wage parity, or union review of wage surveys.

There are a number of instances, however, where contracts specify which job classifications are assigned to each pay grade and the wage levels or ranges for those grades. The contract between American Federation of State, County, and Municipal Employees (AFSCME) Local 521 and the city of Harrisburg, Pennsylvania, is such a case. A recent analysis of thirty-five labor agreements involving employees of local governments in Indiana found that twenty-seven (77 percent) included a negotiated pay schedule with wage rates prescribed by job classification.[9] The BLS study of 624 bargaining agreements found that 80 percent (497) specified the basic wage structure.[10] This occurred in 65 percent (forty-five) of the agreements covering state employees, 80 percent (225) of the agreements covering county workers, and 83 percent (195) of the agreements cover-

8. See, for instance, Katzell and Yankelovich, *Work, Productivity, and Job Satisfaction.*

9. "Analysis of Labor Agreements—Indiana Municipalities, 1973," Indiana Association of Cities and Towns (n.d.), p. 5.

10. BLS Bulletin 1947, p. 21.

ing municipal employees. Of the 497 agreements that stipulated the basic wage structure, 131 specified individual wage rates while another 358 stated the permissible ranges for wages. (The other eight specified minimum wage levels.) Where specific rates of pay or pay ranges are given, monetary incentive plans could be in violation of the contract if the resulting compensation levels lead in some instances to wages that do not coincide with the wage scales or ranges specified for each job classification.

PARITY AND WAGE DIFFERENTIAL REQUIREMENTS

Collective bargaining is often used to establish the differentials between various job classes or, conversely, to ensure that wage levels for some jobs are kept at parity with those of other jobs. Wage parity requirements are found most often in contracts covering police and fire employees. A recent BLS survey of 504 such contracts found that about 6 percent included parity provisions.[11] In some instances, parity was even established between job classes in adjoining jurisdictions.

Such provisions can constrain the use of monetary incentive plans that would permit high performing employees to receive wage increases. Or they may add to the cost of the plan by making it necessary to raise the wages of some employees just to maintain the specified salary separation, regardless of the performance of those individuals. In Philadelphia, as noted earlier, supervisors and skilled repairmen in the Water Department's meter division were granted special pay increases to maintain established wage differentials with respect to other employees earning bonuses under a monetary incentive plan.

Stipulations Involving Performance Appraisal and Promotions

Constraints on the criteria or procedures used to evaluate employees—including the stipulation that seniority must be a major consideration in such assessments—can limit efforts to motivate employees by focusing attention on job performance.

---

11. BLS Bulletin 1885, p. 30.

The use of promotions as a reward to encourage improved performance may be similarly constrained.

PERFORMANCE APPRAISAL

Although union contracts in a number of instances support the use of appraisal criteria that emphasize job performance, those same contracts often explicitly incorporate wording to the effect that any revisions (such as the introduction of appraisals oriented more toward results) are subject to negotiation. This is consistent with the widespread concern of public employee organizations about the importance of having fair, objective measures of employee performance and the consequent need to avoid changes that increase managerial arbitrariness in making appraisals. Of the 624 state and local agreements analyzed by the Bureau of Labor Statistics, fifty-six (9 percent) had provisions concerning formal appraisal systems.[12] Stipulations on appraisal procedures may be especially common in agreements with state civil service associations, since these organizations tend to be strong supporters of existing merit system procedures.[13]

State employee contracts in New Jersey illustrate such stipulations. These contracts require the state to use the employee performance appraisal system set up by the state in 1971. More specifically, the contracts require discussions between employees and their supervisors about individual performance criteria, they provide for grievances if the criteria are unilaterally changed or if supervisors and employees cannot reach agreement on them, and they require management to discuss with employee associations any change in the procedure for evaluating employees for their annual merit increments.

PROMOTIONS

In the absence of what they view as fair, objective appraisal criteria (and, correspondingly, the presence of many opportunities for managerial arbitrariness), public employee unions tend to resist any increase in management discretion over promotions and hiring, as well as definitions of merit that stress excellence

---

12. BLS Bulletin 1947, p. 25.
13. Jerry Lelchook, "State Civil Service Employee Associations," Labor-Management Services Administration, U.S. Department of Labor (Washington, D.C., October 1973), p. 70.

rather than simply satisfactory performance.[14] Instead, unions generally favor greater reliance on assessment procedures and criteria that limit management discretion, for instance, by requiring an emphasis on seniority.

Where public employee unions are strong, seniority appears to be replacing traditional merit assessments as a major criterion for promotions, wage increases, and reductions of the work force.[15] Public employee unions assert that present merit system criteria are too subject to bias or political abuse, that recognition of seniority improves employee security and morale, and that seniority-based procedures encourage promotion from within.[16]

The BLS analysis of 504 collective bargaining agreements for police and firefighters found that 48 percent explicitly included seniority as a criterion for determining promotions, while 11 percent used subjective performance ratings and 50 percent utilized examination scores.[17] Many of the clauses on performance ratings provided safeguards to prevent abuse, including requirements that the appraisal be fair and impartial, be presented to the employee in writing, and be subject to grievance procedures in case of disagreement. In a few cases the actual rating criteria were spelled out in the contract.[18]

In a BLS analysis of 318 state and county agreements for the 1972-73 period, it was found that 92 percent specified the factors upon which promotions were to be made.[19] Of these, 49 percent mentioned seniority, 48 percent mentioned skill and

---

14. See, for instance, Nollen, *The Effect of Collective Bargaining*, p. 17. Also, Jerry Wurf, "Collective Bargaining in Public Employment: The AFSCME View," *The County Yearbook 1976*, National Association of Counties and the International City Management Association (Washington, D.C., 1976), pp. 150-159. Similar reactions have been expressed by officials of several state municipal leagues.

15. Horton, Lewin, and Kuhn, "Impacts of Collective Bargaining," p. 508. Of course, many—if not most—traditional procedures for assessing merit focus more on personal traits than on job performance and excellence. Under these circumstances, seniority—or longevity—may be just as valid and useful a criterion.

16. Nollen, *The Effect of Collective Bargaining*, p. 17.

17. BLS Bulletin 1885, p. 78. Some contracts required the use of more than one procedure.

18. Ibid., p. 75. Among the factors to be assessed in one instance were past performance, initiative, ability to complete assignments, effectiveness in oral and written communications, ability to deal effectively with the public, ability to lead and supervise, and ability to get along with others.

19. BLS Bulletin 1920, p. 29.

ability, and 19 percent mentioned examination scores. Where seniority was mentioned, its role vis-a-vis skill and ability (and other factors) varied.[20] In nine agreements (3 percent of the total of 318), seniority was the only factor to be used to determine promotions. In fifty-five (17 percent), seniority was the primary factor—that is, the most senior employee was to be selected from all candidates meeting the minimum qualifications for the position. And in sixty-four agreements (20 percent of the total), seniority was a secondary factor: the most qualified employee was to be chosen, with seniority to be the deciding factor only if the skill and ability of the candidates were relatively equal. These results support the earlier finding by Stanley that union efforts to make seniority the *primary* criterion for promotions have met with mixed success in the public sector.[21]

In the BLS analysis of 624 collective bargaining agreements (which covered a broad spectrum of state and local government employees), it was found that 61 percent (358) had provisions stipulating promotional procedures. This included 86 percent of the sixty-nine agreements covering state employees, 54 percent of the 281 agreements covering county workers, and 58 percent of the 234 agreements covering municipal employees.[22]

The use of seniority as the major basis for determining the order in which employees are laid off has been accepted by the courts so long as seniority is defined broadly to include all prior service in the jurisdiction.[23] While efficiency and other performance ratings can also be used, management must ensure that such ratings are valid, job-related, fair, and part of a regular appraisal program.[24] The difficulty of satisfying these requirements may encourage management to rely almost entirely on seniority (as defined above) for personnel decisions, at least until more objective performance information becomes regularly available.

There are numerous examples of recent attempts by public employee unions to replace merit and performance assessments with seniority criteria. In Joliet, Illinois, for example, unions have argued that since the city's merit system amounted in practice to a system of longevity increases, it should be rewritten

20. Ibid.

21. Reported in Jones, *Public Sector Labor Relations*, p. 230.

22. BLS Bulletin 1947, p. 18.

23. U.S. Civil Service Commission, "Reducing the Effects of Layoffs," p. 7.

24. Ibid., pp. 7-8.

to reflect that fact of life. As noted earlier, recent contracts covering state employees in Pennsylvania explicitly preclude the use of performance ratings for awarding promotions; management must select the most senior employee within five points of the top score obtained on the promotional examination.

There are other provisions besides seniority which limit or de-emphasize merit considerations in favor of relatively automatic procedures. For example, in New York City, public employee union pressures have led to the institution of a "rule-of-one" whereby administrators must choose the candidate with the highest score as indicated by appropriate tests and rating mechanisms. This eliminates the limited discretion that existed under the previous system, which permitted management to select from among the three candidates with the highest performance ratings.[25]

Stipulations Concerning Paid Leave

Most contracts covering public sector employees have provisions concerning paid leave—vacation, holidays, sick leave, etc. The Bureau of Labor Statistics found at one point that 59 percent of 624 agreements studied contained provisions specifying the maximum amount of vacation available to employees.[26] Sixty-seven percent contained provisions specifying the total number of paid holidays, and 77 percent contained explicit sick leave provisions. Of 504 contracts covering police and firefighters, 71 percent specified vacation allowances, 75 percent specified paid holidays, and 79 percent specified paid sick leave.[27]

The frequent incorporation of leave provisions into public sector contracts implies that management is likely to be restricted in using additional leave as an incentive reward without first negotiating with the union or employee association. Union readiness to modify contracts to allow the use of additional leave as an incentive differs widely. An official of one state employee union indicated that he would be willing to consider such modifications (and would be much more positive toward them than toward cash incentive rewards). But the head of

25. Horton, Lewin, and Kuhn, "Impacts of Collective Bargaining," pp. 508, 514.
26. BLS Bulletin 1947, p. 34.
27. BLS Bulletin 1885, pp. 55-56.

another state employee organization saw additional vacation or personal leave in the same light as monetary incentive rewards; he was opposed to both, insisting that any additions to leave allotments be provided equally to all employees.

It should be noted, however, that a substantial number of the contracts examined in the BLS studies did not cite maximum figures for leave allotments but instead merely referred to local ordinances or civil service regulations. Under such circumstances, management may be able to alter leave allotments without having to renegotiate them (that is, by changing the appropriate ordinance or regulation). There are also indications that a number of contracts merely restate local or state laws on leave allotments.[28] Thus, the question of whether management must negotiate subsequent changes in leave allotments will have to be determined on a case-by-case basis.

Stipulations Concerning Working Hours

The great majority of contracts covering state and local government employees appear to include explicit provisions fixing the hours of work and the length of the work week. The BLS analysis of 624 agreements found that 67 percent (416) included stipulations on the number of weekly working hours.[29] Thirty percent of the agreements referred to a forty-hour week as the standard. Some contracts spelled out the hours for various work shifts.

Stipulations such as the foregoing may require management to negotiate any effort to introduce variations in working hours, such as flexitime or a four-day week with ten-hour days. Under the Minnesota Public Employment Labor Relations Act, for instance, employees can bargain over the minimum number of work hours per day and per week before overtime must be paid.[30] Under such conditions, programs involving a ten-hour day (with three-day weekends) or a nine-hour day (with a three-day weekend every other week) could necessitate payment

---

28. Paul F. Gerhart, "The Scope of Bargaining in Local Government Labor Negotiations," *Labor Law Journal*, vol. 20 (August 1969), pp. 545-552.

29. BLS Bulletin 1947, p. 27.

30. Cyrus Smythe, Jr., "Work Schedules, Work Hours; What's Bargainable," *Minnesota Municipalities*, vol. 59 (August 1974), pp. 27-28.

of overtime unless the union agreed to an exception. For instance, 59 percent of the state and county agreements examined in one study required overtime to be paid for work in excess of eight hours in a twenty-four-hour day, forty hours in a week, or similar fixed standards.[31] In the BLS analysis of 624 contracts, fourteen included explicit provisions permitting flexible work week arrangements while 229 (37 percent) required overtime pay for work in excess of eight hours.[32]

The need to renegotiate a contract in order to introduce variations in working hours may or may not pose a problem. Public employee unions have been relatively positive toward the use of flexitime, but some unions, including the American Federation of State, County, and Municipal Employees, have taken a strong position against programs that lengthen the work day.[33]

Stipulations Involving Job Classifications and Work Rules

Contractual provisions concerning work standards, work practices, work schedules, job classifications, and work assignments can affect the introduction of such motivational programs as performance targets (e.g., those based on work standards), monetary incentives (which may necessitate specification of new work standards or work procedures), and job enrichment (e.g., job redesign, job rotation, and similar innovations that may require modifications to existing job classifications or assignments). These types of stipulations are discussed below.

WORK STANDARDS AND WORK PRACTICES

Public employee contracts have from time to time included provisions specifying a number of different kinds of work standards and practices, including minimum staffing levels (e.g., for police patrol cars), output levels (e.g., daily collection of at least four truckloads of trash), and workload levels (e.g., minimum

---

31. BLS Bulletin 1920, p. 38. The study reported no cases of guaranteed levels of overtime, a stipulation sometimes included in private sector contracts.

32. BLS Bulletin 1947, pp. 27, 29.

33. "AFSCME Resolves," *LMRS Newsletter*, vol. 7, no. 9 (September 1976), p. 1.

case loads for social workers). In Flint, Michigan, a recent contract specified the number of collection stops that constituted a standard route for waste collectors, the definition of a "stop," and the procedures to be used by a union-management team in counting stops on contested routes.[34] Some contracts include a "past practices clause" that preserves the status quo regarding work practices, work rules, and working conditions.[35] Such stipulations may fix the size and composition of work units, making it difficult to alter them to reflect changes in jobs or demands.

On the whole, however, the indications are that contract stipulations on workload and manning have been infrequent, except for a few publicized cases involving professional employees.[36] The BLS study of 504 police and firefighter contracts found that only 11 percent included stipulations on minimum vehicle manning.[37] While contractual stipulations on work standards and practices may not be common at present, however, this may not be true in the future. The executive director of AFSCME District Council 37 in New York City has urged greater worker and union involvement in determining work standards and practices, and has called for the development of "national standards for performance." [38] It seems likely that

34. "Supplemental Agreement for Members of the Waste Collection Division, between AFSCME Local 1600 and the City of Flint, Michigan" (effective July 1, 1975—June 30, 1977). (This contract was recently renewed for three years.) Although the presence of monetary incentives and productivity bargaining with waste collectors in Flint appears to have increased union concern regarding what constituted a "fair day's work," the elaborate contract stipulations on collection standards actually grew out of a dispute over a provision in the 1975 contract that defined the standard collection route as involving 550 to 585 stops per day. When management subsequently recounted the number of residential collection stops, it found that the average number of stops per route had fallen to 544 and that by eliminating one route (and hence one crew), the average would rise only to 574, still within the limits provided by the contract. Attempts to eliminate the route led to a one-day walkout by waste collectors and an arbitrator's decision that the standard number of collection stops— and the related issue of how those stops should be counted—be addressed during the next round of contract negotiations. See Greiner et al., *Monetary Incentives*, pp. 51-52.

35. David E. Northup, "Management's Cost in Public Sector Collective Bargaining," *Public Personnel Management*, vol. 5 (September 1976), pp. 328-334.

36. Jones, *Public Sector Labor Relations*, p. 231.

37. BLS Bulletin 1885, p. 68.

38. Gotbaum and Handman, "A Conversation."

work standards and contractually defined work procedures will increasingly have to be dealt with in connection with the introduction of motivational plans.

WORK SCHEDULES

Although the establishment of work schedules is usually seen as a management right,[39] work schedules have been addressed in a number of labor agreements involving public employees. Several observers have concluded that public sector unions have achieved some success in tying shift assignments to seniority,[40] and the U.S. Civil Service Commission has noted that efforts to reschedule employees in state and local governments often require close attention to contractual provisions.[41] Thus, motivational techniques such as job enrichment (which often requires the revision of work schedules) may be constrained by such contract stipulations.

JOB DESCRIPTIONS AND CLASSIFICATIONS

Contract stipulations on job descriptions and classifications can be a potentially important constraint on the introduction of job enrichment programs. It has been observed that "negotiated job classifications and work rules . . . place practical limits on the kinds and amount of changes that can be made in job content."[42] Public sector unions have often pressed for narrow specifications of job classifications, with detailed listings of job duties for each title and provisions that would eliminate the possibility of union members working below their skill level.[43] As noted in Part Four, attempts to have specialized inspectors undertake several different types of inspections and attempts to introduce public safety officers to handle both fire and police responsibilities have both encountered union resistance at times.

WORK ASSIGNMENTS

Restrictive work rules may limit management's flexibility in assigning public employees. Indeed, there is evidence that unions

---

39. Smythe, "Work Schedules," p. 28.
40. See Jones, *Public Sector Labor Relations*, p. 231.
41. U.S. Civil Service Commission, "Reducing the Effects of Layoffs," p. 4.
42. Monczka and Reif, "A Contingency Approach."
43. Jones, *Public Sector Labor Relations*, p. 231.

have had some success in ensuring that desirable shifts or locations are assigned by seniority.[44] Officials of Pueblo, Colorado, for example, have pointed out that seniority considerations limit their ability to employ job rotation. The BLS analysis of 504 police and firefighter contracts found that 9.5 percent of them conferred on employees the right to choose shift assignments—usually on the basis of seniority—provided it did not detract from departmental effectiveness.[45]

Contractual restrictions on out-of-class work—e.g., by requiring premium pay or by prohibiting such assignments entirely—can also affect efforts to introduce job redesign or job rotation. Unions apparently have had some success in negotiating constraints on out-of-class work. The BLS study of 504 police and firefighter agreements found that one-third of them regulated temporary assignments out of rank.[46] Although these provisions usually involved the pay of employees while serving in a higher classification, some of them prescribed selection criteria or procedures—e.g., the need to take seniority into account or to select from a prescribed list of eligibles. In the BLS analysis of 318 agreements with state and county employees, 44 percent covered temporary promotional transfers. Of these, 26 percent addressed pay during assignments to a higher classification, 8 percent prescribed time limits for such assignments, and 10 percent dealt with both topics.[47] Some contract provisions also constrained assignments to lower job classifications.

There are some signs, however, that these restrictions may be loosened in the future. New York City has attempted to "broadband" job classifications by grouping together narrowly defined jobs of similar complexity, responsibility, experience requirements, and salary grades in order to permit greater flexibility in assignments. In a recent address the president of the American Federation of State, County, and Municipal Employees offered to work for relaxation of some of these constraints, noting that "there's much to be said about the wisdom of loosening up job classifications and putting public employees to work where they can do the most efficient and effective job." [48]

44. Ibid.
45. BLS Bulletin 1885, p. 67.
46. Ibid., p. 73.
47. BLS Bulletin 1947, p. 22.
48. Jerry Wurf, "Labor Views the Cities," *SPEER Newsletter*, National League of Cities, vol. 1, no. 2 (January 1978), p. 1ff.

The Scope of Bargaining

As can be seen from the preceding sections of this chapter, most of the traditional subjects of negotiations in the private sector—wages, salaries, fringe benefits, retirement plans, union security, and working conditions—have been accepted as valid topics for public sector negotiations. But when motivational programs in the public sector involve less traditional or more controversial bargaining areas, the precise scope of bargaining becomes especially important. The Committee for Economic Development points out that the greatest degree of controversy concerning what is or is not bargainable (and hence potentially covered by a contract) usually centers on the distinction between management prerogatives and conditions of work.[49] In some cases, government managers have argued that joint labor-management determination of such conditions as safety, schedules, workload, and exertion is illegal and represents a violation of the trust which the community has conferred on its public officials.[50] Nevertheless, there is evidence that over time negotiations and contracts tend to address such traditional management "rights" as the assignment of tasks, workload, and other decisions regarding job descriptions and procedures.[51] Thus, the question of whether or not management will seek to bargain over a motivational plan may depend on how it interprets the scope of bargaining at any particular time.

There are usually a number of laws and regulations that can be used to define the scope of negotiations. Most collective bargaining laws at the state level indicate in general terms what is or is not subject to negotiation with public employee organizations. Both the inclusion and the exclusion of certain items can affect the introduction of motivational techniques. For example, the collective bargaining law in Massachusetts permits bargaining over productivity and performance standards.[52] This may serve to encourage the use of productivity bargaining and shared

---

49. Committee for Economic Development, *Improving Management,* p. 78.

50. Gerhart, "The Scope of Bargaining," p. 547.

51. See David T. Stanley, *Managing Local Government Under Union Pressure* (Washington, D.C.: The Brookings Institution, 1972), p. 67 (quoted in Jones, *Public Sector Labor Relations,* p. 227).

52. Robert Goetzl, "Productivity Bargaining Under the New Massachusetts Public Employee Collective Bargaining Law," Massachusetts League of Cities and Towns (Boston, Massachusetts, August 12, 1974).

savings techniques (the approach favored by many public sector unions) while discouraging the application of performance targets or work standards. The Massachusetts League of Cities and Towns, however, has discerned no such trends to date.

Many state collective bargaining laws give management fairly broad authority to implement motivational programs unilaterally. Sixteen states appear to incorporate such authority in the fairly broad management rights clauses contained in their public employee bargaining laws,[53] and similar authority is sometimes embodied in federal executive orders, municipal home rule statutes, or civil service regulations.[54] But the degree to which state and local governments actually exercise those rights, especially with regard to motivational programs, appears to vary considerably.

Another important technique for limiting the scope of bargaining involves the inclusion of a management rights clause in the negotiated agreement itself. Such clauses specify the issues not subject to negotiation. In the BLS analysis of 624 agreements, it was found that 64 percent included management rights clauses—86 percent of the sixty-nine agreements covering state employees, 55 percent of the 281 agreements covering county workers, and 69 percent of the 234 agreements covering municipal employees.[55] In the earlier study of 504 agreements covering police and fire personnel, it was found that 55 percent included management rights clauses.[56]

Such clauses are usually one of two types. Either they are broad, general assertions of "residual" rights (i.e., that management retains all rights concerning matters not explicitly addressed in the contract), or they are lists of items excluded from negotiations. A recent report by the Committee for Economic Development has suggested that the following are legitimate items for a list of management rights:[57]

- Agency goals and objectives
- Approaches to meeting goals and objectives
- The work to be performed, and how it is to be performed
- Organizational structure

53. Hal Kooistra, "Municipal Labor Relations: What's Ahead for Missouri," Part I, *Missouri Municipal Review*, vol. 40, no. 1 (January 1975) pp. 18-19.

54. Jones. *Public Sector Labor Relations*, p. 98.

55. BLS Bulletin 1947, p. 15.

56. BLS Bulletin 1885, p. 25.

57. Committee for Economic Development, *Improving Management*, p. 78.

- The tools, machines, and equipment necessary to perform the work
- Budgets and appropriations to agencies and programs
- Selection of supervisors
- The need for increasing or decreasing the number of employees, or for overtime work
- Employment standards, the selection of new employees, promotion policies, and discipline.

The New York Conference of Mayors and Municipal Officials has urged that the following management rights be included in contracts:[58]

- The right to determine the size and composition of the work force
- The right to allocate and assign work
- The right to transfer work out of a bargaining unit
- The right to lay off for lack of work
- The right to restrict union activities on municipal property and on municipal time
- The right to contract out.

A study of thirty-five local government contracts in Indiana suggests the diversity of management rights clauses. Eight of the agreements had no management rights clauses, another eight had a brief general statement of management rights, twelve had lists noting certain management prerogatives, and seven included comprehensive enumerations of management rights.[59]

Statements of "residual" rights are likely to include the authority to introduce many types of motivational programs (i.e., those not explicitly addressed by the contract). And in some instances a list of management rights will include personnel actions, such as the examination, selection, recruitment, hiring, appraisal, training, promotion, and assignment of employees.[60] Such a list would seem to imply the right of management to introduce a wide range of motivational programs unilaterally (again, so long as they do not touch on such traditional bargaining areas as wages, hours, and fringe benefits). However, there does not appear to be any information on the frequency with which clauses listing management rights include provisions relevant to the introduction of motivational programs.

---

58. "Management Rights Pointers," *Labor Relations Newsletter*, Supplement No. 2, vol. 58, no. 7 (March 28, 1977).
59. "Analysis of Labor Agreements—Indiana Municipalities," p. 4.
60. BLS Bulletin 1920, p. 5.

It should, of course, be emphasized that the right of management to make such a decision unilaterally does not mean that management is wise to make the decision without prior consultation with employees.

Note, too, that the formal scope of bargaining may bear little resemblance to what actually takes place. Gerhart has found that the formal scope of bargaining often exceeds the real scope,[61] while other investigators have concluded that statutory restrictions on the scope of bargaining often do not limit that scope in practice.[62] These contradictory observations indicate that it is risky to rely on formal statements as true indications of the scope of bargaining.

In any case, it would appear that the scope of bargaining will be enlarged in the future despite the presence of management rights clauses and other formal limitations.[63] Some new state bargaining laws have expanded the scope of negotiations, as have court verdicts in disputes over what constitutes a negotiable working condition and what constitutes a management prerogative.[64] In addition, public sector unions have sometimes sought to persuade legislators to modify the law in a way that broadens the scope of bargaining.[65] Greater use of productivity bargaining is also likely to increase the scope of negotiations. Recent studies indicate that when productivity bargaining continues over a period of time, more and more considerations relating to the content of work, its organization, and how it is to be evaluated are drawn into the negotiations.[66]

Public employee unions—especially those that include numerous professional employees—represent another force tending to increase the scope of bargaining. Public sector unions have generally shown more interest in management policy issues than their private sector counterparts, arguing that they have a legitimate concern with the missions of public agencies. Teachers want to help choose the curriculum, nurses seek to affect

---

61. Gerhart, "The Scope of Bargaining," p. 546.

62. Jones, *Public Sector Labor Relations*, p. 98.

63. Ibid., p. 100.

64. Ibid., p. 98. A recent example is provided by the city of Vallejo, California. The California Supreme Court ruled that, contrary to a city ordinance, issues such as personnel reductions, vacancies, promotions, and schedules were indeed negotiable. See "Vallejo, California Loses on Arbitration Tiff," *LMRS Newsletter,* vol. 6, no. 1 (January 1975), p. 1.

65. Jones, *Public Sector Labor Relations*, p. 101; Gerhart, "The Scope of Bargaining," p. 549.

66. Greiner et al., *Monetary Incentives*, p. 77.

decisions about health care delivery, and some social workers have even gone on strike to express their concern over the level of benefits provided to clients.[67] Consequently, it is no surprise that labor organizations representing these workers have sought to negotiate such things as class sizes, patient treatment, and case loads. Furthermore, employee concern with quality and effectiveness may contribute to resistance to the introduction of certain motivational techniques. Some employee organizations representing state employment service personnel, for example, have argued that monetary incentives for local office staff are incompatible with the agency's objective of serving all applicants equally (their fear being that such incentives may encourage staff to concentrate on easy-to-place clients). Recent union statements, such as AFSCME's call for negotiations over the methods for delivering public services, also point toward an increased scope of bargaining.[68]

Thus, while there is no information on how often management rights clauses have protected the implementation of motivational programs, the indications are that despite such provisions the scope of bargaining is likely to expand. Consequently, it seems likely that the implementation of motivational programs will be increasingly constrained by contractual stipulations requiring negotiations between labor and management.

The Relationship Between Public Employee Contracts and Civil Service or Merit System Regulations

The degree to which contractual stipulations may limit motivational programs is also determined by the extent to which such stipulations are superseded by laws and regulations governing civil service or merit systems. In several states, the law gives priority to merit systems by excluding them from negotiations.[69]

67. Committee for Economic Development, *Improving Management*, p. 78.

68. Resolution on Productivity in the Public Service adopted by the American Federation of State, County and Municipal Employees at its 1972 Annual Convention.

69. The following states currently exclude the merit system from negotiations for some or all government employees: California, Hawaii, Illinois, Kansas, Maine, New Hampshire, Vermont, Washington, and Wisconsin.

And in a number of other instances, management rights clauses exclude the merit system or the merit principle from bargaining. As noted above, however, formal assertions of the supremacy of civil service or merit system rules may be undercut by other factors. Although California law, for example, gives civil service rules precedence over negotiated contracts, court rulings have often favored contracts. And although civil service rules are supposed to take precedence over contracts covering New Jersey state employees, a recent contract stipulates that efforts must be made to modify the rules to conform with the contracts when conflicts are found.[70]

Other states give clear priority to negotiated agreements. Laws in Alaska and Connecticut, for instance, stipulate that negotiated contract provisions supersede civil service regulations. (In the case of Connecticut, there are some exceptions concerning rules on hiring and promotion.)

In still another group of state and local governments, priorities are mixed or changing. Thus, state employee organizations in Washington may negotiate binding contracts over non-wage issues, but determination of compensation remains under the control of the legislature and the Department of Personnel. In Michigan, contract stipulations supersede civil service regulations for local government employees, but for state employees the Civil Service Commission has almost complete control over wages and other personnel matters. And, as noted earlier in this chapter, unions in several jurisdictions have recently waived merit raises in favor of across-the-board increases to all covered employees.

In a number of areas, the goals of civil service systems and public employee organizations are quite similar. Both unions and civil service commissions tend to support formal job classification systems; both oppose political patronage; both encourage promotion from within; and both tend to resist giving management greater discretion.[71] Where a new motivational approach clashes with these goals, resistance can be expected from both the civil service agency and the unions.

---

70. "Agreement: The State of New Jersey, New Jersey Civil Service Association, and New Jersey State Employees Association—Professional Unit" (July 1, 1977—June 30, 1979), Article III.

71. Committee for Economic Development, *Improving Management*, p. 50.

In general, public employee organizations support the merit principle but are skeptical of merit systems. One union leader has described civil service and merit systems as "first, second, and finally, management's personal tool."[72] Furthermore, unions have taken the position that "merit" refers to the use of standards to make an objective judgment of an applicant's ability to handle a job.[73] The union view is that merit standards should measure the ability of a candidate to perform a job at a minimal level. The merit system, in other words, should be used to reject incompetence rather than to determine relative performance or exceptional ability:

> Merit procedures must be used to assure that a job applicant can do the job—not necessarily that he or she can do it better than anyone, anywhere. If one must, to qualify for a typist position, type 60 words per minute, that is well and good. But it does not follow that an applicant typing 70 or 80 words a minute is the better qualified. . . . it is sufficient that the merit criteria measure the health and fitness of the applicant for the job.[74]

Thus, in some cases unionization has tended to dilute the meaning of merit as "excellence."

The impact of this rather subtle change in emphasis has been substantial. Increasingly, seniority (or seniority plus minimal competence) has been used as the basis for personnel decisions. Some public employee unions have opposed merit raises even if no more than lip service is given to the concepts of relative ability and excellence. And, as noted previously, several employee organizations have resisted efforts to use appraisals as a means of scrutinizing job performance more intensively. Consequently, some motivational techniques can be expected to run into problems arising from their emphasis on "merit" as "excellence" because the encouragement of better performance—a fundamental objective of the motivational techniques considered here—runs counter to the conception of "merit" held by some public employee unions.

One final question, and one which has not been resolved, concerns which environment is more amenable to the introduction of motivational programs—a situation where civil service

---

72. Wurf, "Collective Bargaining," p. 152.
73. Ibid., pp. 152-153.
74. Ibid., p. 154.

regulations take precedence, one where contract stipulations take precedence, or some combination of both. In view of the foregoing findings, it would appear that a general answer cannot be given—the answer will vary in different states and different local governments.

Chapter 28
OTHER POTENTIAL IMPLEMENTATION OBSTACLES

This chapter reviews a number of other potential obstacles that can hamper the introduction of motivational programs. These obstacles include civil service and personnel policies, legal restrictions, performance appraisal inadequacies, and political factors.

Civil Service and Personnel Policies

Although civil service and merit system procedures have come under considerable study and criticism during the past few years, little attention has been given to the obstacles which they sometimes pose to motivational programs. It is ironic that systems created to deal with personnel matters often serve as one of the greatest impediments to improving employee motivation and job satisfaction.

As with labor-related issues, the constraints posed by civil service and personnel systems vary considerably from state to state. (Federal merit system standards impose only minimal requirements and thus allow considerable diversity.) However, nearly every type of motivational approach can be affected in one way or another by civil service and personnel rules and policies.

In some state and local governments, personnel laws and regulations explicitly prohibit or limit the use of monetary rewards for public employees. Six states forbid such rewards entirely, and eleven more have legal restrictions that limit their use. Moreover, civil service officials in a number of states take the position that they would not attempt to establish monetary incentive programs without a law explicitly authorizing their use. At present, only seven states have such a law.

Probably the greatest potential obstacle involves civil service or personnel department rules that require employee compensation to be uniform and comparable. This has been interpreted by many state personnel agencies as meaning that any monetary incentive plan must be made available to all employees or that special authorization must be obtained before such incentives are used in a single agency or operation.

A less stringent interpretation of comparability is that pay rates and opportunities for compensation must be uniform for all employees within a given job class. Thus, incentive plans restricted to a single agency may be feasible only for job classes unique to the agency. Even this interpretation, however, would preclude the possibility of group incentives, since most agencies include at least some persons in jurisdiction-wide job classifications (e.g., clerks, typists, etc.). On the other hand, some government officials (especially in local governments) have taken the position that they can authorize monetary incentive plans for limited groups of employees and then leave it up to other employee groups wishing to earn incentive pay to devise a comparable plan.

Another form of civil service constraint may arise in connection with rules on pay. Civil service rules frequently specify that all employees shall be paid only at the levels (steps) prescribed for their job class. These requirements can constrain monetary incentive plans (1) by limiting incentive rewards to multiples of one salary step (thereby precluding plans with variable rewards), (2) by putting a ceiling on incentive rewards (so that no one's compensation exceeds the top step), (3) by requiring that prescribed pay differentials (e.g., between job classes or between management and nonmanagement employees) be maintained, (4) by limiting the frequency of rewards and prohibiting temporary step increases, and (5) by specifying rigid review periods.

Civil service rules sometimes constrain the use of other types of incentive rewards, such as extra vacation or personal leave. The state of Washington, for example, requires statewide uniformity in employee vacation benefits. Personnel officials in some states felt that attempts to use extra fringe benefits as incentives would encounter the same obstacles as cash awards. In others, however, the use of fringe benefit awards was believed to be less tightly constrained. Motivational programs involving nonmonetary rewards, such as certificates, pins, or trophies, are generally unaffected by civil service rules and practices.

Fewer civil service constraints are likely to be encountered in connection with job enrichment programs, although civil service regulations that narrowly define job classifications may hamper efforts to redesign jobs. Personnel officials in Tacoma, Washington, reported that civil service regulations made it difficult for them to undertake such restructuring. And in states like Michigan, where state law specifies certain features of local police and firefighter personnel systems, the introduction of public safety officers may require voter approval of a referendum abolishing the separate civil service systems for fire and police departments and the substitution of a new system for a consolidated public safety department.[1]

To avoid such problems as ambiguous responsibilities and inequitable pay scales (among other things), it appears important to couple job redesign with reexamination and redefinition of job classifications. In the case of police paraprofessionals, the more successful programs have utilized job descriptions clearly differentiating the prerogatives and responsibilities of civilians and sworn officers.[2] On the other hand, anticipation of difficulties in getting personnel departments to modify job classifications to reflect redesigned positions may inhibit further efforts to restructure jobs. The Public Works Department in Kansas City, Missouri, and the Building Department in Detroit experienced delays of two to four years in getting new job descriptions and salaries approved for employees in redesigned jobs. In Tacoma and Minneapolis, on the other hand, where the job redesign efforts were undertaken by and for Personnel Department employees, officials reported no such delays.

In some instances the difficulty of changing job classifications has been linked to contractual and other union-related constraints on the definition of those job classes. These have hampered a number of different job enrichment approaches.

---

1. Citizens Research Council of Michigan, *Saving Taxpayer Dollars*, p. 11.
2. Schwartz et al., *Employing Civilians for Police Work*.

However, as noted previously, there have recently been efforts by some unions and personnel departments to loosen narrowly defined classifications.

Although they may require employee performance appraisals, civil service laws do not usually specify the content of such appraisals. Traditionally, appraisals have focused on assessing the performance of individuals rather than groups. Most, however, do not include—or do not emphasize—the use of objective, results-oriented performance criteria. In some cases, personnel departments have given management greater discretion in evaluating employees in the hope that this would result in more performance-oriented appraisals. In general, however, such efforts appear to be counterproductive.

Few civil service constraints on the use of performance targets seem to exist, possibly because they are often viewed as a management, rather than as a personnel, technique. To the extent that performance targeting would be more effective if tied to monetary rewards, however, civil service constraints on monetary incentives will indirectly affect the use of performance targets. This has not prevented a number of governments from adopting performance targeting in the form of appraisal by objectives, and other governments appear to be moving in that direction.

In addition to the formal constraints which civil service and personnel systems impose, the frequent need to have any incentive program approved by civil service or personnel officials can introduce an informal obstacle. Most civil service officials appear to take a conservative attitude toward incentives; they are willing to attempt only what is explicitly permitted under law and insist on having prior information about the likely effectiveness of an incentive plan.

Civil service officials have remarked that civil service rules and regulations are generally designed to encourage uniformity (e.g., equal pay for equal work) and to protect employees. Thus, the system has been set up to deal with employees as individuals and by job class. Incentive plans which reflect this orientation—i.e., individual incentives and incentives focused on an entire job classification—were viewed as being most compatible with existing rules and policies, and therefore easiest to implement. Group appraisals, group incentives, and incentives limited to a given organizational unit were viewed as likely to be inherently difficult for civil service systems to handle.

As a result of such attitudes, there often appears to be a reluctance on the part of other governmental agencies to consider certain types of motivational programs (especially monetary incentives). Agency officials have assumed that such programs would automatically be prohibited or opposed by the civil service or personnel department, and they have had no great desire to fight for the programs. Furthermore, civil service and personnel departments have sometimes joined public employee unions to oppose changes associated with motivational programs. Civil service commissions often include representation from private sector labor unions willing to support the positions of public employee organizations regarding the use of motivational techniques.

There have been some promising signs, however, that civil service and personnel system barriers may decline in the future. Personnel departments in a few states have assumed at least partial responsibility for improving the productivity of state employees. They are likely to be pushed further in that direction by proposed reforms of the federal civil service structure. In addition, the revised federal standards for state and local government merit systems encourage innovation and experimentation (e.g., by providing for temporarly suspension of the standards to permit new approaches to be tried). Indeed, the proposed federal merit system standards explicitly authorize the provision of rewards for superior performance.

Miscellaneous Legal Restrictions

In addition to union contracts and civil service rules (both of which often have legal standing), other types of laws can constrain the use of motivational efforts. Federal wage and hour laws (and their overtime provisions) can limit experiments with variations in working hours; EEO requirements can constrain performance appraisal techniques; and requirements for the return of unspent federal grant funds may interfere with the use of shared savings plans. As noted earlier, state laws sometimes restrict the use of public funds, e.g., by prohibiting their use in connection with incentive plans or by forbidding the provision of awards to employees out of cost savings.

Legally mandated benefits and certification requirements can make it difficult to undertake some types of job enlargement and redesign that would involve consolidation of jobs falling under different regulations. For instance, a construction code recently approved by the state of New Jersey requires local government inspectors to be certified by the state's Department of Community Affairs for each type of inspection they perform (e.g., health, fire, plumbing, and other specialized inspections). This has caused at least one jurisdiction to suspend efforts to introduce generalist building inspectors. Many states have medical practices acts which allow only physicians and nurses to perform such functions as cardiac defibrillation, intravenous therapy, drug administration, intubation, and electronic telemetry.[3] Local jurisdictions in these states may have to obtain special legal authority to create paramedical positions for the provision of advanced emergency care involving services such as these. The use of paraprofessionals to relieve police officers has also been constrained at times by laws that prevent civilians from performing certain police functions.[4]

The most serious obstacles to job redesign appear to involve public safety officers. The states of Massachusetts and Pennsylvania, for instance, have laws restricting the unification of police and fire departments in cities over a certain size.[5] In Louisiana, a bill to permit local fire and police boards to authorize public safety officer positions was recently blocked by a committee of the state legislature.[6] In other states, laws restrict the duties that can be performed by police officers and firefighters, making consolidation difficult or impossible. Florida law, for instance, requires employees involved in firefighting to devote 100 percent of their time to firefighting duties; this and other restrictive state laws contributed greatly to St. Petersburg's decision to abandon its public safety officer program.[7] And in a 1971 decision granting an injunction sought by firefighters to prevent the city of South Bend, Indiana, from using a public safety officer approach, the appellate court ruled that the city's home rule authority did not extend to altering the duties of fire and police employees.[8]

---

3. "Is Your Paramedic Program Legal?" *Fire Command*, vol. 43, no. 10 (October 1976), pp. 28-29.
4. Schwartz et al., *Employing Civilians for Police Work*, p. 34.
5. Hayman, *Public Safety Departments*, p. 3.
6. "New Concept for Old Roles: The Public Safety Officer," *Louisiana Municipal Review* (May-June 1977), pp. 15-16.
7. Hayman, *Public Safety Departments*, p. 14.
8. Ibid., p. 3.

Differences between laws applying to police officers and firefighters have also inhibited the use of public safety officers in some states. In Wisconsin, for instance, legally mandated pension benefits are different for police officers and for firefighters; thus, consolidation of police and fire positions might mean that one of the groups would lose its full pension rights.[9] (This problem led Shorewood, Wisconsin, to limit its job redesign effort to giving additional fire prevention responsibilities to firemen.) A related problem was noted in model legislation designed to facilitate police-fire consolidation and the use of public safety officers in New York State:

> Present general laws relating only to policemen or only to firemen and containing different provisions or requirements make an orderly consolidation of police and fire departments legally impossible notwithstanding studies (that) show that efficiencies and economies in the performance of the public safety functions may be achieved by such consolidation.[10]

Technical Problems

Among the major technical obstacles to motivational programs are the determination of the coverage of the plan, the performance criteria to be used and their measurement, the selection of rewards, the standards and groupings to be used in assessing performance, equity problems and ways to compensate for changes in external conditions, and costs. These problems—and their resolution—often take on extra importance when monetary incentives are involved. Inability to resolve these issues satisfactorily can preclude the possibility of an acceptable motivational plan.

Probably the most serious of these problems is the adequacy of performance criteria and appraisal procedures. Although these criteria and procedures constitute the heart of many techniques designed to improve productivity, serious deficiencies in them appear to exist among state and local governments. The lack of acceptable performance criteria was cited by a number of government officials as hampering the introduction of performance

---

9. Ibid.
10. Section 3 of legislation proposed by the New York Conference of Mayors and Municipal Officials in 1975.

target plans; it was also reported to have been a major problem in half of the performance bonus plans terminated by state and local governments.

Due in part to limitations in the measurements currently available for gauging public sector effectiveness and efficiency, as well as the lack of regularly collected data, employee appraisals and assessments have more often than not relied on personal traits and subjective ratings. Some researchers have concluded that appraisals based on such criteria may actually be counterproductive and result in poorer performance. Under such circumstances, the concern of public employee unions about the lack of objective criteria and the danger of giving managers increased discretion is probably not without justification.[11]

In general, performance appraisal systems are not fixed by laws and regulations as to their content and format, although federal equal employment opportunity laws require that they be valid and job-related. Most governments are free to change their appraisal systems, and some alternatives have appeared. Although they do not emphasize objective measures of work quantity, quality, or effectiveness, the newer procedures offer some promise. These appraisal techniques (appraisal by objectives and behaviorally based instruments) also face obstacles, however, in the form of the cost and time required to develop them.

Although job redesign does not rely on performance criteria, it too can involve difficult technical issues. The task of redesigning the jobs of public employees may demand an investment of time and expertise that some governments are unwilling or unable to make. For example, job redesign must sometimes be preceded by an extensive task analysis. This procedure, time-consuming and expensive, often must be conducted by outside consultants. Another type of technical problem was faced by Building Department officials in Detroit. In designing the position of generalist inspector, these officials found it necessary to develop inspection standards consistent with state and local regulations as well as with the limited skills and experience of the persons expected to fill the new positions. Heating inspec-

---

11. In recent years, however, there have been a number of efforts to develop improved procedures for assessing the performance of a number of state and local government services, including various "human services." These developments appear likely to alleviate this problem somewhat.

tions created special difficulties, since there was no simple test for assessing the safety of furnaces. Eventually the department decided that furnaces over fifteen years old were the most hazardous and developed a quick and easy sodium ion test to assess furnace safety.

Training employees to handle their new jobs is another critical element of most job redesign efforts. Jurisdictions that have introduced consolidated inspections have reported training that ranged from informal sessions to the formalized instruction provided in Los Angeles. There, supervisors conducted morning classes using materials developed by senior inspectors, and this classroom instruction was reinforced through field visits in the afternoon.[12] In Washington, D.C., the training efforts that would have been needed to implement a job redesign program for blue-collar workers in the city's Division of Printing and Reproduction were so extensive that department officials judged the program to be impractical over the short term.[13]

Employee aptitudes and capabilities also may limit the scope of job redesign. Despite the fact, for example, that inspectors in Detroit and Phoenix were given tasks of increasing difficulty as their expertise improved, some inspection tasks were still believed to be too complex for them.

Other Potential Obstacles

Political Constraints. Legislative authorization for some types of motivational efforts has sometimes been resisted by legislators. City council opposition has been a relatively common reason for abandonment of monetary bonuses, and state legislatures in several instances have been reluctant to tie pay to performance. City council reluctance to surrender control over wage increases has sometimes interfered with the introduction of monetary incentives, and council lack of interest has sometimes hampered efforts to introduce and maintain target-setting procedures. In a few instances, monetary incentive plans have provoked opposition from the public.

---

12. The Los Angeles Department of Building and Safety encouraged the Los Angeles Trade and Technical College to devise a two-year curriculum leading to a certificate for all phases of construction inspection.
13. Wilson, *Job Analysis*, p. 21.

Financial Constraints. The financial difficulties of state and local governments have sometimes hampered the introduction and use of motivational programs. As budgets shrink, cost-of-living adjustments are usually paid first, with the result that there is little left for performance or merit increases. In other instances, the money for initiating a motivational program may simply not be available. Sometimes the appropriate funds are controlled by outside sources, such as a CETA prime sponsor, or a state or federal agency. This may further inhibit efforts to try new motivational techniques.

General Skepticism and Reluctance to Innovate. Legislators and chief executives may be inherently reluctant to approve the use of monetary incentives. There is always some risk in undertaking such a plan—the possibility of labor strife, exorbitant or undeserved rewards, public outcries, or the failure of the plan to produce improvements in productivity. In addition, evaluative information on the desirability and practicality of motivational plans is limited. This absence of information may lead to additional reluctance when it comes to approving an incentive effort. A good example of this occurred in Virginia, where a special committee of the state's General Assembly—although cognizant of the value of improved monetary incentives—recommended only that such incentives be given further study by yet another committee.[14] Without strong evidence from other jurisdictions that a particular motivational approach will work, public officials may be reluctant to shoulder the necessary risks.

---

14. Commonwealth of Virginia, "A Study on Personnel Management," p. 87.

Part Six:

OVERALL FINDINGS, CONCLUSIONS, AND RECOMMENDATIONS

Chapter 29

OVERALL FINDINGS

This work has focused on four major ways to motivate state and local government employees to improve their productivity: monetary incentives (including performance bonuses, merit increases, and shared savings plans), performance targeting (including management by objectives), performance appraisal, and job enrichment (including the use of teams, participative decision making, job rotation, and job redesign). This chapter summarizes the findings on the use of these motivational techniques by state and local governments, the impact of the techniques on productivity and employee job satisfaction, and the factors that affect the implementation of such programs.

Findings on Frequency of Use

MONETARY INCENTIVES

With the exception of certain merit system procedures, efforts to tie pay to performance have not been common in the public sector. *Performance bonuses* are quite rare in state and local governments: a total of twenty-three such plans were identified, an increase of over 40 percent since 1974. Eight of these plans were for management only. Twelve other performance bonus plans were terminated after implementation or rejected before implementation, usually because of the absence of adequate performance criteria or resistance by unions or city councils. *Piecework incentives* (a type of performance bonus) were identified as being used by nine local and two state governments, an increase of five programs since 1974. Three more governments were considering the introduction of such plans. Piecework incentives have usually been applied to jobs with well-defined, measurable outputs clearly attributable to an individual worker, such as water meter repairs, keypunching, and maintenance operations.

Nearly all of the foregoing plans involved individual rather than group incentives. Another monetary incentive approach, primarily used for groups, is the *shared savings program*, a form of bonus plan. A total of nine shared savings plans were identified, eight of which were designed to use group rewards. Of the nine programs, one was primarily for management personnel. Six of these programs were successful in generating savings, resulting in rewards for employees (however, in one case the savings and the bonuses were quite small). In two of the three programs that did not generate rewards, the joint labor-management committees responsible for the program could not agree on ways to increase productivity and save money (five of the shared savings plans involved such committees). All nine programs were implemented in unionized jurisdictions, in every case but one (the program primarily for management personnel) as a result of negotiations between labor and management. Shared savings plans thus appear to be an especially promising way to involve public employee unions in motivational efforts.

Suggestion awards, a relative of shared savings programs, are fairly common, having been implemented by at least twenty-six states and 128 local governments. Most are quite similar in design, although efforts have been made in a few jurisdictions to focus the plans more sharply on productivity improvement.

The most common type of monetary incentive in the public sector is the *performance-based wage increase*, usually provided through a merit system. Our survey of performance appraisal procedures in the fifty states and a sample of fifty local governments found that twenty-seven states (54 percent) and twenty-four local governments (48 percent) linked superior appraisals to a special raise or bonus. Of these, seventeen governments (fifteen states and two local governments) were using appraisal by objectives (ABO) or behavioral rating scales to assess performance. Twenty-six (eight states and eighteen local governments) of the remaining thirty-four jurisdictions that provided wage increases for superior performance used performance appraisals based largely on narratives and subjective ratings of personal traits. The indications are that in such situations merit increases for "superior performance" do not serve as effective incentives, due in large part to the inadequacies of the appraisal systems.

Numerous efforts to tinker with merit system procedures to focus them more directly on actual job performance were identified. The most promising improvements, however, appeared to be the attempts of a few jurisdictions to achieve fundamental changes by linking bonuses or wage increases to appraisals based on objective effectiveness and efficiency criteria. This has often involved an effort lasting several years, first to develop service objectives and measures of effectiveness; then, after such measures and the necessary data collection procedures are well-established, to use them as the basis for setting performance targets (through MBO or ABO); and finally, to link such targets to monetary rewards. Two governments that have used this approach—Dayton, Ohio, and Palo Alto, California—have applied such incentives only to managers.

PERFORMANCE TARGETING

The setting of performance targets—explicit statements of the desired performance of an individual or group (in quantitative terms, where possible)—is a management device that can potentially serve as a motivator in and of itself. In state and local governments, performance targeting usually occurs in connection with three types of efforts: (1) management procedures, such as MBO and program budgeting; (2) employee performance appraisal processes, such as ABO; and (3) work measurement or work standards programs. In the 1976 ICMA survey, 41 percent of the responding cities and 40 percent of the counties reported using MBO and related performance targeting procedures in at least one agency. Although these percentages are probably high (telephone interviews of twenty-five reported current or past users who responded to the ICMA survey found that only twenty-two had actually used target setting), the indications are that MBO and program budgeting (both of which involve the use of targets) were being used in as many as a third of the jurisdictions responding to the ICMA survey, while ABO was utilized by about 18 percent. The latter figure is supported by the results of a 1976 survey by the International

Personnel Management Association, in which 20 percent of the respondents reported using ABO. All of the users of performance targeting identified through our telephone interviews had begun to use targets within the previous seven years; most had introduced them in the previous three years. (On the other hand, follow-up calls to governments reporting the use of MBO have frequently revealed that the application of MBO was, in fact, minimal. In some cases, "use" of MBO involved nothing more than having all managers sit through several training sessions.)

Despite the widespread interest in performance targets in recent years, however, there has been little emphasis on effectiveness or efficiency in the targets specified. Among the twenty-five reported users surveyed, only seven reported the use of effectiveness targets; only two reported using efficiency measures. The performance targets used in connection with MBO were usually process-oriented, focusing on workload, level of effort, and due dates, while targets associated with ABO leaned toward project completion and personal development goals. Again, however, there were indications that many of the responding jurisdictions were moving slowly in the direction of using better-defined targets supported by more adequate measurement procedures more frequently focused on effectiveness and efficiency.

The use of work standards appears to have spurred in the last several years. The 1973 UI/ICMA/NGC survey indicated that only 12 percent of the responding cities, 18 percent of the counties, and 10 percent of the states were using work standards, while the 1976 ICMA survey reported that 51 percent of the cities and 46 percent of the counties were using such standards in at least one agency. (No comparable information was available for the states.) It was not possible to tell, however, if these standards were being used for motivational purposes or if they were being used primarily for planning, scheduling, and budgeting.

PERFORMANCE APPRAISAL

There appear to be few performance appraisal systems that emphasize the use of objective, output-oriented measures of employee job performance. Twenty-three state governments (46 percent) rely on rating scales or narratives that do not incorporate objective standards and are not tailored to specific jobs.

The situation appears to be even worse at the local government level. In a survey of twenty-five randomly selected counties and an equal number of cities, over half of the respondents (56 percent of the counties and 52 percent of the cities) based their appraisals on narratives or rating scales involving subjective assessments of traits and similar criteria neither tailored to the job nor focused on results. In addition, 26 percent of the states and 42 percent of the local governments examined had *no* formal, government-wide procedures for appraising employees.

On the other hand, thirteen states (26 percent) and two cities (8 percent) reported the use of ABO, that is, joint work planning and goal setting by employee and supervisor, and results-oriented appraisals focusing (at least in part) on goal achievement. In one other state, behavior-based scales and checklists tailored to specific jobs were being used to assess employee performance. None of the counties in the sample reported the use of these or any other output-oriented appraisal techniques, but one county reported that one of its departments was using peer group appraisals to supplement its traditional individual rating procedures.

Overall, there appears to be a slow but steady trend among state and local governments toward greater use of objective setting and measurement of results in connection with performance appraisal. Many of these governments are developing procedures to support the use of performance targets, MBO, and ABO.

JOB ENRICHMENT

Job enrichment programs attempt to improve employee motivation and job satisfaction by altering the content of the job, usually by increasing the employee's autonomy, the variety of the skills used or tasks performed, the completeness (i.e., the lack of fragmentation) of the employee's tasks, and the amount of direct feedback on results.[1] A total of 309 job enrichment programs were reported—twenty-four in counties, eighteen in states, and 267 in cities.[2] This was an increase of almost 180

1. Preenrichment efforts, such as organizational development and team building, were not included in this study.
2. Many of the programs in these tallies were included on the basis of reports from the jurisdictions involved. From the limited follow-up calls we made, it appears likely that the actual number of existing, substantive programs may be considerably smaller.

percent over the total number of programs reported in 1973. Over 25 percent of the reported programs were in California. New York, Illinois, Michigan, New Jersey, and Florida also had a relatively large number of job enrichment efforts. Job enrichment has most frequently affected police (about half of the reported programs involved police personnel or services), although no single outside factor (such as federal funding) seems to have been responsible for this concentration. Programs involving police jobs also comprised forty-one of the fifty-six job enrichment efforts known to have been terminated.

Job enrichment in the public sector has taken four major forms: the use of teams (129 of the 309 reported programs), job redesign (ninety-three reported programs), participative decision making (fifty-six programs), and job rotation (thirty-one programs). About 60 percent (175) of the reported programs involved major changes in the way employees handled their day-to-day work. Among the most popular techniques were team policing (seventy-one programs), joint labor-management committees (forty programs), public safety officers cross-trained to handle both police and fire responsibilities (thirty-six programs), and problem-oriented teams and task forces (twenty-nine programs). Less common techniques included team management, job enlargement, and certain forms of job restructuring. Although team policing constituted the largest application of teamwork, teams for conducting day-to-day operations in other agencies had been introduced in at least eleven other jurisdictions. The service areas involved ranged from health care to custodial services.

Findings on Impact

MONETARY INCENTIVES

Although there have been numerous assessments of the impact of monetary incentives on employee productivity and job satisfaction in the private sector, information on the impact of public sector incentives is quite limited. The results of laboratory and private sector research indicate that individual monetary rewards are effective in increasing employee productivity. Group rewards are also effective, but less so than individual rewards.

Many studies indicate that one of the most important factors in whether a monetary incentive plan has an impact on productivity is the degree to which pay is explicitly dependent on performance.

In the public sector, the few existing evaluations of monetary incentives indicate that the use of shared savings plans, piecework, and, to some extent, other types of performance bonuses in state and local governments has produced some significant improvements in productivity and cost savings, especially when programs have been based on objective criteria focusing on job performance. These successes have been confined largely to areas where objective information on performance has been fairly readily available, such as sanitation, police, vehicle maintenance, water meter repair, and data processing. Large savings have also been reported in connection with suggestion awards, but it is often unclear whether these are real or "paper" savings. Although group incentives appear to be particularly appropriate for public sector motivational efforts where individual contributions are difficult to measure, their use to date has been limited.

The most common type of monetary incentive in the public sector—the merit increase—appears to have received the least amount of evaluation. No systematic assessment of such procedures was found. Research findings from the private sector, however, indicate that such raises are likely to have little or no motivational power under current appraisal systems. Another disadvantage of merit increases is that, unlike bonuses, they usually cannot be withdrawn once they are given, even if performance subsequently decreases. In short, the overall long-term incentive value of merit increases has yet to be demonstrated.

What little private sector research there is on the relationship between monetary rewards and job satisfaction has not produced a consistent relationship. Apparently, job satisfaction depends on numerous factors specific to each case. Public sector results are equally sparse. However, a recent study of the use of monetary incentives in three local governments concluded that employee job satisfaction had suffered no long-term damage (although short-term dissatisfaction did develop in a few cases), and in some instances job satisfaction actually improved. As for the various merit increase procedures, there have been few if any formal assessments of the impact of these on job satisfaction.

PERFORMANCE TARGETING

Research in the private sector indicates that setting specific goals can lead to improved employee performance. There is some evidence that such targets are motivating in and of themselves without being linked to rewards. However, the effectiveness of target-setting procedures apparently depends on many factors, including (a) the quality of the targets (they should be specific, challenging yet realistic, and prioritized), (b) participation by subordinates in the setting of goals, and (c) the provision of frequent, relevant, and constructive feedback on progress toward goal achievement. Where performance targets are tied to significant monetary rewards, private sector research indicates that employees will respond by setting—or accepting—higher targets. One finding of special significance for governments contemplating the introduction of performance targets is that the creation of a successful target-setting system usually requires several years.

There have been virtually no systematic studies of the effectiveness of target-setting procedures in improving state and local government productivity. Most analyses have been limited to case studies of the use of MBO or work standards. A 1975 assessment of the use of work standards and performance targets in five local governments found that productivity improvements attributable to the use of standards occurred only where the standards were associated with monetary rewards. Since most targets used in connection with ABO and MBO in state and local governments appear to focus on process goals rather than efficiency and effectiveness, one might expect that the impact of such target-setting efforts on productivity would be limited; this hypothesis has yet to be tested.

Users of performance targets in local governments tend to believe that improvements in productivity and management decision making have occurred, that whatever negative effects were produced were not serious, and that the cost of these programs has been low (with the exception of work standards efforts). Without more substantial evidence, however, these apparent benefits can be questioned.

There also appear to have been few systematic studies of the impact of performance targeting on job satisfaction. But there is some evidence from other research that identifying specific goals increases employee satisfaction. In the 1975 study of the use of work standards and performance targets in five local governments, some dissatisfaction was found when the standards were established as personal performance requirements and used as the basis of appraisals; when management subsequently de-emphasized the use of work standards as performance targets in favor of using them to help in planning and scheduling work, employee dissatisfaction subsided and no long-term damage was sustained. Of 125 jurisdictions contacted concerning performance appraisal and target setting, only one reported having conducted a survey of employee job satisfaction. In that investigation (conducted about a year after the implementation of an ABO system), employees reported feeling positive about the procedure and the increased objectivity of their performance appraisal. Subjective assessments by officials in a number of other jurisdictions also indicated increased job satisfaction in connection with the use of performance targets.

PERFORMANCE APPRAISAL

On the basis of the evidence available, it does not appear possible to say conclusively whether the performance appraisal methods used by state and local governments contribute to improved productivity. There have been few direct studies of the impact of appraisals on productivity per se, especially in the public sector. (Of the 100 state and local governments contacted in the course of our investigation of performance appraisal techniques, only five had conducted systematic assessments of their appraisal procedures, and these had focused on the validity of the appraisals and on job-relatedness rather than on productivity.)

Fifty of the 100 jurisdictions relied on nonobjective appraisal techniques, such as annual ratings by supervisors based on subjective judgments and focused on characteristics unrelated to specific job responsibilities. Yet, even in these cases—cases in which the validity of the appraisals was doubtful—rewards could be withheld for unsatisfactory performance, although superior performance usually resulted in the same reward as satisfactory performance. Laboratory and private sector research, as well as court opinions, do not indicate that such nonobjective appraisal procedures are valid, helpful for employee development, legally defensible, or likely to motivate improved employee performance and productivity.

There are some indications that other performance appraisal approaches may improve employee performance, but there is little hard evidence of this as yet. Thus, checklists and rating scales based on observable behavior (rather than personal traits) and tailored to individual jobs seem to be an improvement. They are, however, costly and time-consuming. Appraisal by objectives, in which performance is rated against preestablished job objectives, is also promising, but there is insufficient research for an informed judgment and the procedure does have some drawbacks (e.g., difficulties in specifying quantitative, controllable targets for all major responsibilities, and problems with comparing the performance of different individuals).

An oft-cited benefit of most performance appraisal techniques is that they can serve as incentives without the need for rewards while also stimulating supervisor-employee communication and employee self-development. The existing research, however, indicates that realization of such benefits is predicated on adequate training of supervisors in appraisal practices, the focusing of appraisals on specific job behavior, and the preparation of appraisals frequently enough so that the time between employee actions and their evaluation is not unduly long.

Some laboratory and private sector research indicates that the traditional performance appraisal techniques (narratives and subjective rating scales) may actually be counterproductive, producing hostility, loss of self-esteem, and poorer performance. If true for the public sector, this would imply that it may not be advisable to link such traditional appraisals to rewards. What has not been adequately tried or evaluated is the use of performance appraisals based on objective, results-oriented measures and linked to clear rewards (or penalties). Nor have there been adequate efforts to explore the use and effectiveness of appraisals of work groups. In some ways, groups may constitute a more rational basis for appraising the work of government employees.

While there do not appear to have been any systematic assessments of employee job satisfaction in connection with the use of performance appraisals (in either the public or private sectors), there have been widespread reports of employee and union dissatisfaction with merit system procedures and other performance appraisal techniques. Moreover, some private sector research indicates that many appraisal procedures are likely to create dissatisfaction among employees, due largely to the likelihood that the supervisor's assessment will fall below the employee's expectation. One of the ways suggested for coping with this problem involves divorcing the appraisal from the determination of rewards and using it primarily as a tool for employee development.

JOB ENRICHMENT

With the exception of a few special types of programs, there has been little documentation of the impact of job enrichment in the public sector. While there has been considerable private sector research concerning the relationship between job enrichment and productivity, the results are generally inconclusive and complicated by the presence of many intervening factors. An exception is job redesign, where private sector research generally points to the likelihood of productivity improvements. However, because of the many intervening factors, the applicability of the private sector results to the public sector is questionable.

A priori, one might expect the greatest productivity improvements from job enrichment that involves job restructuring or the use of teams. Both of these approaches have a direct impact on work procedures (analogous to the methods improvement techniques used in conjunction with work standards). Where evaluative data are available (e.g., in connection with police teams, public safety officers, and a few similar public sector programs), the data generally do indicate improved efficiency and effectiveness, although in some cases the results are mixed.

There have been few evaluations of the effect of giving public employees increased opportunities to participate in decision making or in contributing advice to management. The assessments that have been conducted indicate that such programs can stimulate ideas that may yield lower costs or increased effectiveness, although it is often difficult to attribute those improvements directly to the use of greater employee participation. This, however, is a general problem in assessing job enrichment efforts. These programs are often combined with other changes, making it hard to distinguish the impact of the enrichment program alone. Although the cost of such programs generally appears to be low (with the exception of some job redesign efforts), very little information is available on the complete costs.

Although one of the major objectives of job enrichment is to improve employee job satisfaction, systematic assessments of job satisfaction have only been conducted in connection with a few types of public sector enrichment efforts. (Private sector results have been surprisingly inconclusive, again indicating the presence of many intervening factors.) Evaluations of the impact of team policing (and related efforts to redesign the job of the patrol officer into that of a "generalist officer") have yielded mixed results in terms of job satisfaction. Improvements in job satisfaction have been modest where there were any at all, and some supervisors and patrol officers have been dissatisfied with the new arrangements. Among the sources of dissatisfaction was the frustration of the officers at seeing how little they could do to control or prevent crime (this became clear to them when they were given responsibility for following up on initial contacts), as well as increased boredom in areas where police teams appeared to be successful in reducing crime.

Studies of other types of job enrichment in the public sector have found mixed results regarding changes in morale and job satisfaction. Assessments of two public sector programs to increase employee participation in decision making and management deliberations found that job satisfaction increased for most participants, although it decreased for some supervisors. Most job enrichment programs reported increased employee enthusiasm and initiative, which might be interpreted as an indication of increased job satisfaction. Instances of dissatisfaction among supervisors were relatively common, since job enrichment often tended to threaten their established roles and attitudes.

Findings on Factors Affecting Implementation

Successful introduction of motivational techniques can be affected by a number of factors. The implementation concerns identified in the course of this investigation, however, clustered around three major areas: performance assessment criteria and procedures, employee labor organizations, and civil service rules and regulations. Other important considerations included state laws and resistance from supervisory and line employees.

PERFORMANCE ASSESSMENT CRITERIA AND PROCEDURES

The absence of adequate performance criteria and appraisal procedures appears to be a major obstacle to the development and introduction of motivational techniques. The lack of objective, valid, results-oriented performance criteria or standards focusing on work quantity and quality has been a major weakness of most current performance appraisal and performance-targeting efforts, and has often been cited by government and labor officials as an obstacle to the development of fair and effective motivational plans, such as monetary incentives. Due in part to limitations in the current state of the art with regard to measurement, as well as the lack of regularly collected data, employee appraisals and assessments in state and local governments have more often than not been based on personal traits and subjective ratings. Some researchers have concluded that appraisals based on such criteria may actually be counterproductive and result in poorer performance. Under such circumstances, the concerns of public employee organizations about the potential dangers of giving managers increased discretion are understandable.

There appears to be a great need for objective, reliable, results-oriented performance measures that are accepted as reasonable by employees, unions, and the courts. Most governments are legally free to change their appraisal systems, as long as the new systems are valid and job-related. While some promising alternatives have appeared (e.g., appraisal by objectives and behaviorally based rating instruments), these techniques usually have not emphasized objective measures of work quantity, work quality, or service effectiveness; moreover, their cost and the time required to develop them often pose serious obstacles.

UNIONS AND EMPLOYEE ASSOCIATIONS

The presence of public employee organizations and collective bargaining can affect the introduction of motivational programs in a number of ways.

Contract stipulations resulting from collective bargaining may require management either to adjust the proposed motivational program to make it compatible with contract provisions, or else negotiate modifications of those provisions. Moreover, the presence of large bargaining units may mean that motivational plans must cover many different types of employees, a requirement that may increase the difficulty of designing an effective plan while greatly diluting the rewards provided. But the alternative—to apply the plan only to some of the employees in the bargaining unit—may be resisted on the basis of equity considerations. Finally, there is concern among some public employee organizations that productivity improvement and motivational techniques may produce inequities, create conflicts within the bargaining unit, cause speedups, damage morale, encourage unhealthy competition, and lead to loss of jobs.

Nearly every type of motivational plan can potentially be affected by some type of labor-related issue or contract constraint. However, the frequency with which such constraints are encountered varies considerably. The use of monetary incentives and other rewards can be affected by contract specifications covering wage rates, working hours, and leave or vacation allotments. Job enrichment efforts can be affected by contract provisions covering job specifications, temporary assignments, and out-of-class work, as well as the fears of union officials that enrichment programs will weaken the role of the union. Performance appraisal procedures can be affected by contract provisions emphasizing seniority rather than performance in awarding promotions and wage increases. In a few instances, performance appraisal techniques have actually been prescribed by contract stipulations. The use of target-setting procedures can be constrained by contract provisions stipulating work standards and appraisal procedures.

It should be stressed, however, that most of the foregoing represent potential barriers; in general, there is little systematic information on the actual impact of public employee organization concerns on the implementation of motivational programs. While there have been examples of overt union obstruction (e.g., in connection with the use of performance bonuses and public safety officer positions), there have also been a number of examples of cooperation. Public employee organizations seem to be particularly interested in shared savings plans, joint labor-management committees, and quality-of-worklife experiments, although opinions among labor organizations are by no means unanimous.

The foregoing suggests that early involvement of employee organizations in the planning and implementation of motivational programs is highly desirable. Joint labor-management committees appear to represent a promising mechanism for that involvement. Not only is early, meaningful participation by public employee organizations likely to facilitate the resolution of contractual and other labor-related issues, but it may also improve the quality of the resulting effort and develop active support for the program that emerges.

CIVIL SERVICE AND PERSONNEL SYSTEMS

Although constraints vary considerably from state to state, nearly every major type of motivational approach can be affected in one way or another by civil service and personnel rules and policies. Monetary incentives appear to be more affected by such constraints than other types of motivational plans. Constraints on the use of monetary incentives include (1) laws and regulations that explicitly prohibit or restrict the use of monetary rewards for public employees; (2) civil service rules (especially for state employees) requiring that compensation be uniform and comparable for all employees in the jurisdiction or for all employees within a given job class (this may mean that a monetary incentive plan must be made available to all employees or that special authorization for trying such incentives in a single agency or operation must be obtained from the civil service commission or the legislature); (3) rules specifying that all employees must be paid only at the levels (steps) prescribed for their job class (thereby precluding, among other things, the possibility of incentive rewards for persons at the top step); and (4) restrictions that limit the frequency with which rewards can be granted and that prohibit temporary step increases. In some cases, civil service rules constrain the use of other types of incentive rewards, such as extra vacation or personal leave. On the other hand, a number of states felt that the use of fringe benefit awards would be less tightly constrained than cash incentives.

Fewer civil service constraints are likely to be encountered in connection with job enrichment programs. Most of those which do exist appear to apply to job redesign (e.g., restrictive job classifications). Civil service laws do not usually fix the content of employee performance appraisals, and there seem to be few civil service constraints on the use of performance targets. Motivational programs involving nonmonetary rewards, such as certificates, pins, or trophies, are generally unaffected by civil service rules.

In addition to the constraints already discussed, the frequent need to have any motivational program approved by civil service or personnel officials can introduce an informal obstacle. Civil service officials tend to take a conservative attitude toward incentives; they are often willing to attempt only what is explicitly permitted under law (only seven states explicitly authorize the use of monetary incentives). As a result, there often appears to be a reluctance on the part of other agencies even to consider motivational programs (especially monetary incentives).

OTHER FACTORS

A number of other factors that can inhibit the introduction of motivational programs have been identified in the course of this study. Among the most serious are opposition from line employees (due to concern over possible speedups, loss of job security, and program inequities) and resistance from management and supervisors (including reluctance to make distinctions between employees based on subjective assessments, opposition to work standards, resistance to the time demands and paperwork associated with some motivational efforts, and concern over loss of their own job security and authority). Other barriers include legal restrictions, technical problems, political constraints, citizen opposition, and financial constraints.

Chapter 30

CONCLUSIONS AND RECOMMENDATIONS

Conclusions

1. In general, state and local governments have made little use of the motivational approaches that appear most likely to encourage employees to improve productivity. Few performance appraisal systems in state and local governments have emphasized objective, output-oriented measures of individual or group performance. Performance-targeting procedures, such as management by objectives, have been more widely accepted, but they have generally failed to emphasize explicit productivity concerns and have encountered technical difficulties in implementation. Few use targets and performance measures focusing on effectiveness and efficiency. Monetary incentives tied to job performance are also rare. Although merit procedures for determining wage increases are fairly widespread, their linkage to employee performance tends to be weak, and they do not appear to serve as incentives for better performance. Job enrichment has been tried by a number of state and local governments, especially in police departments. But many of these efforts have been limited in scope and in the degree of enrichment provided, with little prospect for significant improvements in productivity.

2. In part, the limited use of motivational approaches likely to stimulate improved productivity reflects the difficulties faced by state and local governments in introducing such plans. It appears that monetary (cash) incentives face the most serious implementation obstacles. The major factors affecting implementation of such programs appear to be civil service and personnel

rules and regulations, plus public employee organizations (and contracts involving them). Employee opposition is also an important factor to contend with. Note that labor-related constraints on the introduction of shared savings plans are likely to be much less severe than for other monetary incentives. Finally, certain technical issues—the development of objective measures of productivity, valid performance appraisal techniques, and the like—have hampered past efforts to motivate improved productivity. These problems are only now beginning to be overcome.

3. Incentive plans involving additional fringe benefits, such as extra vacation, are probably somewhat easier to implement than those providing extra dollars, although their motivational power is likely to be less than that of cash. Nonmonetary incentive plans and performance targeting could be used widely, but their effectiveness in improving productivity—both in the short run and over the long term—has not yet been established. Job enrichment programs also appear to face fewer obstacles than incentives involving cash or fringe benefits, although they are probably harder to introduce than performance targets and nonmonetary incentives. The major barriers faced by performance appraisal techniques appear to be more technical—the state of the art of performance measurement, the absence of systematic information on the effectiveness of the procedures (especially in terms of improving productivity), and the large amounts of time and dollars needed to develop promising techniques.

4. There is a serious lack of evaluative information on the impacts of most of the foregoing motivational techniques. Only for certain types of monetary incentives and a few job enrichment efforts, such as the use of police teams and public safety officers, is satisfactory information available. Few systematic assessments were found of the effectiveness of other job enrichment approaches being used in the public sector, or of the performance appraisal and performance-targeting techniques being tried by state and local governments. And in no case has a clear, consistent relationship between any of these techniques and employee job satisfaction been established.

5. Despite the many problems and controversies surrounding monetary incentives for government employees, the evidence (although highly limited) indicates that monetary incentives linked to objective performance criteria focusing on job outcomes and productivity appear to have had the most significant positive effects on productivity, at least in the short run (one to two

years after introduction). These successes, however, have been confined largely to services about which objective information on performance has been fairly readily available (e.g., sanitation, police, vehicle maintenance, water meter repair, and data processing). On the other hand, there appears to be no evidence to indicate that the merit increase procedures now used by many state and local governments serve as an incentive.

6. *Three major conditions appear to be required for significant productivity improvements: (a) the performance of individuals or groups must be assessed in a valid, objective manner, emphasizing the public purposes of the services provided by those employees; (b) such assessment should be closely linked to some type of reward or penalty, whether monetary or nonmonetary; and (c) there should be both early, meaningful involvement by employee organizations as well as adequate advance participation and training for those affected, including supervisory as well as nonsupervisory employees.*

Almost all existing attempts to use performance appraisals, performance targeting, and merit increases appear to have major defects with respect to one or more of these conditions. The evidence, although quite limited, suggests that in most cases those attempts did not yield significantly improved productivity. While job enrichment techniques may in some instances provide an alternate way to achieve this goal without fulfilling the first two conditions, the magnitude of the productivity improvement seems to be smaller than for monetary incentives. On the other hand, job enrichment programs are probably easier to introduce than monetary incentives.

Recommendations[1]

1. We do not believe that attempts to tinker with merit increase procedures in order to tie them more closely to job performance represent a fruitful approach. Instead, more basic changes and improvements are needed in merit system criteria and procedures. We believe there is a need for (a) extensive development, testing, and evaluation of motivational techniques that utilize more objective, results-oriented performance criteria

---

1. These and other recommendations to federal, state, and local governments and other interested organizations are elaborated in the Appendix.

(i.e., focusing on the employee's contribution to service efficiency and effectiveness), and (b) performance appraisal techniques that can make extensive use of such information. Clearer definitions of minimum acceptable levels of performance and reasonable, yet challenging, performance targets are needed. Sanctions, training, and other actions contingent on low performance should be balanced by rewards to provide a positive incentive for high performance. The use of work groups as the focus for performance appraisals and incentive plans may be an especially promising direction. In any case, meaningful participation by employees prior to plan introduction is vital.

2. Until individual performance criteria and appraisal techniques are greatly improved, we recommend that governments desiring to increase employee motivation concentrate on designing and implementing management incentives or, for nonmanagement employees, group incentives. These programs should probably not be linked to existing appraisal procedures, given the inadequacies of the latter. Although management and group incentives are not without certain problems, the state of the art for measuring the performance of groups (and hence, of managers of those groups) in state and local governments is better developed than that for individuals, and the obstacles to such plans are likely to be fewer. Management incentives would avoid many of the issues that worry unions and line employees (while addressing union concerns about the need for improved supervision). Furthermore, a number of civil service officials have indicated that approval of management incentives would be much easier to obtain.

3. Some forms of job enrichment have shown promise for improving productivity, especially (a) those that involve the systematic redesign of the employee's day-to-day job, and (b) those that provide for increased participation in decision making by employees, especially concerning activities related to their own jobs. Examples of such programs include the creation of police and other teams for performing day-to-day operations, the consolidation of related jobs, the restructuring of certain jobs to provide responsibility for a "complete" task, and the introduction of joint labor-management committees that include line employees. Such efforts merit systematic testing and evaluation.

4. The lack of adequate information on the effects of the various types of motivational approaches on productivity and job satisfaction has often been cited. This can and should be

corrected. State and local governments should get into the habit of providing objective, systematic evaluations of the productivity and job satisfaction impacts of any new motivational approaches they try.

Government employees, both managerial and nonmanagerial, are a vital element of government services. Much work needs to be done to improve their motivational environment. Yet our knowledge of public sector motivational plans—which ones work, which ones do not, and the reasons why—is in its infancy. Many of the early results, though limited, are promising. Indeed, the stakes are too high for governments not to explore further the use of motivational approaches to enhance service productivity and employee job satisfaction. Through improved productivity and job satisfaction, both the public and the public employee will be better served.

APPENDIX

SOME RECOMMENDATIONS FOR IMPROVING EMPLOYEE MOTIVATION OVER THE LONG RUN

A number of forces are helping to reduce the barriers that now exist to the use of motivational techniques. Several state legislatures and city councils have urged or required changes designed to improve employee motivation, such as the introduction of performance standards and monetary incentive plans. Increasingly, public employee organizations are realizing that they must take some responsibility for dealing with the fiscal problems of their governments and the ability of those governments to provide jobs and wage increases. This has meant a greater involvement by unions in efforts to improve productivity. And by both word and deed the federal government has begun to express its concern with employee productivity at all levels of government and the need for innovative efforts to improve that productivity.

Nevertheless, we believe that if the most promising motivational techniques are to be widely and effectively harnessed to the task of improving government productivity, a concerted effort must be made to identify and reduce the barriers that remain. This is likely to require a variety of efforts, including changes in state and local civil service and personnel regulations and practices, consultation or negotiation with public employee organizations, and—in some cases—revision of state and local laws. Probably one of the most effective steps would be to conduct carefully evaluated tests of motivational programs in jurisdictions where there are few obstacles. Dissemination of the results of such tests would provide the information needed to

417

make informed judgments about the applicability of these procedures elsewhere.

The following are our recommendations, based on this investigation. Many of these are aimed particularly at the federal government and other large organizations where resources for undertaking these tasks are most likely to be available.

1. The first priority should be to explore ways to improve performance appraisal. Correct assessment of employee performance lies at the heart of many, if not most, motivational techniques. The lack of objective, valid performance indicators is a major obstacle to motivating public sector employees. Thus, the development of improved appraisal techniques and objective, job-related performance measures should be one of the first orders of business for federal, state, and local governments interested in improving employee productivity. Such recent developments as appraisal-by-objectives techniques, and the growing availability of measures and measurement procedures for regularly assessing service effectiveness, should be drawn on in any effort to develop, test, and evaluate new approaches to performance evaluation. Wherever possible, such measures should be incorporated into performance appraisal and target-setting processes. It may be helpful to establish a joint labor-management committee to supervise the development of such criteria in order to make sure that they are acceptable to labor, management, and the courts.

2. Until improved performance measures are developed, it seems best to use appraisals mainly for employee development and, where possible, target setting (without rewards). Where a better linkage between pay and performance is desired, it may be easier and more appropriate to provide managerial and group incentives tied to the (more readily measurable) performance of organizational units.[1] Systematic efforts to develop adequate performance data should be encouraged, as well as use of that data to prepare performance targets. Only after performance measures and data are well-established should governments consider linking targets and the associated appraisal system to rewards.

---

1. Of course, group incentives and management incentives based on group performance are both subject to certain problems of their own. And in a period when wage increases for nonmanagement personnel have been limited by tight budgets, the introduction of management bonuses can be expected to meet considerable resistance from public employees and their organizations.

3. An effort should be made to identify needed revisions in civil service rules and policies that constrain the introduction of motivational programs. The purpose should be to encourage rules and policies that provide more flexibility for program experimentation without damaging merit principles. (For example, recent revisions of the Federal Merit System Standards permit temporary suspension of the standards to allow experiments with new personnel approaches.) Among the changes that should be considered are the elimination of laws prohibiting the use of monetary rewards, the enactment of laws with explicit provisions permitting monetary and other rewards for outstanding performance, and the elimination or relaxation of wage comparability requirements that prevent the use of monetary incentives (and related programs) in one agency if they are not also provided in others.

4. Promising monetary incentive techniques, such as shared savings programs, performance bonuses, and management or supervisory incentives, should be tested and evaluated. Where nonmanagement personnel are involved, emphasis should be placed on group incentives. Such efforts should be kept separate from regular employee appraisal activities. Job enrichment methods should also be tested and evaluated, especially those that involve the systematic redesign of the employee's day-to-day job, the restructuring of certain jobs to provide responsibility for a complete task, or increased participation in decision making by employees, especially concerning their own jobs. The development of public sector Scanlon Plans, which combine monetary rewards (shared savings) with increased employee participation, is a promising direction for future testing and evaluation.

5. An active effort should be made to obtain the support and participation of public employee organizations in facilitating the introduction of motivational programs and in developing plans acceptable to all parties. Such efforts should include joint labor-management committees, with participation by line personnel as well as union officials.

6. Any government contemplating the use of a new motivational program should make an effort to assess, in a systematic way, the impact of the program on productivity (service effectiveness and efficiency) and employee job satisfaction. The importance of making careful, systematic assessments cannot be overemphasized. Although state and local governments usually cannot afford the thorough evaluations recommended later in

this appendix, they have an obligation to themselves and to the public to assess the plans they try. At a minimum, a separate record of program costs should be maintained, and data on the cost and quality of services and on employee job satisfaction should be obtained before implementation and again after implementation (allowing a sufficient period of time for the identification of long-term effects). A simple questionnaire can be used to assess job satisfaction and to determine how the program has actually affected the way employees do their work. A small effort such as this can provide an objective and reasonably complete picture of the value of the approach and whether it is worth continuing.

The Special Role of the Federal Government

The complexity of the problem of motivation, the diversity of the governments and activities likely to be involved, and the expense associated with systematic testing and evaluation of new approaches all argue for a major role by the federal government. Such involvement would complement and support the current effort to reform the federal civil service system. The federal government's role should include the following:

1. *Support for the Development of Adequate Performance Appraisal Techniques.* As noted at the beginning of this appendix, improvement in performance appraisal procedures seems crucial. Among the matters that merit potential federal support are the following:

- Efforts to determine the validity, cost, and effectiveness of such appraisal techniques as ABO and ABO plus checklists or behavioral rating scales. The impact of these and other promising appraisal procedures on employee productivity and job satisfaction, and their ability to satisfy court requirements, should be systematically assessed. This might include comparative studies of the effects of using different appraisal frequencies, different types of criteria, different job classifications and work sites, and different levels of supervisor training.
- Efforts to develop objective, results-oriented performance criteria that are satisfactory to management, employees, public employee organizations, and the courts. Active

participation by employee organizations in such efforts should be encouraged. The types of supplementary information needed in conjunction with such measures should also be determined.

2. *Support for Efforts to Evaluate Existing and Proposed Motivational Techniques.* The absence of information on the cost and impact of various motivational techniques seriously hampers efforts to make improvements. The federal government should support systematic, in-depth studies of the impact of innovative motivational programs on productivity and job satisfaction. Federal funds are needed for this to be done properly. The following types of programs seem most appropriate for such evaluative efforts: monetary incentive plans, including shared savings efforts and performance-based bonuses (or wage increases), especially those that involve ABO or MBO; programs involving non-monetary rewards; performance-targeting procedures; joint labor-management committees involving substantial participation by line employees; and certain other types of job enrichment, especially those involving the systematic redesign of the employee's day-to-day job or increased participation in decision making by employees. Programs that combine several of these approaches may also be effective.

In addition, the federal government should encourage state and local governments to undertake their own evaluations of such programs. It would probably be quite useful if the federal government supported the development of a guidebook that provided state and local governments with suggestions for simple, low-cost evaluation approaches for these types of motivational programs. Federal funds should probably not be used to assess efforts to merely tinker with traditional appraisal and merit systems.

3. *Support for the Development and Testing of New Motivational Approaches.* This would involve new experiments to test the effectiveness of such potentially promising techniques as performance bonuses, shared savings plans, and more participation by individual workers in improving job procedures, as well as combinations of such approaches (e.g., a public sector Scanlon Plan). The establishment of long-term efforts (three to five years) in several jurisdictions should be given special consideration. Each effort should involve the development and implementation of individual and group performance measures focused on output, effectiveness, and efficiency; the subsequent introduction

of target-setting techniques based on those measures; and finally the introduction of incentives tied to target achievement.

4. *Support for Basic Research and Specialized Investigations.* A number of specialized research questions also need further investigation. They include the following:

- Do performance targets focusing on results, efficiency, and effectiveness lead to greater improvement in productivity than traditional, process-oriented targets?
- To what extent does the addition of monetary incentives to a performance target system enhance productivity and job satisfaction? And what is the effect of the size and type of reward on the magnitude of any improvements?
- To what extent would a group emphasis in work design and organization, performance appraisal, and target setting improve productivity and job satisfaction while reducing obstacles to change? For instance, do group targets have a better effect on productivity than individual targets?
- Are certain types of incentives more appropriate for certain types of employees?
- How does the degree to which participation involves making decisions rather than just giving advice affect the impact of participation programs on productivity and job satisfaction?
- To what extent does the substitution of fringe benefit rewards for cash rewards affect the feasibility and effectiveness of monetary incentives?
- How do the effectiveness and applicability of motivational approaches compare with the effectiveness and applicability of other major productivity improvement strategies, such as innovations in technology, improvements in operational procedures, revision of organizational structures, and improvement of management skills and techniques?

Situational differences in the answers to these questions—e.g., for different levels of government, different organizational units, different types of jobs, different management styles, and different labor environments—should also be explored.

5. *Support for Efforts to Examine and Reduce the Obstacles to Motivational Techniques.* The following activities seem needed:

- A systematic, in-depth examination of the actual frequency, magnitude, and impact of legal, civil service, contractual, labor-related, fiscal, and political constraints affecting the use of motivational programs;

- An exploration of techniques that state and local governments might use to lower the more significant barriers; and
- Development of training programs to provide both labor and management representatives with the knowledge and skills necessary to deal with motivational issues.

BIBLIOGRAPHY

Aaron, Benjamin. "Reflections on Public Sector Collective Bargaining." *Labor Law Journal*, vol. 5 (July-August 1976), pp. 234-238.

Adams, J. Stacy. "Toward an Understanding of Inequity." *Journal of Abnormal and Social Psychology*, vol. 67 (1963), pp. 422-436.

"AFSCME Resolves." *LMRS Newsletter*, vol. 7, no. 9 (September 1976), p. 1.

"Agreement Between Commonwealth of Pennsylvania and American Federation of State, County, and Municipal Employees, AFL-CIO" (July 1, 1973 to June 30, 1976).

"Agreement: The State of New Jersey, New Jersey Civil Service Association, and New Jersey State Employees Association—Professional Unit" (July 1, 1977 to June 30, 1979).

"Agreement: The State of New Jersey, New Jersey Civil Service Association, and New Jersey State Employees Association—Administrative and Clerical Services Unit" (July 1, 1974 to June 30, 1977).

Alber, Antone F. "Job Enrichment Programs Seen Improving Employee Performance, But Benefits Not Without Cost." *World of Work Report*, vol. 3, no. 1 (January 1978), pp. 8-9f.

Alderfer, C. P. "An Empirical Test of a New Theory of Human Needs." *Organizational Behavior and Human Performance*, vol. 4 (1969), pp. 142-175.

Allan, Peter, and Rosenberg, Stephen. "The Development of a Task-Oriented Approach to Performance Evaluation in the City of New York." *Public Personnel Management*, vol. 7, no. 6 (January/February 1978), pp. 26-32.

_____. "New York City's Approach to Civil Service Reform: Implications for State and Local Governments." *Public Administration Review*, vol. 38, no. 6 (November-December 1978), pp. 579-584.

Allen, Raymond. "Individual vs. Group Incentive Systems: Research and Practice." Term paper, University of Maryland. College Park, Spring 1972.

Alter, Joseph D., and Maher, Betty M. "Cincinnati: Making the Team Work." *Urban Health*, vol. 3 (February 1973), pp. 21-23ff.

Altman, Bruce A. "Department Head Incentive Plan." City of Simi Valley, Calif., August 11, 1972.

_____. "A New City, Unfettered by Tradition, Breaks New Ground in Management." *Nation's Cities* (June 1973), p. 37.

_____. "A 'New Image' Police Department." *The American City* (March 1972), pp. 89-90.

_____. "1972-73 Salary Adjustments." City of Simi Valley, Calif., July 21, 1972.

_____. "Simi Valley—The City of the Seventies." *Public Management,* vol. 55, no. 5 (May 1973), pp. 5-6.

"Analysis of Labor Agreements—Indiana Municipalities, 1973." Indiana Association of Cities and Towns, n.d.

"Analysis of NYC Productivity Program Shows 'Erosion' of the Concept, Some Successes." *Daily Labor Report,* Bureau of National Affairs, no. 148 (August 8, 1977).

Annual Statistical Report. Chicago: National Association of Suggestion Systems (issued annually).

Aplin, John C., Jr., and Schoderbek, Peter P. "How to Measure MBO." *Public Personnel Journal,* vol. 5, no. 2 (March/April 1976), pp. 88-95.

_____. "MBO: Requisites for Success in the Public Sector." *Human Resource Management,* vol. 15 (Summer 1976), pp. 30-36.

Arizala, Andy; Dwarshuis, Louis; Kolton, Marilyn; and Mader, Gerald. *Team Management in Local Government.* Management Information Service, vol. 5, no. 7. Washington, D.C.: International City Management Association, July 1973.

Arnstein, Sherry R. "A Ladder of Citizen Participation." *Journal of the American Institute of Planners,* vol. 35, no. 4 (July 1969), pp. 216-224.

Bailey, Shirley A. "Administrative Aide Survey." Department of Personnel, County of Montgomery, Rockville, Md., 1974.

Barnett, James H. "A Study of Police and Fire Department Integration in Selected Cities of North America." Special report no. 35. Bureau of Governmental Affairs, University of North Dakota. Grand Forks, January 1973.

Barrett, Richard S. *Performance Rating.* Chicago: Science Research Associates, 1966.

Battelle Memorial Institute. "An Evaluation of the Bellevue Police Department's Experiment in Team Policing." Seattle, Washington, December 1976.

Baumler, J. V. "Defined Criteria of Performance in Organizational Control." *Administrative Science Quarterly,* vol. 16 (1971), pp. 340-350.

"Beame's Management Team Says Fire and Highway Workers Who Produced More Deserve Raise." *New York Times,* November 5, 1976, p. B3.

Bell, James, and Horst, Pamela. "Neighborhood Team Policing in

Multnomah County, Oregon: A Case Study." Contract Report 5054-13. Washington, D.C.: The Urban Institute, December 1977.

_____. "Neighborhood Team Policing in Santa Ana, California: A Case Study." Contract Report 5054-15. Washington, D.C.: The Urban Institute, December 1977.

Bellows, William C. "Productivity Management in the Department of Transportation." *PREP News: Productivity Improvement in North Carolina*, North Carolina State University, vol. 1, no. 2 (November 1976), pp. 1-5.

Berenbaum, Esai. *Police-Fire Consolidation: A Case Study*. Management Information Service Report, vol. 6, no. 3-A. Washington, D.C.: International City Management Association, March 1974.

Berger, Stephen. "Issues Regarding the Payment of Cost of Living Adjustments Open to Municipal Employees Under the Productivity Program." Emergency Financial Control Board for the City of New York. New York, March 22, 1977.

"Bill Donaldson Shakes Up Cincinnati." *LMRS Newsletter*, vol. 9, no. 11 (November 1978), p. 6.

Birkenstock, John; Kurtz, Ronald; and Phillips, Steven. "Career Executive Assignments—Report on a California Innovation." *Public Personnel Management*, vol. 4, no. 3 (May-June 1975), pp. 151-155.

Bishop, Ronald C. "The Relationship Between Objective Criteria and Subjective Judgments in Performance Appraisal." *Academy of Management Journal*, vol. 17, no. 3 (September 1974), pp. 558-563.

Bishop, Ronald C., and Hill, James W. "Effects of Job Enlargement and Job Change on Contiguous but Nonmanipulated Jobs as a Function of Workers' Status." *Journal of Applied Psychology*, vol. 56 (1971), pp. 175-181.

"Blazers on the Beat Bring New Attitudes." *Washington Post*, July 1, 1973, p. E8.

Blick, Larry N. "Cost Savings Plan Averts Strike, Builds Bonus." *LMRS Newsletter*, vol. 7, no. 5 (May 1976), pp. 2-3.

_____. "Cost Savings Plan Breaks Impasse." *Public Management*, vol. 58, no. 9 (September 1976), pp. 20-21.

Block, Peter B., and Specht, David I. *Evaluation of Operation Neighborhood*. Washington, D.C.: The Urban Institute, 1973.

_____. *Neighborhood Team Policing*. Washington, D.C.: U.S. Department of Justice, National Institute of Law Enforcement and Criminal Justice, December 1973.

Block, Peter B., and Ulberg, C. *Auditing Clearance Rates*. Washington, D.C.: The Police Foundation, December 1974.

_____. "The Beat Commander Concept." *The Police Chief*, vol. 39, no. 9 (September 1972), pp. 55-63.

Bockman, Valerie M. "The Herzberg Controversy." *Personnel Psychology,* vol. 24 (1971), pp. 155-189.

Bolin, David C., and Kivens, Laurence. "Evaluation in a Community Mental Health Center: Huntsville, Alabama." *Evaluation,* vol. 2, no. 1 (1974), pp. 26-35.

Bonin, John P. "On the Design of Managerial Incentive Structures in a Decentralized Planning Environment." *American Economic Review,* vol. 66, no. 4 (September 1976), pp. 682-687.

Bons, Paul M., and Fiedler, Fred E. "Changes in Organizational Leadership and the Behavior of Relationship- and Task-Motivated Leaders." *Administrative Science Quarterly,* vol. 21 (September 1976), pp. 453-473.

Bornstein, Tim. "Unions and Bargaining: The Perennial Critics." *AFL-CIO American Federationist,* vol. 84 (February 1977), pp. 16-20.

Boydstun, J. E., and Sherry, M. E. *Final Evaluation Report of the San Diego Police Department's Community Profile Project.* Santa Monica, Calif.: System Development Corporation, March 25, 1975.

Brady, Rodney H. "MBO Goes to Work in the Public Sector." *Harvard Business Review,* vol. 51, no. 2 (March/April 1973), pp. 65-74.

Brooks, George W. "Negotiating for Productivity in Sanitation." Strengthening Local Government Through Better Labor Relations, no. 15. Washington, D.C.: Labor-Management Relations Service, June 1973.

Brown, F. Gerald, and Heimovics, Richard. "What Municipal Employees Want from Work." Paper presented at the National Conference of the American Society for Public Administration, April 1973, Los Angeles.

Brown, Lee P. "Neighborhood Team Policing and Management by Objectives." *The Police Chief,* vol. 41, no. 11 (November 1976), pp. 72-76.

Bryan, Judith F., and Locke, Edwin A. "Goal Setting as a Means of Increasing Motivation." *Journal of Applied Psychology,* vol. 51, no. 3 (1967), pp. 274-277.

Burkhalter, David A., and Coffman, Jerry B. "Charlotte/Management by Objectives." *Public Management,* vol. 56, no. 6 (June 1974), pp. 15-16.

Burpo, John H. "Improving Police Agency and Employee Performance Through Collective Bargaining." *The Police Chief,* vol. 41, no. 2 (February 1974), pp. 36-38.

Byrd, Richard E., and Cowan, John. "MBO: A Behavioral Science Approach." *Personnel,* vol. 51, no. 2 (March/April 1974), pp. 42-50.

Cahoon, Allan R., and Epstein, Marc J. "Performance Appraisal in Management by Objectives." *Studies in Personnel Psychology,* vol. 4, no. 2 (October 1972), pp. 35-44.

Calkins, Myron D. "A Municipal Safety Program That Works." *The American City* (August 1971), pp. 67-68.

Campbell, H. "Group Incentive Payment Schemes: The Effects of Lack of Understanding and Group Size." *Occupational Psychology,* vol. 26 (1952), pp. 15-21.

Campbell, John P.; Dunnette, Marvin D.; Arvey, Richard D.; and Hellervik, Lowell V. "The Development and Evaluation of Behaviorally Based Rating Scales." *Journal of Applied Psychology,* vol. 57, no. 1 (1973), pp. 15-22.

Campbell, John P.; Dunnette, Marvin D.; Lawler, Edward E. III; and Weick, Karl E., Jr. *Managerial Behavior, Performance, and Effectiveness.* New York: McGraw-Hill Book Company, 1970.

Candeub, Fleissig, and Associates. *Evaluation of Changes in Police and Resident Attitudes: Neighborhood Police Unit Project, Albany, New York.* Albany, N.Y.: Albany Police Department, August 1972.

Cann, W. "Our 4/40 Basic Team Concept." *The Police Chief,* vol. 39, no. 12 (December 1972), pp. 56-60f.

Capozzola, John M. "Productivity Bargaining: Problems and Prospects." *National Review,* vol. 65, no. 4 (April 1976), pp. 176-186.

Carroll, Stephen J., and Tosi, Henry L. "Goal Characteristics and Personality Factors in a Management-by-Objectives Program." *Administrative Science Quarterly,* vol. 15, no. 3 (September 1970), pp. 295-305.

_____. *Management by Objectives: Applications and Research.* New York: Macmillan Publishing Company, 1973.

_____. "The Relationship of Characteristics of the Review Process as Moderated by Personality and Situational Factors to the Success of the 'Management by Objectives' Approach." *Academy of Management Proceedings,* vol. 11 (1969), pp. 139-143.

_____. "The Relationship of Characteristics of the Review Process to the Success of the 'Management by Objectives' Approach." *Journal of Business,* vol. 44, no. 3 (1971), pp. 299-305.

Cayer, N. Joseph. "Is Productivity Bargaining All You Ever Wanted It to Be?" *IPMA News,* International Personnel Management Association (March 1977), pp. 6-7.

Chaiken, Jan. *The Criminal Investigation Process.* Vol. II, *Survey of Municipal and County Police Departments.* Report no. R-1777-DOJ. Santa Monica, Calif.: The Rand Corporation, October 1975.

Champagne, Paul J., and Tausky, Curt. "When Job Enrichment Doesn't Pay." *Personnel,* vol. 55, no. 1 (January/February 1978), pp. 30-40.

Cherrington, D. J.; Reitz, H. J.; and Scott, W. E. "Effects of Contingent and Non-Contingent Reward on the Relationship Between Satisfaction and Task Performance." *Journal of Applied Psychology,* vol. 55 (1971), pp. 531-536.

Cherry, Robert. "Performance Reviews: A Note on Failure." *Personnel Journal,* vol. 49, no. 5 (May 1970), pp. 398-403.

Chickering, A. Lawrence, ed. *Public Employee Unions: A Study of the Crisis in Public Sector Labor Relations.* San Francisco: Institute for Contemporary Studies, 1976.

Citizens Research Council of Michigan. *Saving Taxpayer Dollars Through Consolidated Police and Fire Services.* Memorandum no. 227. Detroit, Michigan, October 1975.

Citizens Union. "Promoting Efficiency in Government: Proposals for a New Personnel System for the City of New York." New York, July 1976.

City of Albany, N.Y. "Neighborhood Police Units." Albany Police Department, n.d.

City of Columbus, Ohio. "Columbus/American Federation of State, County and Municipal Employees Quality of Working Life Program." July 1978.

City of Durham, N.C. "A Review of Durham's Public Safety Officer Program After the First Three Years." November 5, 1973.

City of Flagstaff, Arizona. "Police/Fire Specialists." Report no. 19232. Report Clearinghouse, Management Information Service, International City Management Association. Washington, D.C., 1975.

City of Los Angeles. *An Evaluation of the Team 28 Experiment.* Los Angeles Police Department, April 1976.

City of New York. "Improving Productivity in Municipal Agencies: A Labor-Management Approach." New York City Productivity Council, n.d.

City of Pacifica, Calif. "Pacifica Police Department Annual Report 1976." Pacifica Police Department, February 1977.

City of Palo Alto, Calif. "Management Compensation Plan." April 1977.

City of Simi Valley, Calif. "Rotation of Department Heads." Office of the City Manager, December 21, 1971.

Cizanckas, Victor. "Experiment in Police Uniforms: An Interim Report." *The Police Chief,* vol. 37, no. 4 (April 1970), pp. 28-29.

Cizanckas, Victor; Fabbri, John; Hart, George; Marchand, Claude; Murphy, Robert; and Zurcher, James. "Increased Regional Cooperation in Policing: The Bay Area Middle Management Exchange." *The Police Chief,* vol. 42, no. 11 (November 1975), pp. 22-23f.

Clark, Timothy B. "Senior Executive Service—Reform from the Top." *National Journal,* vol. 10, no. 39 (September 30, 1978), pp. 1542-1546.

"Coast Cities Try Job Rotation." *LMRS Newsletter,* vol. 4, no. 7 (July 1973), p. 5.

"Columbus, Ohio: Experiment in Labor-Management Cooperation," *The NLC SPEER Newsletter,* vol. 1, no. 10 (November 1978), pp. 6-7.

Committee for Economic Development. *Improving Management of the Public Work Force: The Challenge to State and Local Government.* New York, 1978.

Commonwealth of Pennsylvania, Department of Labor and Industry. "Pennsylvania Bureau of Employment Security Personnel Incentive Plan." Harrisburg: Bureau of Employment Security, n.d.

Commonwealth of Virginia. "A Study on Personnel Management Within the Commonwealth of Virginia." House Document no. 12. Richmond, 1977.

Connellan, Thomas K. *Management by Objectives in Local Government: A System of Organizational Leadership.* Management Information Service Report, vol. 7, no. 2A. Washington, D.C.: International City Management Association, February 1975.

Cox, John Howell. "Time and Incentive Pay Practices in Urban Areas." *Monthly Labor Review,* vol. 94, no. 12 (December 1971), pp. 53-56.

Cox, Loron. "Developing a Conceptual Framework for Organizational-Team Development and Responsive Personnel Administration Practices." Final Report, IPA State Plan Project Number 31. City of Simi Valley, Calif., September 1974.

Cresap, McCormick and Paget, Inc. *Albany Police Department: A Management Evaluation of the Arbor Hill Neighborhood Police Unit.* Washington, D.C.: Cresap, McCormick and Paget, Inc., April 1974.

Cummings, L. L., and Schwab, D. P. *Performance in Organizations: Determinants and Appraisal.* Glenview, Ill.: Scott, Foresman and Company, 1973.

Davis, Louis E. "Job Satisfaction Research: The Post-Industrial View." *Industrial Relations,* vol. 10 (1971), pp. 179-193.

Davis, Louis E., and Taylor, James C., eds. *Design of Jobs.* Hammondsworth, Middlesex, England: Penguin Books, 1972.

Day, Howard F. "Job Satisfaction, Motivation, and Job Performance: A Case Study." Department of Personnel, City of Little Rock, Arkansas, February 1976.

Deci, Edward L. "The Effects of Contingent and Noncontingent Rewards and Controls on Intrinsic Motivation." *Organizational Behavior and Human Performance,* vol. 8 (1972), pp. 217-229.

_____. "The Hidden Costs of Rewards." *Organizational Dynamics,* vol. 4, no. 3 (Winter 1976), pp. 61-72.

Dembart, Lee. "But Are Productivity Raises Productive?" *New York Times,* April 14, 1977, p. B8.

"Detroit, Phoenix and Los Angeles Try New Inspections." *LMRS Newsletter,* vol. 8, no. 6 (June 1977), pp. 3-4.

"Development of a Methodology for the Application of Job-Related Criteria to Performance Monitoring and Appraisal." Project report by S.S.S. Consulting to City of Trotwood, Ohio. May 1976.

Dillon, C. R. "MBO, Part 1: Setting Objectives." *Supervisory Management,* vol. 21, no. 4 (April 1976), pp. 18-22.

Dince, Robert R. "Coping with Civil Service." *Fortune* (June 5, 1978), pp. 132-135.

Ditzhazy, J. Andrew. "Another View of Team Policing Program Management." *The Police Chief,* vol. 44, no. 5 (May 1977), pp. 39-40.

Doherty, Robert E. "Implications of the Increasing Power of Public Employee Unions." *State Government,* vol. 49 (Autumn 1976), pp. 234-238.

Donaldson, William V. "Participatory Management—Employees Are Creative!" Strengthening Local Government Through Better Labor Relations, no. 16. Washington, D.C.: Labor-Management Relations Service, June 1973.

Downey, Edward H., and Balk, Walter L. *Employee Innovation and Government Productivity: A Study of Suggestion Systems in the Public Sector.* Personnel Report no. 763. Chicago: International Personnel Management Association, 1976.

Downing, M. Scott. "The Virtues and Vices of MBO." *Government Executive,* vol. 10, no. 4 (April 1978), pp. 39-42.

Drucker, Peter F. "What Results Should You Expect? A Users' Guide to MBO." *Public Administration Review,* vol. 36, no. 1 (January/February 1976), pp. 12-19.

Duerr, Edwin C. "The Effect of Misdirected Incentives on Employee Behavior." *Personnel Journal,* vol. 53 (December 1974), pp. 890-893.

Dunnette, Marvin D. "A Note on *The* Criterion." *Journal of Applied Psychology,* vol. 47, no. 4 (1963), pp. 251-254.

Duttagupta, D. "An Empirical Evaluation of Management by Objectives." Unpublished Master's Thesis, Baruch College. New York, 1975.

"EDP Leads the Thirteen 'Most Popular' Management Techniques." *Administrative Management,* vol. 34, no. 6 (June 1973), pp. 26-29ff.

Eilon, Samuel. "Goals and Constraints." *Journal of Management Studies,* vol. 8 (October 1971), pp. 292-303.

Elliott, J. F. "Crime Control Teams: An Alternative to the Conventional Operational Procedures of Investigating Crimes." *Journal of Criminal Justice,* vol. 6 (1978), pp. 11-23.

Ellis, William G. "Neighborhood Team Policing." *The Police Chief,* vol. 44, no. 5 (May 1977), p. 38f.

Ellis, William G., and Arcand, Garnett G. "Career Development in Police Organizations." Police Department, City of Bellevue, Wash., n.d.

"Employee Award Programs: How Well Do They Work?" *Rural and Urban Roads,* vol. 13, no. 8 (August 1975), pp. 26-27.

"Employee Performance Standards and Appraisals." *State and County Administrator,* vol. 1, no. 4 (July/August 1976), pp. 16-20.

Emrich, Robert L. "The Simi Valley Community Safety Agency." Report to the Board of Directors. Washington, D.C.: The Police Foundation, November 1971.

Fan, Liang Shing. "On the Reward System." *American Economic Review,* vol. 65, no. 1 (March 1978), pp. 226-229.

Farr, James L. "Incentive Schedules, Productivity, and Satisfaction in Work Groups: A Laboratory Study." *Organizational Behavior and Human Performance,* vol. 17 (October 1976), pp. 159-170.

_____. "Task Characteristics, Reward Contingency, and Intrinsic Motivation." *Organizational Behavior and Human Performance,* vol. 16 (August 1976), pp. 294-307.

Fay, Peter P., and Beach, David N. "Management by Objectives Evaluated." *Personnel Journal,* vol. 53, no. 10 (October 1974), pp. 767-769f.

Feigenbaum, Charles. "Civil Service and Collective Bargaining: Conflict or Compatibility?" In *A New World: Readings on Modern Public Personnel Management.* Jay M. Shafritz, ed. Chicago: International Personnel Management Association, 1975, pp. 41-49.

Feild, Hubert S., and Holley, William H. "Performance Appraisal— An Analysis of State-Wide Practices." *Public Personnel Management,* vol. 4, no. 3 (May-June 1975), pp. 145-150.

_____. "Traits in Performance Ratings—Their Importance in Public Employment." *Public Personnel Management,* vol. 4 (September/October 1975), pp. 327-330.

Fein, Mitchell. "Improving Productivity by Improved Productivity Sharing." *The Conference Board RECORD,* vol. 13, no. 7 (July 1976), pp. 44-49.

_____. "Let's Return to MDW Incentives." *Industrial Engineering,* vol. 11, no. 1 (January 1979), pp. 34-37.

_____. *Motivation for Work.* Monograph No. 4. New York: American Institute of Industrial Engineers, May 1971.

_____. *Rational Approaches to Raising Productivity.* Monograph no. 5. Norcross, Ga.: American Institute of Industrial Engineers, 1974.

Ferster, C. B., and Skinner, B. F. *Schedules of Reinforcement.* New York: Appleton-Century-Crofts, 1957.

Fiedler, Judith, and Scontrino, M. Peter. "A Study of the King County Merit Award Program." Report IER-193. University of Washington. Seattle, May 1974.

Flynn, John M. "Productivity." Report by the Senate Task Force on Critical Problems, State of New York. Albany, October 1975.

Ford, R. N. *Motivation Through the Work Itself.* New York: American Management Association, 1969.

Forer, R., and Farrell, R. A. *The Impact of the Neighborhood Police Unit on the Arbor Hill Community of Albany, New York: A Sociological Evaluation.* Albany, N.Y.: R. Forer and R. A. Farrell, 1973.

Frank, E. R. "Motivation by Objectives—A Case Study." *Research Management,* vol. 12 (November 1969), pp. 391-400.

French, John R. P., Jr.; Kay, Emanuel; and Meyer, Herbert H. "Participation and the Appraisal System." *Human Relations,* vol. 19 (February 1966), pp. 3-19.

French, W. L., and Hollmann, R. W. "Management by Objectives: The Team Approach." *California Management Review,* vol. 17 (Spring 1975), pp. 13-22.

Fri, Robert W. "How to Manage the Government for Results: The Rise of MBO." *Organizational Dynamics,* vol. 2, no. 4 (1974), pp. 19-33.

Friedman, Steven C. "3600 Ways to Evaluate." *Public Management,* vol. 60, no. 5 (May 1978), pp. 12-15.

Funkhouser, W. H. "Obstacles to Team Policing." *Current Municipal Problems,* vol. 18, no. 1 (Summer 1976), pp. 61-68.

Garner, Gerald W. "Lakewood, Colorado: Evolution of an Innovative Police Agency." *The Police Chief,* vol. 45, no. 11 (November 1978), pp. 57-65.

Garrett, John, and Walker, S. D. *Management by Objectives in the Civil Service.* CAS Occasional Paper no. 10. London: Her Majesty's Stationery Office, 1969.

Gay, William G.; Day, H. Talmadge; and Woodward, Jane P. *Neighborhood Team Policing.* Phase I Summary Report. Washington, D.C.: National Institute of Law Enforcement and Criminal Justice, Law Enforcement Assistance Administration, February 1977.

Gay, William G.; Woodward, Jane P.; Day, H. Talmadge; O'Neil, James P.; and Tucker, Carl J. *Issues in Team Policing: A Review of the Literature.* Washington, D.C.: National Institute of Law Enforcement and Criminal Justice, Law Enforcement Assistance Administration, September 1977.

Gazell, James A. "MBO in the Public Sector." *University of Michigan Business Review,* vol. 27 (July 1975), pp. 29-35.

Gerhart, Paul F. "The Scope of Bargaining in Local Government Labor Negotiations." *Labor Law Journal,* vol. 20 (August 1969), pp. 545-552.

Ghiselli, Edwin E. "Dimensional Problems of Criteria." *Journal of Applied Psychology,* vol. 40, no. 1 (February 1956), pp. 1-4.

Gibson, Frank K., and Teasley, Clyde E. "The Humanistic Model of Organizational Motivation: A Review of Research Support." *Public Administration Review,* vol. 33, no. 1 (January/February 1973), pp. 89-96.

Gilbert, Thomas W., and Baird, H. Robert. "Another Failure for Peer Comparison Ratings." *The Bureaucrat,* vol. 7, no. 3 (Fall 1978), pp. 38-42.

Gilley, James. "Seeking 'Productivity' Changes in Simi Valley Police Services." *Western City* (August 1975), p. 17f.

Giovannetti, Andrew, and Opperwall, Theodore. "Detroit's Sanitation Productivity Plan." Department of Public Works, City of Detroit, January 1974.

Glaser, Edward M. *Productivity Gains Through Worklife Improvements.* New York: Harcourt, Brace, and Jovanovich, 1976.

_____. "State-of-the-Art Questions About Quality of Worklife." *Personnel,* vol. 53, no. 3 (May/June 1976), pp. 39-47.

Goddard, E. E. "Change—and Management by Objectives—in the Greater London Council." *Local Government Studies,* vol. 1 (October 1971), pp. 33-39.

Goetzl, Robert. "Productivity Bargaining Under the New Massachusetts Public Employee Collective Bargaining Law." Massachusetts League of Cities and Towns. Boston, Mass., August 12, 1974.

Goldberg, Joseph; Greenberg, Leon; Horvitz, Wayne; Tchirkow, Peter; Hunter, Lawrence; Kleingartner, Archie; Azevedo, Ross; McKersie, Robert; Oswald, Rudolph; Sayles, Leonard; Bairstow, Leonard; and Zagoria, Sam. *Collective Bargaining and Productivity.* Madison, Wis.: Industrial Relations Research Association, 1975.

Goldoff, Anna C. "The Perceptions of Participants in a Joint Productivity Program." *Monthly Labor Review,* vol. 101, no. 7 (July 1978), pp. 33-34.

Goldoff, Anna C., with Tatage, David C. "Joint Productivity Committees: Lessons of Recent Initiatives." *Public Administration Review,* vol. 38, no. 2 (March/April 1978), pp. 184-186.

Goldoff, Anna C., and Tatage, David C. "Union-Management Cooperation in New York." *Public Productivity Review,* vol. 3, no. 2 (Summer/Fall 1978), pp. 35-47.

Goldstein, Harold M., and Horowitz, Morris A. "Paramedical Manpower: A Restructuring of Occupations." Department of Eco-
nomics, Northeastern University. Boston, Mass., October 1971.
_____. *Restructuring Paramedical Occupations: A Case Study.*
Boston, Mass.: Northeastern University, Department of Eco-
nomics, January 1972.

Gomez, Luis R., and Mussio, Stephen J. "An Application of Job
Enrichment in a Civil Service Setting: A Demonstration Study."
Public Personnel Management, vol. 4 (January-February 1975),
pp. 49-54.

Goodin, Robert. "Labor Contracts: How a Village Preserved Its
Management Rights." *Rural and Urban Roads,* vol. 14 (September 1976), pp. 30-34.

Goodman, P. S., and Friedman, A. "An Examination of Adams'
Theory of Inequity." *Administrative Science Quarterly,* vol. 16
(1971), pp. 271-286.

Gotbaum, Victor, and Handman, Edward. "A Conversation with
Victor Gotbaum." *Public Administration Review,* vol. 38, no. 1
(January/February 1978), pp. 19-20.

Gotbaum, Victor; Zuccotti, John E.; and Schrank, Robert E. "The
Joint Labor Management Productivity Committee Program to
Fund the Cost of Living Adjustments for the Period October 1,
1976, to March 31, 1977." Office of the Mayor, City of New York.
December 1976.

Graves, Clare W. "Levels of Existence: An Open System Theory of
Values." *Journal of Humanistic Psychology,* vol. 10 (Fall 1970),
pp. 131-155.

Greenberg, David; Lipson, Al; and Rostker, Bernard. "Technical
Success, Political Failure: The Incentive Pay Plan for California
Job Agents." *Policy Analysis,* vol. 2, no. 4 (Fall 1976), pp. 545-
575.

Greenwood, Peter W.; Chaiken, Jan; Petersilia, Joan; and Prusoff,
Linda. *The Criminal Investigation Process.* Vol. III, *Observations
and Analysis.* Report no. R-1778-DOJ. Santa Monica, Calif.:
The Rand Corporation, October 1975.

Greenwood, Peter W., and Petersilia, Joan. *The Criminal Investigation Process.* Vol. I, *Summary and Policy Implications.* Report
no. R-1776-DOJ. Santa Monica, Calif.: The Rand Corporation,
October 1975.

Gregg, Peter. "Work in the Public Service—How Employees View
Their Jobs." *Network News,* National Training and Development
Service, vol. 3, no. 1 (Winter 1975), p. 1f.

Grego, Roger. "Street Sweeping Bonus." City of Jersey City, N.J.,
May 1, 1974.

Greiner, John M. *Tying City Pay to Performance: Early Reports on*

Orange, California and Flint, Michigan. Washington, D.C.: Labor-Management Relations Service, December 1974.

Greiner, John M.; Bell, Lynn; and Hatry, Harry P. *Employee Incentives to Improve State and Local Government Productivity.* Washington, D.C.: National Commission on Productivity and Work Quality, March 1975.

Greiner, John M.; Dahl, Roger E.; Hatry, Harry P.; and Millar, Annie P. *Monetary Incentives and Work Standards in Five Cities: Impacts and Implications for Management and Labor.* Washington, D.C.: The Urban Institute, 1977.

Greiner, John M., and Wright, Virginia B. "Employee Incentives for Local Offices of the Employment Service: Prospects and Problems." Project report to the U.S. Department of Labor, Employment and Training Administration. Washington, D.C.: The Urban Institute, December 1977.

Guion, Robert M. *Personnel Testing.* New York: McGraw-Hill Book Company, 1965.

Hackman, J. Richard. "Improving the Quality of Work Life: Work Design." U.S. Department of Labor. Washington, D.C., June 1975.

_____. "Is Job Enrichment Just a Fad?" *Harvard Business Review,* vol. 53, no. 5 (September/October 1975), pp. 129-138.

_____. "On the Coming Demise of Job Enrichment." In *Man and Work in Society.* Eugene L. Cass and Frederick G. Zimmor, eds. New York: Van Nostrand Reinhold Company, 1975, pp. 97-115.

Hackman, J. R., and Lawler, E. E. III. "Employee Reactions to Job Characteristics." *Journal of Applied Psychology,* vol. 55 (1971), pp. 259-286.

Hackman, J. Richard, and Oldham, Greg R. "Motivation Through the Design of Work: Test of a Theory." *Organizational Behavior and Human Performance,* vol. 16 (1976), pp. 250-279.

Hackman, Richard C. *The Motivated Working Adult.* New York: American Management Association, 1969.

Hall, John R., Jr.; Karter, Michael J., Jr.; Koss, Margo; and Schainblatt, Alfred H. "Fire Code Inspection Practices: Results of a 1977 Survey." Project report to the National Fire Prevention and Control Administration. Washington, D.C.: The Urban Institute, March 1978.

Hamby, Wiley G. "Development of Behaviorally Anchored Rating Scales—'BARS'—for Employee Evaluation." U.S. Civil Service Commission, Atlanta Region, n.d.

Hamilton, Tara. *Team Building.* Washington, D.C.: National League of Cities, n.d.

Harriman, Philip L. *Handbook of Psychological Terms.* Totowa, N.J.: Littlefield, Adams and Company, 1969.

Havemann, Joel A. "Administrative Report/OMB Begins Major Program to Identify and Attain Presidential Goals." *National Journal Reports,* vol. 5 (June 1973), pp. 783-793.

——————. "Can Carter Chop Through the Civil Service System?" *National Journal,* vol. 9, no. 17 (April 23, 1977), pp. 616-624.

——————. "Executive Report/OMB Nears Second Phase, Linking Goals to Budget Process." *National Journal Reports,* vol. 6 (April 1974), pp. 609-618.

——————. "White House Report/OMB's 'Management-by-Objective' Produces Goals of Uneven Quality." *National Journal Reports,* vol. 5 (August 1973), pp. 1201-1210.

Havens, Harry S. "MBO and Program Evaluation, or Whatever Happened to PPBS?" *Public Administration Review,* vol. 36 (January/February 1976), pp. 40-45.

Hayes, Frederick O'R. *Productivity in Local Government.* Lexington, Mass.: Lexington Books, D. C. Heath and Company, 1977.

Hayman, Marie. *Public Safety Departments: Combining the Police and Fire Functions.* Management Information Service Report, vol. 8, no. 7. Washington, D.C.: International City Management Association, July 1976.

Hegarty, William G., and Kissinger, C. Samuel. "A Proposal to Improve Police Services Without Increasing Municipal Operating Costs." *Journal of Police Science and Administration,* vol. 5, no. 4 (1977), pp. 390-392.

Heisel, W. Donald. "The Personnel Revolution: An Optimist's View." *Public Personnel Management,* vol. 5 (July-August 1976), pp. 234-238.

Herrick, Neal Q. "Institutional Views on the Quality of Working Life." Draft report. Washington, D.C.: National Center for Productivity and Quality of Working Life, June 1977.

——————. *The Quality of Work and Its Outcomes.* Columbus, Ohio: The Academy for Contemporary Problems, September 1975.

——————. "Six Interviews on the Quality of Working Life." Draft report. Washington, D.C.: National Center for Productivity and Quality of Working Life, July 1977.

Herzberg, Frederick. "One More Time: How Do You Motivate Employees?" *Harvard Business Review,* vol. 46, no. 1 (January/February 1968), pp. 54-63.

——————. *Work and the Nature of Man.* Cleveland, Ohio: World Publishing Company, 1966.

Herzberg, F.; Mausner, B.; and Snyderman, B. B. *The Motivation to Work.* New York: John Wiley and Sons, 1969.

Herzberg, Frederick, and Zautra, Alex. "Orthodox Job Enrichment: Measuring True Quality in Job Satisfaction." *Personnel,* vol. 53, no. 5 (September/October 1976), pp. 54-68.

Hills, Ann. "Committee of 100 Implementation Committee Files Report." *Spectrum*, New Jersey Department of Labor and Industry, vol. 1, no. 5 (August 1976), pp. 2-5.

Hobbs, Daniel G. "Productivity in Rockville, Maryland." City of Rockville, December 6, 1977.

Hodgson, J. S. "Management by Objectives—the Experience of a Federal Government Department." *Canadian Public Administration*, vol. 16, no. 3 (Fall 1973), pp. 422-431.

Hoffman, Frank O. " 'Team Spirit' As It Affects Productivity." *Personnel Administration*, vol. 16, no. 3 (May/June 1971), pp. 11-14.

Holley, William H., Jr. "Performance Appraisal in Public Sector Arbitration." *Public Personnel Management*, vol. 7, no. 6 (January/February 1978), pp. 1-5.

Holley, William H., Jr., and Feild, Hubert S. "Performance Appraisal and the Law." *Labor Law Journal*, vol. 26, no. 7 (July 1975), pp. 423-430.

Holley, William H., Jr.; Feild, Hubert S.; and Barnett, Nona J. "Analyzing Performance Appraisal Systems: An Empirical Study." *Personnel Journal*, vol. 55 (September 1976), pp. 457-463.

Hollmann, Robert W. "Applying MBO Research to Practice." *Human Resource Management*, vol. 15, no. 4 (Winter 1976), pp. 28-36.

Honig, W. K., ed. *Operant Behavior: Areas of Research and Application*. New York: Appleton-Century-Crofts, 1966.

Hopkins, Anne H.; Rawson, George E.; and Smith, Russell L. "Individuals, Unionization, the Work Situation and Job Satisfaction: A Comparative Study." Bureau of Public Administration, University of Tennessee. Knoxville, 1976.

Horton, Raymond D. "Productivity and Productivity Bargaining in Government: A Critical Analysis." *Public Administration Review*, vol. 36, no. 4 (July-August 1976), pp. 407-414.

Horton, Raymond D.; Lewin, David; and Kuhn, James W. "Some Impacts of Collective Bargaining on Local Government: A Diversity Thesis." *Administration and Society*, vol. 7, no. 4 (February 1976), pp. 497-514.

"How Management by Objectives Works for Government Administrators." *State and County Administrator*, vol. 1, no. 3 (May/June 1976), pp. 24-29.

Howard, Edward N. "The Orbital Organization." *Library Journal*, vol. 95, no. 9 (May 1, 1970), pp. 1712-1715.

Howenstine, E. Jay; Isler, Morton; and Dietrich, John. "Public Housing Maintenance Productivity Improvement in the United Kingdom." Paper no. 222-51-1. Washington, D.C.: The Urban Institute, 1974.

Hulin, C. L. "Individual Differences and Job Enrichment—The Case Against General Treatments." In *New Perspectives in Job Enrichment.* J. R. Maher, ed. New York: Van Nostrand Reinhold, 1971, pp. 159-191.

Hunady, R. J., and Varney, G. H. "Salary Administration: A Reason for MBO." *Training and Development Journal,* vol. 28 (September 1974), pp. 24-28.

"Improving Productivity and Quality of Worklife in the Public Sector: Pioneering Initiatives in Labor-Management Cooperation." Second report on Project Network. Management and Behavioral Science Center, University of Pennsylvania. Philadelphia, July 15, 1978.

Institute for Local Self-Government. *Alternatives to Traditional Public Safety Delivery Systems: Civilians in Public Safety Services.* PSDS report no. 5. Berkeley, Calif., September 1977.

_____. *Alternatives to Traditional Public Safety Delivery Systems: Public Safety Inspection Consolidation.* PSDS report no. 3. Berkeley, Calif., September 1977.

International City Management Association. *The Guide to Management Improvement Projects in Local Government,* vols. 1 and 2 (1977, 1978).

_____. *Guide to Productivity Improvement Projects.* 3rd ed. Washington, D.C., 1976.

_____. "The Status of Local Government Productivity." Washington, D.C., March 1977.

"Is Your Paramedic Program Legal?" *Fire Command,* vol. 43, no. 10 (October 1976), pp. 28-29.

Ivancevich, John M. "Changes in Performance in a Management by Objectives Program." *Administrative Science Quarterly,* vol. 19, no. 4 (December 1974), pp. 563-574.

_____. "A Longitudinal Assessment of Management by Objectives." *Administrative Science Quarterly,* vol. 17, no. 1 (March 1972), pp. 126-138.

_____. "The Theory and Practice of Management by Objectives." *Michigan Business Review,* vol. 21 (March 1969), pp. 13-16.

Ivancevich, John M.; Donnelly, James H.; and Lyon, Herbert L. "A Study of the Impact of Management by Objectives on Perceived Need Satisfaction." *Personnel Psychology,* vol. 23 (Summer 1970), pp. 139-151.

Jacques, Elliot. *Equitable Payment.* New York: John Wiley and Sons, 1961.

Janka, Katherine. *People, Performance . . . Results.* Washington, D.C.: National Training and Development Service Press, 1977.

Jarrett, James E., and Howard, Dick. *Incentives and Performance:*

Minnesota's Management Plan. Lexington, Ky.: The Council of State Governments, 1978.

Jehring, J. J. "Increasing Productivity in Hospitals: A Case Study of the Incentive Program at Memorial Hospital of Long Beach." Center for the Study of Productivity Motivation, University of Wisconsin. Madison, 1966.

_____. "Participation Bonuses." *Public Administration Review,* vol. 32, no. 5 (September/October 1972), pp. 539-543.

_____. "The Use of Subsystem Incentives in Hospitals: A Case Study of the Incentive Program at Baptist Hospital, Pensacola, Florida." Center for the Study of Productivity Motivation, University of Wisconsin. Madison, 1968.

Jerkins, Bob. "Merit Pay, or, Violating the Law of Averages." *Municipal Reporter,* vol. 77, no. 7 (July 1977), pp. 5-6.

Jones, Ralph T. *Public Sector Labor Relations: An Evaluation of Policy-Related Research.* Belmont, Mass.: Contract Research Corporation, 1975.

Kalleberg, Arne L. "Work Values and Job Rewards: A Theory of Job Satisfaction." *American Sociological Review,* vol. 42 (February 1977), pp. 124-143.

Katzell, Raymond A.; Bienstock, Penny; and Faerstein, Paul H. *A Guide to Worker Productivity Experiments in the United States: 1971-1975.* New York: New York University Press, 1977.

Katzell, Raymond A., and Yankelovich, Daniel. *Work, Productivity, and Job Satisfaction: An Evaluation of Policy-Related Research.* New York: The Psychological Corporation, 1975.

Kearney, William J. "The Value of Behaviorally Based Performance Appraisals." *Business Horizons,* vol. 19 (June 1976), pp. 75-83.

Kerr, Steven. "On the Folly of Rewarding A, While Hoping for B." *Academy of Management Journal,* vol. 18, no. 4 (December 1975), pp. 769-783.

Kimmel, Wayne A.; Dougan, William R.; and Hall, John R. *Municipal Management and Budget Methods: An Evaluation of Policy Related Research.* Washington, D.C.: The Urban Institute, 1974.

King, Albert S. "Expectation Effects in Organization Change." *Administrative Science Quarterly,* vol. 19, no. 2 (June 1974), pp. 221-230.

_____. "Management's Ecstasy and Disparity Over Job Enrichment." *Training and Development Journal,* vol. 30, no. 3 (March 1976), pp. 3-8.

King, N. "Clarification and Evaluation of the Two-Factor Theory of Job Satisfaction." *Psychological Bulletin,* vol. 74 (1970), pp. 18-31.

Kiracofe, John H. "A Systems Approach: Urban Management by Objectives." *Michigan Municipal Review,* vol. 47, no. 12 (December 1974), pp. 325-327.

Kirchhoff, Bruce A. "A Diagnostic Tool for Management by Objectives." *Personnel Psychology,* vol. 28 (1975), pp. 351-364.

Kirkpatrick, Donald L. "MBO and Salary Administration." *Training and Development Journal,* vol. 27 (September 1973), pp. 3-5.

Kleber, Thomas P. "Forty Common Goal-Setting Errors." *Human Resource Management,* vol. 11 (Fall 1972), pp. 10-13.

Klevickis, A. C. "The Rights and Wrongs of Management by Objectives." *Industrial Engineering,* vol. 5, no. 7 (July 1973), pp. 16-19.

Kochan, Thomas A., and Wheeler, Hoyt N. "Municipal Collective Bargaining: A Model and Analysis of Bargaining Outcomes." *Industrial and Labor Relations Review,* vol. 29, no. 1 (October 1975), pp. 44-66.

Kolb, D. A.; Winters, S.; and Berlew, D. "Self-Directed Change: Two Studies." *Journal of Applied Behavioral Science,* vol. 4 (1968), pp. 453-473.

Kooistra, Hal. "Municipal Labor Relations: What's Ahead for Missouri." Part I. *Missouri Municipal Review,* vol. 40, no. 1 (January 1975), pp. 18-19.

Korman, A. K. "Toward an Hypothesis of Work Motivation." *Journal of Applied Psychology,* vol. 54 (1970), pp. 31-41.

Kuhn, David G.; Slocum, John W.; and Chase, Richard B. "Does Job Performance Affect Employee Satisfaction?" *Personnel Journal,* vol. 50, no. 6 (June 1971), pp. 455-459f.

Kunde, James. "Task Force Management." *Nation's Cities* (October 1973), pp. 33-36.

Labor-Management Policies for State and Local Government. Report A-35. Washington, D.C.: Advisory Commission on Intergovernmental Relations, September 1969.

Larson, James S. "Participative Management: Why Has It Failed?" *IPMA News,* International Personnel Management Association (July 1977), pp. 2-4.

Lasagna, John B. "Make Your MBO Pragmatic." *Harvard Business Review,* vol. 49, no. 6 (November/December 1971), pp. 64-69.

Latham, Gary P., and Baldes, J. James. "The 'Practical Significance' of Locke's Theory of Goal Setting." *Journal of Applied Psychology,* vol. 60, no. 1 (1975), pp. 122-124.

Latham, Gary P., and Dossett, Dennis L. "Designing Incentive Plans for Unionized Employees: A Comparison of Continuous and Variable Ratio Reinforcement Schedules." *Personnel Psychology,* vol. 31 (1978), pp. 47-61.

Latham, Gary P., and Kinne, Sidney B. III. "Improving Job Performance Through Training in Goal Setting." *Journal of Applied Psychology,* vol. 59, no. 2 (1974), pp. 187-191.

Latham, Gary P.; Mitchell, Terence R.; and Dossett, Dennis L. "Importance of Participative Goal Setting and Anticipated Rewards on Goal Difficulty and Job Performance." *Journal of Applied Psychology,* vol. 63, no. 2 (1978), pp. 163-171.

Latham, Gary P., and Wexley, Kenneth N. "Behavioral Observation Scales for Performance Appraisal Purposes." *Personnel Psychology,* vol. 30 (1977), pp. 255-268.

Latham, Gary P., and Yukl, Gary A. "Assigned Versus Participative Goal Setting with Educated and Uneducated Woods Workers." *Journal of Applied Psychology,* vol. 60, no. 3 (1975), pp. 299-302.

_____. "A Review of Research on the Application of Goal Setting in Organizations." *Academy of Management Journal,* vol. 18 (December 1975), pp. 824-845.

Lathrop, James K. "Public Safety Inspectors Program a Success." *Fire Command,* vol. 45, no. 9 (September 1978), p. 34.

Lawler, Edward E. III. "How Much Money Do Executives Want?" In *American Bureaucracy.* Warren G. Bennis, ed. Chicago: Aldine Publishing Company, 1970, pp. 65-83.

_____. "Improving the Quality of Work Life; Reward Systems." U.S. Department of Labor. Washington, D.C., June 1975.

_____. *Pay and Organizational Effectiveness: A Psychological View.* New York: McGraw-Hill Book Company, 1971.

Lawshe, C. H. "A Quantitative Approach to Content Validity." *Personnel Psychology,* vol. 28 (1975), pp. 563-575.

Lelchook, Jerry. "State Civil Service Employee Associations." Labor Management Services Administration, U.S. Department of Labor. Washington, D.C., October 1973.

Lelchook, Jerry, and Lahne, Herbert J. *Collective Bargaining in Public Employment and the Merit System.* Washington, D.C.: U.S. Department of Labor, Labor Management Services Administration, April 1972.

Levinson, Harry. "Appraisal of What Performance?" *Harvard Business Review,* vol. 54, no. 4 (July/August 1976), pp. 125-134.

_____. "Asinine Attitudes Toward Motivation." *Harvard Business Review,* vol. 51, no. 1 (January/February 1973), pp. 70-76.

_____. "Management by Objectives: A Critique." *Training and Development Journal,* vol. 26 (April 1972), pp. 3-8.

_____. "Management by Whose Objectives?" *Harvard Business Review,* vol. 48, no. 4 (July/August 1970), pp. 125-134.

Levitan, Sar A., and Johnston, William B. "Job Redesign, Reform, Enrichment—Exploring the Limitations." *Monthly Labor Review,* vol. 96, no. 7 (July 1973), pp. 35-41.

Lewin, David. "Collective Bargaining Impacts on Personnel Administration in the Public Sector." *Labor Law Journal,* vol. 27 (July 1976), pp. 426-436.

Lewin, David; Feuille, Peter; and Kochan, Thomas A. *Public Sector Labor Relations: Analysis and Readings.* New York: Thomas Horton and Daughters, 1977.

Liberman, Aaron; Barrera, Fred; Kargl, Gilard; Crenshaw, Lawrence; Farias, George; Spigner, Reedy Macque; and Williams, Eugene. "The Employee Service Review: Worker Perceptions of the System." *Public Personnel Management,* vol. 6 (March/April 1977), pp. 84-92.

Likert, R. *The Human Organization.* New York: McGraw-Hill Book Company, 1967.

—————. "Measuring Organizational Performance." *Harvard Business Review,* vol. 36, no. 2 (March/April 1958), pp. 41-50.

—————. *New Patterns of Management.* New York: McGraw-Hill Book Company, 1961.

Likert, Rensis, and Fisher, M. Scott. "MBGO: Putting Some Team Spirit into MBO." *Personnel,* vol. 54, no. 1 (January/February 1977), pp. 40-47.

Lloyd, Penelope A. *Incentive Payment Schemes.* Management Survey Report no. 34. London: British Institute of Management, 1976.

Locke, Edwin A. "Job Satisfaction and Job Performance: A Theoretical Analysis." *Organizational Behavior and Human Performance,* vol. 5 (September 1970), pp. 484-500.

—————. "Motivational Effects of Knowledge of Results: Knowledge or Goal Setting?" *Journal of Applied Psychology,* vol. 51, no. 4 (1967), pp. 324-329.

—————. "The Relationship of Intentions to Level of Performance." *Journal of Applied Psychology,* vol. 50 (1966), pp. 60-66.

—————. "Toward a Theory of Task Motivation and Incentives." *Organizational Behavior and Human Performance,* vol. 3 (1968), pp. 157-189.

Locke, Edwin A.; Bryan, Judith F.; and Kendell, Lorne M. "Goals and Intentions as Mediators of the Effects of Monetary Incentives on Behavior." *Journal of Applied Psychology,* vol. 52, no. 2 (1968), pp. 104-121.

Locke, Edwin A.; Cartledge, Norman; and Knerr, Claramae S. "Studies of the Relationship Between Satisfaction, Goal-Setting, and Performance." *Organizational Behavior and Human Performance,* vol. 5 (1970), pp. 135-158.

Longhini, Greg. "How Three Cities Fared in One-Stop Permitting." *Planning,* vol. 44, no. 9 (October 1978), p. 31.

Lorenzini, Arthur L., Jr., and Fukuhara, Rackham S. *Management Evaluation and Compensation.* Municipal Management Innovation Series, no. 13. Washington, D.C.: International City Management Association, December 1976.

Lucas, Norman A. "Developing an Employee Pay Plan." *Public Management,* vol. 61, no. 10 (October 1979), pp. 7-8.

Luthans, Fred. "How to Apply MBO." *Public Personnel Management,* vol. 5, no. 2 (March/April 1976), pp. 83-87.

Luthans, Fred, and Reif, William E. "Job Enrichment: Long on Theory, Short on Practice." *Organizational Dynamics,* vol. 2, no. 3 (1974), pp. 30-38ff.

McCaffery, Jerry. "MBO and the Federal Budgetary Process." *Public Administration Review,* vol. 36, no. 1 (January/February 1976), pp. 33-39.

McConkey, Dale D. "Applying Management by Objectives to Non-Profit Organizations." *SAM Advanced Management Journal,* vol. 38, no. 3 (January 1973), pp. 10-20.

_____. *How to Manage by Results.* Rev. ed. New York: American Management Association, 1967.

_____. "Twenty Ways to Kill Management by Objectives." *Management Review,* vol. 61 (October 1972), pp. 4-13.

McGregor, Douglas. *The Human Side of Enterprise.* New York: McGraw-Hill Book Company, 1960.

_____. "An Uneasy Look at Performance Appraisal." *Harvard Business Review,* vol. 35 (May/June 1957), pp. 89-94.

McKersie, Robert B., and Hunter, L. C. *Pay, Productivity and Collective Bargaining.* London: Macmillan, St. Martin's Press, 1973.

McNamar, Tim. "White Collar Job Enrichment: The Pay Board Experience." *Public Administration Review,* vol. 33, no. 6 (November-December 1973), pp. 563-568.

McNamara, Charles. "Community Resources Management Approach Reports Success with New Team Concept." *American Journal of Correction,* vol. 39, no. 4 (July-August 1977), pp. 32-36f.

Macri, Vincent J. "Nassau Offers Unique Productivity Pay Plan." *LMRS Newsletter,* vol. 6, no. 2 (February 1975), pp. 4-5.

_____. "Productivity Benefit Increase: Questions and Answers." Department of General Services, County of Nassau, Mineola, N.Y., n.d.

Macri, Vincent J., and Paul, Dina D. "Multi-Municipal Productivity Project Attitudinal Program." County of Nassau, Mineola, N.Y., June 1974.

Maher, J. R., ed. *New Perspectives in Job Enrichment.* New York: Van Nostrand Reinhold, 1971.

Mahler, Walter R. "Management by Objectives: A Consultant's Viewpoint." *Training and Development Journal,* vol. 26 (April 1972), pp. 16-19.

Maiben, Dean H., and Schwabe, Charles J. "Government by Objectives: A Management System." *Governmental Finance,* vol. 3, no. 1 (February 1974), pp. 2-5.

Malek, Frederick V. "Managing for Results in the Federal Government." *Business Horizons,* vol. 17 (1974), pp. 23-28.

"Management Performance Appraisal Programs." PPF Survey No. 104. Washington, D.C.: Bureau of National Affairs, January 1974.

"Management Rights Pointers." *Labor Relations Newsletter,* vol. 58, no. 7, supp. 2 (March 28, 1977).

Mann, Gary. "How States Cope with Collective Bargaining." *County News,* National Association of Counties, vol. 7 (May 5, 1975), p. 7f.

Marrow, A. J.; Bowers, D. G.; and Seashore, S. E. *Management by Participation.* New York: Harper and Row, 1967.

Maslow, Abraham. *Motivation and Personality.* New York: Harper and Row, 1954.

Meyer, Herbert H. "The Pay-for-Performance Dilemma." *Organizational Dynamics,* vol. 3, no. 3 (Winter 1975), pp. 39-50.

Meyer, Herbert H.; Kay, Emanuel; and French, John R. P., Jr. "Split Roles in Performance Appraisal." *Harvard Business Review,* vol. 43 (January/February 1965), pp. 123-129.

Millar, Jean. "Motivational Aspects of Job Enrichment." *Management International Review,* vol. 16, no. 2 (1976), pp. 37-46.

Millard, Cheedle W.; Luthans, Fred; and Ottemann, Robert L. "A New Breakthrough for Performance Appraisal." *Business Horizons,* vol. 19 (August 1976), pp. 66-73.

Miller, Ernest C. *Objectives and Standards: An Approach to Planning and Control.* AMA Research Study 74. New York: American Management Association, 1966.

Miller, Louis. "The Use of Knowledge of Results in Improving the Performance of Hourly Operators." Crotonville, N.Y.: Behavioral Research Service, General Electric Company, 1965.

Mills, Ted. "Human Resources: Why the New Concern?" *Harvard Business Review,* vol. 53, no. 2 (March/April 1975), pp. 120-134.

Miner, John B., and Dachler, H. Peter. "Personnel Attitudes and Motivation." In *Annual Review of Psychology,* vol. 24. Paul H. Mussen and Mark R. Rosenzweig, eds. Palo Alto, Calif.: Annual Reviews, Inc., 1973, pp. 375-401.

Mobley, W. H. "The Link Between MBO and Merit Compensation." *Personnel Journal,* vol. 53, no. 6 (June 1974), pp. 423-427.

Molander, C. F. "Management by Objectives in Perspective." *Journal of Management Studies,* vol. 9 (February 1972), pp. 74-81.

Monczka, Robert M., and Reif, William E. "A Contingency Approach to Job Enrichment Design." *Human Resource Management,* vol. 12, no. 4 (Winter 1973), pp. 9-17.

Monohan, Terrance O. "Management Merit-Compensation Plan." Municipality of Metropolitan Seattle. Seattle, Washington, July 1976.

Moore, Perry. "Rewards and Public Employees' Attitudes Toward Client Service." *Public Personnel Management,* vol. 6, no. 2 (March/April 1977), pp. 98-105.

Morgenstern, Marty. "Collective Bargaining for Public Workers?" *State and County Administrator,* vol. 1 (July/August 1976), p. 15.

_____. "Merit Principle, Civil Service and Collective Bargaining." *State Government Administration,* vol. 12, no. 1 (January 1977), p. 7.

Morrisey, George L. "MBO Questions and Answers." *Public Personnel Management,* vol. 5, no. 2 (March/April 1976), pp. 96-102.

Murphy, Richard J., and Sackman, Morris, eds. *The Crisis in Public Employee Relations in the Decade of the Seventies.* Washington, D.C.: Bureau of National Affairs, 1970.

Murray, William J. "Management by Objectives: A Pilot Project for the Division of Family Services." Division of Family Services, State of Utah. Salt Lake City, December 1977.

Mushkin, Selma J. "Personnel Management in the Cities as a Component of Administrative Services." Public Services Laboratory, Georgetown University. Washington, D.C., November 1976.

Mushkin, Selma J., and Sandifer, Frank H. "Personnel Management and Productivity in City Government." Public Services Laboratory, Georgetown University. Washington, D.C., March 1978.

Mussio, Stephen J., and Smith, Mary K. "Content Validity: A Procedural Manual." Civil Service Commission, Division of Personnel Research, City of Minneapolis, n.d.

Mustafa, Husain. "Performance Rating Revisited." *Civil Service Journal,* vol. 9, no. 4 (April-June 1969), pp. 29-31.

Myers, M. S. *Every Employee a Manager.* New York: McGraw-Hill Book Company, 1970.

National Center for Productivity and Quality of Working Life. *Directory of Labor-Management Committees.* Washington, D.C. Edition 1, October 1976, and Edition 2, Spring 1978.

_____. *Improving Government Productivity: Selected Case Studies.* Washington, D.C., 1977.

_____. *Managing Inspections for Greater Productivity.* Washington, D.C., 1977.

National Commission on Productivity. *Report of the Advisory Group on Productivity in Law Enforcement on Opportunities for Improving Productivity in Police Services.* Washington, D.C., 1973.

National Commission on Productivity and Work Quality. *Improving Municipal Productivity: The Detroit Refuse Collection Incentive Plan.* Washington, D.C., 1974.

_____. *Labor-Management Committees in the Public Sector.* Washington, D.C., November 1975.

Nelson, M. R. "Pacifica Police Department Project: Community Contact Patrol." City of Pacifica, Calif., January 1971.

Nelson, Nels E. "Union Security in the Public Sector." *Labor Law Journal,* vol. 27 (June 1976), pp. 334-342.

Neubacher, James. "Detroit Sanitation Productivity—Everyone Wins." Strengthening Local Government Through Better Labor Relations, no. 18. Washington, D.C.: Labor-Management Relations Service, November 1973.

"New Concept for Old Roles: The Public Safety Officer." *Louisiana Municipal Review* (May-June 1977), pp. 15-16.

Newland, Chester A. "Policy/Program Objectives and Federal Management: The Search for Government Effectiveness." *Public Administration Review,* vol. 36, no. 1 (January/February 1976), pp. 20-27.

_____. "Public Personnel Administration: Legalistic Reforms vs. Effectiveness, Efficiency, and Economy." *Public Administration Review,* vol. 36, no. 5 (September/October 1976), pp. 529-537.

Newland, Chester A.; Cole, John D. R.; Porter, Elsa A.; Ingrassia, Anthony F.; Horton, Raymond D.; and Macri, Vincent J. *MBO and Productivity Bargaining in the Public Sector.* Public Employee Relations Library, no. 45. Chicago: International Personnel Management Association, 1974.

"New Method of Rating Goddard Employees." *The Washington Star,* February 7, 1977, p. F2.

Newstrom, John W.; Reif, William E.; and Monczka, Robert M. "Motivating the Public Employee: Fact vs. Fiction." *Public Personnel Management,* vol. 5, no. 1 (January/February 1976), pp. 67-72.

Nollen, Stanley D. *The Effect of Collective Bargaining on Municipal Personnel Systems: A Research Review.* Staffing Services to People in the Cities, no. 2. Washington, D.C.: Public Services Laboratory, Georgetown University, 1975.

Nord, W. R. "Beyond the Teaching Machine: The Neglected Area of Operant Conditioning in the Theory and Practice of Management." *Organizational Behavior and Human Performance,* vol. 4 (1969), pp. 375-401.

"Normal and Bloomington, Illinois, Share Administrative Staff." *The Municipal Attorney,* vol. 17, no. 1 (January 1976), pp. 26-27.

Northup, David E. "Management's Cost in Public Sector Collective Bargaining." *Public Personnel Management,* vol. 5 (September 1976), pp. 328-334.

Norton, Steven D. "Management by Results in the Public Sector." *Public Productivity Review,* vol. 2, no. 1 (Fall 1976), pp. 20-31.

"N.Y.C. Cites Gains from Productivity." *LMRS Newsletter,* vol. 8, no. 5 (May 1977), p. 4.

O'Brien, John T. "The Neighborhood Task Force in New Brunswick, New Jersey." *The Police Chief,* vol. 42, no. 6 (June 1975), pp. 48-49.

Odiorne, George S. *Management by Objectives: A System of Managerial Leadership.* New York: Pitman Publishing Corporation, 1969.

_____. "MBO in State Government." *Public Administration Review,* vol. 36 (January/February 1976), pp. 28-33.

_____. "The Politics of Implementing MBO." *Business Horizons,* vol. 17 (June 1974), pp. 13-21.

Ohio Law Enforcement Planning Agency. "Continuation of Community Centered Team Policing Program." Discretionary Grant Progress Report. Dayton, Ohio: Dayton Police Department, March 1972.

Oldham, G. R.; Hackman, J. R.; and Pearce, J. L. "Conditions Under Which Employees Respond Positively to Enriched Work." *Journal of Applied Psychology,* vol. 61, no. 4 (1976), pp. 395-403.

Olsen, Kristin. "Suggestion Schemes Seventies Style." *Personnel Management,* vol. 8 (April 1976), pp. 36-39.

Olson, David H. "Integrated Police and Fire Service: Gladstone Experience." *Missouri Municipal Review,* vol. 39, no. 4 (April 1974), pp. 9-11.

Osterman, Melvin H., Jr. "Productivity Bargaining in New York State—What Went Wrong?" Paper presented at the Tenth Annual Conference on Management Analysis in State and Local Government, October 19, 1973, Windsor Locks, Conn.

Oswald, Rudolph. "Enhancing and Measuring the Productivity of Public Employees." Draft paper. Madison, Wis.: Industrial Relations Research Association, December 28, 1973.

_____. "Public Productivity Tied to Bargaining." *AFL-CIO American Federationist,* vol. 83 (March 1976), pp. 20-22.

Owen, John D. "Flexitime: Some Problems and Solutions." *Industrial and Labor Relations Review,* vol. 30 (January 1977), pp. 152-160.

Palmer, Walter W., and Dean, Charles C. "Increasing Employee Productivity and Reducing Turnover." *Training and Development Journal,* vol. 27 (March 1973), pp. 53-55.

Patchen, Martin. *The Choice of Wage Comparisons.* Englewood Cliffs, N.J.: Prentice-Hall, 1961.

Patten, Thomas H., Jr. "Linking Financial Rewards to Employee Performance: The Roles of OD and MBO." *Human Resource Management,* vol. 15, no. 4 (1976), pp. 2-17.

_____. "OD, MBO, and the Reward System." In *OD—Emerging Dimensions and Concepts.* Thomas H. Patten, Jr., ed. Madison, Wis.: American Society for Training and Development, 1973, pp. 9-31.

_____. "OD, MBO, and the R/P System: A New Dimension

in Personnel Administration." *Personnel Administration,* vol. 35 (March/April 1972), pp. 14-23.

Patz, Alan L. "Performance Appraisal: Useful But Still Resisted." *Harvard Business Review,* vol. 53 (May/June 1975), pp. 74-80.

Peach, Len. "Personnel Management by Objectives." *Personnel Management,* vol. 7 (March 1975), pp. 20-23f.

Peart, Leo E. "A Management by Objective Plan for a Municipal Police Department." *The Police Chief,* vol. 38, no. 6 (June 1971), pp. 34-40.

Peirce, Neal R. "Civil Service Systems Experience Quiet Revolution." *National Journal,* vol. 7, no. 48 (November 29, 1975), pp. 1643-1648.

_____. "Employment Report/Public Employee Unions Show Rise in Membership, Militancy." *National Journal,* vol. 7, no. 35 (August 30, 1975), pp. 1239-1249.

Phelps, Lourn G., and Harmon, Lorne. "Team Policing—Four Years Later." *FBI Law Enforcement Bulletin,* vol. 41, no. 12 (December 1972), pp. 2-5f.

"PIE Story: Town of Hempstead, Department of Public Works." Multi-Municipal Productivity Project, Mineola, N.Y., n.d.

Piper, C. Erwin. "Establishment of a Total Compensation Program for General Managers." City of Los Angeles, June 8, 1978.

_____. "Executive Compensation Plan." City of Los Angeles, June 1978.

_____. "Memo to the Heads of All Departments of City Government." City of Los Angeles, June 18, 1973.

_____. "Proposed Performance Evaluation Program for Department Managers and Bureau Heads." City of Los Angeles, July 20, 1971.

"Plainfield, New Jersey, Fire Division Meets the Challenge of the 70's with a Fire Safety Patrol." Report 18511. Report Clearinghouse, Management Information Service, International City Management Association. Washington, D.C., June 1974.

Platty, Robert A. "Local Government Structure and Organization." Discussion paper. Washington, D.C.: National League of Cities, International City Management Association, and National Association of Counties, n.d.

"Police and Fire Consolidation: In the Interest of Public Safety." *Uptown.* Municipal Association of South Carolina (February 1978).

The Police Foundation. *A Conference on Managing the Patrol Function.* Washington, D.C., 1974.

Porter, Lyman W., and Lawler, Edward E. III. *Managerial Attitudes and Performance.* Homewood, Ill.: Irwin, 1968.

Porter, Lyman W.; Lawler, Edward E. III; and Hackman, J. Richard. *Behavior in Organizations.* New York: McGraw-Hill Book Company, 1975.

Poulter, William E., and Sadacca, Robert. "Work Incentives in Public Housing: A Proposed Demonstration Program." Working Paper 223-62-1. Washington, D.C.: The Urban Institute, 1976.

Powell, Reed M., and Schlacter, John L. "Participative Management —A Panacea?" *Academy of Management Journal,* vol. 14 (June 1971), pp. 165-171.

"Power to the Public Worker." *State Government News,* vol. 18 (August 1975), pp. 2-6.

President's Reorganization Project. "Final Staff Report: Personnel Management Project." Vol. 1. Washington, D.C., December 1977.

Presley, Jane, and Keen, Sally. "Better Meetings Lead to Increased Productivity: A Case Study." *Management Review,* vol. 64, no. 4 (April 1975), pp. 16-22.

Prien, Erich P.; Jones, Mark A.; and Miller, Louise M. "A Job-Related Performance Rating System." Office of Personnel Management, State of Arkansas. Little Rock, 1976.

Pritchard, R. D. "Equity Theory: A Review and Critique." *Organizational Behavior and Human Performance,* vol. 4 (1969), pp. 176-211.

Pritchard, R. D., and Curtis, M. I. "The Influence of Goal Setting and Financial Incentives on Task Performance." *Organizational Behavior and Human Performance,* vol. 10 (1973), pp. 175-183.

"Public Sector Labor-Management Relations." Chapter in *State Actions in 1975.* Washington, D.C.: Advisory Commission on Intergovernmental Relations, July 1976, pp. 103-118.

"Public Sector Labor Relations." Special issue of *State Government,* vol. 49, no. 4 (Autumn 1976).

Public Sector Labor Relations: Recent Trends and Developments. Lexington, Ky.: The Council of State Governments, January 1975.

Public Services Laboratory, Georgetown University. *Do Productivity Measures Pay Off for Employee Performance?* Staffing Services to People in the Cities, no. 9. Washington, D.C., 1975.

_____. *Is Employee Classification Effective in the Cities?* Staffing Services to People in the Cities, no. 7. Washington, D.C., 1975.

_____. *What Determines City Employees Compensation?* Staffing Services to People in the Cities, no. 8. Washington, D.C., 1975.

Public Technology, Inc. *Improving Productivity Using Work Measurement.* Washington, D.C., 1977.

"Public Workers Put the Pressure On." *The American City* (January 1975), p. 8.

Pudinski, Walter. "Managing for Results." *The Police Chief,* vol. 40, no. 1 (January 1973), pp. 38-39f.

Quinn, Robert P.; Mangione, Thomas W.; and Baldi de Mandilo-
vitch, Martha S. "Evaluating Working Conditions in America."
Monthly Labor Review, vol. 96, no. 11 (November 1973), pp. 32-
41.

Raia, Anthony P. "Goal Setting and Self-Control." *Journal of
Management Studies,* vol. 2 (February 1965), pp. 34-53.

_____. *Managing by Objectives.* Glenview, Ill.: Scott, Fores-
man and Company, 1974.

_____. "A Second Look at Management Goals and Controls."
California Management Review, vol. 8 (Summer 1966), pp. 49-
58.

Regan, Katrina. "Neighborhood Team Policing in Elizabeth, New
Jersey: A Case Study." Contract Report 5054-12. Washington,
D.C.: The Urban Institute, December 1977.

"Restructuring Paramedical Jobs." *Manpower,* vol. 5, no. 3 (March
1973), pp. 3-7.

Ridgway, V. F. "Dysfunctional Consequences of Performance Measurements." *Administrative Science Quarterly,* vol. 1 (September
1956), pp. 240-247.

Riebock, Thomas W. "Decatur's Experience with Labor-Management Productivity Workshops." Office of the City Manager, City
of Decatur, Ill., December 1976.

Rieder, George A. "Performance Review—A Mixed Bag." *Harvard
Business Review,* vol. 51 (July/August 1973), pp. 61-67.

Riggs, Joseph E., and Gaddis, Richard K. "Increasing Patrol Status:
Myth or Reality." *The Police Chief,* vol. 45, no. 12 (December
1978), pp. 50-52.

Roberts, Markley. "Sharing the Benefits of Productivity." *AFL-
CIO American Federationist,* vol. 79 (October 1972), pp. 19-23.

Rock, Milton L., ed. *Handbook of Wage and Salary Administration.*
New York: McGraw-Hill Book Company, 1972.

Ronan, W. W.; Anderson, Charles L.; and Talbert, Terry L. "A
Psychometric Approach to Job Performance: Fire Fighters."
Public Personnel Management, vol. 5, no. 6 (November/Decem-
ber 1976), pp. 409-422.

Ronan, W. W.; Latham, Gary P.; and Kinne, S. B. III. "Effects of
Goal Setting and Supervision on Worker Behavior in an Industrial Situation." *Journal of Applied Psychology,* vol. 58, no. 3
(1973), pp. 302-307.

Ronan, W. W., and Prien, Erich P., eds. *Perspectives on the Measurement of Human Performance.* New York: Appleton-Century-
Crofts, 1971.

Rosen, Gerald R. "Is Civil Service Outmoded?" *Dunn's Review,*
vol. 10, no. 5 (November 1977), pp. 46-50.

Ross, Doris. *'76 Update: Collective Bargaining in Education.* Report no. 78. Denver, Colo.: Education Commission of the States, January 1976.

Rothe, H. F. "Does Higher Pay Bring Higher Productivity?" *Personnel,* vol. 37, no. 4 (July/August 1960), pp. 20-27.

Rubenstein, Sidney P. "Participative Problem-Solving: How to Increase Organizational Effectiveness." *Personnel,* vol. 54, no. 1 (January/February 1977), pp. 30-39.

Rush, Harold M. F. *Job Design for Motivation.* New York: The Conference Board, 1971.

Rutstein, Jacob J. "Survey of Current Personnel Systems in State and Local Government." *Good Government,* vol. 87, no. 1 (Spring 1971).

Ryan, Raymond M. "Employee Relations Key in Washington State Productivity." *LMRS Newsletter,* vol. 7, no. 7 (July 1976), pp. 3-5.

Ryan, T. A. *Intentional Behavior: An Approach to Human Motivation.* New York: Ronald, 1970.

Savas, E. S., and Ginsburg, Sigmund G. "The Civil Service: A Meritless System?" *The Public Interest,* vol. 32 (June 1973), pp. 70-85.

Schlesinger, Leonard A., and Walton, Richard E. "The Process of Work Restructuring and Its Impact on Collective Bargaining." *Monthly Labor Review,* vol. 100 (April 1977), pp. 52-56.

Schneier, Craig Eric. "Multiple Rater Groups and Performance Appraisal." *Public Personnel Management,* vol. 6, no. 1 (January/February 1977), pp. 13-20.

Schrader, Albert W. "Let's Abolish the Annual Performance Review." *Management of Personnel Quarterly,* vol. 8, no. 3 (Fall 1969), pp. 20-28.

Schrank, Robert. "Work in America: What Do Workers Really Want?" *Industrial Relations,* vol. 13 (May 1974), pp. 124-129.

Schuster, Fred E., and Kindall, Alva F. "Management by Objectives Where We Stand—A Survey of the Fortune 500." *Human Resource Management,* vol. 13 (Spring 1974), pp. 8-11.

Schuster, J. R. "Management-Compensation Policy and the Public Interest." *Public Personnel Management,* vol. 3 (November/December 1974), pp. 510-523.

Schwab, D. P., and Cummings, L. L. "Theories of Performance and Satisfaction: A Review." *Industrial Relations,* vol. 9 (October 1970), pp. 408-430.

Schwab, Donald P.; Heneman, Herbert A. III; and DeCotiis, Thomas A. "Behaviorally Anchored Rating Scales: A Review of the Literature." *Personnel Psychology,* vol. 28 (1975), pp. 549-562.

Schwartz, Alfred I., and Clarren, Sumner N. *The Cincinnati Team Policing Experiment: A Summary Report.* Washington, D.C.: The Police Foundation, 1977.

Schwartz, Alfred I.; Clarren, Sumner, N.; Fischgrund, T.; Hollins, E.; and Nalley, Paul. "Evaluation of Cincinnati's Community Sector Team Policing Program—A Progress Report After One Year, Summary of Major Findings." Working Paper 3006-18. Washington, D.C.: The Urban Institute, March 10, 1975.

Schwartz, Alfred I.; Vaughn, Alease M.; Waller, John D.; and Wholley, Joseph S. *Employing Civilians for Police Work.* Paper no. 5012-03-1. Washington, D.C.: The Urban Institute, 1975.

Sears, P. M., and Wilson, S. *Crime Reduction in Albuquerque: Evaluation of Three Police Projects.* New Mexico University. University Park, 1973.

Seberhagen, Lance W. "What Motivates Civil Service Employees?" *Public Personnel Review,* vol. 31, no. 1 (January 1970), pp. 48-50.

" 'Secretaries' No More! It's 'Administrative Aides'." *The Washington Evening Star and Daily News,* June 13, 1973, p. E3.

Selberg, Barry. "Management by Objective." *North Dakota League of Cities Bulletin* (April 1975), pp. 2-4.

Shapek, Raymond A. "Federal Influences in State and Local Personnel Management: The System in Transition." *Public Personnel Management,* vol. 5, no. 1 (January/February 1976), pp. 41-51.

Sherman, L. W.; Milton, C. H.; and Kelly, T. V. *Team Policing: Seven Case Studies.* Washington, D.C.: The Police Foundation, August 1973.

Sherwood, Frank P., and Page, William J., Jr. "MBO and Public Management." *Public Administration Review,* vol. 36 (January/February 1976), pp. 5-12.

Singleton, David W. "Firefighting Productivity in Wilmington: A Case History." *Public Productivity Review,* vol. 1 (December 1975), pp. 19-29.

Sirota, David, and Wolfson, Alan D. "Job Enrichment: What Are the Obstacles?" *Personnel,* vol. 49, no. 3 (May/June 1972), pp. 8-17.

_____. "Job Enrichment: Surmounting the Obstacles." *Personnel,* vol. 49, no. 4 (July-August 1972), pp. 8-19.

Skinner, B. F. *Science and Human Behavior.* New York: Macmillan Publishing Co., 1953.

Smith, Bruce A., and Goldlust, Perry F. "A Study of Solid Waste Collection Practices in Wilmington, Delaware." Report 19208. Report Clearinghouse, Management Information Service, International City Management Association. Washington, D.C., May 1974.

Smith, Howard R. "The Half-Loaf of Job Enrichment." *Personnel,* vol. 53, no. 2 (March/April 1976), pp. 24-31.

Smith, Jack; Niedzwiedz, Edward; Davis, Melissa; and Kniesner, Cheryl. *Handbook of Job Proficiency Criteria: A GLAC Research*

Report. Columbus: Ohio Department of State Personnel, July 1973.

Smythe, Cyrus, Jr. "Work Schedules, Work Hours; What's Bargainable." *Minnesota Municipalities,* vol. 59 (August 1974), pp. 27-28.

Somers, Paul, and Sullivan, Daniel J. "Productivity Improvement a Must for Local Government." *Personnel and Labor Relations Bulletin.* Massachusetts League of Cities and Towns. Boston, December 1974.

Srivastva, Suresh; Salipante, Paul F., Jr.; Cummings, Thomas G.; Notz, William W.; Bigelow, John D.; and Waters, James A. *Job Satisfaction and Productivity: An Evaluation of Policy Related Research on Productivity, Industrial Organization and Job Satisfaction.* Cleveland, Ohio: Case Western Reserve University, 1975.

Stafford, Samuel. "In Interior's BOR, Watt's Happening Is an MBO Success." *Government Executive,* vol. 6, no. 4 (April 1974), pp. 42-49.

"Standards for a Merit System of Personnel Administration." *Federal Register,* vol. 44, no. 34 (February 16, 1979), pp. 10238-10263.

Stanley, David T. *Managing Local Government Under Union Pressure.* Washington, D.C.: The Brookings Institution, 1972.

_____, ed. "The Merit Principal Today: A Symposium." *Public Administration Review,* vol. 34, no. 5 (September/October 1974), pp. 425-452.

_____. "Unions and Government Management: New Relationships in Theory and Fact." In *Managing Government's Labor Relations.* Chester A. Newland, ed. Washington, D.C.: Manpower Press, 1972, pp. 12-16.

_____. "What Are Unions Doing to Merit Systems?" *Civil Service Journal,* vol. 12 (January-March 1972), pp. 10-14.

State of California, Employment Development Department, Northern Region. "ES and UI Job Performance Standards." Memorandum no. 75-75-C. Sacramento, California, October 29, 1975.

State of California, Legislative Analyst. "Collective Bargaining in California Public Jurisdictions, Alternatives and Considerations for Implementation." Report no. 75-4. Sacramento, February 1975.

State of Maine, Committee on State Government. "Report of the Committee on State Government on the Necessary Evolution of the State Personnel System." Augusta, December 18, 1974.

State of Maine, House of Representatives. "AN ACT to Establish Pay Scales for Managers and Assistant Managers in State Liquor Stores." Legislative Document 2354. Augusta, January 15, 1974.

State of Minnesota, Legislative Audit Commission. "Department of Personnel." Report to the Minnesota State Legislature. St. Paul, May 1978.

State of New Jersey, Civil Service Commission. "69th Annual Report: 1975-1976." Trenton, 1976.

State of New Jersey, Department of Civil Service, Division of Administration. "Improving Managerial Competence: The Recognition and Selection of Government Executives." Trenton, April 1976.

State of New Jersey, Department of Labor and Industry. "Broadening Employee Involvement in the Department's Management Structure." Report of Committee no. 1, Employee Task Force on Morale, Productivity, and Involvement. Trenton, 1975.

_____. "Distribution of the 1971 Incentive Bonus Award." Administrative Informational Memorandum No. 2. Trenton, October 29, 1971.

_____. "Establishment of an Improved Employee Incentive Plan." Report of Committee no. 7, Employee Task Force on Morale, Productivity, and Involvement. Trenton, 1975.

_____. "Implementation Committee Report on Employee Task Forces' Recommendations." Trenton, August 1976.

_____. "Seminar on Participative Problem-Solving." Trenton, June 1976.

State of New Jersey, Office of Fiscal Affairs. "Administration of the New Jersey State Civil Service System." Trenton, January 1975.

State of North Carolina, General Assembly. "An Act to Determine the Value and Practicality of Providing Incentive Pay for State Employees for Gains in Economy and Efficiency in the Rendering of Governmental Services." Senate Bill 772, 1977 Session. Raleigh, July 1, 1977.

State of Washington, Advisory Council on State Government Productivity. "Final Report." Olympia, 1976.

State of Washington, Department of Printing. "Comments of Public Printer Relative to Performance Audit of the Public Printer." Olympia, 1976.

State of Washington, Legislative Budget Committee. "Performance Audit: The Public Printer." Report no. 76-7. Olympia, 1977.

State of Washington, Office of Program Planning and Fiscal Management. "Report on Inhibitors Questionnaire." Olympia, December 1974.

State of West Virginia, Department of Welfare. "Area Rankings Manual." Charleston, June 1974 and later editions.

Stearns, Robert B. "People, Not Trucks, Make Refuse Vanish." *The American City and County* (October 1978), pp. 83-84.

Stedry, A. C. *Budget Control and Cost Behavior.* Englewood Cliffs, N.J.: Prentice-Hall, 1960.

Stedry, A. C., and Kay, E. *The Effects of Goal Difficulty on Performance.* Crotonville, N.Y.: Behavioral Research Service, General Electric Company, 1964.

Steers, Richard M. "Task Goals, Individual Need Strengths, and Supervisory Performance." Doctoral Dissertation, University of California. Irvine, 1973.

Steers, Richard M., and Porter, Lyman W. "The Role of Task-Goal Attributes in Employee Performance." *Psychological Bulletin,* vol. 81 (1974), pp. 434-452.

Stelluto, George L. "Report on Incentive Pay in Manufacturing Industries." *Monthly Labor Review,* vol. 92, no. 7 (July 1969), pp. 49-53.

Stetson, Damon. "Productivity: More Work for a Day's Pay." Strengthening Local Government Through Better Labor Relations, no. 13. Washington, D.C.: Labor-Management Relations Service, November 1972.

Stieber, Jack. *Public Employee Unionism: Structure, Growth, Policy.* Washington, D.C.: The Brookings Institution, 1973.

Stone, Daniel E. "Work Measurement Applied to Municipal Service." Report no. 18651. Report Clearinghouse, Management Information Service, International City Management Association. Washington, D.C., December 1974.

Stone, Thomas H. "An Examination of Six Prevalent Assumptions Concerning Performance Appraisal." *Public Personnel Management,* vol. 2, no. 6 (November/December 1973), pp. 408-414.

Strauss, George. "Improving the Quality of Work Life: Managerial Practices." U.S. Department of Labor. Washington, D.C., June 1975.

_____. "Management by Objectives: A Critical View." *Training and Development Journal,* vol. 26 (April 1972), pp. 10-15.

Sullivan, Gary; Booms, Bernard H.; and Cohn, Steven M. "Tacoma, Washington Used 'Team Management Approach' to Create Inner-City Plaza; Is Continuing Team Approach for Community Development." *Journal of Housing,* vol. 32, no. 2 (February 1975), pp. 69-72.

"Sunnyvale Rotates Supervisors for 'Total City' Approach." *LMRS Newsletter,* vol. 7, no. 3 (March 1976), p. 4.

"Supplemental Agreement for Members of the Waste Collection Division Between AFSCME Local 1600 and the City of Flint, Michigan" (July 1, 1975 to June 30, 1977).

"Symposium on Collective Bargaining in the Public Service: A Reappraisal." Special issue of *Public Administration Review,* vol. 32, no. 2 (March/April 1972).

T. J. Hourihan Associates. "Report on Municipal Personnel Systems in Massachusetts." Boston: Massachusetts League of Cities and Towns, May 1974.

Tatter, Milton A. "Turning Ideas into Gold." *Management Review,* vol. 64 (March 1975), pp. 4-10.

"Team Policing, Joint Units Described at USCM Session." *LMRS Newsletter,* vol. 8, no. 7 (July 1977), pp. 2-3.

Teresko, John. "Myths and Realities of Job Enrichment." *Industry Week* (November 24, 1975), pp. 39-43.

Thompson, Arthur A. "Employee Participation in Decision Making: The TVA Experience." In *A New World: Readings in Modern Public Personnel Management.* Jay M. Shafritz, ed. Chicago, Ill.: International Personnel Management Association, 1975, pp. 80-86.

Thompson, Paul H., and Dalton, Gene W. "Performance Appraisal: Managers Beware." *Harvard Business Review,* vol. 48 (January/February 1970), pp. 149-157.

Tien, James M., and Larson, Richard C. "Police Service Aides: Paraprofessionals for Police." *Journal of Criminal Justice,* vol. 6 (1978), pp. 117-131.

Tosi, Henry L., and Carroll, Stephen J. "Improving Management by Objectives: A Diagnostic Change Program." *California Management Review,* vol. 16, no. 1 (Fall 1973), pp. 57-66.

_____. "Management by Objectives." *Personnel Administration,* vol. 33 (July/August 1970), pp. 44-48.

_____. "Managerial Reaction to Management by Objectives." *Academy of Management Journal,* vol. 11 (December 1968), pp. 415-426.

_____. "Some Factors Affecting the Success of 'Management by Objectives.'" *Journal of Management Studies,* vol. 7 (May 1970), pp. 209-223.

_____. "Some Structural Factors Related to Goal Influence in the Management by Objectives Process." *MSU Business Topics,* vol. 17 (Spring 1969), pp. 45-50.

Truax, Charles B., and Mitchell, Kevin M. "Research on Certain Therapist Interpersonal Skills in Relation to Process and Outcome." In *Handbook of Psychotherapy and Behavior Change.* A. Bergin and S. Garfield, eds. New York: John Wiley and Sons, 1971, pp. 299-344.

Turner, A. Jack, and Goodson, W. H. "Catch a Fellow Worker Doing Something Good Today." Huntsville-Madison County Mental Health Center. Huntsville, Ala., n.d.

Umstot, Denis D. "MBO + Job Enrichment: How to Have Your Cake and Eat It Too." *Management Review,* vol. 66, no. 2 (February 1977), pp. 21-26.

Umstot, Denis D.; Bell, Cecil H., Jr.; and Mitchell, Terence R. "Effects of Job Enrichment and Task Goals on Satisfaction and Productivity: Implications for Job Design." *Journal of Applied Psychology,* vol. 61, no. 4 (1976), pp. 379-394.

U.S. Bureau of the Census. *Governmental Finances in 1976-77.* Series GF77, no. 5. Washington, D.C., 1978.

_____. *Labor-Management Relations in State and Local Governments: 1975.* Series GSS, no. 81. Washington, D.C., 1977.

U.S. Civil Service Commission. "Collective Bargaining in the Federal Sector." Washington, D.C., 1974.

_____. "Reducing the Effects of Layoffs on Your Affirmative Action Program." EEO for State and Local Governments, issue no. 15. Washington, D.C., n.d.

U.S. Civil Service Commission, Bureau of Intergovernmental Personnel Programs. *Job Analysis: Developing and Documenting Data.* BIPP 152-35. Washington, D.C., December 1973.

_____. *The Productivity of People: Grant Projects in Human Resource Management.* BIPP 152-85. Washington, D.C.: September 1977.

U.S. Department of Health, Education, and Welfare, Health Services and Mental Health Administration. *Employee Incentive System for Hospitals.* DHEW Publication No. HSM 72-6705. Washington, D.C., 1972.

U.S. Department of Labor, Bureau of Labor Statistics. *Characteristics of Agreements in State and Local Governments January 1, 1974.* Bulletin 1861. Washington, D.C., 1975.

_____. *Characteristics of Agreements in State and Local Governments July 1, 1975.* Bulletin 1947. Washington, D.C., 1977.

_____. *Collective Bargaining Agreements for Police and Firefighters.* Bulletin 1885. Washington, D.C., 1976.

_____. *Collective Bargaining Agreements for State and County Government Employees.* Bulletin 1920. Washington, D.C., 1976.

U.S. Department of Labor, Labor Management Services Administration. "A Directory of Public Employee Organizations." Washington, D.C., 1974.

_____. *Summary of Public Sector Labor Relations Policies.* Washington, D.C., 1976.

U.S. General Accounting Office. "Federal Employee Performance Rating Systems Need Fundamental Changes." Report to Congress by the Comptroller General of the United States. No. FPCD-77-80. Washington, D.C., March 1978.

"Vallejo, California Loses on Arbitration Tiff." *LMRS Newsletter,* vol. 6, no. 1 (January 1975), p. 1.

von Kaas, H. K. *Making Wage Incentives Work.* New York: American Management Association, 1971.

Vroom, V. *Work and Motivation.* New York: John Wiley and Sons, 1964.

W. K. Williams and Company. "Job Restructuring Study." Report to the Department of Personnel, City of New York, March 1974.

Walters, Dan. "Is Civil Service About to Become Obsolete?" *California Journal,* vol. 7, no. 6 (June 1976), pp. 185-187.

Warr, Peter B., ed. *Psychology at Work.* Hammondsworth, Middlesex, England: Penguin Books, 1971.

Washington State Nurses Association. "Guidelines for Agency Patient Care/Nursing Practice Committees." Draft. Seattle, Wash., December 1972.

Watkins, Kent. "Quarterly Report: July-September 1977." National Work Incentive Demonstration Program, Institute for Housing Management Innovations. Washington, D.C., 1978.

Watlington, Malchus L. "Getting Involved: The Development of Team Management in Forsyth County." County of Forsyth, Winston-Salem, N.C., March 1974.

Ways, Max. "The American Kind of Worker Participation." *Fortune* (October 1976), pp. 68-71ff.

Weeks, David A. *Compensating Employees: Lessons of the 1970's.* New York: The Conference Board, 1976.

Weihrich, Heinz. "Management by Objectives: Does It Really Work?" *University of Michigan Business Review,* vol. 28 (July 1976), pp. 27-31.

Weinstein, Alan G., and Holzbach, Robert L., Jr. "Impact of Individual Differences, Reward Distribution, and Task Structure on Productivity in a Simulated Work Environment." *Journal of Applied Psychology,* vol. 58, no. 3 (1973), pp. 296-301.

Wellington, Harry H., and Winter, Ralph K., Jr. *The Unions and the Cities.* Washington, D.C.: The Brookings Institution, 1971.

Werne, Benjamin. "Guide to Clauses for Public Sector Labor Contracts." Albany: New York Conference of Mayors and Municipal Officials, 1975.

West, George Edward. "Bureaupathology and the Failure of MBO." *Human Resource Management,* vol. 16, no. 2 (Summer 1977), pp. 33-40.

White, Robert D. "Democratizing the Reward System." *Public Personnel Management,* vol. 3 (September/October 1974), pp. 409-414.

White, Thomas W. "Neighborhood Team Policing in Winston-Salem, North Carolina: A Case Study." Contract Report 5054-16. Washington, D.C.: The Urban Institute, December 1977.

White, Thomas W., and Gillice, Robert A. "Neighborhood Team Policing in Boulder, Colorado: A Case Study." Contract Report 5054-11. Washington, D.C.: The Urban Institute, December 1977.

White, Thomas W.; Horst, Pamela; Regan, Katryna J.; Bell, James; and Waller, John D. "Evaluation of LEAA's Full Service Neighborhood Team Policing Demonstration: A Summary Report." Contract Report 5054-17. Washington, D.C.: The Urban Institute, December 1977.

Wickens, J. D. "Management by Objectives: An Appraisal."

Journal of Management Studies, vol. 5 (October 1968), pp. 365-379.

Widdop, F. R. "Why Performance Standards Don't Work." *Personnel,* vol. 47, no. 2 (March/April 1970), pp. 14-20.

Wikstrom, Walter S. *Managing by—and with—Objectives.* Personnel Policy Study no. 212. New York: National Industrial Conference Board, 1968.

Wildavsky, Aaron. "The Strategic Retreat on Objectives." *Policy Analysis,* vol. 2 (Summer 1976), pp. 499-526.

Williams, Robert J. "The Housing Code: Flexibility, Public Relations, Combined Inspections Are Keys to Successes." *The Building Official and Code Administrator,* vol. 11, no. 1 (January 1977), pp. 16-20.

Wilson, Michael. *Job Analysis for Human Resource Management: A Review of Selected Research and Development.* Manpower Research Monograph No. 36. Washington, D.C.: U.S. Department of Labor, Manpower Administration, 1974.

Winning, Ethan A. "MBO: What's in It for the Individual?" *Personnel,* vol. 51, no. 2 (March/April 1974), pp. 51-56.

Winpisinger, William W. "Job Enrichment: A Union View." *Monthly Labor Review,* vol. 96 (April 1973), pp. 54-56.

Wittenberg, James F. "Personnel." Draft productivity paper. Personnel Division, Department of Administration, State of Nevada. Carson City, 1978.

Wofford, J. C. "The Motivational Bases of Job Satisfaction and Job Performance." *Personnel Psychology,* vol. 24 (1971), pp. 501-518.

Wolf, M. G. "Need Gratification Theory: A Theoretical Reformulation of Job Satisfaction/Dissatisfaction and Job Motivation." *Journal of Applied Psychology,* vol. 54 (1970), pp. 87-94.

Wool, Harold. "What's Wrong with Work in America?—A Review Essay." *Monthly Labor Review,* vol. 96, no. 3 (March 1973), pp. 38-44.

Work in America. Report of a Special Task Force to the Secretary of Health, Education, and Welfare. Cambridge, Mass.: MIT Press, 1973.

Wright, Grace H., ed. *Public Sector Employment Selection: A Manual for the Personnel Generalist.* Chicago: International Personnel Management Association, 1974.

Wurf, Jerry. "Collective Bargaining in Public Employment: The AFSCME View." In *The County Yearbook 1976.* Washington, D.C.: National Association of Counties and International City Management Association, 1976, pp. 150-159.

_____. "Labor Views the Cities." *SPEER Newsletter,* National League of Cities, vol. 1, no. 2 (January 1978), p. 1ff.

_____. "Merit: A Union View." *Public Administration Review,* vol. 34 (September/October 1974), pp. 431-434.

Wycoff, Mary Ann, and Kelling, George L. *The Dallas Experience: Organizational Reform.* Washington, D.C.: The Police Foundation, 1978.

Young, Joseph. "Why AFL-CIO Opposes Those Staggered Workdays." *The Washington Star,* June 3, 1976, p. B2.

Yukl, Gary A., and Latham, Gary P. "Consequences of Reinforcement Schedules and Incentive Magnitudes for Employee Performance: Problems Encountered in an Industrial Setting." *Journal of Applied Psychology,* vol. 60, no. 3 (1975), pp. 294-298.

Yukl, G. A.; Wesley, K. N.; and Seymore, J. D. "Effectiveness of Pay Incentives Under Variable Ratio and Continuous Reinforcement Schedules." *Journal of Applied Psychology,* vol. 56 (1972), pp. 19-23.

Zagoria, Sam. "An Evaluation of the Nassau County Project." Final report to the U.S. Department of Labor on Contract L-74-82. Washington, D.C.: Labor-Management Relations Service, July 30, 1975.

_____. "Are City Workers Bored With Their Jobs?" *The American City* (August 1973), pp. 51-52f.

_____. "In Springfield, Ohio, Pioneering Work Quality Effort Shows Results." *LMRS Newsletter,* vol. 6, no. 8 (August 1975), pp. 2-3.

_____. *Productivity: A Positive Route.* Washington, D.C.: Labor-Management Relations Service, 1978.

Zander, A. *Motives and Goals in Groups.* New York: Academic Press, 1971.

Zenk, Gordon K. "Police-Fire Consolidation." *Nation's Cities* (June 1972), pp. 27-29f.

Zimmerer, Thomas W., and Stroh, Thomas F. "Preparing Managers for Performance Appraisal." *SAM Advanced Management Journal,* vol. 39, no. 3 (July 1974), pp. 36-42.

Zurcher, James A. "The Team Management/Team Policing Organizational Concept." *The Police Chief,* vol. 38, no. 4 (April 1971), pp. 54-56.

Index

Absenteeism, 10, 18

Across-the-board pay increases, 72, 216, 361. *See also* Automatic wage increases; Cost-of-living increases.

Advancement opportunity, 5, 18, 30

American Federation of State, County, and Municipal Employees (AFSCME), 109*n*, 362, 369, 372, 377

Analysis, task, 221-23, 388

Appraisal by objectives (ABO), 8, 125-26, 238
  barriers, 169, 210-11
  costs, 147-48, 222, 228-29, 420
  definition, 134-35, 187
  and job satisfaction impacts, 135, 145-46, 218-20, 401
  measurement problems in, 147, 167, 210
  overall assessment, 210-11, 219-20, 228-30
  overall use, 125-26, 171-72, 195-96, 394, 396
  and performance appraisal, 73, 79, 134, 187, 195, 209-11, 222
  and performance targets, 111, 119, 130, 134-37, 171, 173, 187-88, 209-11, 384, 395-97, 400
  and productivity impacts, 145, 218-20, 228, 393
  recommendations on, 228-30, 418, 420-21

Appraisals. *See* Management appraisal systems; Performance appraisals.

Appropriation laws, 95, 97

Attendance incentives, 30

Automatic wage increases, 361-62. *See also* Across-the-board pay increases.

Autonomy, task, 6, 8, 233, 294, 308, 339, 351, 397

Bargaining. *See* Collective bargaining; Productivity bargaining.

Barriers to use of motivational programs. *See* Implementation obstacles; specific types of programs.

Behavior-based scales, 184-86, 206-207, 229, 397. *See also* Checklists, behavior-based; Rating scales.

Bonuses, 7, 18, 22, 24, 28, 33-46, 107-108, 115, 393. *See also* Monetary incentives; Wage increases; specific types of bonus programs.
  cost of, 49-50, 53-55, 58, 61-63, 103-104, 110
  group, 20-21, 22, 24, 37-38, 39-41, 43, 394
  individual, 20-21, 22, 24, 394
  and job satisfaction impacts, 22, 46, 56, 108-109, 115, 398-99
  obstacles to, 95-98, 100-102, 113, 381-82, 389
  organization-wide, 20, 21-22
  overall assessment of, 19-26, 32, 113-15, 399
  overall use of, 30-33, 37, 43, 107, 393-95
  and productivity impacts, 17-18, 22-24, 108, 112-14, 399
  recommendations on, 113-15, 419, 421
  types of, 28-30, 33-51, 399

Budgetary constraints, 72, 84, 103-104, 390, 408, 423

Building inspections, 254-56, 295, 299, 301-302, 304-305, 307-308, 310

Career development, 30, 127, 134-35, 167, 200, 214, 227, 238, 402-403

Jurisdictional Index

---

1. This index focuses on references to state and local government motivational programs that appear in the text. References appearing in the various lists of motivational programs are not included here.

Jurisdiction	Type of Motivational Program	Pages
Oyster Bay (cont'd.)	Productivity Bargaining	*See* Shared savings.
	Shared Savings	51, 53, 272
Rochester	Operating Teams	249-50, 251, 252
Syracuse	Job Restructuring	321

NORTH CAROLINA

State Government	Shared Savings	51, 59-60, 62, 63
	Suggestion Awards	63
Local Governments		
Charlotte	Operating Teams	250, 253
Durham	Graphic Rating Scales	183
	Job Enlargement	302, 303, 306, 354
Fayetteville	Job Rotation	292
Forsyth County	Problem-Oriented Teams	259, 262, 263, 264
Greensboro	Participative Decision Making	281, 283-84
	Performance-Based Wage Increases	82
Rocky Mount	Job Enlargement	302, 305, 307
	Job Restructuring	322, 325
Winston-Salem	Job Enlargement	303, 306, 354

NORTH DAKOTA

Local Governments		
Fargo	Performance Bonuses	33, 37

OHIO

State Government	Participative Decision Making	281, 282, 283
	Performance Bonuses	39
	Suggestion Awards	65
Local Governments		
Cincinnati	Joint Labor-Management Committees	273, 274
	Operating Teams	250, 251, 252, 253, 256, 257-58, 259, 328
Columbus	Joint Labor-Management Committees	272
Dayton	Job Restructuring	323-24
	Management by Objectives	*See* Performance-based wage increases.
	Operating Teams	252, 253
	Performance-Based Wage Increases	72, 73-74, 84, 88, 114, 395
Oakwood	Job Enlargement	307